English   Spanish
French   Italian
German   Portuguese
Dutch   Turkish
Danish   Greek

Yachtsman's Ten Language Dictionary

Second edition

**Barbara Webb
& Michael Manton** with

ADLARD COLES NAUTICAL
London

This edition published 2000 by Adlard Coles Nautical
an imprint of A & C Black (Publishers) Ltd
35 Bedford Row, London WC1R 4JH
www.adlardcoles.co.uk

Copyright *Yachtsman's Eight Language Dictionary* © Barbara Webb
1965, 1977, 1983
Copyright *Yachtsman's Ten Language Dictionary* © Barbara Webb and
Cruising Association 1995, 2000

First edition *Yachtsman's Eight Language Dictionary* published by
Adlard Coles 1965

Reprinted 1969	Third edition 1983
Second edition 1977	Reprinted 1985, 1988, 1989,
Reprinted 1978	1991, 1994

First edition *Yachtsman's Ten Language Dictionary* published by
Adlard Coles Nautical 1995
Second edition 2000

ISBN 0–7136–52950

A CIP catalogue record for this book is available from the British
Library.

Typeset in Stone Serif 8/8pt by Falcon Oast Graphic Art
Printed and bound in Great Britain by
The Cromwell Press, Trowbridge, Wiltshire

INTRODUCTION

Barbara Webb put together the first edition of her admirable dictionary thirty years ago. Since then we have seen major changes in yachts and their equipment. Nowadays even a modest family cruiser will carry a long inventory of gear which was unusual or unknown then, and a skipper needing repairs or replacements in a foreign port must be able to describe what he wants. I have therefore added over 600 words to the original dictionary, but without sacrificing the vocabulary of the classic wooden boat. Where economies of space had to be found, I have omitted words which can be found in an ordinary tourist phrase book. Rather reluctantly, I have also omitted the racing vocabulary, which perhaps deserves its own specialized dictionary.

Another change is that more skippers venture far afield, and the Eastern Mediterranean is now an important cruising ground. Greek and Turkish have therefore been added to the original eight languages. The Greek alphabet has been used in preference to transliteration, partly because Greek skippers will use the dictionary, and partly because a single transliteration would not be correct for each language. And in Greece, as in all other countries, pointing at a word in the book is an inelegant but effective way of communicating without risking mispronunciation.

Translating around 2750 words into nine other languages offers some 25 000 opportunities for mistakes and misunderstandings, not to mention the likelihood of omissions. Comments, criticisms and corrections from users of this book will be most welcome, so that they can be incorporated in later editions. Meanwhile, the publishers and I have done the best we can, but we cannot be held responsible for the consequences of any errors.

Many proprietary names and trade marks have passed into the language as everyday terms. Where such words have been knowingly included in this dictionary, they are indicated by ™. Unwitting inclusion of further unidentified trade marks does not imply that they have acquired for legal purposes a general significance; their inclusion is regretted, as is any wrong attribution which may have been made. Corrections will be made in subsequent reprints, if substantiated objections are made with adequate notice.

USING THIS BOOK

A multilingual dictionary cannot, of course, be arranged in alphabetical order. To make words easier to find I have grouped them into sections mainly defined by subject or situation. In particular, the first sections list words which may be needed in a hurry – in an emergency and when coming into harbour. But my logic may not be the same as yours, so you are recommended to familiarize yourself with the arrangement of the contents before you need to make a serious search for a word.

Michael Manton

INTRODUCTION

Il y a 30 ans que Barbara Webb a réalisé la première édition de son excellent dictionnaire. Depuis, beaucoup de changements concernant les bateaux de plaisance et leur équipement sont intervenus. De nos jours, même un modeste yacht familial emporte une longue liste de matériel qui aurait été inhabituel ou inconnu à cette époque, et il est indispensable qu'en cas de réparations ou de remplacements de pièces dans un port étranger, un skipper puisse décrire ce dont il a besoin. C'est pourquoi j'ai ajouté plus de 600 mots à la version originale, mais sans pour cela sacrifier le vocabulaire du bateau classique en bois. Où une économie de place était nécessaire, j'ai supprimé les mots que l'on peut trouver dans un lexique ordinaire pour touristes. Avec plus de réticence, j'ai également supprimé le vocabulaire de course qui mérite peut-être son propre dictionnaire spécialisé.

Le fait que beaucoup plus de skippers s'aventurent dans des régions plus éloignées est aussi nouveau et la Méditerranée Orientale est maintenant un lieu important de croisière. C'est pourquoi le Grec et le Turc ont été ajoutés aux huit langues initiales. Nous avons utilisé l'alphabet grec plutôt que la translitération, d'abord parce que des skippers grecs vont utiliser le dictionnaire et ensuite parce qu'une seule translitération ne pourrait être correcte pour chaque langue. Et en Grèce comme dans tous les pays, montrer du doigt un mot dans le livre est une façon inélégante mais efficace de communiquer sans risque de mauvaise prononciation.

Traduire environ 2750 mots dans neuf langues différentes offre quelques 25 000 possibilités d'erreurs ou de malentendus, sans parler des probabilités d'omissions. C'est pourquoi nous serons toujours heureux de recevoir les commentaires, critiques ou corrections des utilisateurs de ce livre, afin de pouvoir les incorporer dans une édition ultérieure. Entre-temps, les éditeurs et moi-même avons fait de notre mieux mais ne pouvons être tenus responsables des conséquences d'erreurs quelles qu'elles soient.

Beaucoup de noms propres et de marques de fabrique sont passés dans le langage courant. Lorsque de tels mots sont sciemment inclus, ils sont marqués™ dans ce dictionnaire. Si certaines marques de fabrique sont mentionnées dans ce livre sans être identifiées, cela ne signifie pas qu'elles aient acquis une importance généralisée du point de vue légal; nous regrettons leur inclusion ainsi que quelqu'autre attribution qui se révèlerait erronée. Nous effectuerons les corrections nécessaires dans les éditions ultérieures, au vu d'objections accompagnées de preuves et présentées avec un préavis suffisant.

COMMENT UTILISER CE LIVRE

Il est évident qu'un dictionnaire en plusieurs langues ne peut être présenté dans l'ordre alphabétique. Pour que les mots soient plus faciles à trouver, je les ai regroupés en sections couvrant principalement un sujet ou une situation. En particulier, les premières sections énumèrent les mots dont on a besoin rapidement – en cas d'urgence et lors d'une arrivée dans un port. Cependant, ma logique n'est pas forcément la même que la vôtre, il est donc recommandé de vous familiariser avec l'arrangement du contenu avant d'avoir besoin de procéder à la recherche sérieuse d'un mot.

Michael Manton

EINFÜHRUNG

Barbara Webb hat die erste Ausgabe dieses beachtlichen Wörterbuches vor 30 Jahren zusammengestellt. Seit dieser Zeit hat sich viel an den Yachten und ihrer Ausrüstung geändert. Heute verfügt sogar ein bescheiden ausgestattetes Familienschiff über ein derartig reichhaltiges Inventar an Ausrüstungsgegenständen, wie es damals nicht üblich oder bekannt war. Ein Skipper muß in der Lage sein, in einem fremden Hafen benötigte Ersatzteile oder Reparaturen beschreiben zu können. Ich habe deshalb 600 Begriffe der Originalausgabe zugefügt, ohne dabei das Vokabular über klassische Holzboote zu verkleinern. Mußte aus Raummangel Platz geschaffen werden, habe ich Worte fortgelassen, die auch in einem gewöhnlichen Wörterbuch für Touristen zu finden sind. Nur mit Widerstreben habe ich außerdem Begriffe aus dem Vokabular des Regattasegelns herausnehmen müssen, das möglicherweise sein eigenes Spezialwörterbuch verdient hätte.

Eine weitere Änderung hat sich dadurch ergeben, daß die Skipper ihren Fahrtenbereich ausgedehnt haben. Das östliche Mittelmeer ist zu einem wichtigen Fahrtengebiet geworden. Deshalb wurden Griechisch und Türkisch den ursprünglichen acht Sprachen zugefügt. Dabei wurde der griechischen Schreibweise der Vorzug vor einer Umschreibung der Begriffe gegeben. Einerseits sollten auch griechische Segler dieses Wörterbuch benutzen können, andererseits läßt sich eine Umschreibung nicht in jede Sprache korrekt übertragen. In Griechenland ist es deshalb sehr praktisch, ähnlich wie in anderen Ländern auch, wenn man zur besseren Verständigung in diesem Buch auf das betreffende Wort zeigt, um Mißverständnisse durch falsche Aussprache zu vermeiden.

Beim Übersetzen von 2750 Begriffen in neun Sprachen könnten sich etwa 25000 Möglichkeiten für Fehler oder Mißverständnisse ergeben. Die Wahrscheinlichkeit, Begriffe vergessen zu haben, ist dabei noch nicht berücksichtigt. Deshalb sind uns Kommentare, Kritiken und Korrekturen sehr willkommen, um sie in späteren Ausgaben berücksichtigen zu können. Der Herausgeber und ich haben soweit unser Bestes getan; für eventuelle Folgen, die durch Irrtümer entstehen könnten, sind wir aber nicht verantwortlich.

Viele Markenbezeichnungen und Warenzeichen sind als Alltagsbegriffe in die Sprachen eingedrungen. Wurden bewußt solche Bezeichungen in dieses Wörterbuch aufgenommen, sind sie mit™ gekennzeichnet. Wurden unwissentlich nicht genau bekannte Warenzeichen mit aufgenommen, bedeutet dies nicht, daß sie rechtlich anerkannt sind. Ihre Aufnahme bedauern wir, wie auch jede andere falsche Zuordnung. Wenn glaubhafte Einwendungen mit entsprechenden Nachweisen vorgetragen werden sollen in den folgenden Auflagen entsprechende Korrekturen erfolgen.

ZUM GEBRAUCH DIESES BUCHES

Ein mehrsprachiges Wörterbuch läßt sich naturgemäß nicht alphabetisch ordnen. Um einzelne Begriffe leichter finden zu können, habe ich sie in Abschnitte eingruppiert, die sich auf den Gegenstand oder die Situation beziehen. In den ersten Abschnitten sind besonders Worte für Situationen aufgeführt, in denen Eile geboten ist, z.B. bei Notfällen oder beim Einlaufen in einen Hafen. Da aber auch andere Eingruppierungen logisch sein können, empfehle ich Ihnen, sich frühzeitig mit dieser Inhaltsanordnung vertraut zu machen, um langwieriges Suchen nach einzelnen Begriffen zu vermeiden.

Michael Manton

VOORWOORD

Barbara Webb stelde de eerste editie van haar bewonderenswaardige woordenboek dertig jaar geleden samen. Sinds die tijd hebben er grote veranderingen in jachten en uitrusting plaatsgevonden. Heden ten dage hebben normale familie-jachten een uitgebreide inventaris en uitrusting hetgeen toen ongebruikelijk of onbekend was. Ten einde de huidige schippers in staat te stellen noodzakelijke reparaties of vervangingen aan te duiden, heb ik 600 woorden aan de originele uitgave toegevoegd, zonder echter de terminologie van de klassieke houten boten daarvoor op te offeren. In verband met ruimtegebrek heb ik woorden, welke in gewone boekjes met uitdrukking voor toeristen kunnen worden gevonden, weggelaten. Node heb ik woorden welke speciaal bij de wedstrijd-zeilsport horen niet opgenomen; hiervoor zou misschien een speciaal woordenboekje moeten komen.

Omdat tegenwoordig steeds meer schippers langere reizen maken en de oostelijke Middellandse Zee een belangrijk vaargebied is geworden heb ik Grieks en Turks aan de originele acht talen toegevoegd. Voor de Griekse sectie heb ik het Griekse alphabet gebruikt, omdat het overzetten naar het voor ons normale alphabet geen goed zou doen aan de andere vertalingen en omdat dit voor de Griekse gebruiker eenvoudiger is. Bovenien is in Griekenland, zoals trouwens ook in andere landen, het aanwijzen van een woord in het boek een onelegante, maar effectieve manier van communicatie, zonder het risico van een verkeerde uitspraak.

Het vertalen van 2.750 woorden in negen andere talen schept de mogelijkheid van ongeveer 25.000 fouten en vergissingen, met daarnaast nog de mogelijkheid van weglatingen.

Opmerkingen, kritiek en verbeteringen zijn van harte welkom, zodat hiermede in volgende uitgaven rekening kan worden gehouden. Ofschoon de uitgevers en ik ons uiterste best hebben gedaan kunnen wij niet verantwoordelijk worden gesteld voor eventuele fouten in dit bookje.

Vele merk- en handelsnamen worden tegenwoordig als dagelijkse geïbruiksnamen gebezigd. Daar waar zulke woorden in dit boek zijn gebruikt worden ze aangeduid met ™. Opname van verdere niet gedentificeerde woorden uit onwetendheid, houdt niet in dat deze een algemene betekenis voor wettige doeleinden hebben verkregen; wij betreuren het opnemen hiervan, evenals elke andere verkeerde toeschrijving. Correcties zullen in volgende herdrukken worden opgenomen, indien overtuigende bezwaren zijn gemaakt met voldoende kennisgeving.

HET GEBRUIK VAN DIT BOEK

Het alphabetisch rangschikken van woorden in een meertalig woordenboek is natuurlijk onmogelijk. Ten einde het opzoeken van woorden te vergemakkelijken heb ik gekozen voor groeperen volgens onderwerp of situatie. Speciaal de eerste groepen bevatten woorden welke men snel nodig zou kunnen hebben, in noodgevallen of bij het binnenkomen van een haven. Echter, mijn logica hoeft niet de Uwe te zijn, dus adviseer ik U zich vertrouwd te maken met de rangschikking van de onderwerpen van de inhoud, alvorens zich de noodzaak voordoet van serieus gebruik.

Michael Manton

FORORD

For tredive år siden udarbejdede Barbara Webb den første udgave af denne fortrinlige ordbog. Siden er der sket store forandringer med lystfartøjer og deres udrustning. I dag medbringer selv en beskeden familiebåd en hel masse grej, som var usædvanligt eller ukendt dengang, og en skipper, der har brug for reparation eller reservedele i en fremmed havn, må være i stand til at beskrive, hvad han ønsker. Jeg har derfor tilføjet over 600 ord til den oprindelige udgave, dog uden at ordforrådet for klassiske træbåde. Nogle steder måtte der spares på pladsen, og jeg har udeladt ord, som kan findes i en almindelig turistordbog. Modstræbende har jeg også slettet kapsejladsterminologien, som sikkert fortjener sin egen specialordbog.

En anden forandring er, at et større antal sejlere kommer langt omkring og det østlige Middlehav er i dag et betydende langtursområde. Følgelig er græsk og tyrkisk føjet til de oprindelige otte sprog. Det græske alfabet er anvendt uden omskrivning; dels fordi græske sejlere vil benytte ordbogen, dels fordi en omskrivning ikke fungerer korrekt ved alle sprog. Og i Grækenland – som i alle andre lande – er metoden med at pege på et ord i bogen en mindre elegant, men effektiv måde at kommunikere på uden at risikere misforståelser.

Oversættelsen af omkring 2.750 ord til andre sprog giver ca. 25.000 muligheder for fejltagelser, misforståelser eller ikke mindst udeladelser. Brugerne af bogen er velkomne til at kommentere, kritisere eller korrigere indholdet til gavn for senere udgaver. Udgiverne og jeg har gjort arbejdet så godt vi kunne, men kan ikke holdes ansvarlige for følgerne af eventuelle fejl.

Mange beskyttede firmanavne og varemærker er gledet ind i hverdagssproget. Hvor sådanne betegnelser med forsæt er medtaget i ordbogen, er det tilkendegivet med ™. Hvis lignende uidentificerede betegnelser er sluppet med, betyder det ikke, at de i legal forstand har fået en generel betydning. Det er beklageligt, hvis de er smuttet med og eventuelt er tillagt en forkert betydning. Rettelser vil blive bragt i efterfølgende oplag, hvis dokumenterede indvendelser gøres med rimeligt varsel.

OM BOGENS BRUG

En flersproget ordbog kan efter sagens natur ikke opstilles i alfabetisk rækkefølge. For at lette eftersøgningen, er ordene grupperet i afsnit, der stort set er defineret af genstand eller situation. Specielt indeholder de første afsnit gloser, som måske skal bruges i en fart – i en nødsituation eller ved anløb af havn. Men min logik er måske ikke den samme som Deres, så jeg anbefaler, at man gør sig fortrolig med indholdets gruppering før man begynder at lede efter ord.

Michael Manton

INTRODUCCIÓN

Barbara Webb redactó la primera edición de su admirable diccionario hace treinto años. Desde entonces ha habido importantes cambios en los yates y su equipamiento. Hoy en día incluso el más modesto yate estará equipado con instrumentos y aparejos no usuales o desconocidos en aquella época, y un skipper que necesite reparaciones o recambios en un puerto extranjero debe ser capaz de describir lo que desea. Por lo tanto he añadido unas 600 palabras al diccionario original, pero sin tocar el vocabulario de los barcos clásicos de madera. Donde se debía economizar espacio, he omitido palabras que pueden encontrarse en un libro turístico corriente de frases hechas. Más a regañadientes también he omitido el vocabulario de regatas, que quizá precise su propio diccionario especializado.

Otro cambio es que más skippers emprendan viajes más lejanos y el Mediterráneo oriental es ahora una importante zona de cruceros. Por lo tanto se han añadido el Griego y el Turco a las ocho lenguas originales. El alfabeto Griego se ha usado preferentemente a la transcripción, en parte porque los skippers Griegos usarán el diccionario, y en parte porque una simple transcripción no será corecta para cada lengua. Y en Grecia como en todos los demas países, senalar una palabra en el libro es una manera poco elegante pero efectiva para comunicarse sin riesgo de pronunciar mal.

Traducir unas 2750 palabras a otras nueve lenguas ofrece algo así como 25000 oportunidades de errores y faltas de comprensión, sin mencionar la posibilidad de las omisiones. Comentarios, críticas y correcciones de los usuarios de este libro serán muy bien recibidas, ya que podrán ser incorporadas en ediciones posteriores. Mientras tanto, los editores y yo hemos hecho todo lo mejor que hemos podido, pero no podemos responsabilizarnos por las consecuencias de cualquier error.

Muchas nombres propios y marcas registradas han pasado como términos de lenguaje diario. Cuando tales palabras han sido incluídas deliberadamente en este diccionario, están indicados con un™. La inclusíon inconsciente de otras marcas registradas no implicar que hayan adquirido un significado general con propósitos legales; se lamenta su inclusíon así como cualquier atribución errónea que pueda haber sido hecha. Se efectuarán correcciones en futuras ediciones si se hacen objeciones justificadas con la suficiente antelación.

UTILIZACIÓN DE ESTE LIBRO

Un diccionario multilingüe no puede por supuesto presentarse por orden alfabético. Para facilitar el buscar las palabras las he agrupado en secciones preferentemente definidas por temas o situación. En concreto, las primeras secciones catalogan palabras que pueden necesitarse con urgencia o de emergencia y al llegar a puerto. Pero mi lógica puede no ser la misma que la suya, por lo tanto se le recomienda que se familiarice usted mismo con la presentación de los contenidas antes de que usted necesite buscar en serio una palabra.

Michael Manton

INTRODUZIONE

Barbara Webb compilò la prima edizione del suo ammirevole dizionario trent'anni fa. Da allora si sono viste imponenti innovazioni negli yacht e nelle loro attrezzature. Oggigiorno anche una modesta barca de crociera familiare ha un lungo inventario di materiali che erano insoliti o ignoti a quei tempi, e uno skipper che abbia bisogno di riparazioni o ricambi in un porto straniero deve essere in grado di descrivere quel che gli serve. Ho quindi aggiunto oltre 600 parole al dizionario originale, ma senza sacrificare il vocabolario della barca di legno classica. Ove si richiedevano economie di spazio, ho tralasciato parole che si possono trovare in un normale frasario turistico. Con riluttanza, ho anche omesso il vocabolario di regata, che forse merita un proprio dizionario specializzato.

Un altro cambiamento è che sempre più skipper si avventurano in luoghi lontani, e il Mediterraneo Orientale è diventato ormai un importante campo di crociere. Abbiamo perciò aggiunto il greco e il turco alle otto lingue originali. Si è usato l'alfabeto greco in preferenza alla traslitterazione, in parte perché useranno il dizionario anche gli skipper greci, e in parte perché un'unica traslitterazione non sarebbe corretta per ogni lingua. Inoltre in Grecia, come in tutti gli altri paesi, quello di indicare una parola nel libro è un modo, forse non elegante ma certo efficace, di comunicare senza rischio di sbagliare la pronuncia.

Tradurre circa 2.750 parole in nove altre lingue crea qualcosa come 25.000 occasioni di errori ed equivoci, senza contare la probabilità di omissioni. Tutti i commenti, critiche e correzioni da parte degli utenti di questo volume saranno benvenute, e potranno essere incorporate in edizioni successive. Nel frattempo, gli editori e io stesso abbiamo fatto del nostro meglio, ma non possiamo essere considerati responsabili delle conseguenze di eventuali errori.

Molti nomi proprietari e marchi sono entrati nella lingua come termini quotidiani. Ove si sono consapevolmente introdotti nel dizionario termini di questo tipo, essi sono indicati con ™. L'inclusione inconsapevole di altri marchi non identificati non implica che essi abbiano acquisito un significato generico dal punto di vista legale, e anzi ci scusiamo dell'inclusione, come di qualsiasi falsa attribuzione che possiamo aver fatto. Verranno fatte correzioni nelle ristampe, se ci verranno presentate obiezioni comprovate con preavviso adeguato.

USO DI QUESTO VOLUME

Un dizionario multilingue non può evidentemente essere disposto in ordine alfabetico. Per rendere le parole più facili da trovare le ho raggruppate in sezioni definite essenzialmente per soggetto o per situazione. In particolare, le prime sezioni elencano parole che possono servire in fretta: in un'emergenza, o entrando in porto. Ma la mia logica può non essere uguale alla vostra: Vi raccomandiamo quindi di familiarizzar Vi colla disposizione del contenuto prima che abbiate bisogno di cercare davvero una parola.

Michael Manton

INTRODUÇÃO

Barbara Webb compilou a primeira edição do seu admirável dicionário, faz trinta anos. Desde essa altura assistiu-se a grandes mudanças nos iates e no seu equipamento. Actualmente até um modesto barco de cruzeiro familiar tem um largo inventário de equipamento ou palamenta que não era vulgar ou não existia naquele tempo, mas as necessidades de reparação ou substituição daqueles em portos estrangeiros obriga o «patrão» a saber descrever o que pretende. Por isso acrescentei cerca de 600 palavras ao dicionário original, mas sem sacrificar o vocabulário usado para os barcos de madeira clássicos. Onde houve necessidade de economia de espaço, omiti as palavras que podem ser encontradas em qualquer dicionário turístico. Relutantemente omiti também o vocabulário utilizado nas regatas, que talvez mereça um dicionário da especialidade.

Outra mudança deve-se a que os patrões dos nossos barcos se aventuram cada vez mais longe e o Mediterrâneo de Leste é hoje uma importante zona de cruzeiro. A lingua Grega e Turca foram por isso acrescentadas às oito linguas originais. Demos preferencia a utilização do alfabeto grego em vez de usarmos uma transliteração, por um lado porque os «patrões» Gregos usam o dicionário, por outro porque a simples transliteração poderia não estar correcta em cada lingua. Na Grécia, como em outros países, apontar para uma palavra no livro não é uma maneira elegante mas é efectiva quando se pretende comunicar sem correr o risco de má pronúncia.

A tradução de cerca de 2750 palavras em 9 linguas corresponde a 25000 oportunidades de erros ou má compreensão isto sem falar da possibilidade de haver omissões. Comentários, criticas e correcções a fazer pelos utilizadores deste livro serão benvindas, de modo a poderem ser inseridas nas próximas edições. Entretanto, o editor e eu fizemos o melhor que pudemos, mas não nos consideramos responsáveis pelas consequências de quaisquer erros.

Muitos nomes patenteados e marcas registadas passaram a pertencer à linguagem corrente. Quando estas palavras forem incluídas neste dicionário, estarão indicadas por ™. A inclusão involuntária de outras marcas registadas desconhecidas não implica que tenham adquirido, para fins legais, um significado generalizado. Lamentamos a sua inclusão, pois qualquer má atribuição pode ter sido feita. As correcções serão feitas nas próximas edições se as objecções se revelarem adequadas e forem feitas acompanhadas de uma informação válida.

UTILIZAÇÃO DO LIVRO

É evidente que um dicionário multi-linguas não pode estar organizado por ordem alfabética. Para facilitar a consulta agrupei-o em secções sobretudo definidas pelo assunto ou situação. Especialmente no que respeita a primeira lista de palavras, que podem ser necessárias com urgência numa emergência ou nas entradas dos portos. Mas a minha maneira de ver pode não coincidir com a vossa, por isso recomendamos que se familiarize com a estrutura e o conteúdo da obra antes que lhe seja necessário fazer uma consulta urgente procurando uma palavra.

Michael Manton

öNSöZ

Barbara Webb otuz yıl önce bu harika sözlüğünün ilk baskısını yapmıştı. O günden beri yatlarda ve kullanılan malzemelerde büyük değişiklikler meydana geldi. Bugünlerde normal bir yelkenli yat dahi malzemelerin listelendiği uzun bir envanter taşımaktadır. Bu bizim alışmadığımız ve bilmediğimiz bir şeydi. Günümüzde tamirat yada bazı değişiklikler isteyen bir yatın sorumlusu, yabancı bir limanda ne istediğini daha iyi bir şekilde açıklamak zorunda kalmaktadır. Bu nedenle, klasik ahşap teknelerle ilgili bölümü değiştirmeden 600 yeni kelimeyi ilk sözlüğe ilave ettim. Yer kazanmak amacı il ede turistik kitaplarda bulunabilecek kelimeleri çıkarttım. Ayrıca özel bir sözlükte yayınlanmalarının daha iyi olacağını düşünerek, istemeyerek de olsa, yarışla ilgili sözcükleri de iptal ettim.

Başka bir değişiklik de, daha çok sayıda yatçının uzak bölgelere seyretmek için cesaret bulmaları idi ve buna paralel olarak Doğu Akdeniz önemli bir gezi bölgesi haline geldi. Bu yeni gelişme doğrultusunda Yunanca ve Türkçe dillerini mevcut sekiz dile ekledik. Biraz Yunanlı yatçıların kullanım kolaylığı biraz da çevirinin tam doğru yapılamayacağı düşünceleri ile Yunan alfabesi kullanım için seçildi. Diğer tüm dillerde olduğu gibi Yunan dilinde de, kitaptaki bir kelimeyi işaretle göstermenin belki biraz kabaca da olsa yanlış anlamaları ortadan kaldıracağı için çok faydalı bir iletişim yolu olacağını düşünüyoruz.

Yaklaşık 2.750 kelimeyi 9 ayrı dile çevirmek yaklaşık 25.000 hata ve yanlış anlama ihtimalini ortaya çıkarmaktadır. Yorumlar, eleştiriler ve değişiklik tekliflerini bekliyoruz ve ancak bu bilgilerle bundan sonraki baskılarda gerekli düzeltmeleri yapabiliriz. Basımevi ve ben elimizden gelenin en iyisini yaptık fakat hataların ortaya çıkaracağı olumsuz sonuçlardan sorumlu tutulamayacağımızı özellikle belirtmek isterim.

Birçok firma isimleri ve ticari markaları günlük terimler olarak dilimize yerleşmiştir. Bu sözlükte bu tür kelimeler farkedildiği kadarı ile '™' işareti ile belirlenmişlerdir. Bazı markalarıın,™ markası ile işaretlenmesinin istenmeyerek unutulması, bunların genel anlamda ve kanuni bir şekilde kulanılabileceği anlamına gelmez. Bu kelimelerin kullanımından dolayı meydana gelebilecek olumsuz gelişmeler üzüntü ile karşılanacaktır. Gerekliliği belirlendiği taktirde, yapılan düzeltmeler gelecek baskılarda yenilenecektir.

KİTABIN KULLANIMI

Birden fazla dili içeren bir sözlük doğal olarak alfabetik sıraya göre yapılamıyor. Kelimelerin daha kolay bulunabilinmesi için durumlarına yada konularına göre bölümlerin ayırarak gruplandırma yaptım. Detay olarak, ilk bölümlerin liste kelimeleri limana girişlerde ve acil durumlarda ihtiyaç duyulabilecek kelimelerden ibarettir. Fakat sizin ve benim yaklaşımlarımız arasında fark olabilir ve aradığınız bir kelime için ciddi bir araştırma yapmadan önce içeriklerin yerleştirmesi için uyguladığımız düzenlemeyi tanımanızı ve alışmanızı tavsiye ederim.

Michael Manton | 11

ΕΙΣΑΓΩΓΗ

Η Barbara Webb επιμελήθηκε την πρώτη έκδοση του θαυμάσιου λεξικού της πριν τριάντα χρόνια. Από τότε έχουν γίνει βασικές αλλαγές στα σκάφη αναψυχής και τον εξοπλισμό τους. Τη σημερινή εποχή, ακόμη και ένα απλό οικογενειακό σκάφος αναψυχής έχει ένα πλούσιο εξοπλισμό, ο οποίος παλαιότερα ήταν ασυνήθιστος ή τελείως άγνωστος και ο καπετάνιος που χρειάζεται να κάνει επισκευές ή να αντικαταστήσει κάτι σε ένα ξένο λιμάνι πρέπει να είναι σε θέση να περιγράψει αυτό που θέλει. Για το λόγο αυτό έχω προσθέσει πάνω από 600 λέξεις στο αρχικό λεξικό χωρίς όμως να θυσιάσω το λεξιλόγιο που αφορά το κλασσικό ξύλινο σκάφος. Όπου έπρεπε να κάνω οικονομία χώρου, έχω παραλείψει λέξεις οι οποίες περιέχονται σε απλούς τουριστικούς οδηγούς. Έχω επίσης παραλείψει, μάλλον απρόθυμα, το λεξιλόγιο που αφορά την αγωνιστική ιστιοπλοΐα, το οποίο αξίζει να περιληφθεί σε ένα εξειδικευμένο λεξικό.

Μία άλλη αλλαγή είναι ότι όλο και περισσότεροι καπετάνιοι τολμούν να πλεύσουν σε πιο μακρινά μέρη και η Ανατολική Μεσόγειος έχει γίνει ελκυστική περιοχή για κρουαζιέρες. Έτσι τα Ελληνικά και τα Τουρκικά έχουν προστεθεί στις αρχικές οκτώ γλώσσες. Το Ελληνικό αλφάβητο έχει χρησιμοποιηθεί αυτούσιο και όχι η ηχητική του απόδοση, αφ'ενός διότι Έλληνες καπετάνιοι θα χρησιμοποιήσουν το λεξικό και αφ' ετέρου διότι μία μόνο ηχητική απόδοση δε θα ήταν σωστή για κάθε γλώσσα χωριστά.

Εξ άλλου, στην Ελλάδα, όπως και σε κάθε άλλη χώρα, το να δείξεις μια λέξη στο λεξικο, μπορεί να είναι ένας άκομψος τρόπος επικοινωνίας, σίγουρα όμως δεν αφήνει περιθώρια παρανοήσεων.

Μεταφράζοντας περίπου 2.750 λέξεις σε εννέα άλλες γλώσσες σου προσφέρονται περί τις 25.000 ευκαιρίες για λάθη και παρανοήσεις, χωρίς να αναφέρω την πιθανότητα παραλείψεων. Σχόλια, κριτικές και διορθώσεις από χρήστες αυτού του βιβλίου θα είναι πολύ ευπρόσδεκτες έτσι ώστε να μπορούν να ενσωματωθούν σε μελλοντικές εκδόσεις. Εν τω μεταξύ, οι εκδότες και εγώ κάναμε ό, τι καλύτερο μπορούσαμε αλλά μη μας θεωρείτε υπεύθυνους για τις συνέπειες των όποιων λαθών μας.

Πολλά ονόματα εταιριών και σήματα κατατεθέντα έχουν περάσει στη γλώσσα σαν καθημερινοί όροι. Όπου έχουν περιληφθεί τέτοιες λέξεις συνειδητά σε αυτό το λεξικό συμβολίζονται με τα αρχικά ™. Εάν τυχαία έχουμε περιλάβει και άλλα μη αναγνωρίσιμα σήματα κατατεθέντα, δεν υπονοείται ότι έχουν αποκτήσει νομικό έρεισμα. Λυπόμαστε για το ότι τα συμπεριλάβαμε όπως και για οποιαδήποτε λανθασμένη απόδοση. Διορθώσεις θα γίνουν σε μελλοντικές ανατυπώσεις του λεξικού, εάν υπάρξουν έγκαιρα τεκμηριωμένες αντιρρήσεις.

ΧΡΗΣΙΜΟΠΟΙΩΝΤΑΣ ΑΥΤΟ ΤΟ ΒΙΒΛΙΟ

Οι λέξεις που περιλαμβάνονται σε ένα πολύγλωσσο λεξικό δεν μπορεί φυσικά να ταξινομηθούν αλφαβητικά. Για να διευκολυνθεί ο χρήστης, οι λέξεις έχουν οργανωθεί κατά ομάδες ανάλογα με το θέμα ή την περίσταση. Ειδικά οι πρώτες ενότητες αφορούν λέξεις οι οποίες χρησιμοποιούνται σε περίπτωση ανάγκης ή προσέγγισης σε λιμάνι.

Επειδή η δική μου λογική μπορεί να μην είναι ίδια με τη δική σας, σας συνιστώ να εξοικειωθείτε με τη διάταξη των περιεχομένων προτού βρεθείτε στην ανάγκη να ψάξετε για μια λέξη.

Michael Manton

ACKNOWLEDGEMENTS

Eight language edition

French:	Mme L van de Wiele
German:	Hr Otto Albrecht Ernst and Hr Ludwig Dinklage
Dutch:	Ir M F Guning
Danish	Redaktør G Strømberg
Italian:	Sr Adolfo Grill
Spanish	Contralmirante Julio Guillen and Duque de Arion
Portuguese	Antonio and Patricia Potier

Ten language edition

Greek:	Hellenic Offshore Racing Club
	A Krallis and E Panayotou
Turkish:	Capt A Muhittin Öney and Hasan Kaçmaz*
French:	Janine Kempton*
German:	Dr Med Meinhard Kohfahl* and Wolfgang Mertz
Dutch:	Capt M H Loos* and J van Vroonhoven
Danish	Royal Danish Yacht Club
	Eyvind Peetz*
Italian:	dr ing Carlo Spandonari
Spanish	Capt Jeffrey Kempton* and Sra Catalina Ginart Vidal
Portuguese	Joaquim L F Pinto Basto*

* Cruising Association Honorary Local Representatives

My friends and fellow CA members gave me invaluable help and advice in compiling the additions to the English master text, and in particular Keith Kilburn , Roger Powley and Andrew Turner.

CONTENTS

TABLE DES MATIERES

INHALTSVERZEICHNIS

INHOUDSOPGAVE

20

INDHOLDSFORTEGNELSE

LISTA DE MATERIAS

INDICE DELLA MATERIA

LISTA DE ASSUNTOS

İÇİNDEKİLER

ΠΕΡΙΕΧΟΜΕΝΑ

ENGLISH	FRANÇAIS	DEUTSCH	NEDERLANDS	DANSK
1 EMERGENCIES	**1 URGENCES**	**1 NOTFÄLLE**	**1 NOODGEVALLEN**	**1 NØDSITUATIONER**
Asking for help	**Demandes de secours**	**Hilferuf**	**Vragen om hulp**	**Anmode om hjælp**
1 Mayday	1 Mayday	1 May day	1 Mayday	1 Mayday
2 Pan Pan	2 Pan Pan	2 Pan Pan	2 pan pan	2 Pan Pan
3 emergencies	3 urgence	3 Notfall	3 noodsituatie	3 nødstilfælde
4 present position	4 position actuelle	4 gegenwärtige Position	4 huidige positie	4 nuværende position
5 very urgent	5 très urgent	5 sehr dringend	5 zeer dringend	5 meget vigtigt
6 please come	6 venez s'il vous plaît	6 bitte kommen	6 kom alstublieft	6 kom venligst
7 please hurry	7 dépêchez-vous s'il vous plaît	7 bitte beeilen	7 haast u alstublieft	7 skynd dem
8 please help	8 à l'aide s'il vous plaît	8 bitte helfen	8 helpt u alstublieft	8 hjælp ønskes
9 not understood	9 pas compris	9 nicht verstanden	9 niet verstaan, niet begrepen	9 ikke forstået
10 yes	10 oui	10 ja	10 ja	10 ja
11 no	11 non	11 nein	11 neen	11 nej
12 thank you	12 merci	12 danke	12 dank u	12 tak
Problems	**Problèmes**	**Probleme**	**Problemen**	**Problemer**
1 collision	1 abordage	1 Kollision	1 aanvaring	1 kollision
2 shipwreck	2 naufrage	2 Schiffbruch	2 schipbreuk	2 skibbrud
3 man overboard	3 homme à la mer	3 Mann über Bord	3 man overboord	3 mand overbord
4 capsize	4 chavirer	4 kentern	4 omslaan	4 kæntring
5 stove in, holed	5 défoncé, troué	5 eingedrückt, Loch in	5 ingedrukt, lek	5 lækage
6 explosion	6 explosion	6 Explosion	6 explosie	6 eksplosion
7 fire	7 feu	7 Feuer	7 brand	7 brand
8 smoke	8 fumée	8 Rauch	8 rook	8 røg
9 gas	9 gaz	9 Gas	9 gas	9 gas
10 danger	10 danger	10 Gefahr	10 gevaar	10 fare
11 pollution	11 pollution	11 Verunreinigung	11 vervuiling	11 forurening
12 fouled anchor	12 l'ancre surjalée	12 unklarer Anker	12 onklaar anker	12 ankeret fisker
13 dragging anchor	13 chasser sur l'ancre	13 der Anker schliert	13 krabbend anker	13 ankeret holder ikke
14 to run aground	14 échouer	14 auf Grund laufen	14 aan de grond lopen	14 gå på grund
15 lee shore	15 côté sous le vent	15 Legerwall, Leeküuste	15 lage wal	15 læ kyst
16 to founder	16 couler	16 sinken	16 vergaan, zinken	16 rystelser

ESPAÑOL	ITALIANO	PORTUGUÊS	TÜRKÇE	ΕΛΛΗΝΙΚΑ
1 EMERGENCIAS	**1 EMERGENZA**	**1 EMERGÊNCIAS**	**1 ACİL DURUMLAR**	**1 ΕΠΕΙΓΟΥΣΕΣ ΚΑΤΑΣΤΑΣΕΙΣ**
Pidiendo ayuda	**Richiesta d'aiuto**	**Pedido de socorro**	**Yardım isteme/yardım çağırısı**	**ΒΟΗΘΕΙΑ**
1 Mayday	1 Mayday	1 Mayday	1 Mayday	1 ΜΕΙΝΤΕΙ
2 Pan Pan	2 Pan Pan	2 Pane Pane	2 Panpan	2 ΠΑΝ-ΠΑΝ
3 urgencia	3 Pan Pan	3 emergência	3 acil durum	3 ΕΠΕΙΓΟΥΣΑ ΚΑΤΑΣΤΑΣΗ
	3 emergenza			
4 situación actual	4 posizione attuale	4 posição actual	4 bulunulan mevki-konum	4 ΠΑΡΟΥΣΑ ΘΕΣΗ
5 muy urgente	5 urgentissimo	5 muito urgente	5 çok acele	5 ΠΟΛΥ ΕΠΕΙΓΟΝ
6 por favor acudan	6 prego venite	6 por favor venha	6 lütfen cevap verin	6 ΠΑΡΑΚΑΛΩ ΕΛΑΤΕ
		7 venha depressa	7 lütfen acele edin	7 ΠΑΡΑΚΑΛΩ ΒΙΑΣΤΕΙΤΕ
7 por favor apresurense	7 prego affrettatevi			
8 ayuda por favor	8 prego soccorreteci	8 favor ajudem-nos	8 lütfen yardım edin	8 ΠΑΡΑΚΑΛΩ ΒΟΗΘΕΙΣΤΕ
9 no comprendido	9 non ho capito	9 não entendido	9 anlaşılmadı	9 ΔΕΝ ΚΑΤΑΛΑΒΑ
10 si	10 sì	10 sim	10 evet	10 ΝΑΙ
11 no	11 no	11 não	11 hayır	11 ΟΧΙ
12 gracias	12 grazie	12 obrigado	12 teşekkür ederim	12 ΕΥΧΑΡΙΣΤΩ
Problemas	**Problemi**	**Problemas**	**Problemler**	**ΠΡΟΒΛΗΜΑΤΑ**
1 colisión, abordaje	1 collisione	1 colisão abalroamento	1 çatışma	1 ΣΥΓΚΡΟΥΣΗ
2 naufragio	2 relitto	2 naufrágio	2 gemini batması	2 ΝΑΥΑΓΙΟ
3 hombre al agua	3 uomo in mare	3 homem ao mar	3 denize adam düştü	3 ΑΝΘΡΩΠΟΣ ΣΤΗ ΘΑΛΑΣΣΑ
4 zozobrado	4 capovolgersi (scuffiare)	4 virar-se	4 alabora	4 ΑΝΑΠΟΔΟΓΥΡΙΣΜΑ
5 desfondado	5 sfondato	5 porão	5 karinada delik, ezilme	5 ΕΜΒΟΛΙΣΜΕΝΟΣ
6 explosion	6 esplosione	6 explosão	6 infilak	6 ΕΚΡΗΞΗ
7 fuego, incendio	7 incendio	7 fogo	7 yangın	7 ΦΩΤΙΑ
8 humo	8 fumo	8 fumo	8 duman	8 ΚΑΠΝΟΣ
9 gas	9 gas	9 gás	9 gaz	9 ΑΕΡΙΟ
10 peligro	10 pericolo	10 perigo	10 tehlike	10 ΚΙΝΔΥΝΟΣ
11 contaminación	11 inquinamento	11 poluição	11 kirlenme	11 ΜΟΛΥΝΣΗ
12 ancla encepada	12 ancora impigliata	12 ferro preso	12 demir takıldı	12 ΜΠΕΡΔΕΜΕΝΗ ΑΓΚΥΡΑ
13 ancla garreando	13 ancora che ara	13 ferro agarrar	13 tarayan demir	13 ΑΓΚΥΡΑ ΠΟΥ ΞΕΣΕΡΝΕΙ
14 varar, encallar	14 incagliarsi	14 encalhar	14 kıyıya oturma	14 ΠΡΟΣΑΡΑΞΗ
15 costa de sotavento	15 costa sottovento	15 terra a sotavento	15 rüzgar altında seyir	15 ΠΡΟΣΗΝΕΜΟΣ ΑΚΤΗ
16 hundir	16 affondare	16 afundar	16 batmak	16 ΒΟΥΛΙΑΖΩ

ENGLISH	FRANÇAIS	DEUTSCH	NEDERLANDS	DANSK
1 EMERGENCIES	**1 URGENCES**	**1 NOTFÄLLE**	**I NOOGEVALLEN**	**1 NØDSITUATIONER**

Weather	**Le temps**	**Wetter**	**Weer**	**Vejr**
1 gale	1 coup de vent	1 stürmischer Wind	1 harde wind	1 hårdkuling
2 strong gale	2 fort coup de vent	2 Sturm	2 storm	2 stormende kuling
3 storm	3 tempête	3 schwerer Sturm	3 zware storm	3 storm
4 violent storm	4 violente tempête	4 orkanartiger Sturm	4 zeer zware storm	4 stærk storm
5 hurricane	5 ouragan	5 Orkan	5 hurricane, orkaan	5 orkan
6 breaking seas	6 lames déferlantes	6 brechende Seen	6 brekers, brekende zeeën	6 brydende søer
7 lightning strike	7 foudre	7 Blitzschlag	7 blikseminslag	7 lynnedslag

Damage	**Dégâts**	**Schaden**	**Schade**	**Skader**
1 stove in, holed	1 défoncé, troué	1 eingedrückt, Loch in	1 ingedrukt, lek	1 lækage
2 dismasted	2 démâté	2 entmastet	2 ontmast	2 tabt masten
3 broken rudder	3 gouvernail cassé	3 Ruderbruch	3 gebroken roer	3 brækket ror
4 broken keel	4 quille cassée	4 Kielbruch	4 gebroken kiel	4 brækket køl
5 to make water	5 faire de l'eau	5 Wasser machen	5 lek zijn	5 trække vand
6 to ship water	6 embarquer de l'eau	6 vollschlagen	6 water maken	6 tage vand ind
7 to pump the bilges	7 pomper, vider, assécher	7 Bilge lenzen	7 bilges leegpompen	7 pumpe læns
8 to bail out	8 écoper	8 ausösen	8 hozen	8 øse
9 engine failure	9 panne de moteur	9 Störung der Maschine	9 motorstoring	9 motorstop
10 electrical failure	10 panne d'électricité	10 Störung der Elektrik	10 elektrische storing	10 elektrisk fejl

Safety equipment	**Equipement de sécurité**	**Sicherheitsausrüstung**	**Veiligheidsuitrusting**	**Sikkerhedsudstyr**
1 fire extinguisher	1 extincteur d'incendie	1 Feuerlöscher	1 brandblusser	1 brandslukker
2 fog horn	2 corne de brume	2 Nebelhorn	2 misthoorn	2 tågehorn
3 bell	3 cloche	3 Glocke	3 bel	3 klokke
4 radar reflector	4 réflecteur radar	4 Radarreflektor	4 radarreflector	4 radar reflektor
5 distress flares	5 feux de détresse, fusées	5 Notsignalfeuer	5 vuurpijlen, noodsignalen	5 nødblus

ESPAÑOL	ITALIANO	PORTUGUÊS	TÜRKÇE	ΕΛΛΗΝΙΚΑ
1 EMERGENCIAS	**1 EMERGENZA**	**1 EMERGÊNCIAS**	**1 ACİL DURUMLAR**	**1 ΕΠΕΙΓΟΥΣΕΣ ΚΑΤΑΣΤΑΣΕΙΣ**
El tiempo	**Condizioni atmosferiche**	**Tempo**	**Hava**	**ΚΑΙΠΟΣ**
1 duro	1 burrasca	1 vento muito forte	1 fırtına	1 ΘΥΕΛΛΑ
2 muy duro	2 burrasca forte	2 vento tempestuoso	2 kuvvetli fırtına	2 ΙΣΧΥΡΗ ΘΥΕΛΛΑ
3 temporal	3 tempesta	3 temporal	3 tam fırtına	3 ΚΑΤΑΙΓΙΔΑ
4 borrasca	4 tempesta forte	4 temporal desfeito	4 çok şiddetli fırtına	4 ΙΣΧΥΡΗ ΚΑΤΑΙΓΙΔΛΑ
5 huracán	5 uragano	5 furacão	5 kasırga	5 ΑΝΕΜΟΘΥΕΛΛΑ
6 rompientes	6 frangenti	6 arrebentacão	6 kırılan dalgalar	6 ΑΦΡΙΣΜΕΝΑ ΚΥΜΑΤΑ
7 rayo	7 colpo di fulmine	7 relâmpago	7 yıldırım çarpması	7 ΚΕΡΑΥΝΟΣ
Averias	**Danni**	**Avarias**	**Hasar**	**ΖΗΜΙΑ**
1 desfondado	1 sfondato	1 porão	1 teknenin delinmesi	1 ΕΜΒΟΛΙΣΜΟΣ
2 desarbolado	2 disalberato	2 partir o mastro	2 direk kırmak	2 ΞΑΛΜΠΟΥΡΩΜΑ
3 timón averíado	3 timone in avaria	3 leme partido	3 dümenin kırılması	3 ΣΠΑΣΜΕΝΟ ΤΙΜΟΝΙ
4 quilla averíada	4 chiglia rotta	4 quilha partida	4 salma kırılması	4 ΣΠΑΣΜΕΝΗ ΚΑΡΙΝΑ
5 hacer agua	5 fare acqua	5 fazer água	5 su yapmak	5 ΚΑΝΩ ΝΕΡΑ
6 embarcar agua	6 imbarcare acqua	6 meter água	6 teknenin su alması	6 ΠΑΙΡΝΩ ΝΕΡΑ
7 achicar la sentina	7 svuotare la sentina	7 esgotar com bomba	7 sintineleri pompalamak	7 ΑΝΤΛΩ ΣΕΝΤΙΝΕΣ
8 achicar	8 sgottare	8 esgotar com bartedouro	8 suyu kovayla boşaltmak	8 ΑΔΕΙΑΖΩ ΝΕΡΑ
9 fallo de motor	9 guasto al motore	9 falha no motor	9 motor arızası	9 ΒΛΑΒΗ ΜΗΧΑΝΗΣ
10 fallo eléctrico	10 guasto elettrico	10 falha electrica	10 elektrik arızası	10 ΗΛΕΚΤΡΙΚΗ ΒΛΑΒΗ
Equipamiento de seguridad	**Dispositivi di sicurezza**	**Equipamento de segurança**	**Güvenlik donanımı (ekipman)**	**ΕΞΟΠΛΙΣΜΟΣ ΑΣΦΑΛΕΙΑΣ**
1 extintor	1 estintore	1 extintor	1 yangın söndürücü	1 ΠΥΡΟΣΒΕΣΤΗΡΑΣ
2 bocina de niebla	2 corno (da nebbia)	2 sereia de nevoeiro	2 sis düdüğü	2 ΜΠΟΥΡΟΥ
3 campana	3 campana	3 sino	3 çan	3 ΚΑΜΠΑΝΑ
4 reflector de radar	4 riflettore radar	4 reflector de radar	4 radar reflektörü	4 ΑΝΑΚΛΑΣΤΗΡΑΣ PANTAP
5 bengala	5 razzi di soccorso	5 fachos luminosos de socorro	5 tehlike fişekleri	5 ΦΩΤΟΒΟΛΙΔΕΣ

ENGLISH	FRANÇAIS	DEUTSCH	NEDERLANDS	DANSK
1 EMERGENCIES	**1 URGENCES**	**1 NOTFÄLLE**	**I NOODGEVALLEN**	**1 NØDSITUATIONER**
Safety equipment	**Equipement de sécurité**	**Sicherheitsausrüstung**	**Veiligheidsuitrusting**	**Sikkerhedsudstyr**
6 inflatable liferaft	6 radeau de survie	6 aufblasbare Rettungsinsel	6 opblaasbaar reddingvlot	6 oppustelig gummiflåde
7 safety harness	7 harnais, ceinture de sécurité	7 Sicherheitsgurt	7 veiligheidsgordel	7 sikkerhedssele
8 lifebelt	8 brassière	8 Rettungsring	8 veiligheidsgordel	8 redningsbælte
9 lifejacket	9 gilet de sauvetage	9 Schwimmweste	9 reddingvest	9 redningsvest
10 lifebuoy	10 bouée en fer à cheval	10 Rettungsboje	10 reddingboei	10 redningskrans
11 danbuoy	11 perche IOR	11 Bergungsboje	11 danbuoy	11 redningsbøje
12 floating line	12 ligne flottante	12 Schwimmleine	12 drijvende lijn	12 flydeline
13 EPIRB	13 balise de détresse	13 Seenotfunkboje	13 EPIRB	13 EPIRB
14 search & rescue transponder	14 balise émettrice	14 Seenotfunkboje	14 opsporings en reddings transponder	14 eftersøgnings og redningsoperation
15 bung/plug	15 bouchon	15 Leckpfropfen	15 stop, plug	15 prop

ESPAÑOL	ITALIANO	PORTUGUÊS	TÜRKÇE	EΛΛHNIKA
1 EMERGENCIAS	**1 EMERGENZA**	**1 EMERGÊNCIAS**	**1 ACİL DURUMLAR**	**1 ΕΠΕΙΓΟΥΣΕΣ ΚΑΤΑΣΤΑΣΕΙΣ**
Equipamiento de seguridad	**Dispositivi di sicurezza**	**Equipamento de segurança**	**Güvenlik donanımı (ekipman)**	**ΕΞΟΠΛΙΣΜΟΣ ΑΣΦΑΛΕΙΑΣ**
6 balsa salvavidas	6 zattera gonfiabile	6 jangada pneumática de salvação	6 şişme can salı	6 ΝΑΥΑΓΟΣΩΣΤΙΚΗ ΣΧΕΔΙΑ
7 cinturón de seguri-dad	7 cintura di sicurezza	7 cinto de segurança	7 emniyet kemeri	7 ΕΞΑΡΤΗΣΗ ΑΣΦΑΛΕΙΑΣ
8 salvavidas	8 salvagente	8 bóia de salvação	8 can kemeri	8 ΖΩΝΗ ΑΣΦΑΛΕΙΑΣ
9 chaleco salvavidas	9 giubbotto di salvataggio	9 cinto, colete de salvação	9 can yeleği	9 ΣΩΣΙΒΙΟ
10 salvavidas abierto	10 salvagente a ferro di cavallo con luce	10 bóia de ferradura	10 can simidi	10 ΠΕΤΑΛΟ – ΣΩΣΙΒΙΟ
11 boya de socorro	11 gavitello	11 bóia de sinalização de homem ao mar	11 can simidi göstergesi	11 ΑΝΘΡΩΠΟΣ ΣΤΗ ΘΑΛΑΣΣΑ
12 cabo que flota	12 cima galleggiante	12 retenida flutuante	12 yüzen (batmayan) halat	12 ΣΧΟΙΝΙ ΠΟΥ ΕΠΙΠΛΕΕΙ
13 radio baliza para local-ización de sinistros	13 EPIRB	13 EPIRB	13 EPİRB	13 ΕΠΙΡΜΠ
14 transpondador de busca y salvamenta	14 trasponditore di ricerca e salvataggio	14 busca e salvamento	14 elektronik arama ve tarama aygıtı (transponder)	14 ΜΕΤΑΔΟΤΗΣ ΑΝΑΖΗΤΗΣΗΣ ΚΑΙ ΔΙΑΣΩΣΗΣ
15 tapón	15 foro d'allievo/tappo	15 bujão de boeira	15 tıpa, miçoz	15 ΤΑΠΑ

ENGLISH	FRANÇAIS	DEUTSCH	NEDERLANDS	DANSK
2 MEDICAL EMERGENCIES	**2 URGENCES MEDICALES**	**2 MEDIZINISCHE NOTFÄLLE**	**2 MEDISCHE NOODGEVALLEN**	**2 FØRSTEHJÆLP**
Asking for help	**Demandes de secours**	**Hilferuf**	**Vragen om hulp**	**Anmode om hjælp**
1 please can you direct me to … ?	1 s'il vous plaît, où puis- je trouver …?	1 Bitte zeigen Sie mir den Weg …	1 Kunt u me de weg wijzen naar …?	1 hvor finder jeg…?
2 the doctor	2 le médecin	2 zum Arzt	2 de dokter	2 lægen
3 the hospital	3 l'hôpital	3 zum Krankenhaus	3 het ziekenhuis	3 hospitalet
4 the dentist	4 le dentiste	4 zum Zahnarzt	4 de tandarts	4 tandlægen
5 the chemist	5 le pharmacien	5 zur Apotheke	5 de apotheker	5 apoteket
6 the optician	6 l'opticien	6 zum Optiker	6 de oogarts	6 optikeren
7 someone is injured	7 quelqu'un est blessé	7 jemand ist verletzt	7 er is iemand gewond	7 en mand er såret
8 someone is ill	8 quelqu'un est malade	8 jemand ist krank	8 er is iemand ziek	8 en mand er syg
Symptoms	**Symptômes**	**Symptome**	**Symptomen**	**Symptomer**
1 burn	1 brûlure	1 Brandwunde	1 brandwond	1 brandsår
2 scald	2 échaudure	2 Verbrennung	2 verbranding	2 skoldet
3 shock	3 traumatisme, choc	3 Schock	3 shock	3 chok
4 broken	4 cassé	4 gebrochen	4 gebroken	4 brækket
5 fracture	5 fracture	5 Fraktur, Bruch	5 breuk	5 brud
6 compound fracture	6 fracture compliquée	6 komplizierter Bruch	6 gecompliceerde breuk	6 kompliceret brud
7 swelling	7 enflure, hypertrophie	7 Schwellung	7 zwelling	7 hævelse
8 bruise	8 contusion	8 Prellung	8 kneuzing	8 kvæstelse
9 to cut open	9 faire une incision	9 aufschneiden	9 opensnijden	9 skære op
10 bleeding	10 saignement	10 blutend	10 bloeden	10 blødende
11 haemorrhage	11 hémorragie	11 Blutung	11 bloeding	11 blødning
12 internal haemorrhage	12 hémorragie interne	12 innere Blutung	12 interne bloeding	12 indvendig blødning
13 low blood pressure	13 tension basse	13 niedriger Blutdruck	13 lage bloeddruk	13 lavt blodtryk
14 to drown, drowning	14 se noyer, noyade	14 Ertrinken	14 verdrinken	14 drukne
15 hypothermia	15 hypothermie	15 Unterkühlung	15 onderkoeling	15 hypotermia

ESPAÑOL	ITALIANO	PORTUGUÊS	TÜRKÇE	ΕΛΛΗΝΙΚΑ
2 URGENCIAS MEDICAS	**2 EMERGENZA MEDICA**	**2 EMERGÊNCIAS MÉDICAS**	**2 TIBBİ ACİL DURUMLAR**	**2 ΙΑΤΡΙΚΑ ΕΠΕΙΓΟΝΤΑ**
Pidiendo ayuda	**Richiesta d'aiuto**	**Pedido de socorro**	**Yardım isteme/yardım çağirisi**	**ΖΗΤΩ ΒΟΗΘΕΙΑ**
1 ¿Por favor puede Ùsted guiarme...?	1 per favore, può indicarmi ...?	1 faz favor indicat-me	1 lütfen beni ... e yönlendirin	1 ΠΑΡΑΚΑΛΩ ΜΠΟΡΕΙΤΕ ΝΑ ΜΕ ΟΔΗΓΕΙΣΤΕ ΠΡΟΣ
2 al médico	2 il dottore	2 um médico	2 doktor	2 ΤΟΝ ΓΙΑΤΡΟ
3 al hospital	3 l'ospedale	3 um hospital	3 hastane	3 ΤΟ ΝΟΣΟΚΟΜΕΙΟ
4 al dentista	4 il dentista	4 um dentista	4 dişçi	4 ΤΟΝ ΟΔΟΝΤΟΓΙΑΤΡΟ
5 al farmacéutico	5 la farmacia	5 uma farmácia	5 eczacı	5 ΤΟ ΦΑΡΜΑΚΕΙΟ
6 al Optico	6 l'oculista	6 oftalmologista	6 göz doktoru	6 ΤΟΝ ΟΦΘΑΛΜΙΑΤΡΟ
7 alguien esta herido	7 qualcuno è ferito	7 temos alguém ferido	7 yaralanan var	7 ΚΑΠΟΙΟΣ ΕΙΝΑΙ ΠΛΗΓΩΜΕΝΟΣ
8 alguien esta enfermo	8 qualcuno sta male	8 temos um doente	8 hasta var	8 ΚΑΠΟΙΟΣ ΕΙΝΑΙ ΑΡΡΩΣΤΟΣ
Simptomas	**Sintomi**	**Sintomas**	**Belirtiler**	**ΣΥΜΠΤΩΜΑΤΑ**
1 quemadura	1 ustione	1 queimadura	1 yanık	1 ΕΓΚΑΥΜΑ
2 escaldado	2 scottatura	2 escaldadura	2 haşlanmak	2 ΚΑΨΙΜΟ
3 shock	3 shock	3 choque	3 sok	3 ΣΟΚ
4 roto	4 rotto	4 partido	4 parçalanmak, kopmak, kesilmek	4 ΣΠΑΣΜΕΝΟ
5 fractura	5 frattura	5 fractura	5 kırık, kemik, kırığı	5 ΚΑΤΑΓΜΑ
6 fractura conminuta	6 frattura composta	6 fractura múltipla	6 İhtilâtlı kırık	6 ΠΟΛΛΑΠΛΟ ΚΑΤΑΓΜΑ
7 hinchazón, hinchado	7 gonfiore	7 inchação	7 şiş	7 ΠΡΗΞΙΜΟ
8 cardenal, chichón	8 escoriazione	8 contusão	8 bere	8 ΚΑΚΩΣΗ
9 hacer una incisión	9 tagliarsi profondamente	9 cortar para abrir	9 yarmak	9 ΚΟΒΩ – ΑΝΟΙΓΩ
10 sangrando	10 sanguinare	10 sangrar	10 kanama	10 ΑΙΜΟΡΡΑΓΙΑ
11 hemorragia	11 emorragia	11 hemorragia	11 hemoraji, kanama	11 ΑΙΜΟΡΡΑΓΙΑ
12 hemorragia interna	12 emorragia interna	12 hemorragia interna	12 iç kanama	12 ΕΣΩΤΕΡΙΚΗ ΑΙΜΟΡΡΑΓΙΑ
13 tensión baja	13 bassa pressione sanguigna	13 baixa de tensão	13 düşük kan basıncı	13 ΧΑΜΗΛΗ ΠΙΕΣΗ
14 ahogarse	14 annegare	14 afogar-se	14 boğulmak, boğulma	14 ΠΝΙΓΜΟΣ
15 hypotermia	15 ipotermia	15 hipotermia	15 hipotermi	15 ΥΠΟΘΕΡΜΙΑ

ENGLISH	FRANÇAIS	DEUTSCH	NEDERLANDS	DANSK
2 MEDICAL EMERGENCIES	**2 URGENCES MEDICALES**	**2 MEDIZINISCHE NOTFÄLLE**	**2 MEDISCHE NOODGEVALLEN**	**2 FØRSTEHJÆLP**
Symptoms	**Symptômes**	**Symptome**	**Symptomen**	**Symptomer**
16 carbon monoxide poisoning	16 asphyxie ou empoisonnement par l'oxyde de carbonne	16 Kohlenmonoxid-vergiftung	16 koolmonoxyde vergiftiging	16 kulilte-forgiftning
17 suffocation	17 asphyxie	17 Erstickung	17 verstikking	17 kvælning
18 breathing problem	18 problème de respiration	18 Atemprobleme	18 ademhalings-probleem	18 åndedrætsbesvær
19 electric shock	19 décharge électrique	19 elektrischer Schlag	19 elektrische schok	19 elektrisk chok
20 unconscious	20 évanoui, inconscient, comateux	20 ohnmächtig, beuwußtlos	20 buiten bewustzijn, bewusteloos	20 bevidstløs
21 sunstroke	21 coup de soleil	21 Sonnenstich	21 zonnesteek	21 solstik
22 heatstroke	22 coup de chaleur	22 Hitzschlag	22 zonnesteek, bevangen zijn	22 hedeslag
23 sunburn	23 brúlure par le soleil	23 Sonnenbrand	23 zonnebrand	23 solskoldet
24 illness	24 maladie	24 Krankheit	24 ziekte	24 dårligt tilpas
25 high temperature, fever	25 fièvre	25 Fieber	25 verhoging, koorts	25 høj temperatur, feber
26 pain	26 douleur	26 Schmerz	26 pijn	26 smerte
27 infection	27 infection	27 Infektion	27 infectie	27 infektion
28 septic	28 septique	28 septisch	28 septisch	28 betændelse
29 paralysis	29 paralysie	29 Lähmung	29 verlamming	29 lammelse
30 heart attack/pain	30 crise/douleur cardiaque	30 Herzanfall/Herzschmerzen	30 hartaanval/pijn	30 hjerteanfald
31 allergy	31 allergie	31 Allergie	31 allergie	31 allergi
32 rash	32 éruption	32 Hautausschlag	32 uitslag (huiduitslag)	32 udslæt
33 insect bite/sting	33 piqúre d'insecte	33 Insektenbiß/Insektenstich	33 insektebeet/steek	33 insektbid/stik
34 poisoning	34 empoisonnement	34 Vergiftung	34 vergiftiging	34 forgiftning
35 diarrhoea	35 diarrhée	35 Durchfall	35 diarree, buikloop	35 diarré
36 stomach upset	36 digestion dérangée	36 Bauchbeschwerden, Magenbeschwerden	36 maag van streek	36 mavepine
37 stomach ache	37 mal au ventre	37 Magenschmerzen	37 buikpijn	37 mavesmerter
38 vomiting	38 vomissement	38 Brechreiz	38 overgeven, braken	38 opkast
39 dehydration	39 déshydration	39 Austrocknung	39 uitdrogings-verschijnselen	39 tørst

ESPAÑOL	ITALIANO	PORTUGUÊS	TÜRKÇE	ΕΛΛΗΝΙΚΑ
2 URGENCIAS MEDICAS	**2 EMERGENZA MEDICA**	**2 EMERGÊNCIAS MÉDICAS**	**2 TIBBİ ACİL DURUMLAR**	**2 ΙΑΤΡΙΚΑ ΕΠΕΙΓΟΝΤΑ**
Simptomas	**Sintomi**	**Sintomas**	**Belirtiler**	**ΣΥΜΠΤΩΜΑΤΑ**
16 envenenamiento por óxido de carbono	16 avvelenamento da monossido di carbonio	16 intoxicação por gaz de óxido de carbono	16 karbon monoksit zehirlenmesi	16 ΔΗΛΗΤΗΡΙΑΣΗ ΑΠΟ ΜΟΝΟΞΕΙΔΙΟ ΑΝΘΡΑΚΑ
17 asfixia	17 soffocamento	17 sufocaçao	17 nefessiz kalma	17 ΑΣΦΥΞΙΑ
18 problema respiratorio	18 problema di respirazione	18 problema de respiração	18 solunum sorunu	18 ΠΡΟΒΛΗΜΑ ΑΝΑΠΝΟΗΣ
19 descarga eléctrica	19 shock elettrico	19 choque eléctrico	19 elektrik çarpması, şoku	19 ΗΛΕΚΤΡΙΚΟ ΣΟΚ
20 sin conocimiento	20 svenuto	20 sem sentidos	20 bilinçsiz	20 ΑΝΑΙΣΘΗΤΟΣ
21 insolación	21 colpo di sole	21 insolação	21 güneş çarpması	21 ΗΛΙΑΣΗ
22 insolación	22 colpo di calore	22 insolação derido ao calôr	22 sıcak çarpması	22 ΘΕΡΜΟΠΛΗΞΙΑ
23 quemadura del sol	23 scottatura da sole	23 queimadura de sol	23 güneş yanığı	23 ΕΓΚΑΥΜΑ ΑΠΟ ΤΟΝ ΗΛΙΟ
24 enfermedad	24 malore	24 doença	24 hastalık	24 ΑΡΡΩΣΤΙΑ
25 fiebre alta	25 febbre	25 temperatura alta, febre	25 yüksek ateş, ateş	25 ΠΥΡΕΤΟΣ
26 dolor	26 dolore	26 dôr	26 ağrı,acı	26 ΠΟΝΟΣ
27 infección	27 infezione	27 infecção	27 enfeksiyon	27 ΜΟΛΥΝΣΗ
28 séptico	28 settico	28 aceptico	28 septik	28 ΜΟΛΥΣΜΕΝΟ
29 parálisis	29 paralisi	29 paralisia	29 felç	29 ΠΑΡΑΛΥΣΗ
30 ataque cardiaco/angina de pecho	30 attacco/dolore cardiaco	30 ataque de coração/dor	30 kalp krizi, ağrısı	30 ΚΑΡΔΙΑΚΗ ΠΡΟΣΒΟΛΗ – ΠΟΝΟΣ
31 alergia	31 allergia	31 alergia	31 allerji	31 ΑΛΛΕΡΓΙΑ
32 urticaria	32 eruzione	32 erupçâo de sangue	32 isilik	32 ΕΞΑΝΘΗΜΑ
33 picadura de insecto	33 morso/puntura d'insetto	33 picada de insecto/ferrão	33 böcek sokması	33 ΤΣΙΜΠΗΜΑ ΕΝΤΟΜΟΥ
34 envenenamiento	34 avvelenamento	34 envenenamento	34 zehirlenme	34 ΔΗΛΗΤΗΡΙΑΣΗ
35 diarrea	35 diarrea	35 diarreia	35 diarre, ishal	35 ΔΙΑΡΡΟΙΑ
36 mal de estómago	36 stomaco scombussolato	36 cólicas	36 mide bozukluğu	36 ΣΤΟΜΑΧΙΚΗ ΔΙΑΤΑΡΑΧΗ
37 dolor de estómago	37 mal di stomaco	37 dor de estômago	37 mide sancısı	37 ΣΤΟΜΑΧΟΠΟΝΟΣ
38 vomitos	38 vomito	38 vomitar	38 kusma, kay	38 ΕΜΕΤΟΣ
39 deshidratación	39 disidratazione	39 desidratação	39 su kaybı	39 ΑΦΥΔΑΤΩΣΗ

ENGLISH	FRANÇAIS	DEUTSCH	NEDERLANDS	DANSK
2 MEDICAL EMERGENCIES	**2 URGENCES MEDICALES**	**2 MEDIZINISCHE NOTFÄLLE**	**2 MEDISCHE NOODGEVALLEN**	**2 FØRSTEHJÆLP**
Symptoms	**Symptômes**	**Symptome**	**Symptomen**	**Symptomer**
40 constipation	40 constipation	40 Verstopfung	40 verstopping	40 forstoppelse
41 urine	41 urine	41 Urin	41 urine	41 urin
42 toothache	42 rage de dents	42 Zahnschmerzen	42 kies/tandpijn	42 tandpine
43 abscess	43 abcès	43 Abszeß	43 gezwel, abces	43 bylder
44 backache	44 mal au dos	44 Rückenschmerzen	44 rugpijn	44 rygsmerter
45 earache	45 mal à l'oreille	45 Ohrenschmerzen	45 oorpijn	45 ørepine
46 concussion	46 traumatisme crânien	46 Erschütterung	46 hersenschudding	46 hjernerystelse
47 headache	47 mal à la tête	47 Kopfschmerzen	47 hoofdpijn	47 hovedpine
48 migraine	48 migraine	48 Migräne	48 migraine	48 migræne
49 sore throat	49 mal de gorge	49 Halsschmerzen	49 zere keel, keelpijn	49 ondt i halsen
50 pregnant	50 enceinte	50 schwanger	50 zwanger, in verwachting	50 gravid
51 epilepsy	51 épilepsie	51 Epilepsie	51 epilepsie	51 epilepsi
52 diabetes	52 diabète	52 Diabetes, Zuckerkrankheit	52 suikerziekte	52 sukkersyge
Treatment	**Traitement**	**Behandlung**	**Behandelingen**	**Behandling**
1 artificial respiration	1 respiration artificielle	1 künstliche Beatmung	1 kunstmatige ademhaling	1 kunstigt åndedræt
2 pulse	2 pouls	2 Puls	2 pols, polsslag	2 puls
3 to dress a wound	3 faire un bandage, poser un pansement	3 einen Verband anlegen	3 een wond verbinden	3 forbinde et sår
4 antiseptic cream	4 onguent antiseptique	4 antiseptische Salbe	4 desinfecterende zalf	4 anticeptisk creme
5 aspirin tablets	5 aspirine	5 Aspirin	5 aspirinetabletten	5 hovedpinetabletter
6 paracetamol	6 paracetamol	6 Paracetamol	6 paracetamol	6 paracetamol
7 painkillers	7 analgésiques	7 Schmerztabletten	7 pijnstillers	7 smertestillende midler
8 anaesthetic	8 anesthésie	8 gefühllos	8 verdoving	8 bedøvelse
9 sleeping pills	9 somnifère, sédatif	9 Schlaftabletten	9 slaappillen	9 sovetabletter
10 laxative	10 laxatif, purgatif	10 Abführmittel	10 laxeermiddel	10 afføringsmidler
11 suppositories	11 suppositoires	11 Zäpfchen	11 zetpil	11 søsygepiller
12 anti-seasickness pills	12 remède contre le mal de mer	12 Medikament gegen Seekrankheit	12 zeeziektepillen	12 stikpiller

ESPAÑOL	ITALIANO	PORTUGUÊS	TÜRKÇE	ΕΛΛΗΝΙΚΑ
2 URGENCIAS MEDICAS	**2 EMERGENZA MEDICA**	**2 EMERGÊNCIAS MÉDICAS**	**2 TIBBİ ACİL DURUMLAR**	**2 ΙΑΤΡΙΚΑ ΕΠΕΙΓΟΝΤΑ**
Simptomas	**Sintomi**	**Sintomas**	**Belirtiler**	**ΣΥΜΠΤΩΜΑΤΑ**
40 estreñimiento	40 stitichezza	40 mal da barriga	40 kabızlık	40 ΔΥΣΚΟΙΛΙΟΤΗΣ
41 orina	41 urina	41 urina	41 sidik	41 ΟΥΡΑ
42 dolor de muelas	42 mal di denti	42 dôr dos dentes	42 diş ağrısı	42 ΠΟΝΟΔΟΝΤΟΣ
43 abceso, flemón	43 ascesso	43 abcesso	43 abse	43 ΦΟΥΣΚΑΛΑ
44 dolor de espalda	44 mal di schiena	44 dor nas costas	44 sırt ağrısı	44 ΠΟΝΟΣ ΣΤΗΝ ΠΛΑΤΗ
45 dolor de oidos	45 mal d'orecchi	45 dor de ouvidos	45 kulak ağrısı	45 ΠΟΝΟΣ ΣΤΟ ΑΥΤΙ
46 conmoción	46 concussione	46 concussão	46 başa darbe	46 ΔΙΑΣΕΙΣΗ
47 dolor de cabeza	47 mal di testa	47 dor de cabeça	47 başağrısı	47 ΠΟΝΟΚΕΦΑΛΟΣ
48 jaqueca	48 emicrania	48 enxaqueca	48 migren	48 ΗΜΙΚΡΑΝΙΑ
49 dolor de garganta	49 mal di gola	49 dor de garganta	49 boğaz ağrısı	49 ΠΟΝΟΛΑΙΜΟΣ
50 embarazo	50 incinta	50 grávida	50 hamile	50 ΕΓΚΥΟΣ
51 epilepsia	51 epilessia	51 epilepsia	51 epilepsi, sara	51 ΕΠΙΛΗΨΙΑ
52 diabetes	52 diabete	52 diabetes	52 diabet	52 ΔΙΑΒΗΤΗ
Tratamiento	**Cure**	**Tratamento**	**Tıbbı yardım ve tedavi**	**ΘΕΡΑΠΕΙΑ**
1 respiración artificial	1 respirazione artificiale	1 respiração artificial	1 suni solunum	1 ΤΕΧΝΗΤΗ ΑΝΑΠΝΟΗ
2 pulso	2 polso	2 pulso	2 nabız	2 ΣΦΥΓΜΟΣ
3 curar una herida	3 medicare una ferita	3 tratar uma ferida	3 yara pansumanı	3 ΕΠΙΔΕΣΗ
4 pomada de sulfamidas	4 pomata antisettica	4 pomada antiséptica	4 antiseptik merhem	4 ΑΝΤΙΣΗΠΤΙΚΗ ΚΡΕΜΑ
5 pastillas de aspirina	5 compresse d'aspirina	5 compromidos de aspirina	5 aspirin tabletleri	5 ΔΙΣΚΙΑ ΑΣΠΙΡΙΝΗΣ
6 paracetamol	6 paracetamolo	6 paracetamol	6 paracetamol	6 ΠΑΡΑΚΕΤΑΜΟΛΗ
7 analgesicos	7 antidolorifico	7 analgésico	7 ağrı dindiriciler	7 ΑΝΑΛΓΗΤΙΚΑ
8 anestesia	8 anestetico	8 anestésico	8 anastezik	8 ΑΝΑΙΣΘΗΤΙΚΑ
9 pildoras somniferas	9 sonnifero	9 compromidos para dormir	9 uyku hapları	9 ΥΠΝΩΤΙΚΑ ΧΑΠΙΑ
10 laxante	10 lassativo	10 laxativo	10 laksatif	10 ΚΑΘΑΡΤΙΚΑ
11 supositorios	11 supposte	11 supositórios	11 süppozituarlar, fitille	11 ΥΠΟΘΕΤΑ
12 pildoras contra el mareo	12 pillole contro il mal di mare	12 compromidos para não enjoar	12 deniz tutmasına karşı hap	12 ΔΙΣΚΙΑ ΓΙΑ ΤΗΝ ΝΑΥΤΙΑ

ENGLISH	FRANÇAIS	DEUTSCH	NEDERLANDS	DANSK
2 MEDICAL EMERGENCIES	**2 URGENCES MEDICALES**	**2 MEDIZINISCHE NOTFÄLLE**	**2 MEDISCHE NOODGEVALLEN**	**2 FØRSTEHJÆLP**
Treatment	**Traitement**	**Behandlung**	**Behandelingen**	**Behandling**
13 anti-histamine	13 anti-histamine	13 Antihistamine	13 anti-histamine	13 anti-histamin
14 anti-diarrhoea	14 anti-diarrhée	14 Durchfallmittel	14 anti-diarree	14 midler mod diarré
15 antibiotic	15 antibiotique	15 Antibiotika	15 antibiotica	15 antibiotika
16 anti-tetanus	16 anti-têtanos	16 Tetanusschutzimpfung	16 anti-tetanus	16 stivkrampemidler
17 eye lotion	17 Optrex™	17 Augentropfen	17 oogdruppels	17 øjensalve
18 ear drops	18 goûttes pour l'oreille	18 Ohrentropfen	18 oordruppels	18 øjendråber
19 inhaler	19 inhalateur	19 Inhalator	19 respirator	19 inhalator
20 rehydration	20 réhydratation	20 Flüssigkeitsausgleich	20 bevochtiger	20 genhydrering
21 splint	21 attelle	21 Schiene	21 splinter/spalk	21 splint
22 injection	22 piqûre	22 Injektion	22 injectie	22 insprøjtning
23 insulin	23 insuline	23 Insulin	23 insuline	23 insulin
Equipment	**Equipement**	**Ausrüstung**	**Uitrusting**	**Udstyr**
1 first aid box	1 pharmacie de bord	1 Bordapotheke	1 EHBO kist	1 Førstehjælpskasse
2 wound dressing	2 pansement stérilisé	2 Notverband	2 verbandgaas	2 at forbinde et sår
3 cotton wool	3 ouate, coton hydrophile	3 Watte	3 pluksel, watten	3 vat
4 sticking plaster	4 pansement adhésif, sparadrap	4 Heftpflaster	4 pleister, leukoplast	4 hæfteplaster
5 bandage	5 bandage	5 Binde, Verband	5 verbandwindsel	5 forbinding
6 elastic bandage	6 bandage élastique	6 elastische Binde	6 elastisch verband	6 elastikbind
7 scissors	7 ciseaux	7 Schere	7 schaar	7 saks
8 safety pin	8 épingle de sureté	8 Sicherheitsnadel	8 veiligheidsspeld	8 sikkerhedsnåle
9 tweezers	9 pince à echardes	9 Pinzette	9 pincet	9 pincet
10 thermometer	10 thermomètre	10 Thermometer	10 thermometer	10 termometer
11 disinfectant	11 désinfectant	11 Desinfektionsmittel	11 ontsmettingsmiddel	11 desinfektionsvand
12 stretcher	12 brancard	12 Trage	12 draagbaar	12 båre
13 spectacles	13 lunettes	13 Brille	13 bril	13 briller
14 contact lens	14 verres de contact	14 Kontaktlinse	14 contactlens	14 kontaktlinser
15 sterile hypodermic	15 seringue stérile	15 steril unter die Haut…	15 steriel gaasje	15 steril sprøjte

ESPAÑOL	ITALIANO	PORTUGUÊS	TÜRKÇE	ΕΛΛΗΝΙΚΑ
2 URGENCIAS MEDICAS	**2 EMERGENZA MEDICA**	**2 EMERGÊNCIAS MÉDICAS**	**2 TIBBİ ACİL DURUMLAR**	**2 ΙΑΤΡΙΚΑ ΕΠΕΙΓΟΝΤΑ**
Tratamiento	**Cure**	**Tratamento**	**Tıbbi yardım ve tedavi**	**ΘΕΡΑΠΕΙΑ**
13 antihistaminico	13 antistaminico	13 anti-hestaminico	13 antihistaminik	13 ΑΝΤΙΙΣΤΑΜΙΝΙΚΑ
14 antidiarreco	14 anti-diarrea	14 anti-diarreia	14 ishal kesici	14 ΕΝΑΝΤΙΟΝ ΤΗΣ ΔΙΑΡΡΟΙΑΣ
15 antibiotico	15 antibiotico	15 antibiótico	15 antibiyotik	15 ΑΝΤΙΒΙΟΤΙΚΑ
16 antitetanico	16 antitetanico	16 antitetânico	16 tetanos aşısı	16 ΑΝΤΙΤΕΤΑΝΙΚΑ
17 colirio	17 collirio	17 anticongestivo	17 göz losyonu	17 ΟΦΘΑΛΜΙΚΟ ΥΓΡΟ
18 gotas para los oidos	18 gocce per l'otite	18 gotas para os ouvidos	18 göz damlası	18 ΣΤΑΓΟΝΕΣ ΓΙΑ ΤΑ ΑΥΤΙΑ
19 inhalador	19 inalatore	19 inalador	19 nefes açıcı	19 ΣΠΡΕΙ ΕΙΣΠΝΟΩΝ
20 rehidratación	20 reidratazione	20 rehidratação	20 su kaybını gidermek	20 ΕΠΑΝΥΔΑΤΩΣΗ
21 tablilla	21 stecca	21 colocar em talas	21 kırık sargısı	21 ΝΑΡΘΗΚΑΣ
22 inyección	22 iniezione	22 injecção	22 enjeksiyon	22 ΕΝΕΣΗ
23 insulina	23 insulina	23 insulina	23 ensulin	23 ΙΝΣΟΥΛΙΝΗ
Equipamiento	**Materiali**	**Equipamento**	**Ekipman**	**ΕΞΟΠΛΙΣΜΟΣ**
1 botiquin	1 cassetta di pronto soccorso	1 caixa de medicamentes para socorro	1 ilk yardım kutusu	1 ΚΟΥΤΙ ΠΡΩΤΩΝ ΒΟΗΘΕΙΩΝ
2 gasa	2 medicazione	2 penso	2 yara pansumanı	2 ΓΑΖΕΣ
3 algodón hydrófilo	3 cotone idrofilo	3 algodão	3 hidrofil pamuk	3 ΒΑΜΒΑΚΙ
4 esparadrapo	4 cerotto	4 adesivo	4 yara bandı	4 ΛΕΥΚΟΠΛΑΣΤΗΣ
5 venda	5 benda	5 ligadura	5 sargı	5 ΕΠΙΔΕΣΜΟΣ
6 venda de elástico	6 benda elastica	6 ligadura elástica	6 elastik sargı, bandaj	6 ΕΛΑΣΤΙΚΟΣ ΕΠΙΔΕΣΜΟΣ
7 tijeras	7 forbici	7 tesoura	7 makas	7 ΨΑΛΙΔΙ
8 imperdibles	8 spilla di sicurezza	8 alfinetes de dama	8 çengelli iğne	8 ΠΑΡΑΜΑΝΑ
9 pinzas	9 pinzette	9 pinças	9 cımbız	9 ΤΣΙΜΠΙΔΑΚΙ
10 termómetro	10 termometro	10 termómetro	10 termometre	10 ΘΕΡΜΟΜΕΤΡΟ
11 desinfectante	11 disinfettante	11 desinfectante	11 dezenfektan, mikrop öldürücü	11 ΑΠΟΛΥΜΑΝΤΙΚΟ
12 camilla	12 barella	12 maca	12 sedye	12 ΦΟΡΕΙΟ
13 gafas	13 occhiali	13 óculos	13 gözlük	13 ΓΥΑΛΙΑ
14 lentillas	14 lente a contatto	14 lentes de contacto	14 kontakt lens	14 ΦΑΚΟΙ ΕΠΑΦΗΣ
15 aguja hipodérmica esteilizada	15 siringa ipodermica sterile	15 agulha esterelizada	15 steril hipotermik iğne	15 ΣΥΡΙΓΓΑ ΜΙΑΣ ΧΡΗΣΕΩΣ

ENGLISH	FRANÇAIS	DEUTSCH	NEDERLANDS	DANSK
3 FORMALITIES	**3 FORMALITES**	**3 FORMALITÄTEN**	**3 FORMALITEITEN**	**3 FORMALITETER**
1 harbourmaster	1 Capitaine du port	1 Hafenkapitän	1 havenmeester	1 havnefoged
2 harbour dues	2 Droits de port	2 Hafengebühren	2 havengeld	2 havnepenge
3 port police	3 Police du port	3 Hafenpolizei	3 (haven) politie	3 havnepoliti
4 immigration	4 Immigration	4 Grenzschutz, Einwanderungsbehörde	4 immigratie-ambtenaar	4 immigration
5 customs	5 Douanes	5 Zoll	5 douane	5 told
6 health authority	6 Autorités sanitaires	6 hafenärztlicher Dienst	6 gezondheidsdienst	6 sundhedstilsyn
7 boat name	7 nom du bateau	7 Schiffsname	7 scheepsnaam	7 bådenavn
8 length overall/LOA	8 longueur hors-tout	8 Länge über Alles/LüA	8 lengte over alles/LOA	8 længde overalt/LOA
9 skipper	9 skipper	9 Schiffsführer	9 schipper	9 skipper
10 owner	10 propriétaire	10 Eigner	10 eigenaar	10 ejer
11 address	11 adresse	11 Adresse	11 adres	11 adresse
12 beam	12 largeur	12 Schiffsbreite	12 breedte	12 bredde
13 draught	13 tiran d'eau	13 Tiefgang	13 diepgang	13 dybgang
14 sailing yacht	14 voilier	14 Segelyacht	14 zeiljacht	14 sejlbåd
15 motor yacht	15 motor yacht	15 Motoryacht	15 motorjacht	15 motorbåd
16 auxiliary engine	16 moteur auxiliaire	16 Hilfsmotor	16 hulpmotor	16 hjælpemotor
17 wooden construction	17 construction en bois	17 Holzbauweise	17 houtbouw	17 trækonstruktion
18 glass reinforced plastic/GRP	18 polyester renforcé fibre de verre	18 glasfaserverstärkter Kunststoff/GFK	18 polyester	18 glasfiberarmeret polyester
19 steel	19 acier	19 Stahl	19 staal	19 stål
20 aluminium	20 aluminium	20 Aluminium	20 aluminium	20 aluminium
21 ferro-cement	21 ferro-ciment	21 Ferrozement	21 ferro-cement	21 ferro-cement
22 diesel	22 diesel	22 Diesel	22 dieselolie/gasolie	22 diesel
23 petrol	23 essence	23 Benzin	23 benzine	23 benzin
24 horsepower	24 cheval vapeur (CV)	24 Pferdestärken	24 paardekracht	24 hestekræfter
25 flag/nationality	25 pavillon/nationalité	25 Flagge/Nationalität	25 natonaliteit	25 flag/nationalitet
26 port of registry	26 port d'attache	26 Heimathafen	26 registratiehaven, thuishaven	26 hjemmehavn
27 registration number	27 numéro d'immatriculation	27 Registriernummer	27 registratienummer	27 registreringsnummer
28 last port of call	28 dernière escale	28 zuletzt angelaufener Hafen	28 laatste aanloophaven	28 forrige anløbshavn

ESPAÑOL	ITALIANO	PORTUGUÊS	TÜRKÇE	ΕΛΛΗΝΙΚΑ
3 FORMALIDADES	**3 FORMALITA**	**3 FORMALIDADES**	**3 FORMALİTELER**	**3 ΔΙΑΤΥΠΩΣΕΙΣ**
1 Capitán de puerto	1 capitano del porto	1 director da marina	1 liman başkanı	1 ΛΙΜΕΝΑΡΧΗΣ
2 derechos de puerto	2 diritti portuali	2 taxas	2 liman harçları	2 ΛΙΜΕΝΙΚΟ ΤΕΛΟΣ
3 policia de puerto	3 polizia marittima	3 policia marítima	3 liman polisi	3 ΛΙΜΕΝΙΚΗ ΑΣΤΥΝΟΜΙΑ
4 inmigración	4 immigrazione	4 emigração	4 pasaport polisi	4 ΑΛΛΟΔΑΠΩΝ
5 aduana	5 dogana	5 alfândega	5 gümrük	5 ΤΕΛΩΝΕΙΟ
6 Autoridad sanitaria del puerto	6 autorità sanitaria	6 direcção de saúde	6 sahil sıhhiye	6 ΙΑΤΡΙΚΕΣ ΑΡΧΕΣ
7 nombre del barco	7 nome della barca	7 nome do barco	7 tekne adı	7 ΟΝΟΜΑ ΣΚΑΦΟΥΣ
8 eslora total	8 lunghezza fuori tutto (LFT)	8 comprimento fora a fora	8 tekne tam boyu	8 ΟΛΙΚΟ ΜΗΚΟΣ
9 patrón	9 skipper	9 comandante	9 skipper, kaptan	9 ΚΥΒΕΡΝΗΤΗΣ
10 propietario	10 proprietario	10 proprietário	10 yacht sahibi	10 ΙΔΙΟΚΤΗΤΗΣ
11 dirección	11 indirizzo	11 morada	11 adres	11 ΔΙΕΥΘΥΝΣΗ
12 manga	12 larghezza massima	12 boca	12 azami tekne eni	12 ΠΛΑΤΟΣ
13 calado	13 pescaggio	13 calado	13 çektiği su	13 ΒΥΘΙΣΜΑ
14 velero	14 barca a vela, veliero	14 iate à vela	14 yelkenli yat	14 ΙΣΤΙΟΦΟΡΟ ΘΑΛΑΜΗΓΟ
15 lancha, bote a motor	15 barca a motore	15 iate a motor	15 motorlu yat	15 ΜΗΧΑΝΟΚΙΝΗΤΟ ΘΑΛΑΜΗΓΟ
16 motor auxiliar	16 motore ausiliario	16 motor auxiliar	16 yardımcı motor	16 ΒΟΗΘΗΤΙΚΗ ΜΗΧΑΝΗ
17 buque de madera	17 costruzione in legno	17 construção em madeira	17 ahşap inşaat	17 ΞΥΛΙΝΗ ΚΑΤΑΣΚΕΥΗ
18 poliéster con fibra de vidrio	18 vetroresina	18 fibra de vidro	18 GRP/camelyafı takfiyeli	18 ΕΝΙΣΧΥΜΕΝΟΣ ΠΟΛΥΕΣΤΕΡΑΣ
19 acero	19 acciaio	19 ferro	19 çelik	19 ΑΤΣΑΛΙΝΟ
20 aluminio	20 alluminio	20 aluminio	20 alüminyum	20 ΑΛΟΥΜΙΝΕΝΙΟ
21 hierro y cemento	21 ferro-cemento	21 ferrocimento	21 betonarme	21 ΕΝΙΣΧΥΜΕΝΟ ΣΚΥΡΟΔΕΡΜΑ
22 diesel	22 diesel	22 gasoleo	22 dizel	22 ΠΕΤΡΕΛΑΙΟ
23 gasolina	23 benzina	23 gasolina	23 benzin	23 ΒΕΝΖΙΝΗ
24 caballo de vapor	24 potenza	24 cavalos força	24 beygirgücü	24 ΙΠΠΟΔΥΝΑΜΗ
25 bandera/nationalidad	25 bandiera/nazionalità	25 bandeira/ nacionalidade	25 bayrak/milliyet	25 ΣΗΜΑΙΑ/ΕΘΝΙΚΟΤΗΣ
26 puerto de matrícula	26 porto d'immatricolazione	26 porto de registo	26 kayıt limanı	26 ΛΙΜΗΝ ΝΗΟΛΟΓΗΣΕΩΣ
27 matrícula	27 numero d'immatricolazione	27 número do registo	27 kütük numarası	27 ΑΡΙΘΜΟΣ ΝΗΟΛΟΓΙΟΥ
28 ultima escala	28 ultimo scalo	28 último porto tocado	28 geldiği liman	28 ΤΕΛΕΥΤΑΙΟ ΛΙΜΑΝΙ ΕΙΣΟΔΟΥ

ENGLISH	FRANÇAIS	DEUTSCH	NEDERLANDS	DANSK
3 FORMALITIES	**3 FORMALITES**	**3 FORMALITÄTEN**	**3 FORMALITEITEN**	**3 FORMALITETER**
29 next port of call	29 prochaine escale	29 nächster anzulaufender Hafen	29 volgende aanloophaven	29 næste anløbshavn
30 ship's papers, etc	30 papiers de bord	30 Schiffspapiere	30 scheepspapieren	30 skibspapirer
31 certificate of registry	31 certificat de francisation, lettre de mer	31 Registrierungs-Zertifikat	31 registratiepapieren	31 registreringscertifikat
32 rating certificate	32 certificat de jauge	32 Meßbrief	32 meetbrief	32 målebrev
33 ship's articles	33 rôle d'equipage	33 Musterrolle	33 scheepswetten	33 besætningsliste
34 ship's log	34 livre de bord	34 Schiffstagebuch, Logbuch	34 logboek, journaal	34 logbog
35 bill of health	35 patente de santé	35 Gesundheitspaß	35 gezondheidsverklaring	35 sundhedscertifikat
36 radio licence	36 licence radio	36 Funkerlaubnis	36 zendmachtiging	36 radiolicens
37 radio call sign	37 indicatif radio	37 Rufzeichen	37 radioroepnaam	37 radiokaldesignal
38 pratique	38 libre-pratique	38 freie Verkehrserlaubnis	38 inklaren, inklaring	38 sejltilladelse
39 insurance certificate	39 certificat d'assurance	39 Versicherungspolice	39 verzekeringspolis	39 forsikringspolice
40 VAT certificate	40 attestation de TVA	40 Mehrwertsteuer-bescheinigung	40 BTW-papieren	40 told/MOMS-dokument
41 charter party	41 charte-partie	41 Chartervertrag	41 huurovereenkomst	41 certeparti
42 customs clearance	42 libre-sortie, congé de douane	42 Zollabfertigung	42 douaneverklaring	42 toldklarering
43 bonded stores	43 provisions entreposées, en franchise, sous douane	43 unter Zollverschluß	43 verzegelde waren	43 varer fra frilager
44 passport	44 passeport	44 Reisepaß	44 paspoort	44 pas
45 visa	45 visa	45 Visum	45 visum	45 visa
46 crew list	46 liste d'équipage	46 Besatzungsliste	46 bemanningslijst	46 mandskabsliste
47 crew change	47 changement d'équipage	47 Besatzungswechsel	47 bemanningswissel	47 mandskabsbytte
48 transit log/temporary importation permit	48 permis d'importation temporaire	48 Durchreisegenehmigung / befristete Einfuhrgenehmigung	48 doorvoerpapieren	48 transitbevis/midlertidig importtilladelse
49 master's certificate	49 diplôme de capitaine	49 Kapitänspatent	49 vaarbevoegdheids-papieren	49 eksamensbevis for skippere
50 certificate of competence	50 permis bateau	50 Befähigungszeugnis	50 getuigschrift	50 dueligshedscertifikat

50

ESPAÑOL	ITALIANO	PORTUGUÊS	TÜRKÇE	ΕΛΛΗΝΙΚΑ
3 FORMALIDADES	**3 FORMALITA**	**3 FORMALIDADES**	**3 FORMALİTELER**	**3 ΔΙΑΤΥΠΩΣΕΙΣ**
29 proxima escala	29 prossimo scalo	29 próximo porto	29 gideceği ilk liman	29 ΕΠΟΜΕΝΟ ΛΙΜΑΝΙ
30 documentación	30 documenti di bordo	30 documentação do barco	30 gemi belgeleri	30 ΕΓΓΡΑΦΑ ΣΚΑΦΟΥΣ
31 Patente de Navigación	31 certificato d'immatricolazione	31 Certificado de Registo	31 kayıt belgesi	31 ΕΓΓΡΑΦΟ ΕΘΝΙΚΟΤΗΤΟΣ
32 certificado de 'Rating' (ventaja)	32 certificato di stazza	32 certificado de abôno	32 rating belgesi	32 ΠΙΣΤΟΠΟΙΗΤΙΚΟ ΚΑΤΑΜΕΤΡΗΣΕΩΣ
33 rol	33 clausole d'ingaggio	33 rol da equipagem	33 gemi mürettebat alıştırma rolesi	33 ΠΕΡΙΕΧΟΜΕΝΑ
34 cuaderno de bitácora	34 libro di bordo	34 diário de bordo	34 gemi jurnali	34 ΗΜΕΡΟΛΟΓΙΟ ΣΚΑΦΟΥΣ
35 Patente de Sanidad	35 certificato sanitario	35 certificado de saúde	35 sağlık belgesi	35 ΠΙΣΤΟΠΟΙΗΤΙΚΟ ΥΓΕΙΟΝΟΜΙΚΟΥ
36 certificado radioeléctrico	36 licenza radio	36 licença de rádio	36 telsiz kullanma ruhsatı	36 ΑΔΕΙΑ ΡΑΔΙΟΣΤΑΘΜΟΥ
37 distintivo de llamada	37 nominativo radio	37 indicativo de chamada	37 telsiz çağırma işareti	37 ΣΗΜΑ ΡΑΔΙΟΣΤΑΘΜΟΥ
38 plática	38 libera pratica	38 livre prática	38 sağlık kontrolü	38 ΙΔΙΟΤΗΣ ΣΚΑΦΟΥΣ
39 póliza de seguro	39 polizza d'assicurazione	39 certificado de seguro	39 sigorta belgesi	39 ΠΙΣΤΟΠΟΙΗΤΙΚΟ ΑΣΦΑΛΙΣΕΩΣ
40 certificado IVA	40 certificato IVA	40 certificado de IVA	40 KDV belgesi	40 ΠΙΣΤΟΠΟΙΗΤΙΚΟ ΦΠΑ
41 contrato de flete	41 contratto di noleggio	41 fretador	41 charter müşterisi,	41 ΟΜΑΔΑ ΝΑΥΛΩΣΕΩΣ
42 despacho de aduana	42 sdoganamento	42 despacho	42 gümrüklerden çıkış izni	42 ΕΚΤΕΛΩΝΣΜΟΣ
43 víveres precintados	43 magazzini doganali	43 mantimentos des alfandegados	43 gümrük antrepolarında bulundurulan yiyecekler	43 ΑΠΟΤΑΜΙΕΥΜΕΝΑ ΑΓΑΘΑ (ΤΡΑΝΖΙΤ)
44 pasaporte	44 passaporto	44 passaporte	44 pasaport	44 ΔΙΑΒΑΤΗΡΙΟ
45 visado	45 visto	45 visto	45 vize	45 ΒΙΖΑ
46 lista de tripulación	46 ruolo dell'equipaggio	46 lista da tripulação	46 mürettebat listesi	46 ΛΙΣΤΑ ΠΛΗΡΩΜΑΤΟΣ
47 cambio de tripulación	47 variazione dell'equipaggio	47 mudança de tripulação	47 mürettebat değişimi	47 ΑΛΛΑΓΗ ΠΛΗΡΩΜΑΤΟΣ
48 permis temporal de importación	48 permesso d'importazione temporanea	48 licença de estadia/ licença de importação temporária	48 transit log/geçici	48 ΠΡΟΣΩΡΙΝΗ ΑΔΕΙΑ ΕΙΣΑΓΩΓΗΣ
49 titulo del capitán	49 certificato di proprietà	49 carta de patrão	49 ithal izni	49 ΔΙΠΛΩΜΑ ΚΥΒΕΡΝΗΤΗ
50 titulo	50 attestato di competenza	50 certificado de competência	50 yeterlilik belgesi	50 ΔΙΠΛΩΜΑ ΙΚΑΝΟΤΗΤΟΣ

ENGLISH	FRANÇAIS	DEUTSCH	NEDERLANDS	DANSK
4 IN HARBOUR	**4 AU PORT**	**4 IM HAFEN**	**4 IN DE HAVEN**	**4 I HAVN**
Anchoring	**Jeter l'ancre**	**Ankern**	**Ankeren**	**Ankring**
1 anchor	1 ancre	1 Anker	1 anker	1 anker
2 to drop/let go	2 jeter l'ancre	2 fallen lassen	2 laat vallen/lekko	2 kaste/lade gå
3 to weigh	3 lever l'ancre	3 auslaufen	3 ophalen	3 lette anker
4 chain	4 chaine	4 Kette	4 ketting	4 kæde
5 anchor warp	5 aussière/câblot	5 Ankerleine	5 ankerketting	5 ankertrosse
6 fouled	6 surjalée	6 unklar	6 onklaar	6 i bekneb
7 to drag	7 chasser	7 schlieren	7 krabben	7 drive
8 to anchor off	8 ancrer au large de	8 Ankerauf gehen	8 ankeren nabij	8 ankre ud for
9 upwind	9 au vent	9 gegen den Wind	9 in de wind	9 mod vinden
10 downwind	10 sous le vent	10 mit dem Wind	10 voor de wind	10 med vinden
11 up-tide	11 en amont du courant de marée	11 gegen die Tide	11 tegenstrooms	11 med tidevandet
12 down-tide	12 en aval du courant de marée	12 mit der Tide	12 voor de stroom	12 mod tidevandet
13 to swing	13 rappeler sur son ancre	13 schwojen	13 zwaaien	13 at svaje
14 to anchor	14 mouiller	14 ankern	14 ankeren	14 at ankre
15 to let go anchor	15 jeter l'ancre	15 Anker fallen lassen	15 het anker laten vallen	15 kaste anker
16 to run out the anchor	16 faire porter l'ancre par un canot	16 einen Anker ausfahren	16 ketting (bij) steken	16 varpe ankeret ud
17 fouled	17 surjalée, surpattée	17 unklar	17 onklaar	17 uklar/i bekneb
18 dragging anchor	18 chasser sur l'ancre	18 der Anker schliert	18 krabbend anker	18 i drift for ankeret
19 holding anchor	19 l'ancre croche, tient	19 der Anker hält	19 houdend anker	19 ankeret holder
20 to lie to an anchor	20 être au mouillage	20 vor Anker liegen	20 ten anker liggen	20 at ligge for anker
21 to break out an anchor	21 décrocher, déraper l'ancre	21 den Anker ausbrechen	21 een anker losbreken	21 at brække ankeret løs
22 to weigh anchor	22 appareillage	22 Anker aufgehen, Anker hieven oder lichten	22 anker inhalen	22 lette anker
23 to slip the anchor	23 filer par le bout	23 den Anker lippen	23 anker laten uitvieren	23 stikke ankeret fra sig med bøje på

ESPAÑOL	ITALIANO	PORTUGUÊS	TÜRKÇE	ΕΛΛΗΝΙΚΑ
4 EN EL PUERTO	**4 NEL PORTO**	**4 NO PORTO**	**4 LİMANDA**	**4 ΣΤΟ ΛΙΜΑΝΙ**
Fondear	**Ancoraggio**	**Ancorar**	**Demirleme**	**ΑΓΚΥΡΟΒΟΛΙΑ**
1 ancla	1 ancora	1 âncora/ferro	1 demir	1 ΑΓΚΥΡΑ
2 fondear el ancla	2 gettare/mollare	2 largar o ferro/deixar ir	2 funda demir/demir atmak	2 ΡΙΧΝΩ ΤΗΝ ΑΓΚΥΡΑ
3 levar ancla	3 salpare	3 pesar	3 demir almak	3 ΣΗΚΩΝΩ
4 cadena	4 catena	4 amarra/amarreta	4 zincir	4 ΑΛΥΣΣΙΔΑ
5 cabo del ancla	5 gomena per ancora	5 cabo do ferro	5 demir haladı	5 ΑΓΚΥΡΟΣΧΟΙΝΟ
6 ancla enredada	6 impigliata	6 unhado	6 demir zincirinin çapariz alması	6 ΜΠΛΕΓΜΕΝΗ
7 garrear el ancla	7 arare	7 à garra	7 demir taramak	7 ΞΕΣΕΡΝΕΙ
8 fondear en rada	8 levare l'ancora	8 levantar o ferro	8 demirlemek	8 ΦΟΥΝΤΑΡΩ ΜΑΚΡΥΑ
9 barlovento	9 controvento	9 barlavento	9 rüzgâra karşı	9 ΠΡΟΣΗΝΕΜΑ
10 sotovento	10 sottovento	10 sotavento	10 rüzgâr altına	10 ΥΠΗΝΕΜΑ
11 barlovento de marea	11 contro la marea	11 barlacorrente	11 akıntıya karşı	11 ΠΡΟΣ ΤΗΝ ΠΑΛΙΡΡΟΙΑ
12 sotovento de marea	12 con la marea	12 sotacorrente	12 akıntıyla birlikte	12 ΜΕ ΤΗΝ ΠΑΛΙΡΡΟΙΑ
13 bornear	13 girare sull'ancora	13 rabiar	13 salmak	13 ΓΥΡΝΩ ΠΑΝΩ ΣΤΗΝ ΑΓΚΥΡΑ
14 fondear	14 ancorarsi	14 fundear	14 demirlemek	14 ΑΓΚΥΡΟΒΟΛΩ
15 dar fondo	15 dare fondo all'ancora	15 largar o ferro	15 demir atmak, demirlemek	15 ΡΙΧΝΩ ΤΗΝ ΑΓΚΥΡΑ
16 atoar el ancla	16 stendere l'ancora	16 espiar um ferro	16 demiri bir botla götürmek	16 ΑΦΗΝΩ ΑΛΥΣΣΙΔΑ
17 encepada	17 ancora impigliata, inceppata	17 ferro prêso, ensarilhado	17 zincirin demire sarması	17 ΜΠΛΕΓΜΕΝΗ
18 ancla garreando	18 ancora che ara	18 ferro a garrar	18 demirin taraması	18 ΞΕΣΕΡΝΕΙ
19 ancla agarrada	19 ancora che agguanta	19 ferro unhado	19 demirin tutması	19 ΚΡΑΤΑΕΙ
20 aguantarse con un ancla	20 essere alla fonda	20 fundeado	20 tek demirle yatmak	20 ΣΤΕΚΟΜΑΙ/ΚΡΑΤΙΕΜΑΙ ΑΠΟ ΤΗΝ ΑΓΚΥΡΑ
21 desatrincar	21 spedare un'ancora	21 arrancar o ferro	21 demiri (dipten) koparmak	21 ΞΕΚΑΡΦΩΝΩ ΤΗΝ ΑΓΚΥΡΑ
22 levar el ancla	22 levare l'ancora, salpare	22 suspender a amarra	22 demir kaldırmak, hareket etmek	22 ΣΗΚΩΝΩ ΑΓΚΥΡΑ
23 perder el ancla	23 sferrare l'ancora	23 picar a amarra	23 demir döşemek, zincir kaçırmak	23 ΣΕΡΝΩ ΤΗΝ ΑΓΚΥΡΑ

ENGLISH	FRANÇAIS	DEUTSCH	NEDERLANDS	DANSK
4 IN HARBOUR	**4 AU PORT**	**4 IM HAFEN**	**4 IN DE HAVEN**	**4 I HAVN**
Mooring up	**Amarrage**	**Festmachen**	**Afmeren**	**Fortøjning**
1 quay	1 quai	1 Kaje, Kai	1 kade	1 kaj
2 jetty	2 jetée	2 Anlegesteg	2 pier, steiger	2 dækmole
3 mooring buoy	3 bouée de corps mort	3 Festmachetonne	3 meerboei	3 fortøjningsbøje
4 laid mooring	4 corps mort	4 ausgebrachte Festmachertonnen	4 verankerde afmeerplaats	4 fast fortøjning
5 finger pontoon	5 catway	5 Schwimmstege mit Auslegern	5 vingersteiger	5 finger-ponton
6 pile	6 poteau	6 Dalben	6 steigerpaal	6 pæl
7 bollard	7 bollard	7 Poller	7 bolder	7 pullert
8 mooring ring	8 anneau d'amarrage	8 Festmachering	8 afmeerring	8 fortøjningsring
9 depth	9 profondeur	9 Wassertiefe	9 diepte	9 dybde
10 is there enough water?	10 est-ce qu'il y a assez d'eau?	10 Ist dort genug Wasser?	10 staat daar genoeg water?	10 er der vand nok?
11 where can I moor?	11 où est-ce que je peux m'amarrer?	11 Wo kann ich festmachen?	11 waar kan ik afmeren?	11 hvor kan jeg fortøje?
12 to dry out	12 s'échouer	12 trocken fallen	12 droogvallen	12 tør ved lavvande
13 stern-to	13 arrière à quai	13 heckwärts	13 met het achterschip naar	13 hækken til
14 bows-to	14 avant à quai	14 bugwärts	14 met de boeg naar	14 stævnen til
15 alongside	15 le long de	15 längsseits	15 langs, langszij	15 langskibs
16 to raft up	16 amarrer à couple	16 im Päckchen festmachen	16 langszij vastmaken	16 fortøje på siden
17 warp/line	17 amarre	17 Verholleine	17 lijn	17 kasteline
18 breast-rope	18 traversière	18 Querleine	18 dwarslijn	18 fortøjning
19 spring	19 garde	19 Spring	19 spring	19 spring
20 make fast	20 frapper	20 festmachen	20 vastmaken	20 sætte fast
21 let go/cast off	21 larguer	21 loswerfen	21 losgooien, ontmeren	21 lade gå

ESPAÑOL	ITALIANO	PORTUGUÊS	TÜRKÇE	ΕΛΛΗΝΙΚΑ
4 EN EL PUERTO	**4 NEL PORTO**	**4 NO PORTO**	**4 LİMANDA**	**4 ΣΤΟ ΛΙΜΑΝΙ**
Amarrar	**Ormeggio**	**Atracação**	**Bağlama**	**ΠΡΟΣΔΕΣΗ**
1 muelle, desembarcadero	1 banchina	1 cais	1 rıhtım	1 ΝΤΟΚΙ
2 muelle, dique, escollera, pantalán	2 molo	2 molhe	2 iskele	2 ΠΡΟΒΛΗΤΑ
3 boya de amarre	3 boa d'ormeggio	3 bólia de atracação	3 bağlama şamandırası	3 ΣΗΜΑΔΟΥΡΑ ΠΡΟΣΔΕΣΗΣ
4 muerto de amarre	4 corpo morto	4 estaleiro permanente	4 bağlama halatı	4 ΑΓΚΥΡΟΒΟΛΗΜΕΝΗ ΣΗΜΑΔΟΥΡΑ
5 pantalán	5 pontile a pennello	5 pontão com fingers	5 parmak iskele	5 ΠΑΚΤΩΝΑΣ-ΠΟΝΤΟΝΙ
6 estaca	6 pilone	6 estaca	6 bağlama kazığı	6 ΣΤΥΛΟΣ
7 bolardo	7 bitta	7 abita	7 baba, bağlama babası	7 ΚΑΠΟΝΙ-ΔΕΣΤΡΑ ΜΩΛΟΥ
8 argolla de amarre	8 anello d'ormeggio	8 argola de amarração	8 bağlama anelesi	8 ΚΡΙΚΟΣ ΠΡΟΣΔΕΣΗΣ
9 profundidad	9 profondità	9 fundura	9 derinlik	9 ΒΑΘΟΣ
10 ¿hay bastante calado?	10 c'è abbastanza acqua?	10 tenho àgua suficiente?	10 orada yeterli derinlik var mı?	10 ΕΧΕΙ ΑΡΚΕΤΟ ΒΑΘΟΣ
11 ¿donde puedo amarrar?	11 dove posso ormeggiare?	11 onde posso atracar?	11 nereye bağlayabilirim?	11 ΠΟΥ ΜΠΟΡΩ ΝΑ ΔΕΣΩ
12 sentado en seco	12 seccare	12 secar	12 gel-git nedeniyle karaya oturmak	12 ΒΓΑΖΩ ΣΚΑΦΟΣ ΣΤΗ ΣΤΕΡΙΑ
13 amarrar a popa	13 in andana	13 à popa	13 kıçtan kara	13 ΜΕ ΤΗΝ ΠΡΥΜΝΗ
14 amarrar a proa	14 di prua	14 à proa	14 baştan kara	14 ΜΕ ΤΗΝ ΠΛΩΡΗ
15 al costado	15 di fianco, all'inglese	15 paralelo a …	15 aborda olmak, yanaşmak	15 ΜΕ ΤΗΝ ΠΛΕΥΡΑ
16 amarrar de costada	16 far zattera con un'altra barca	16 içar a balsa	16 borda, bordaya bağlamak	16 ΔΕΝΩ ΤΟ ΣΚΑΦΟΣ ΣΕ ΝΤΑΝΑ
17 cabo	17 cime d'ormeggio	17 espia	17 palamar (tel veya halat)	17 ΚΑΒΟΣ
18 través	18 traversino	18 cabo com seio	18 omuzluk palamarı	18 ΜΟΥΣΤΑΚΙΑ-ΚΟΥΤΟΥΚΙΑ
19 esprín	19 spring	19 rejeira	19 açmaz, spring halatı, pürmeçe halatı	19 ΣΧΟΙΝΙΑ ΠΡΟΣΔΕΣΕΩΣ
20 amarrar firme	20 dar volta	20 depressa	20 bağlamak	20 ΣΙΓΟΥΡΕΥΩ-ΠΡΟΣΔΕΝΟΜΑΙ
21 largar amarras	21 mollare (l'ormeggio)	21 folgar/atira	21 halatı boşlamak, boşkoymak	21 ΑΦΗΝΩ

55

ENGLISH	FRANÇAIS	DEUTSCH	NEDERLANDS	DANSK
4 IN HARBOUR	**4 AU PORT**	**4 IM HAFEN**	**4 IN DE HAVEN**	**4 I HAVN**
Mooring up	**Amarrage**	**Festmachen**	**Afmeren**	**Fortøjning**
22 to single up a rope	22 garder une seule amarre	22 alle Leinen bis auf eine loswerfen	22 dubbele lijnen wegnemen	22 kvejle op
23 to slip a rope	23 larguer	23 Leine loswerfen	23 een lijn laten vieren	23 kaste los
24 to shorten up	24 raccourcir	24 aufkürzen	24 overbodige lijnen weghalen	24 korte op
25 to slack off/ease	25 choquer	25 fieren, Lose geben	25 vieren	25 lade gå
Manoeuvring	**Faire des manœuvres**	**Manövrieren**	**Manœuvreren**	**Manøvrering**
1 bow	1 proue	1 Bug	1 boeg	1 stævn
2 stern	2 poupe	2 Heck	2 hek, achterschip	2 hæk
3 amidships	3 milieu	3 mittschiffs	3 midscheeps	3 midtskibs
4 port	4 babord	4 backbord	4 bakboord	4 bagbord
5 starboard	5 tribord	5 steuerbord	5 stuurboord	5 styrbord
6 to go ahead	6 aller en avant	6 voraus gehen	6 vooruitgaan	6 gå frem
7 to go astern	7 aller en arrière	7 zurück gehen	7 achteruitgaan	7 bakke
8 propeller	8 hélice	8 Propeller	8 schroef	8 skrue
9 stop engine!	9 arrêter le moteur	9 Maschine stopp!	9 stop motor	9 stop motoren
10 start engine!	10 démarrer le moteur	10 Maschine starten!	10 start motor	10 start motoren
11 fast	11 vite	11 schnell	11 snel	11 hurtigt
12 slowly	12 lentement	12 langsam	12 langzaam	12 langsomt
13 bow thruster	13 propulseur d'étrave	13 Bugstrahlruder	13 boegschroef	13 bovpropel
14 fender	14 défense	14 Fender	14 fender	14 fender
15 to fend off	15 écarter	15 abfendern	15 afhouden	15 fendre af
16 boathook	16 gaffe	16 Bootshaken	16 bootshaak, pikhaak	16 bådshage

ESPAÑOL	ITALIANO	PORTUGUÊS	TÜRKÇE	ΕΛΛΗΝΙΚΑ
4 EN EL PUERTO	**4 NEL PORTO**	**4 NO PORTO**	**4 LİMANDA**	**4 ΣΤΟ ΛΙΜΑΝΙ**
Amarrar	**Ormeggio**	**Atracação**	**Bağlama**	**ΠΡΟΣΔΕΣΗ**
22 aligerar las amarras	22 disporre a doppino una cima	22 cabo singelo	22 (voltayı) tek halata indirmek voltayı azaltmak	22 ΠΑΙΡΝΩ ΜΕΣΑ ΣΧΟΙΝΙ ΚΑΙ ΜΕΤΖΑΒΟΛΤΑ
23 largar, lascar la amarra	23 filare una cima	23 deslizar o cabo	23 halatı kaydırmak	23 ΑΦΗΝΩ ΤΟ ΣΧΟΙΝΙ
24 acortar	24 accorciare	24 encurtar	24 halatın boşunu almak	24 ΜΑΖΕΥΩ-ΚΟΝΤΕΝΩ ΤΟ ΣΧΟΙΝΙ
25 amollar	25 allentare	25 folgar	25 halatı lâşka etmek	25 ΧΑΛΑΡΩΝΩ ΤΟ ΣΧΟΙΝΙ
Maniobras	**Manovre**	**Manobrar**	**Manevra**	**ΧΕΙΡΙΣΜΟΙ**
1 proa	1 prua	1 proa	1 pruva, baş	1 ΠΛΩΡΗ
2 popa	2 poppa	2 popa	2 pupa, kıç	2 ΠΡΥΜΝΗ
3 en medio del buque	3 a mezzanave	3 través	3 tekne vasadı (ortası)	3 ΣΤΟ ΚΕΝΤΡΟ ΤΟΥ ΣΚΑΦΟΥΣ
4 babor	4 sinistra	4 bombordo	4 iskele	4 ΑΡΙΣΤΕΡΗ ΠΛΕΥΡΑ
5 estribor	5 dritta	5 estibordo	5 sancak	5 ΔΕΞΙΑ ΠΛΕΥΡΑ
6 ir avante	6 andare avanti	6 à vante	6 ileri yol	6 ΠΡΟΣΩ
7 dar marcha atras	7 andare indietro, sciare	7 à ré	7 geri yol, tornistan	7 ΑΝΑΠΟΔΑ
8 hélice	8 elica	8 hélice	8 pervane	8 ΠΡΟΠΕΛΛΑ
9 ¡ parar la maquina!	9 ferma il motore!	9 parar o motor	9 motor stop	9 ΚΡΑΤΕΙ, ΣΒΥΣΕ ΜΗΧΑΝΗ
10 ¡ arrancar la maquina!	10 accendi il motore!	10 ligar o motor	10 motor çalıştır	10 ΑΝΑΨΕ ΜΗΧΑΝΗ
11 rápido	11 veloce	11 depressa	11 hızlı	11 ΓΡΗΓΟΡΑ
12 despacio	12 lento	12 devagar	12 yavaş, yavaşça	12 ΑΡΓΑ
13 hélice de proa	13 elica trasversale di prua	13 bow thruster	13 bodoslama pervanesi	13 ΠΡΟΠΕΛΛΑ ΠΛΩΡΗΣ
14 defensa	14 parabordo	14 defensa	14 usturmaça	14 ΜΠΑΛΟΝΙ
15 abrir el bote del costado	15 scostare	15 por as defensas	15 teknenin dokunmasını önlemek	15 ΑΒΑΡΑΡΩ
16 bichero	16 gaffa, mezzomarinaio	16 croque	16 kanca, bot kancası	16 ΓΑΝΤΖΟΣ

ENGLISH	FRANÇAIS	DEUTSCH	NEDERLANDS	DANSK
4 IN HARBOUR	**4 AU PORT**	**4 IM HAFEN**	**4 IN DE HAVEN**	**4 I HAVN**
Supplies	**Avitaillement**	**Versorgungsgüter**	**Voorzieningen**	**Forsyninger**
1 water	1 eau	1 Wasser	1 water	1 vand
2 hose	2 tuyau	2 Schlauch	2 slang	2 slange
3 hose connector	3 embout de tuyau	3 Schlauchanschluß	3 slangaansluiting	3 slangeforskruning
4 electricity	4 électricité	4 Elektrizität	4 stroom, elektriciteit	4 elektricitet
5 electric cable	5 câble électrique	5 Elektrokabel	5 snoer, elektriciteitskabel	5 elektrisk ledning
6 electric plug	6 prise de courant	6 Elektrostecker	6 stekker	6 elstik
7 fuelling station	7 station de carburant	7 Tankstelle	7 bunkerplaats	7 benzinstation
8 garbage	8 ordures	8 Küchenabfälle	8 afval	8 affald

ESPAÑOL	ITALIANO	PORTUGUÊS	TÜRKÇE	ΕΛΛΗΝΙΚΑ
4 EN EL PUERTO	**4 NEL PORTO**	**4 NO PORTO**	**4 LİMANDA**	**4 ΣΤΟ ΛΙΜΑΝΙ**
Suministros	**Rifornimenti**	**Mantimentos**	**İkmaller**	**ΠΡΟΜΗΘΕΙΕΣ**
1 agua	1 acqua	1 àgua	1 su	1 ΝΕΡΟ
2 manguera	2 manichetta	2 mangueira	2 hortum	2 ΣΩΛΗΝΑΣ-ΛΑΣΤΙΧΟ
3 conexión de manguera	3 raccordo per manichetta	3 ligação da mangueira	3 hortum bağlantısı	3 ΕΝΩΤΙΚΟ ΣΩΛΗΝΑ-ΡΑΚΟΡ
4 electricidad	4 elettricità	4 electricidade	4 elektrik	4 ΗΛΕΚΤΡΙΚΟ
5 cable eléctrico	5 cavo elettrico	5 cabo electrico	5 elektrik kablosu	5 ΗΛΕΚΤΡΙΚΟ ΚΑΛΩΔΙΟ
6 enchufe	6 spina elettrica	6 ficha electrica	6 elektrik fişi	6 ΠΡΙΖΑ
7 surtidor	7 stazione di rifornimento carburante	7 estação de serviço	7 akaryakıt ikmal istasyonu	7 ΣΤΑΘΜΟΣ ΚΑΥΣΙΜΩΝ
8 basuras	8 pattume	8 lixo	8 çöp	8 ΣΚΟΥΠΙΔΙΑ

ENGLISH	FRANÇAIS	DEUTSCH	NEDERLANDS	DANSK
5 THE BOAT	**5 LE BATEAU**	**5 DAS BOOT**	**5 DE BOOT, HET SCHIP**	**5 BÅDEN**
Basic vocabulary	**Vocabulaire de base**	**Grundbegriffe**	**Basiswoordenlijst**	**Nøgleord**
1 hull	1 coque	1 Rumpf	1 romp	1 skrog
2 deck	2 pont	2 Deck	2 dek	2 dæk
3 mast	3 mât	3 Mast	3 mast	3 mast
4 keel	4 quille	4 Kiel	4 kiel	4 køl
5 rudder	5 gouvernail	5 Ruder	5 roer	5 ror
6 bow	6 proue	6 Bug	6 boeg	6 stævn
7 stern	7 poupe	7 Heck	7 achterschip	7 hæk
8 port	8 babord	8 backbord	8 bakboord	8 bagbord
9 starboard	9 tribord	9 steuerbord	9 stuurboord	9 styrbord
10 ahead	10 en avant	10 voraus	10 vooruit	10 frem
11 astern	11 en arrière	11 zurück	11 achteruit	11 bak
12 mooring	12 amarre	12 Liegeplatz	12 afmeren	12 fortøjning
13 anchor	13 ancre	13 Anker	13 anker	13 anker
14 rope	14 cordage	14 Leine	14 touw	14 tovværk
Yachts & rigs	**Yachts et leur gréement**	**Yachten und Takelagen**	**Jachten en tuigage**	**Fartøjer og rigning**
1 masthead cutter	1 cotre en tête de mât	1 Kutter mit Hochtakelung	1 kotter, masttoptuig	1 mastetop-rig
2 bermudan sloop	2 sloop bermudien	2 Slup	2 sloep, torentuig	2 bermudarig
3 gaff cutter	3 cotre franc, aurique	3 Gaffelkutter	3 kotter, gaffeltuig	3 gaffelrigget kutter
4 bermudan yawl	4 yawl bermudien	4 Yawl	4 yawl, torentuig	4 bermudarigget yawl
5 bermudan ketch	5 ketch bermudien	5 Ketsch	5 kits, torentuig	5 bermuda-ketch
6 staysail schooner	6 goélette à voile d'étai	6 Stagsegelschoner	6 stagzeilschoener	6 stagsejls skonnert
7 brig	7 brick	7 Brigg	7 brik	7 brig
8 barque	8 barque	8 Bark	8 bark	8 bark
9 cruiser	9 bateau de croisière	9 Fahrtenyacht	9 toerschip	9 tursejler
10 racer	10 bateau de course	10 Rennyacht	10 wedstrijdschip	10 kapsejler
11 ocean racer	11 bateau de course-croisière	11 Hochseerennyacht	11 zeegaand wedstrijdschip	11 havkapsejler
12 racing dinghy	12 dériveur de course	12 Rennjolle	12 open wedstrijdboot	12 kapsejladsdjolle

ESPAÑOL	ITALIANO	PORTUGUÊS	TÜRKÇE	ΕΛΛΗΝΙΚΑ
5 EL BARCO	**5 LA BARCA**	**5 DO BARCO**	**5 TEKNE**	**5 ΤΟ ΣΚΑΦΟΣ**

Vocabulario básico	**Vocabolario basilare**	**Vocabulário básico**	**Ana lügatçe/sözlük**	**ΒΑΣΙΚΟ ΛΕΞΙΛΟΓΙΟ**
1 casco	1 carena	1 casco	1 karina	1 ΚΥΤΟΣ/ΓΑΣΤΡΑ
2 cubierta	2 ponte	2 convés	2 güverte	2 ΚΑΤΑΣΤΡΩΜΑ
3 palo, mástil	3 albero	3 mastro	3 direk	3 ΚΑΤΑΡΤΙ
4 quilla	4 chiglia	4 quilha	4 omurga	4 ΚΑΡΙΝΑ
5 timón	5 timone	5 leme	5 dümen	5 ΠΗΔΑΛΙΟ
6 proa	6 prua, prora	6 proa	6 pruva, baş	6 ΠΛΩΡΗ
7 popa	7 poppa	7 popa	7 pupa, kıç	7 ΠΡΥΜΝΗ
8 babor	8 sinistra	8 bombordo	8 iskele	8 ΑΡΙΣΤΕΡΑ
9 estribor	9 dritta	9 estibordo	9 sancak	9 ΔΕΞΙΑ
10 por la proa	10 proravia, avanti	10 à proa	10 ileri	10 ΠΡΟΣΩ
11 por la popa	11 poppavia, indietro	11 à popa	11 geri, tornistan	11 ΑΝΑΠΟΔΑ
12 amarradero	12 ormeggio	12 atracar	12 tekneyi bağlama, bağlama yeri	12 ΑΓΚΥΡΟΒΟΛΙΟ
13 ancla	13 àncora	13 ferro	13 demir, çipa	13 ΑΓΚΥΡΑ
14 cabo	14 cima	14 cabo	14 halat	14 ΣΧΟΙΝΙ

Yates y aparejos	**Yachts e attrezzature**	**Iates e armação**	**Yatlar ve armalar**	**ΤΥΠΟΙ ΙΣΤΙΟΦΟΡΩΝ**
1 balandra de mas-telero	1 cutter con fiocco in testa d'albero	1 cuter	1 markoni cutter, kotra	1 ΚΟΤΤΕΡΟ (ΔΥΟ ΠΡΟΤΟΝΟΙ)
2 balandro de Bermudas	2 sloop (Marconi)	2 sloop	2 markoni sloop	2 ΜΟΝΟΚΑΤΑΡΤΟ
3 cachemarin	3 cutter a vele auriche	3 cuter de Carangueja	3 randa armalı cutter, randa armalı kotra	3 ΚΟΤΤΕΡΟ ΜΕ ΠΙΚΙ
4 balandro de baticulo	4 yawl o iolla (Marconi)	4 yawl Marconi	4 markoni yawl	4 ΓΙΟΛΑ
5 queche bermudo	5 ketch (Marconi)	5 ketch Marconi	5 markoni ketch	5 ΚΕΤΣ
6 goleta a la americana	6 goletta a vele di taglio	6 palhabote	6 velena yelkenli uskuna	6 ΣΚΟΥΝΑ ΜΕ ΔΥΟ ΦΛΟΚΟΥΣ
7 bergantin	7 brigantino	7 brigue	7 brik	7 ΜΠΡΙΚΙ
8 barca	8 brigantino a palo	8 barca	8 barka	8 ΜΠΑΡΚΟ
9 yate crucero	9 barca da crociera	9 barco de cruzeiro	9 gezi yatı	9 ΚΡΟΥΖΕΡ
10 yate de regatas	10 barca da regata	10 barco de regata	10 yarış yatı	10 ΑΓΩΝΙΣΤΙΚΟ
11 yate de regatas oceánica	11 barca da regata oceanica	11 barco de regatas oceânicas	11 okyanus/açıkdeniz yarış yatı	11 ΑΓΩΝΙΣΤΙΚΟ ΩΚΕΑΝΟΥ
12 barco de regatas	12 deriva da regata	12 dinghy de regata	12 salma omurgalı yarış teknesi	12 ΑΓΩΝΙΣΤΙΚΟ ΜΙΚΡΟ ΣΚΑΦΟΣ

ENGLISH	FRANÇAIS	DEUTSCH	NEDERLANDS	DANSK
5 THE BOAT	**5 LE BATEAU**	**5 DAS BOOT**	**5 DE BOOT, HET SCHIP**	**5 BÅDEN**
Types of vessel	**Types de bateau**	**Schiffstyp**	**Scheepstypen**	**Fartøjstyper**
1 motorboat	1 bateau à moteur	1 Motoryacht	1 motorboot	1 motorbåd
2 motorsailer	2 bateau mixte, motor-sailer	2 Motorsegler	2 motorsailer	2 motorsejler
3 dinghy	3 youyou, dinghy, canot	3 Beiboot, Dingi	3 open bootje	3 jolle
4 launch	4 vedette	4 Barkasse	4 barkas	4 chalup
5 rescue launch	5 bateau de sauvetage	5 Bergungsfahrzeug	5 reddingboot	5 følgebåd
6 lifeboat	6 canot de sauvetage	6 Rettungsboot	6 reddingboot	6 redningsbåd
7 pilot cutter	7 bateau pilote	7 Lotsenfahrzeug	7 loodsboot	7 lodsbåd
8 ship	8 navire	8 Schiff	8 schip	8 skib, fregat
9 tug	9 remorqueur	9 Schlepper	9 sleepboot	9 bugserbåd
10 sailing yacht	10 voilier	10 Segelyacht	10 zeilboot	10 sejlbåd
11 barge	11 péniche	11 Schute	11 dekschuit, schuit	11 pram
12 fishing boat	12 bateau de pêche	12 Fischereifahrzeug	12 vissersschip	12 fiskerbåd
13 ferry	13 ferry/bac (rivière)	13 Fähre	13 veerboot	13 færge
14 warship	14 navire de guerre	14 Kriegsschiff	14 oorlogsschip	14 krigsskib
15 coastguard	15 garde-côtes	15 Küstenwache	15 kustwacht	15 kystvagt
Construction	**Construction**	**Bauweise**	**Constructie**	**Konstruktion**
Hull design & construction	*Plan de coque et construction*	*Rumpfkonstruktion und Bauweise*	*Romp- ontwerp en-constructie*	*Skrogkonstruktion*
1 naval architect	1 architecte naval	1 Schiffbauingenieur	1 scheepsarchitect	1 skibskonstruktør
2 designer	2 architecte naval	2 Konstrukteur	2 ontwerper	2 skibskonstruktør
3 surveyor	3 expert maritime	3 Gutachter	3 inspecteur	3 synsmand
4 builder	4 constructeur	4 Bootsbauer	4 bouwer	4 skibsbygmester
5 light displacement	5 déplacement léger	5 Leichtdeplacement	5 licht,met weing waterverplaatsing	5 let deplacement
6 heavy displacement	6 déplacement lourd	6 Schwerdeplacement	6 zwaar, veel waterver-plaatsing	6 deplacement
7 clinker	7 à clins	7 klinker	7 klinker, overnaadse bouw	7 klinkbygget
8 carvel	8 à franc-bord	8 karweel oder kraweel	8 karveel	8 kravelbygget
9 moulded plywood	9 contreplaqué moulé	9 formverleimtes Sperrholz	9 gevormd plakhout	9 limet finer

ESPAÑOL	ITALIANO	PORTUGUÊS	TÜRKÇE	ΕΛΛΗΝΙΚΑ
5 EL BARCO	**5 LA BARCA**	**5 DO BARCO**	**5 TEKNE**	**5 ΤΟ ΣΚΑΦΟΣ**
Tipos de barco	**Tipi di natante**	**Tipos de embarcação**	**Tekne tipleri**	**ΤΥΠΟΙ ΣΚΑΦΩΝ**
1 motora	1 barca a motore	1 barco a motor	1 motorbot	1 ΜΗΧΑΝΟΚΙΝΗΤΟ
2 moto-velero	2 motor sailer	2 barco a motor e à vela	2 motorlu yelken teknesi	2 ΜΗΧΑΝΟΚΙΝΗΤΟ ΜΕ ΠΑΝΙΑ
3 bote, chinchorro	3 deriva	3 escaler	3 dingi, bot	3 ΒΑΡΚΑΚΙ
4 lancha	4 lancia	4 lancha	4 İşkampavya	4 ΛΑΝΤΖΑ
5 bote de salvamento	5 lancia di salvataggio	5 barco de socorro	5 can kurtarma işkampavyası	5 ΛΑΝΤΖΑ ΔΙΑΣΩΣΕΩΣ/ ΝΑΥΑΓΟΣΩΣΤΙΚΟ
6 bote salvavidas	6 scialuppa	6 barco salva vidas	6 can filikası	6 ΣΩΣΙΒΙΑ ΛΕΜΒΟΣ
7 bote del práctico	7 pilotina	7 embarcação dos pilôtos	7 kılavuz teknesi	7 ΠΙΛΟΤΙΝΑ
8 buque	8 nave	8 navio	8 gemi	8 ΚΑΡΑΒΙ
9 remolcador	9 rimorchiatore	9 rebocador	9 römorkör	9 ΡΥΜΟΥΛΚΟ
10 velero	10 yacht a vela, veliero	10 iate à vela	10 yelkenli yat	10 ΙΣΤΙΟΦΟΡΟ
11 gabarra	11 chiatta	11 lancha	11 şalupa	11 ΜΑΟΥΝΑ
12 barco de pesca	12 peschereccio	12 barco de pesca	12 balıkçı teknesi	12 ΨΑΡΑΔΙΚΗ ΒΑΡΚΑ
13 ferry	13 traghetto	13 ferry	13 feribot	13 ΦΕΡΡΥ
14 buque de guerra	14 nave da guerra	14 navio de guerra	14 harpgemisi	14 ΠΟΛΕΜΙΚΟ
15 guardacosta	15 guardacoste	15 policia marítima	15 sahil güvenlik teknesi	15 ΛΙΜΕΝΙΚΟ
Construcción	**Costruzione**	**Construção**	**İnşaat**	**ΚΑΤΑΣΚΕΥΗ**
Diseño y construcción del casco	*Progetto e costruzione della carena*	*Desenho e construção do casco*	*Karina dizaynı ve inşaatı*	*ΣΧΕΔΙΟ ΓΑΣΤΡΑΣ & ΚΑΤΑΣΚΕΥΗ*
1 ingeniero naval	1 architetto navale	1 engenheiro construtor naval	1 gemi inşa mühendisi	1 ΝΑΥΠΗΓΟΣ
2 proyectista	2 progettista	2 projectista	2 tasarımcı	2 ΣΧΕΔΙΑΣΤΗΣ
3 inspector	3 perito marittimo	3 inspector	3 sörveyci, eksper	3 ΕΠΙΘΕΩΡΗΤΗΣ
4 constructor	4 costruttore	4 construtor	4 yapımcı	4 ΚΑΤΑΣΚΕΥΑΣΤΗΣ
5 pequeño desplaza- miento	5 piccola stazza	5 deslocamento pequeno	5 hafif deplasman	5 ΜΙΚΡΟΥ ΕΚΤΟΠΙΣΜΑΤΟΣ
6 gran desplazamiento	6 grande stazza	6 deslocamento grande	6 ağır deplasman	6 ΜΕΓΑΛΟΥ ΕΚΤΟΠΙΣΜΑΤΟΣ
7 tingladillo	7 clinker	7 tabuado trincado	7 bindirme ağaç kaplama	7 ΚΛΙΜΑΚΩΤΗ ΑΡΜΟΛΟΓΙΑ
8 unión a tope	8 a paro	8 tabuado liso	8 armuz kaplama	8 ΛΕΙΑΣ ΑΡΜΟΛΟΓΙΑΣ
9 contrachapado moldado	9 compensato marino	9 contraplacado moldado	9 kalıplanmış kontraplak	9 ΦΟΡΜΑΡΙΣΜΕΝΟ ΚΟΝΤΡΑ-ΠΛΑΚΕ

ENGLISH	FRANÇAIS	DEUTSCH	NEDERLANDS	DANSK
5 THE BOAT	**5 LE BATEAU**	**5 DAS BOOT**	**5 DE BOOT, HET SCHIP**	**5 BÅDEN**
Construction	**Construction**	**Bauweise**	**Constructie**	**Konstruktion**
Hull design & construction	*Plan de coque et construction*	*Rumpfkonstruktion und Bauweise*	*Romp- ontwerp en- constructie*	*Skrogkonstruktion*
10 open	10 non ponté	10 offen	10 open	10 åben
11 half-decked	11 semi-ponté	11 halbgedeckt	11 half open	11 halvdæk
12 cabin yacht	12 cabinier, ponté	12 Kajütyacht	12 kajuitjacht	12 kahytsbåd
13 round bilged	13 en forme	13 Rundspant	13 met ronde kimmen, rondspant	13 rundbundet
14 hard chine	14 à bouchain vif	14 Knickspant	14 knikspant	14 knækspant
15 overhang	15 élancement	15 Überhang	15 overhangend	15 overhang
16 sheer	16 tonture	16 Sprung	16 zeeg	16 spring
17 transom stern	17 arrière à tableau	17 Plattgattheck, Spiegelheck	17 platte spiegel	17 agterspejl
18 canoe stern	18 arrière canoë	18 Kanuheck	18 kano-achtersteven	18 kanohæk
19 counter stern	19 arrière à voûte	19 Yachtheck	19 overhang met kleine spiegel	19 gilling
20 scoop transom	20 arrière à jupe	20 Heck moderner GFK-Yachten, Schaufelheck	20 tableauspiegel	20 negativ hæk
21 spoon bow	21 étrave en cuiller	21 Löffelbug	21 lepelboeg	21 rund stævn
22 trim	22 assiette	22 Trimm, Trimmlage	22 trim, ligging	22 trim
23 mast rake	23 quête, inclinaison	23 Fall des Mastes	23 masttrim, valling	23 mastens hældning
24 sail area	24 surface de voilure	24 Segelfläche	24 zeiloppervlak	24 sejlareal
25 sail plan	25 plan de voilure	25 Segelriß	25 zeilplan	25 sejlplan
26 scantlings	26 échantillonnage	26 Materialstärke, Profil	26 afmeting van constructiedelen	26 scantlings
27 glass reinforced plastic/ GRP	27 polyester renforcé fibre de verre	27 glasfaserverstärkter Kunststoff/GFK	27 polyester	27 glasfiberarmeret plastic
28 moulding	28 moulage	28 Schale	28 mal, vormstuk,	28 støbning
29 lay-up	29 couche	29 auflegen, Gewebelage	29 laag op laag	29 lag
30 rovings	30 rovings	30 Gewebematten	30 roving mat	30 måtter

ESPAÑOL	ITALIANO	PORTUGUÊS	TÜRKÇE	ΕΛΛΗΝΙΚΑ
5 EL BARCO	**5 LA BARCA**	**5 DO BARCO**	**5 TEKNE**	**5 ΤΟ ΣΚΑΦΟΣ**
Construcción	**Costruzione**	**Construção**	**İnşaat**	**ΚΑΤΑΣΚΕΥΗ**
Diseño y construcción del casco	*Progetto e costruzione della carena*	*Desenho e construção do casco*	*Karina dizaynı ve inşaatı*	*ΣΧΕΔΙΟ ΓΑΣΤΡΑΣ & ΚΑΤΑΣΚΕΥΗ*
10 abierto	10 aperto, spontato	10 aberto	10 açık güverteli	10 ΑΝΟΙΚΤΟ
11 con media cubierta, tillado	11 semiappontato	11 meio convez	11 yarım güverteli	11 ΜΙΣΟ ΚΟΥΒΕΡΤΩΜΕΝΟ
12 yate con camara	12 cabinato	12 iate de cabine	12 kamaralı yat	12 ΘΑΛΑΜΗΓΟ
13 pantoque redondo	13 a carena tonda	13 fundo redondo	13 yuvarlak karinalı yat	13 ΣΤΡΟΓΓΥΛΗ ΓΑΣΤΡΑ
14 chine	14 a spigolo	14 hidrocónico	14 köşeli	14 ΓΩΝΙΑΣΜΕΝΗ ΓΑΣΤΡΑ
15 sobresalir	15 slancio	15 lançamento	15 bodoslama, bodoslamanın su üzerindeki kısmının boyu	15 ΠΡΟΕΞΟΧΗ ΤΗΣ ΠΛΩΡΗΣ ΤΟΥ ΣΚΑΦΟΥΣ
16 arrufo	16 cavallino	16 tosado	16 borda veya güverte kavsi çalimı	16 ΚΑΜΠΥΛΟΤΗΣ ΔΙΑΜΗΚΟΥΣ
17 popa de yugo	17 poppa a specchio	17 pôpa arrasada	17 ayna kıç	17 ΠΡΥΜΝΗ ΜΕ ΚΑΘΡΕΠΤΗ
18 popa de canoa	18 poppa a canoa	18 pôpa de canoa	18 kano kıç, karpuz kıç	18 ΜΥΤΕΡΗ ΠΡΥΜΝΗ
19 revés	19 poppa a fetta	19 pôpa de painel	19 ters ayna kıç	19 ΠΡΥΜΝΗ ΜΕ ΚΛΙΣΗ
20 popa de jupette	20 poppa attrezzata	20 vertedouro	20 kepçe kıç	20 ΚΑΜΠΥΛΗ ΠΑΠΑΔΙΑ
21 proa de cuchara	21 prora a cucchiaio	21 proa de colher ou de iate	21 kaşık başlı	21 ΣΤΡΟΓΓΥΛΗ ΠΛΩΡΗ
22 estiba	22 assetto	22 caimento	22 trim, ayar	22 ΖΥΓΙΑΣΜΑ
23 inclinación del palo	23 inclinazione dell'albero	23 inclinação do mastro	23 direk meyli	23 ΚΛΙΣΗ ΚΑΤΑΡΤΙΟΥ
24 superficie vélica	24 superficie velica	24 área de vela	24 yelken alanı	24 ΕΠΙΦΑΝΕΙΑ ΠΑΝΙΩΝ
25 plano de velámen	25 piano velico	25 plano vélico	25 yelken planı	25 ΔΙΑΤΑΞΗ ΠΑΝΙΩΝ
26 escantillón	26 dimensioni	26 dimensões dos materiais	26 tekne eğrilerinin çizimi	26 ΤΕΜΑΧΙΑ ΞΥΛΟΥ
27 poliester	27 vetroresina	27 fibra de vidro	27 cam elyafıyla takviyeli plastik/GRP	27 ΟΠΛΙΣΜΕΝΟΣ ΠΟΛΥΕΣΤΕΡΑΣ
28 moldadura	28 formatura	28 moldagem	28 kalıplama	28 ΚΑΛΟΥΠΩΤΑ ΜΕΡΗ
29 laminar	29 stratificazione	29 planos	29 polyester kaplama	29 ΕΠΙΣΤΡΩΣΗ
30 rovings	30 fibre	30 comissões	30 cam elyafı dokuma	30 ΥΦΑΣΜΕΝΟΣ ΠΟΛΥΕΣΤΕΡΑΣ

ENGLISH	FRANÇAIS	DEUTSCH	NEDERLANDS	DANSK
5 THE BOAT	**5 LE BATEAU**	**5 DAS BOOT**	**5 DE BOOT, HET SCHIP**	**5 BÅDEN**
Construction	**Construction**	**Bauweise**	**Constructie**	**Konstruktion**
Hull design & construction	*Plan de coque et construction*	*Rumpfkonstruktion und Bauweise*	*Romp- ontwerp en- constructie*	*Skrogkonstruktion*
31 mat	31 mât	31 Matte	31 mat	31 måtter
32 chopped strand	32 fibre de verre coupée	32 Spritzverfahren	32 korte vezels, mat	32 fibre
33 balsa cored sandwich	33 sandwich balsa	33 Sandwichbauweise mit Balsakern	33 balsakern sandwich	33 sandwichkonstruktion, balsa
34 foam core	34 noyau de mousse	34 Schaumkern	34 schuimkern	34 skumkerne
35 to laminate	35 laminer	35 laminieren	35 lamineren	35 laminere
36 to bond	36 coller	36 abbinden	36 lijmen, hechten	36 lime
37 carbon fibre	37 fibre de carbonne	37 Kohlefaser	37 koolstofvezel	37 kulfibre
38 Kevlar™	38 Kevlar™	38 Kevlar™	38 Kevlar™	38 Kevlar™
39 steel	39 acier	39 Stahl	39 staal	39 stål
40 aluminium	40 aluminium	40 Aluminium	40 aluminium	40 aluminium
41 ferro-cement	41 ferro-ciment	41 Ferrozement	41 ferrocement	41 ferro-cement
Longitudinal section	*Section longitudinale*	*Längsschnitt*	*Langsdoorsnede*	*Opstalt*
1 stem	1 étrave	1 Vorsteven	1 achtersteven	1 forstævn
2 breasthook	2 guirlande	2 Bugband	2 boegband	2 bovbånd
3 apron	3 contre-étrave	3 Binnenvorsteven	3 binnenvoorsteven	3 inderstævn
4 wood keel	4 quille de bois	4 Holzkiel	4 houten kiel	4 trækøl
5 keelson	5 carlingue	5 Kielschwein	5 kielbalk	5 kølsvin
6 ballast keel	6 lest	6 Ballastkiel	6 ballastkiel	6 ballastkøl
7 keelbolts	7 boulons de quille	7 Kielbolzen	7 kielbouten	7 kølbolte
8 sternpost	8 étambot	8 Achtersteven	8 achterstevenbalk	8 agterstævn
9 horn timber	9 allonge de voûte	9 Heckbalken	9 hekbalk	9 hækbjælke

ESPAÑOL	ITALIANO	PORTUGUÊS	TÜRKÇE	ΕΛΛΗΝΙΚΑ
5 EL BARCO	**5 LA BARCA**	**5 DO BARCO**	**5 TEKNE**	**5 ΤΟ ΣΚΑΦΟΣ**
Construcción	**Costruzione**	**Construção**	**İnşaat**	**ΚΑΤΑΣΚΕΥΗ**

Diseño y construcción del casco	*Progetto e costruzione della carena*	*Desenho e construção do casco*	*Karina dizaynı ve inşaatı*	*ΣΧΕΔΙΟ ΓΑΣΤΡΑΣ & ΚΑΤΑΣΚΕΥΗ*
31 mat	31 stuoia	31 esteira	31 cam elyafı keçe	31 ΥΑΛΟΒΑΜΒΑΚΑΣ ΤΥΧΑΙΑΣ ΠΛΕΞΗΣ
32 fibra troceada	32 stoppini trinciati	32 filamento cortado	32 cam elyaf kırpığı, yünü	32 ΤΡΙΧΑ-ΚΟΜΜΕΝΟΣ ΥΑΛΟΒΑΜΒΑΞ
33 sandwich de balsa	33 sandwich con anima di balsa	33 sanduiche de balsa	33 balsa ile sandviç	33 ΚΑΤΑΣΚΕΥΗ ΣΑΝΤΟΥΙΤΣ ΜΕ ΞΥΛΟ ΜΠΑΛΣΑ
34 sandwich de espuma	34 anima di espanso	34 interior de espuma	34 sert köpükle	34 ΚΑΤΑΣΚΕΥΗ ΣΑΝΤΟΥΙΤΣ ΜΕ ΑΦΡΟ
35 laminar	35 laminare	35 laminar	35 lamine etmek	35 ΕΠΙΣΤΡΩΝΩ
36 ensamblar	36 unire	36 amarrar	36 yapıştırmak	36 ΕΝΩΝΩ-ΚΟΛΛΩ
37 fibra de carbon	37 fibra di carbonio	37 fibra de carbono	37 karbon elyaf	37 ΑΝΘΡΑΚΟΝΗΜΑ
38 Kevlar™	38 Kevlar™	38 Kevlar™	38 Kevlar™	38 ΚΕΒΛΑΡ
39 acero	39 acciaio	39 ferro	39 çelik	39 ΑΤΣΑΛΙ
40 aluminio	40 alluminio	40 aluminio	40 alüminyum	40 ΑΛΟΥΜΙΝΙΟ
41 hierro y cemento	41 ferro-cemento	41 ferrocimento	41 betonarme	41 ΟΠΛΙΣΜΕΝΟ ΕΚΥΡΟΔΕΜΑ

Sección longitudinal	*Sezione longitudinale*	*Secção longitudinal*	*Boyuna (tülani) kesit*	*ΚΑΤΑΜΗΚΟΣ ΤΟΜΗ*
1 roda	1 dritto di prua	1 roda de proa	1 baş bodoslama	1 ΠΡΥΜΝΗ
2 buzarda	2 gola di prua	2 buçarda	2 baş güverte/ bodoslama praçolu	2 ΚΟΡΑΚΙ
3 contrarroda	3 controdritto	3 contra-roda	3 kontra bodoslama	3 ΠΟΔΙΑ
4 quilla de madera	4 chiglia di legno	4 quilha	4 ağaç omurga	4 ΞΥΛΙΝΗ ΚΑΡΙΝΑ
5 sobrequilla	5 paramezzale, controchiglia	5 sobreçame	5 kontra omurga/iç omurga	5 ΣΩΤΡΟΠΙ
6 quilla lastrada	6 chiglia zavorrata	6 patilhão	6 maden omurga	6 ΣΑΒΟΥΡΩΜΕΝΗ ΚΑΡΙΝΑ
7 pernos de quilla	7 bulloni di chiglia	7 cavilhas do patilhão	7 omurga cıvataları maden omurga cıvataları	7 ΤΣΑΒΕΤΕΣ
8 codaste	8 dritto di poppa	8 cadaste	8 kıç bodoslama	8 ΠΟΔΟΣΤΑΜΟ
9 gambota de la limera	9 volta di poppa, dragante	9 cambota	9 kepçe omurgası	9 ΞΥΛΟ (ΚΑΡΙΝΑ) ΠΟΥ ΥΠΟΣΤΗΡΙΖΕΙ ΜΕΤΑ ΤΟ ΤΙΜΟΝΙ

ENGLISH	FRANÇAIS	DEUTSCH	NEDERLANDS	DANSK
5 THE BOAT	**5 LE BATEAU**	**5 DAS BOOT**	**5 DE BOOT, HET SCHIP**	**5 BÅDEN**
Construction	**Construction**	**Bauweise**	**Constructie**	**Konstruktion**
Longitudinal section	*Section longitudinale*	*Längsschnitt*	*Langsdoorsnede*	*Opstalt*
10 stern knee	10 marsouin, courbe de poupe	10 Achterstevenknie	10 stevenknie	10 hæk-knæ
11 deadwood	11 massif	11 Totholz	11 opvulhout, doodhout	11 dødtræ
12 rudder trunk	12 jaumière	12 Ruderkoker	12 hennegatskoker	12 rorbrønd
13 rudder	13 gouvernail, safran	13 Ruder	13 roer	13 ror
14 tiller	14 barre	14 Ruderpinne	14 helmstok	14 rorpind
15 deck	15 pont	15 Deck	15 dek	15 dæk
16 beam	16 barrot	16 Decksbalken	16 dekbalk	16 bjælke
17 shelf	17 bauquière	17 Balkweger	17 balkweger	17 bjælkevæger
18 rib	18 membrure, couple	18 Spant	18 spant	18 spanter
19 bilge stringer	19 serre de bouchain	19 Stringer, Kimmweger	19 kimweger	19 langskibsvæger
20 length overall/LOA	20 longueur hors-tout	20 Länge über Alles, LüA	20 lengte over alles, LOA	20 længde overalt/LOA
21 load waterline/LWL	21 ligne de flottaison	21 Konstruktionswasserlinie (KWL, CWL)	21 lengte waterlijn, LWL	21 vandlinielængde/LWL
22 bilges	22 bouchain, fonds	22 Bilge	22 kim	22 kimingen
23 hull	23 coque	23 Rumpf	23 romp	23 skrog
24 wing keel	24 quille à ailettes	24 Flügelkiel	24 vleugelkiel	24 vingekøl
25 fin keel	25 quille à aileron	25 Flossenkiel	25 vinkiel	25 finnekøl
26 bilge keel	26 biquilles	26 Kimmkiel	26 kimkiel	26 rundbundet
27 long keel	27 quille longue	27 Langkiel	27 langekiel	27 langkølet
28 skeg	28 talon	28 Ruderhacke	28 scheg	28 skeg
29 rudder stock	29 axe de gouvernail	29 Ruderschaft	29 roerkoning	29 rorstamme
30 coachroof	30 roof/rouf	30 Kajütdach	30 kajuitdek	30 kahytstag
31 wheelhouse	31 timonerie abritée	31 Steuerhaus	31 stuurhuis	31 styrehus
32 stemhead	32 étrave	32 Vorstevenende, Bugbeschlag	32 voorluik	32 stærn
33 deckhead	33 tête de pont	33 Kajütdach	33 dekluik	33 hæk

ESPAÑOL	ITALIANO	PORTUGUÊS	TÜRKÇE	ΕΛΛΗΝΙΚΑ
5 EL BARCO	**5 LA BARCA**	**5 DO BARCO**	**5 TEKNE**	**5 ΤΟ ΣΚΑΦΟΣ**
Construcción	**Costruzione**	**Construção**	**İnşaat**	**ΚΑΤΑΣΚΕΥΗ**

Sección longitudinal	*Sezione longitudinale*	*Secção longitudinal*	*Boyuna (tülani) kesit*	*ΚΑΤΑΜΗΚΟΣ ΤΟΜΗ*
10 curva coral	10 bracciolo dello specchio di poppa	10 curva do painel	10 kıç ayna praçolu	10 ΓΩΝΙΑ (ΓΟΝΑΤΟ) ΠΡΥΜΝΗΣ
11 macizo	11 massiccio di poppa	11 coral	11 yığma, kıç yığma, praçol	11 ΠΡΟΣΤΑΤΕΥΤΙΚΗ ΚΟΝΤΡΑ ΚΑΡΙΝΑ
12 limera de timon	12 losca del timone	12 caixão do leme	12 dümen kovanı	12 ΚΟΡΜΟΣ ΤΙΜΟΝΙΟΥ
13 timón	13 timone	13 leme	13 dümen, dümen palası	13 ΠΗΔΑΛΙΟ
14 caña	14 barra (del timone)	14 cana de leme	14 dümen yekesi	14 ΛΑΓΟΥΔΕΡΑ
15 cubierta	15 ponte	15 convez	15 güverte	15 ΚΑΤΑΣΤΡΩΜΑ
16 bao	16 baglio	16 vau	16 kemere	16 ΟΛΙΚΟ ΠΛΑΤΟΣ
17 durmiente	17 dormiente	17 dormente	17 kemere/güverte ıstralyası, güverte kuşağı	17 ΓΩΝΙΑ ΓΑΣΤΡΑ/ ΚΑΤΑΣΤΡΩΜΑ
18 cuaderna	18 ordinata	18 caverna	18 triz	18 ΣΤΡΑΒΟ
19 vagra	19 corrente di sentina	19 escôa	19 alt kuşak	19 ΝΕΥΡΟ ΣΕΝΤΙΝΑΣ
20 eslora total	20 lunghezza fuori tutto (LFT)	20 comprimento fora a fora	20 tam boy, LOA	20 ΟΛΙΚΟ ΜΗΚΟΣ
21 eslora en el plano de flotación	21 linea di galleggiamento	21 comprimento na linha de água	21 dolu iken su hattı	21 ΜΗΚΟΣ ΙΣΑΛΟΥ
22 sentina	22 sentina	22 entre fundo	22 sintine	22 ΣΕΝΤΙΝΕΣ
23 casco	23 scafo, carena	23 casco	23 karina	23 ΓΑΣΤΡΑ
24 quilla con alas	24 chiglia ad alette	24 quilha com asa	24 kanatçıklı maden omurga	24 ΦΤΕΡΩΤΗ ΚΑΡΙΝΑ
25 orza	25 chiglia a pinna, chiglia a bulbo	25 patilhão	25 fin keel	25 ΚΑΡΙΝΑ ΠΤΕΡΥΓΙΟ
26 doble quilla	26 chiglia di rollio	26 quilha dupla	26 çift tarafta omurga	26 ΔΙΠΛΗ, ΠΛΑΙΝΗ ΚΑΡΙΝΑ
27 quilla corrida	27 chiglia lunga	27 quilha corrida	27 uzun omurga	27 ΜΑΚΡΥΑ ΚΑΡΙΝΑ
28 skeg	28 skeg	28 skeg	28 skeg/dumen iğnecikleri bağlantı parçası	28 ΠΤΕΡΥΓΙΟ ΣΤΗΡΙΞΕΩΣ ΤΙΜΟΝΙΟΥ
29 mecha del timón	29 asta del timone	29 madre do leme	29 dümen mili	29 ΑΞΩΝ ΠΗΔΑΛΙΟΥ
30 techo de cabina	30 tetto della tuga	30 tecto da cabine	30 kamara tavanı	30 ΟΡΟΦΗ ΚΑΜΠΙΝΑΣ
31 timonera, caseta del timón	31 timoniera	31 casa do leme	31 dümenevi	31 ΤΙΜΟΝΙΕΡΑ
32 roda	32 dritto di prua	32 roda de proa	32 bodoslama başı	32 ΑΝΩ ΑΚΡΟ ΚΟΡΑΚΙΟΥ
33 techo de cabina	33 cielo della tuga	33 cabeço do convés	33 güverte başı	33 ΥΠΟΚΑΤΩ ΜΕΡΟΣ ΚΑΤΑΣΤΡΩΜΑΤΟΣ

ENGLISH	FRANÇAIS	DEUTSCH	NEDERLANDS	DANSK
5 THE BOAT	**5 LE BATEAU**	**5 DAS BOOT**	**5 DE BOOT, HET SCHIP**	**5 BÅDEN**
Construction	**Construction**	**Bauweise**	**Constructie**	**Konstruktion**
Lateral section	*Section latérale*	*Generalplan*	*Dwarsdoorsnede*	*Halve sektioner*
1 rail	1 liston	1 Reling	1 reling	1 ræling
2 bulwark	2 pavois	2 Schanzkleid	2 verschansing	2 skanseklædning
3 scupper	3 dalot	3 Speigatt	3 spuigat	3 spygatter
4 rubbing strake	4 bourrelet, ceinture	4 Scheuerleiste	4 berghout	4 fenderliste
5 planking	5 bordage	5 Beplankung	5 huid, beplanking	5 rangene
6 skin	6 bordé	6 Außenhaut	6 huid	6 klædning
7 garboard strake	7 virure de galbord	7 Kielgang	7 zandstrook	7 kølplanke
8 king plank	8 faux-étambrai, virure d'axe	8 Fischplanke	8 vissingstuk, schaarstokplank	8 midterfisk
9 covering board	9 plat-bord	9 Schandeck	9 lijfhout, potdeksel	9 skandæk
10 carline	10 élongis	10 Schlinge	10 langsligger	10 kraveller
11 beam	11 barrot	11 Decksbalken	11 dekbalk	11 bjælke
12 tie-rod	12 tirant	12 Stehbolzen	12 trekstang	12 spændebånd
13 knee	13 courbe	13 Knie	13 knie	13 knæ
14 timber, frame	14 membrure	14 Spant	14 spant	14 svøb, fast spant
15 floor	15 varangue	15 Bodenwrange	15 wrang	15 bundstokke
16 cabin sole	16 plancher	16 Bodenbrett	16 vloer	16 dørk
17 limber holes	17 anguillers	17 Wasserlauflöcher	17 waterloopgaten	17 sandspor
18 coaming	18 hiloire	18 Süll	18 opstaande rand	18 lugekarm
19 coachroof	19 rouf	19 Kajütsdach	19 kajuitdek, opbouw	19 ruftag
20 depth	20 creux	20 Raumtiefe	20 holte	20 dybde indvendig

ESPAÑOL	ITALIANO	PORTUGUÊS	TÜRKÇE	ΕΛΛΗΝΙΚΑ
5 EL BARCO	**5 LA BARCA**	**5 DO BARCO**	**5 TEKNE**	**5 ΤΟ ΣΚΑΦΟΣ**
Construcción	**Costruzione**	**Construção**	**İnşaat**	**ΚΑΤΑΣΚΕΥΗ**
Sección lateral	*Sezione laterale*	*Secção lateral*	*Enine (arzani) kesit*	*ΚΑΘΕΤΟΣ ΤΟΜΗ*
1 tapa de regala	1 capodibanda	1 talabardão	1 parampet kapağı/ küpeştesi	1 ΚΟΥΠΑΣΤΗ
2 borda, regala	2 impavesata	2 borda falsa	2 parampet	2 ΥΠΕΡΥΨΩΜΑ ΓΑΣΤΡΑΣ ΠΑΝΩ ΑΠΟ ΚΑΤΑΣΤΡΩΜΑ
3 imbornal	3 ombrinale	3 embornais, portas de mar	3 frengi	3 ΜΠΟΥΝΙ
4 cintón	4 bottazzo	4 cinta, verdugo	4 yumra, borda yumrusu	4 ΠΛΑΙΝΟ ΜΡΟΣΤΑΤΕΥΤΙΚΟ
5 tablazón del casco	5 fasciame	5 tabuado	5 borda-karina kaplama tahtaları	5 ΠΕΤΣΩΜΑ ΜΕ ΣΑΝΙΔΕΣ
6 forro	6 rivestimento	6 querena	6 kaplama/borda ağacı	6 ΠΕΤΣΩΜΑ ΜΕ ΠΟΛΥΕΣΤΕΡΑ
7 aparadura	7 torello	7 tábua de resbôrdo	7 burma tahtası	7 ΔΙΑΚΟΣΜΗΤΙΚΗ ΓΡΑΜΜΗ
8 tabla de crujía	8 tavolato di coperta	8 tábua da mediania	8 güverte kaplaması	8 ΚΕΝΤΡΙΚΟ ΜΑΔΕΡΙ ΚΑΤΑΣΤΡΩΜΑΤΟΣ
9 trancanil	9 trincarino	9 tabica	9 küpeşte, anbar iç kapama tahtası	9 ΞΥΛΙΝΗ ΕΠΙΚΑΛΥΨΗ ΤΩΝ ΝΟΜΕΩΝ
10 gualdera	10 anguilla	10 longarina da cabine	10 kamara kovuşu	10 ΔΙΑΖΥΓΟ-ΜΠΙΜΠΕΚΙΑ
11 bao	11 baglio	11 vau	11 kemere	11 ΠΛΑΤΟΣ
12 tiranta	12 mezzobaglio	12 tirante de ligação	12 öksüz kemere takviye civatası	12 ΞΥΛΑ ΠΟΥ ΕΝΩΝΟΥΝ ΤΟ ΚΟΚΠΙΤ ΜΕ ΤΗΝ ΚΟΥΠΑΣΤΗ
13 curva, curvatón	13 bracciolo	13 curva de reforço	13 praçol, paracol	13 ΓΟΝΑΤΟ
14 madero, pieza	14 ossatura, scheletro	14 caverna	14 kaburga (posta)	14 ΣΤΡΑΒΟ
15 varenga	15 madiere	15 reforços do pé caverna	15 döşek	15 ΠΑΤΩΜΑ
16 plan de la cámara	16 piano di calpestio	16 paneiros	16 kamara farşları	16 ΠΑΝΙΟΛΟ
17 imbornales de la varenga	17 ombrinali	17 boeiras	17 yığma frengi delikleri	17 ΔΙΑΚΕΝΑ ΣΤΗΝ ΚΟΥΠΑΣΤΗ ΓΙΑ ΝΑ ΦΕΥΓΟΥΝ ΤΑ ΝΕΡΑ
18 brazola	18 battente (di boccaporto)	18 braçola	18 kasara	18 ΚΑΣΑ ΚΟΥΒΟΥΣΙΟΥ - ΕΙΣΟΔΟΣ
19 tambucho	19 tetto della tuga	19 teto da cabine	19 kasara tavanı, kamara üstü	19 ΠΕΤΣΩΜΑ ΚΑΜΠΙΝΑΣ
20 puntal	20 altezza, puntale	20 pontal	20 iç derinlik (omurga üstü-kemere üstü derinliği)	20 ΒΑΘΟΣ

71

ENGLISH	FRANÇAIS	DEUTSCH	NEDERLANDS	DANSK
5 THE BOAT	**5 LE BATEAU**	**5 DAS BOOT**	**5 DE BOOT, HET SCHIP**	**5 BÅDEN**
Construction	**Construction**	**Bauweise**	**Constructie**	**Konstruktion**
Lateral section	*Section latérale*	*Generalplan*	*Dwarsdoorsnede*	*Halve sektioner*
21 headroom	21 hauteur sous barrots	21 Stehhöhe	21 stahoogte	21 højde i kahytten
22 draught	22 tirant d'eau	22 Tiefgang	22 diepgang	22 dybgående
23 waterline	23 ligne de flottaison	23 Wasserlinie	23 waterlijn	23 vandlinie
24 topsides	24 œuvres-mortes	24 Überwasserschiff	24 bovenschip	24 højde over vandlinien
25 bottom	25 œuvres-vives, carène	25 Schiffsboden	25 onderwaterschip, bodem, vlak	25 bund
26 freeboard	26 franc-bord	26 Freibord	26 vrijboord	26 fribord
Accommodation plan	*Plan d'aménagements*	*Einrichtungsplan*	*Accommodatieplan*	*Apteringsplan*
1 forepeak	1 pic avant	1 Vorpiek	1 voorpiek	1 forpeak
2 chain locker	2 puits à chaine	2 Kettenkasten	2 kettingbak	2 kædebrønd
3 cabin, saloon	3 carré, cabine	3 Kajüte, Messe	3 kajuit	3 kahyt, salon
4 berth	4 couchette	4 Koje	4 kooi, slaapplaats	4 køje
5 pipecot	5 cadre	5 Gasrohrkoje, Klappkoje	5 pijpkooi	5 klapkøje
6 quarter berth	6 couchette de quart	6 Hundekoje	6 hondekooi	6 hundekøje
7 galley	7 cuisine	7 Kombüse	7 kombuis	7 kabys
8 table	8 table	8 Tisch	8 tafel	8 bord
9 locker, stowage space	9 coffre, placard, surface de rangement	9 Schrank, Stauraum	9 bergruimte, kastje	9 kistebænk, stuverum
10 bosun's locker	10 coffre à outils, cambuse	10 Hellegat	10 kabelgat	10 bådsmandsgrej
11 bulkhead	11 cloison	11 Schott	11 schot	11 skot
12 bridgedeck	12 bridge-deck	12 Brückendeck	12 brugdek	12 brokæk
13 companionway	13 descente	13 Niedergang	13 kajuittrap	13 kahytstrappe
14 engine compartment	14 chambre du moteur	14 Motorenraum	14 motorruimte	14 maskinrum
15 freshwater tank	15 réservoir d'eau douce	15 Frischwassertank	15 drinkwatertank	15 ferskvandstank
16 hatch, sliding hatch	16 écoutille, capot coulissant	16 Luk, Schiebeluk	16 luik, schuifluik	16 skydekappe, luge

ESPAÑOL	ITALIANO	PORTUGUÊS	TÜRKÇE	ΕΛΛΗΝΙΚΑ
5 EL BARCO	**5 LA BARCA**	**5 DO BARCO**	**5 TEKNE**	**5 ΤΟ ΣΚΑΦΟΣ**
Construcción	**Costruzione**	**Construção**	**İnşaat**	**ΚΑΤΑΣΚΕΥΗ**
Sección lateral	***Sezione laterale***	***Secção lateral***	***Enine (arzani) kesit***	*ΚΑΘΕΤΟΣ ΤΟΜΗ*
21 altura de techo	21 altezza in cabina	21 pé direito	21 baş yüksekliği (kamarada farş üstü-kemere altı yüksekliği)	21 ΕΣΩΤΕΡΙΚΟ ΥΨΟΣ
22 calado	22 pescaggio	22 calado	22 çektiği su	22 ΒΥΘΙΣΜΑ
23 linea de flotación	23 linea di galleggiamento	23 linha de água	23 su hattı	23 ΙΣΑΛΟΣ
24 obra muerta	24 opera morta	24 costado, obras mortas	24 su hattı üzerindeki tekne bordaları	24 ΕΞΑΛΑ
25 fondo, carena	25 opera viva	25 fundo, obras vivas	25 karina, teknenin sualtı kesimi	25 ΥΦΑΛΑ
26 franco bordo	26 bordo libero	26 altura do bordo livre	26 fribord, teknenin süüstü kesiminin yüksekliği	26 ΥΠΕΡΚΕΙΜΕΝΗ ΕΠΙΦΑΝΕΙΑ
Acondicionamiento interior	***Pianta degli alloggiamenti***	***Plano de acomodação***	***Yerleşim planı***	*ΣΧΕΔΙΟ ΕΝΔΙΑΙΤΗΣΗΣ*
1 tilla	1 gavone di prua	1 pique de vante	1 baş pik, başaltı	1 ΚΟΡΑΚΙ
2 pañol de cadenas	2 cala delle catene	2 paiol da amarra	2 zincirlik, zincir kuyusu	2 ΣΤΡΙΤΣΙΟ
3 camarote	3 quadrato	3 cabine, salão	3 kamara, salon	3 ΚΑΜΠΙΝΑ
4 litera	4 cuccetta	4 beliche	4 ranza	4 ΚΟΥΚΕΤΑ
5 catre	5 brandina smontabile	5 beliche em tubo desmontável	5 boru çerçeveli ranza	5 ΜΙΚΡΗ ΚΟΥΚΕΤΑ
6 litera del tambucho	6 cuccetta di guardia	6 beliche de quarto	6 vardiye ranzası	6 ΠΛΑΙΝΗ ΚΟΥΚΕΤΑ
7 fogón	7 cambusa	7 cozinha	7 kuzina-galey	7 ΚΟΥΖΙΝΑ
8 mesa	8 tavolo	8 mesa	8 masa	8 ΤΡΑΠΕΖΙ
9 pañol, caja	9 gavone, stivaggio	9 paióis, armários, arrumação	9 dolap	9 ΝΤΟΥΛΑΠΙ
10 pañol contramaestre	10 cala del nostromo	10 paiol do mestre	10 porsun dolabı, alet dolabı	10 ΝΤΟΥΛΑΠΙ ΕΡΓΑΛΕΙΩΝ
11 mamparo	11 paratia	11 antepara	11 bölme	11 ΜΠΟΥΛΜΕΣ
12 puente	12 ponte di comando	12 pavimento da ponte	12 köprüüstü güvertesi	12 ΚΑΤΑΣΤΡΩΜΑ ΓΕΦΥΡΑΣ
13 escalera de la cámara	13 scaletta (di boccaporto)	13 escotilha de passagem	13 ana kaporta, giriş kaportası	13 ΔΙΑΔΡΟΜΟΣ
14 cuarto de máquinas	14 locale motore	14 casa do motor	14 motor dairesi	14 ΧΩΡΟΣ ΜΗΧΑΝΗΣ
15 depósito de agua potable	15 serbatoio d'acqua dolce	15 tanque de aguada	15 tatlısu tankı	15 ΔΕΞΑΜΕΝΗ ΝΕΡΟΥ
16 escotilla, escotilla de corredera	16 boccaporto, tambuccio scorrevol	16 alboi, tampa de escotilha de correr	16 kaporta, sürgülü kaporta	16 ΚΑΣΑΡΟ

ENGLISH	FRANÇAIS	DEUTSCH	NEDERLANDS	DANSK
5 THE BOAT	**5 LE BATEAU**	**5 DAS BOOT**	**5 DE BOOT, HET SCHIP**	**5 BÅDEN**
Construction	**Construction**	**Bauweise**	**Constructie**	**Konstruktion**
Accommodation plan	***Plan d'aménagements***	***Einrichtungsplan***	***Accommodatieplan***	***Apteringsplan***
17 cockpit	17 baignoire, cockpit	17 Plicht	17 kuip	17 cockpit
18 self-draining	18 auto-videur	18 selbstlenzend	18 zelflozend	18 selvlænsende
19 watertight	19 étanche	19 wasserdicht	19 waterdicht	19 vandtæt
20 sail locker	20 soute à voiles	20 Segelkoje	20 zeilkooi	20 sejlkøje
21 bow, forward	21 étrave; avant	21 Bug; vorn	21 boeg, voorsteven	21 stævn, forude
22 stern, aft	22 poupe; arrière	22 Heck; achtern	22 hek, achtersteven	22 hæk, agter
23 beam	23 largeur, bau	23 Breite	23 breedte	23 bredde
24 port	24 bâbord	24 Backbord	24 bakboord	24 bagbord
25 starboard	25 tribord	25 Steuerbord	25 stuurboord	25 styrbord
26 heads	26 WC	26 Toilettenbecken	26 toilet, WC	26 toilet
27 chart table	27 table à cartes	27 Kartentisch	27 kaartentafel	27 kortbord
Joints & fastenings	***Joints et fixations***	***Verbindungselemente***	***Verbindingen en bevestigingen***	***Samlinger og befæstigelser***
1 scarf	1 écart	1 Laschung	1 las	1 lask
2 rabbet	2 râblure	2 Sponung	2 sponning	2 spunding
3 mortise and tenon	3 mortaise et tenon	3 Nut und Zapfen	3 pen en gat	3 notgang & tap af træ, taphul & sportap
4 butted	4 bout à bout	4 Stoß	4 gestuikt	4 stød-plankeender
5 dovetail	5 en queue d'aronde	5 verzahnen, Schwalbenschwanz	5 zwaluwstaart	5 sammensænkning
6 faired	6 caréné, poncé	6 geglättet	6 gestroomlijnd	6 slette efter med skarøkse
7 bolt	7 boulon	7 Bolzen	7 bout	7 bolt
8 nail	8 clou	8 Nagel	8 nagel	8 søm
9 screw	9 vis	9 Schraube	9 schroef	9 skrue
10 rivet	10 rivet	10 Niet	10 ringetje	10 nagle
11 metal dowel	11 goujon	11 Metalldübel	11 metalen pen	11 metal låseprop
12 weld	12 souder	12 schweißen	12 las	12 svejse
13 wooden dowel	13 cheville	13 Holzdübel, Holzpropfen	13 houten plug	13 trædyvel

ESPAÑOL	ITALIANO	PORTUGUÊS	TÜRKÇE	ΕΛΛΗΝΙΚΑ
5 EL BARCO	**5 LA BARCA**	**5 DO BARCO**	**5 TEKNE**	**5 ΤΟ ΣΚΑΦΟΣ**
Construcción	**Costruzione**	**Construção**	**İnşaat**	**ΚΑΤΑΣΚΕΥΗ**
Acondicionamiento interior	*Pianta degli alloggiamenti*	*Plano de acomodação*	*Yerleşim planı*	*ΣΧΕΔΙΟ ΕΝΔΙΑΙΤΗΣΗΣ*
17 bañera	17 pozzetto,	17 poço	17 havuzluk, kokpit	17 ΚΟΚΠΙΤ – ΧΑΒΟΥΖΑ
18 de imbornales	18 autosvuotante	18 com esgoto para o mar	18 frengili havuzluk	18 ΑΥΤΟΑΔΕΙΑΖΟΜΕΝΟ
19 estanca	19 stagno	19 estanque	19 su geçirmez havuzluk	19 ΥΔΑΤΟΣΤΕΓΕΣ
20 pañol de velas	20 cala vele	20 paiol das velas	20 yelkenlik	20 ΑΜΠΑΡΙ ΠΑΝΙΩΝ
21 proa; a proa	21 prua; proravia	21 proa; avante	21 pruva, baş	21 ΠΡΟΣ ΤΗΝ ΠΛΩΡΗ
22 popa; a popa	22 poppa; poppavia	22 pôpa; à ré	22 kıç, arka	22 ΠΡΥΜΗ, ΠΙΣΩ ΜΕΡΟΣ
23 manga	23 larghezza	23 bocadura, bôca	23 en, tekne eni	23 ΠΛΑΤΟΣ
24 babor	24 sinistra	24 bombordo	24 iskele	24 ΑΡΙΣΤΕΡΑ
25 estribor	25 dritta	25 estibordo	25 sancak	25 ΔΕΞΙΑ
26 inodoros	26 WC, cesso	26 cabeças/cabeçotes	26 tuvalet	26 ΤΟΥΑΛΕΤΕΣ
27 mesa de cartas	27 tavolo di carteggio	27 mesa de cartas	27 harita masası	27 ΤΡΑΠΕΖΙ ΧΑΡΤΩΝ
Juntas y ensamblajes	*Giunti*	*Juntas e ferragem*	*Ekler ve bağlantılar*	*ΕΝΩΣΕΙΣ ΚΑΙ ΔΕΣΙΜΑΤΑ*
1 empalme	1 ammorsatura	1 escarva	1 geçme	1 ΜΑΤΙΣΜΑ (ΞΥΛΟ-ΞΥΛΟ)
2 rebajo	2 scanalatura	2 rebaixo	2 bindirme	2 ΓΚΙΝΙΣΙΑ
3 encaje y mecha	3 mortasa e tenone	3 fêmea e espiga	3 lamba ve zıvana	3 ΣΚΑΤΣΑ ΚΑΙ ΔΟΝΤΙ (ΤΟΡΜΟΣ)
4 unido a tope	4 di testa	4 topado	4 uç uca ekleme	4 ΤΕΤΡΑΓΩΝΙΣΜΕΝΟ
5 cola de milano	5 coda di rondine	5 emalhetado	5 güvercin kuyruğu geçmeli	5 ΧΕΛΙΔΟΝΙ - ΨΑΛΙΔΩΤΟΣ ΑΡΜΟΣ
6 encajar	6 carenato	6 desempolado	6 zımparalanmış	6 ΣΤΡΟΓΓΥΛΕΜΕΝΟ
7 perno	7 bullone	7 cavilha	7 civata	7 ΜΠΟΥΛΟΝΙ
8 clavo	8 chiodo	8 prego	8 çivi	8 ΚΑΡΦΙ
9 tornillo	9 vite	9 parafuso	9 vida	9 ΒΙΔΑ
10 remache	10 rivetto	10 rebite	10 perçin	10 ΠΡΙΤΣΙΝΙ
11 espiga de metal	11 spina metallica	11 rôlha metálica	11 metal düvel, metal takoz	11 ΑΚΕΦΑΛΟ ΚΑΡΦΙ
12 soldar	12 saldatura	12 soldar	12 kaynak	12 ΣΥΓΚΟΛΛΩ
13 espiga de madera	13 spina di legno, tassello	13 rôlha	13 ağaç düvel, ağaç takoz	13 ΞΥΛΙΝΗ ΣΦΗΝΑ

ENGLISH	FRANÇAIS	DEUTSCH	NEDERLANDS	DANSK
5 THE BOAT	**5 LE BATEAU**	**5 DAS BOOT**	**5 DE BOOT, HET SCHIP**	**5 BÅDEN**
Rigging & sails	**Gréement et voiles**	**Rigg und Segel**	**Tuigage en zeilen**	**Rigning og sejl**
Mast & boom	*Mât et bôme*	*Mast und Baum*	*Mast en giek*	*Mast og bom*
1 mast	1 mât	1 Mast	1 mast	1 mast
2 truck	2 pomme	2 Masttopp, Mastspitze	2 masttop	2 fløjknap
3 hounds	3 jottereaux, capelage	3 Mastbacken	3 nommerstuk	3 kindbakker
4 partners	4 étambrai	4 Mastfischung	4 mastknie	4 mastefisk
5 step and heel	5 emplanture et pied	5 Mastspur und Mastfuß	5 mastspoor en mastvoet	5 mastespor & hæl
6 wedges	6 cales	6 Mastkeile	6 keggen	6 kiler
7 collar	7 jupe	7 Mastkragen	7 mastbroeking	7 masterkrave
8 crosstrees	8 barres de flèche	8 Saling	8 zaling	8 salingshorn
9 jumper struts	9 guignol	9 Jumpstagspreize	9 knikzaling	9 strutter
10 pinrail	10 râtelier	10 Nagelbank	10 nagelbank	10 naglebænk
11 crutch, gallows	11 support de bôme, portique	11 Baumbock, Baumstütze	11 schaar, vang	11 bomstol
12 boom	12 bôme	12 Baum	12 giek	12 bom
13 boom claw	13 croissant	13 Baumklaue	13 schootring	13 bomklo, lyre
14 gooseneck	14 vit-de-mulet	14 Lümmelbeschlag des Baumes	14 lummel	14 svanehals
15 rod kicker	15 hale-bas rigide	15 starrer Baumniederholer, Rodkicker	15 giekophouder, neerhouder	15 kicking rod
16 spreaders	16 barres de flèche	16 Saling	16 zaling	16 salingshorn
17 keel-stepped	17 mât posé sur la quille	17 durchgehender Mast	17 op de kiel staand (van mast)	17 står på kølen
18 deck-stepped	18 mât posé sur le pont	18 an Deck stehender Mast	18 op het dek staand (van de mast)	18 står på dækket
19 tabernacle	19 jumelles	19 Mastkoker	19 mastkoker	19 tabernakel
20 mast gaiter	20 jupe de mât	20 Mastkragen	20 manchet	20 gamache
21 mast track	21 rail	21 Mastschiene	21 mastrail	21 mastespor
22 slide	22 coulisseau	22 Rutscher, Reiter	22 slede, leuver	22 slæde
23 gate	23 verrou	23 Gatchen	23 wissel zeilinvoer	23 åbning
24 ratchet and pawl	24 rochet à linguet	24 Pallkranz und Pall	24 palrad en pal	24 rebeapparat med skralle
25 worm gear	25 vis sans fin	25 Schneckenreff	25 worm en wormwiel	25 rebeapparat med snekke

ESPAÑOL	ITALIANO	PORTUGUÊS	TÜRKÇE	ΕΛΛΗΝΙΚΑ
5 EL BARCO	**5 LA BARCA**	**5 DO BARCO**	**5 TEKNE**	**5 ΤΟ ΣΚΑΦΟΣ**
Jarcias y velas	**Attrezzatura e vele**	**Massame e velas**	**Arma ve yelkenler**	**ΑΡΜΑΤΩΣΙΑ & ΠΑΝΙΑ**
Palo y botavara	*Albero e boma*	*Mastro e retranca*	*Direk ve bumba*	*ΚΑΤΑΡΤΙ & ΜΑΤΣΑ*
1 palo	1 albero	1 mastro	1 direk	1 ΚΑΤΑΡΤΙ
2 tope	2 formaggetta	2 galope, topo do mastro	2 direk başlığı, tepesi	2 ΣΙΔΗΡΟΔΡΟΜΟΣ
3 cacholas de un palo	3 incappellaggio, maschette	3 calcês	3 direk çarmıh bağlantıları	3 ΣΚΥΛΑΚΙΑ
4 fogonadura	4 mastra	4 enora do mastro	4 güverte trosasında direk ayar siğilleri	4 ΣΤΗΡΙΓΜΑΓΑ (ΛΑΜΠΟΥΡΟΥ)
5 carlinga y coz o mecha	5 scassa e miccia	5 carlinga e pé	5 iskaça ve direk topuğu	5 ΒΑΣΗ ΚΑΤΑΡΤΙΟΥ
6 cuñas	6 cunei	6 cunhas	6 siğiller	6 ΣΦΗΝΕΣ
7 encapilladura	7 collare	7 colar	7 bilezik, direk bileziği	7 ΚΟΛΛΑΡΟ
8 crucetas	8 crocette basse	8 vaus	8 gurcatalar	8 ΣΤΑΥΡΟΣ
9 contrete	9 crocette alte	9 diamante	9 şeytan gurcataları, üst gurcatalar	9 ΞΑΡΤΟΡΙΖΕΣ
10 cabillero	10 cavigliera	10 mesa das malagetas	10 armadora	10 ΡΑΓΑ ΤΟΥ ΤΡΑΚ
11 posa botavara	11 forchetta, capra	11 descanço da retranca	11 Bumba çatalı, çatal yastık	11 ΣΤΗΡΙΓΜΑ ΜΑΤΣΑΣ
12 botavara	12 boma	12 retranca	12 bumba	12 ΜΑΤΣΑ
13 media-luna	13 trozza	13 colar de fixação da escota á retranca	13 bumba boğazı	13 ΔΑΓΚΑΝΑ ΜΑΤΣΑΣ
14 pescante arbotante	14 snodo del boma	14 mangual	14 kazboynu, bumba mafsalı	14 ΕΝΩΣΗ ΜΑΤΣΑΣ ΣΤΟ ΚΑΤΑΡΤΙ
15 contra rigido	15 vang rigido	15 rod kicker	15 bumba basma gubağu	15 ΣΤΡΟΦΕΙΟ PONT
16 crucetas	16 crocette	16 vaus	16 gurcatalar	16 ΣΤΑΥΡΟΙ
17 mastil en quilla	17 posato in chiglia	17 mastro apoiado na quilha	17 omurgaya oturan	17 ΚΑΤΑΡΤΙ ΜΕ ΒΑΣΗ ΣΤΗΝ ΚΑΡΙΝΑ
18 mastil en cubierta	18 posato sul ponte	18 mastro apoiado no convés	18 güverteye oturan	18 ΚΑΤΑΡΤΙ ΜΕ ΒΑΣΗ ΣΤΟ ΚΑΤΑΣΤΡΩΜΑ
19 cajera de palo	19 scassa a perno	19 bitácula	19 aryalı direk ıskaçası tabernakl	19 ΣΚΑΝΤΖΑ
20 funda de fogonadura	20 ghetta dell'albero	20 manga de protecção do mastro	20 direk fistanı	20 ΠΡΟΣΤΑΤΕΥΤΙΚΟ ΑΔΙΑΒΡΟΧΟ ΣΤΗ ΒΑΣΗ
21 gula, carril	21 rotaia	21 calha do mastro	21 direk, yelken rayı	21 ΣΙΔΗΡΟΔΡΟΜΟΣ ΚΑΤΑΡΤΙΟΥ
22 corredera	22 garroccio scorrevole	22 corrediça	22 yelken ray arabası	22 ΓΛΙΣΤΡΑ
23 boca del esnón	23 scambio	23 abertura da calha	23 ray arabası kapısı	23 ΕΙΣΟΔΟΣ
24 catalina y pal	24 cricco e nottolino	24 roquete	24 dişli ve tırnak	24 ΚΑΣΤΑΝΙΑ
25 husillo	25 ingranaggio a vite senza fine	25 sem-fim	25 sonsuz dişli	25 ΚΟΧΛΙΩΤΟ ΓΡΑΝΑΖΙ

ENGLISH	FRANÇAIS	DEUTSCH	NEDERLANDS	DANSK
5 THE BOAT	**5 LE BATEAU**	**5 DAS BOOT**	**5 DE BOOT, HET SCHIP**	**5 BÅDEN**
Rigging & sails	**Gréement et voiles**	**Rigg und Segel**	**Tuigage en zeilen**	**Rigning og sejl**
Spars & bowsprit	*Espars et beaupré*	*Spieren und Bugspriet*	*Rondhouten en boegspriet*	*Rundholter og bovspryd*
1 solid	1 massif, plein	1 voll	1 massief	1 massiv
2 hollow	2 creux	2 hohl	2 hol	2 hul
3 bumpkin	3 queue-de-mallet	3 Heckausleger	3 papegaaiestok	3 buttelur, udligger
4 jib boom	4 bôme de foc ou de trinquette	4 Fock-, Klüverbaum	4 kluiverboom	4 klyverbom
5 spinnaker boom	5 tangon de spi	5 Spinnakerbaum	5 spinnakerboom	5 spilerstage
6 jury mast	6 mât de fortune	6 Notmast	6 noodmast	6 nødmast
7 yard	7 vergue	7 Rah	7 ra	7 rå
8 gaff and jaws	8 corne et mâchoires	8 Gaffel und Gaffelklau	8 gaffel en klem	8 gaffel & klo
9 topmast	9 mât de flèche	9 Toppstenge	9 steng, topmast	9 topmast
10 boom roller	10 enrouleur de bôme	10 Baumrollreff	10 giekrolrif	10 rullebom
11 in-mast roller furling	11 enrouleur de mât	11 Mastrollreff	11 mastrolrif	11 rulle-storsejl
12 roller-furling foresail	12 génois à enrouleur	12 Rollfock	12 voorstagrolrif	12 rullefok
13 drum	13 tambour	13 Trommel	13 trommel	13 tromle
14 bowsprit	14 beaupré	14 Bugspriet	14 boegspriet	14 bovspryd
15 dolphin striker	15 martingale	15 Stampfstock	15 stampstok, spaanse ruiter	15 pyntenetstok
16 bobstay	16 sous-barbe	16 Wasserstag	16 waterstag	16 vaterstag
17 cranze iron	17 collier à pitons	17 Bugsprietnockband	17 boegspriet nokring	17 sprydring med øjer
18 gammon iron	18 liure	18 Bugsprietzurring	18 boegspriet stevenring	18 sprydring
19 traveller	19 rocambeau	19 Bugsprietausholring	19 traveller	19 udhalering

ESPAÑOL	ITALIANO	PORTUGUÊS	TÜRKÇE	ΕΛΛΗΝΙΚΑ
5 EL BARCO	**5 LA BARCA**	**5 DO BARCO**	**5 TEKNE**	**5 ΤΟ ΣΚΑΦΟΣ**
Jarcias y velas	**Attrezzatura e vele**	**Massame e velas**	**Arma ve yelkenler**	**ΑΡΜΑΤΩΣΙΑ & ΠΑΝΙΑ**
Arboladura y botalón	*Antenne e bompresso*	*Mastreação e pau da bujarrona*	*Ahşap direkler, bumbalar ve gurcatalar & civadra*	*ΚΑΤΑΡΤΙΑ - ΜΑΤΣΑ - ΜΠΑΣΤΟΥΝΙ*
1 macizo	1 piene	1 maciço	1 içi dolu, solid	1 ΠΛΗΡΕΣ - ΜΑΣΙΦ
2 hueco	2 cave	2 ôco	2 içiboş	2 ΚΕΝΟ - ΚΟΥΦΙΟ
3 arbotante	3 buttafuori	3 pau da pôpa	3 kıç bastonu	3 ΜΟΥΡΑ ΤΟΥ ΤΡΙΓΚΟΥ
4 tangoncillo de foque	4 tangone del fiocco	4 retranca do estai	4 flok bumbası trinket bumbası	4 ΜΑΤΣΑ ΦΛΟΚΟΥ
5 tangón del espina- quer	5 tangone dello spi	5 pau de spinnaker	5 spinnaker bumbası, gönderi	5 ΣΠΙΝΑΚΟ ΞΥΛΟ
6 palo del jurado	6 albero di fortuna	6 mastro de recurso	6 geçici direk	6 ΠΡΟΧΕΙΡΟ ΚΑΤΑΡΤΙ
7 verga	7 pennone	7 verga	7 çubuk	7 ΑΝΤΕΝΝΑ
8 pico y boca de can- grejo	8 picco e gola	8 carangueja e bôca	8 randa yelken piki, boğazı ve çatalı	8 ΠΙΚΙ ΚΑΙ ΔΑΓΚΑΝΑ
9 mastelero	9 alberetto	9 mastaréu	9 direk çubuğu	9 ΑΝΩ ΜΕΡΟΣ ΑΛΜΠΟΥΡΟΥ
10 enrollador de botavara	10 boma a rullino	10 enrolador na retranca	10 bumba sarma düzeneği	10 ΠΕΡΙΣΤΡΕΦΟΜΕΝΗ ΜΑΤΣΑ
11 mastil enrollable	11 avvolgi-randa nell'albero	11 enrolador no mastro	11 direk içine sarma düzeneği	11 ΤΥΛΙΓΜΑ ΜΕΓΙΣΤΗΣ ΜΕΣΑ ΣΤΟ ΚΑΤΑΡΤΙ
12 enrollador de génova	12 avvolgi-fiocco	12 genoa de enrolar	12 önyelken sarma düzeneği	12 ΤΥΛΙΓΜΑ ΜΠΡΟΣΤΙΝΟΥ ΠΑΝΙΟΥ ΣΤΟΝ ΠΡΟΤΟΝΟ
13 tambor	13 tamburo	13 tambor	13 sarma tambura, makarası	13 ΤΥΜΠΑΝΟ
14 botalón	14 bompresso	14 pau da bujarrona	14 civadra	14 ΜΠΑΣΤΟΥΝΙ
15 moco	15 pennaccino	15 pau de pica peixe	15 civadra bıyığı	15 ΔΕΛΦΙΝΙΕΡΑ
16 barbiquejo	16 briglia	16 cabresto	16 civadra kösteği	16 ΜΟΥΣΤΑΚΙ
17 raca	17 collare	17 braçadeira do pau	17 civadra cunda bileziği	17 ΣΤΕΦΑΝΙ ΣΤΕΡΕΩΣΗΣ ΜΟΥΣΤΑΚΙΟΥ
18 zuncho de botalón	18 trinca	18 braçadeira da prôa	18 civadra güverte bileziği	18 ΒΑΣΗ ΣΤΕΡΕΩΣΗΣ ΜΠΑΛΚΟΝΙΟΥ
19 racamento	19 cerchio (di mura del fiocco)	19 urraca	19 hareketli ve ayarlanabilen civadra bileziği	19 ΒΑΓΟΝΑΚΙ - ΔΙΑΔΡΟΜΕΑΣ

ENGLISH	FRANÇAIS	DEUTSCH	NEDERLANDS	DANSK
5 THE BOAT	**5 LE BATEAU**	**5 DAS BOOT**	**5 DE BOOT, HET SCHIP**	**5 BÅDEN**
Rigging & sails	**Gréement et voiles**	**Rigg und Segel**	**Tuigage en zeilen**	**Rigning og sejl**
Standing rigging	*Gréement dormant*	*Stehendes Gut*	*Staand want*	*Stående rig*
1 topmast, stay	1 grand étai, étai de flèche	1 Toppstag	1 topstag	1 topstag
2 forestay, jib stay	2 étai avant ou de trinquette, draille	2 Vorstag, Fockstag	2 voorstag, fokkestag	2 forstag
3 preventer backstay	3 pataras, étai arrière	3 Achterstag	3 achterstag	3 fast bagstag
4 runner and lever	4 bastaque et levier	4 Backstag und Strecker	4 bakstag en hefboom	4 løst bagstag
5 jumper stay	5 étai de guignol	5 Jumpstag	5 knikstag	5 violinstag
6 shroud	6 hauban	6 Want	6 want	6 vant
7 chain plate	7 cadène	7 Rüsteisen, Pütting	7 putting	7 røstjern
8 bottlescrew, turnbuckle	8 ridoir	8 Wantenspanner	8 wantspanner, spanschroef	8 vantskrue
9 ratlines	9 enflèchures	9 Webelein	9 weeflijnen	9 vævlinger
10 diamonds	10 losanges	10 Diamantwanten	10 diamantverstaging	10 diamant-stag
11 baby stay	11 bas étai	11 Babystag	11 babystag	11 babystag
12 clevis pin	12 axe à anneau brisé	12 Schäkelbolzen	12 borstbout	12 clevis-pind
Running rigging	*Gréement courant*	*Laufendes Gut*	*Lopend want*	*Løbende rig*
1 halyard	1 drisse	1 Fall	1 val	1 fald
2 sheet	2 écoute	2 Schot	2 schoot	2 skøde
3 topping lift	3 balancine	3 Dirk	3 kraanlijn, dirk	3 bomdirk
4 outhaul	4 hale-dehors, étarqueur	4 Ausholer	4 uithaler	4 udhaler
5 downhaul	5 hale-bas	5 Halsstreckertalje	5 neerhaler	5 nedhaler
6 kicking strap, vang	6 hale-bas de bôme	6 Baumniederholer	6 neerhouder	6 kicking strap
7 gybe preventer	7 retenu de bôme	7 Bullentalje, Baumbremse	7 bulletalie	7 ledereb
8 spinnaker guy	8 écoute de tangon	8 Spinnakerachterholer	8 spinnakergei, ophouder buitenschoot	8 spiler guy

ESPAÑOL	ITALIANO	PORTUGUÊS	TÜRKÇE	ΕΛΛΗΝΙΚΑ
5 EL BARCO	**5 LA BARCA**	**5 DO BARCO**	**5 TEKNE**	**5 ΤΟ ΣΚΑΦΟΣ**
Jarcias y velas	**Attrezzatura e vele**	**Massame e velas**	**Arma ve yelkenler**	**ΑΡΜΑΤΩΣΙΑ &ΠΑΝΙΑ**
Maniobra	*Manovre fisse (o dormienti)*	*Aparelho fixo*	*Sabit donanım*	*ΣΤΑΘΕΡΗ ΑΡΜΑΤΩΣΙΑ*
1 estay de tope, estay de galope	1 strallo d'alberetto	1 estai do galope	1 ana ıstralya, direkbaşı ıstralyası	1 ΠΑΤΑΡΑΤΣΟ
2 estay de proa	2 strallo	2 estai real	2 baş ıstralya, flok ıstralyası	2 ΠΡΟΤΟΝΟΣ
3 poparrás	3 paterazzo	3 brandal fixo da pôpa	3 pupa ıstralyası, kıç ıstralya	3 ΕΠΙΤΟΝΟΣ - ΒΑΡΔΡΙΑ
4 burdavolante y palanca	4 sartia volante	4 brandal volante e alavanca	4 pupa çarmıhı ve levyesi	4 ΕΠΑΡΤΗΣ ΜΑΤΣΟΠΟΔΑΡΟ
5 estay de boza	5 controstrallo	5 estai de diamante	5 şeytan çarmıhı	5 ΒΟΗΘΗΤΙΚΟΣ ΠΡΟΤΟΝΟΣ - ΣΤΑΝΤΖΟΣ
6 obenque	6 sartia	6 enxárcia	6 çarmıh	6 ΞΑΡΤΙΑ
7 cadenote	7 landa	7 chapa de fixação do olhal das enxárcias	7 güverte çarmıh landaları	7 ΞΑΡΤΟΡΙΖΕΣ
8 tensor	8 arridatoio	8 esticador	8 dönger, liftin uskur	8 ΕΝΤΑΤΗΡΑΣ
9 flechadura, flechates	9 griselle	9 enfrechates	9 iskalarya	9 ΑΝΕΜΟΣΚΑΛΕΣ
10 losange	10 diamanti	10 diamante	10 şeytan çarmıhları, üst çarmıhlar	10 ΚΕΡΑΤΙΔΙΑ
11 babystay	11 stralletto	11 baby stay	11 iç ıstralya	11 ΕΣΩΤΕΡΙΚΟΣ ΠΡΟΤΟΝΟΣ
12 pasador de seguridad	12 perno di gancio d'attacco	12 perno com troço de argola	12 kopilya	12 ΠΕΙΡΟΣ ΚΛΕΙΔΙΟΥ ΣΧΗΜΑΤΟΣ ΠΕΤΑΛΟΥ
Jarcias de labor	**Manovre correnti**	**Aparelho móvel**	**Hareketli donanım**	**ΣΧΟΙΝΙΑ**
1 driza	1 drizza	1 adriça	1 mandar	1 ΜΑΝΤΑΡΙΑ
2 escota	2 scotta	2 escota	2 iskota	2 ΣΚΟΤΑ
3 amantillo	3 amantiglio	3 amantilho	3 balançina	3 ΜΑΝΤΑΡΙ ΣΠΙΝΑΚΟΞΥΛΟΥ
4 envergue de puño	4 tesabugna	4 talha do punho da escota	4 alt yaka gergisi	4 ΣΥΣΤΗΜΑ ΓΙΑ ΤΕΝΤΩΜΑ ΜΕΓΙΣΤΗΣ ΣΤΗ ΜΑΤΣΑ
5 cargadera	5 caricabasso	5 teque do peão de retranca	5 baskı	5 ΣΥΣΤΗΜΑ ΓΙΑ ΤΕΝΤΩΜΑ ΜΕΓΙΣΤΗΣ ΣΤΟ ΚΑΤΑΡΤΙ
6 trapa	6 vang	6 kicking strap	6 bumba baskı düzeneği	6 ΜΠΟΥΜ ΒΑΝΓΚ
7 trapa	7 ritenuta del boma	7 contra-escota	7 kavança önleyici donanım	7 ΠΡΙΒΕΝΤΕΡ
8 braza de tangón	8 braccio dello spinnaker	8 gaio do pau do spinnaker	8 spinnaker bumba baskısı	8 ΓΚΑΗΣ

ENGLISH	FRANÇAIS	DEUTSCH	NEDERLANDS	DANSK
5 THE BOAT	**5 LE BATEAU**	**5 DAS BOOT**	**5 DE BOOT, HET SCHIP**	**5 BÅDEN**
Rigging & sails	**Gréement et voiles**	**Rigg und Segel**	**Tuigage en zeilen**	**Rigning og sejl**
Sails	*Voiles*	*Segel*	*Zeilen*	*Sejl*
1 mainsail	1 grand-voile	1 Großsegel	1 grootzeil	1 storsejl
2 topsail	2 flèche	2 Toppsegel	2 topzeil	2 topsejl
3 mizzen	3 artimon, tape-cul	3 Besan, Treiber	3 bezaan, druil	3 mesan
4 main staysail	4 grand-voile d'étai	4 Großstagsegel	4 schoenerzeil	4 store mellem stagsejl
5 fisherman staysail	5 voile d'étai de flèche	5 Fischermann-Stagsegel	5 grootstengestagzeil	5 top mellem stagsejl
6 mizzen staysail	6 foc ou voile d'étai d'artimon	6 Besanstagsegel	6 bezaansstagzeil, aap	6 mesan stagsejl
7 jib	7 foc	7 Fock	7 fok	7 fok
8 genoa	8 génois	8 Genua, Kreuzballon	8 genua	8 genua
9 staysail	9 trinquette	9 Stagsegel	9 stagzeil	9 stagsejl
10 genoa staysail	10 foc ballon	10 Raumballon	10 botterfok	10 genuafok
11 yankee	11 yankee	11 grosser Klüver	11 grote kluiver	11 yankee
12 trysail	12 voile de cape	12 Trysegel	12 stormzeil, grootzeil	12 stormsejl
13 spitfire, storm jib	13 tourmentin	13 Sturmfock	13 stormfok	13 stormfok
14 spritsail	14 livarde	14 Sprietsegel	14 sprietzeil	14 sprydsejl
15 wishbone staysail	15 wishbone	15 Spreizgaffel-Stagsegel	15 wishbone-stagzeil	15 wishbone-sejl
16 headsail	16 voile d'avant	16 Vorsegel	16 voorzeil	16 forsejl
17 spinnaker	17 spinnaker	17 Spinnaker	17 spinnaker	17 spiler
18 lugsail	18 voile à bourcet, au tiers	18 Luggersegel	18 loggerzeil, emmerzeil	18 luggersejl
19 gunter	19 houari	19 Huari-, Steilgaffeltakelung	19 houari	19 gunterrig
20 fore-and-aft sail	20 voile longitudinale	20 Schratsegel	20 langsscheeps tuig	20 for og agter sejl
21 square sail	21 voile carrée	21 Rahsegel	21 razeil	21 råsejl
22 working jib	22 foc	22 Arbeitsfock	22 werkfok	22 krydsfok
23 head	23 point de drisse	23 Kopf	23 top	23 top

ESPAÑOL	ITALIANO	PORTUGUÊS	TÜRKÇE	ΕΛΛΗΝΙΚΑ
5 EL BARCO	**5 LA BARCA**	**5 DO BARCO**	**5 TEKNE**	**5 ΤΟ ΣΚΑΦΟΣ**
Jarcias y velas	**Attrezzatura e vele**	**Massame e velas**	**Arma ve yelkenler**	**ΑΡΜΑΤΩΣΙΑ & ΠΑΝΙΑ**
Velas	*Vele*	*Velas*	*Yelkenler*	*ΠΑΝΙΑ*
1 vela mayor	1 randa	1 vela grande	1 anayelken	1 ΜΕΓΙΣΤΗ
2 escandalosa	2 freccia, controranda	2 gaff-tope	2 kontra randa	2 ΦΛΙΤΣΙ
3 mesana	3 mezzana	3 mezena	3 mizana yelkeni	3 ΜΕΤΖΑΝΑ
4 vela de estay mayor	4 fiocco	4 traquete	4 istralya anayelkeni, velenası	4 ΤΖΕΝΟΑ
5 vela alta de estay	5 fisherman	5 extênsola	5 balıkçı yelkeni	5 ΑΡΑΠΗΣ
6 entrepalos	6 carbonera	6 estai entre mastros	6 mizana velenası	6 ΣΤΡΑΛΙΕΡΑ
7 foque	7 fiocco	7 bujarrona	7 flok	7 ΦΛΟΚΟΣ
8 génova	8 genoa	8 genoa	8 genoa, cenova	8 ΤΖΕΝΟΑ
9 vela de estay	9 trinchettina	9 estai	9 trinket	9 ΠΑΝΙ ΣΕ ΠΡΟΤΟΝΟ (ΑΡΑΠΗΣ)
10 foque balón	10 trinchettina genoa	10 estai de genoa	10 balon flok	10 ΣΤΕΙΣΕΙΛ - ΔΕΥΤΕΡΟΣ ΦΛΟΚΟΣ
11 trinquetilla	11 yankee	11 giba	11 yankee yelkeni	11 ΕΣΩ ΦΛΟΚΟΣ - ΓΙΑΝΚΗ
12 vela de capa	12 vela di cappa	12 cachapana	12 fırtına şeytan yelkeni	12 ΜΑΙΣΤΡΑ ΘΥΕΛΛΗΣ
13 foque de capa	13 tormentina, fiocco da burrasca	13 estai de tempo	13 fırtına floku	13 ΦΛΟΚΟΣ ΘΥΕΛΛΗΣ
14 vela tarquina, abanico	14 vela a tarchia	14 vela de espicha	14 açevela gönderli yelken	14 ΦΛΟΚΟΣ ΤΣΙΜΠΟΥΚΙΟΥ
15 vela de pico vacio	15 randa 'wishbone'	15 traquete especial 'wishbone'	15 wishbone yelkeni	15 ΣΤΡΑΛΙΕΡΑ ΜΕ ΜΑΤΣΑ
16 foque, vela de proa	16 vela di prora	16 pano de proa	16 ön yelken, pruva yelkeni	16 ΠΑΝΙΑ ΠΟΥ ΦΤΑΝΟΥΝ ΣΤΗΝ ΚΟΡΥΦΗ ΤΟΥ ΚΑΤΑΡΤΙΟΥ
17 espinaquer	17 spinnaker	17 spinnaker, balão	17 balon yelkeni	17 ΜΠΑΛΟΝΙ
18 vela cangreja, al tercio	18 vela al terzo	18 vela de pendão	18 çeyrek yelken	18 ΤΕΤΡΑΓΩΝΟ ΠΑΝΙ ΧΩΡΙΣ ΜΑΤΣΑ
19 vela de cortina, guaira	19 alla portoghese	19 vela de baioneta	19 sürmeli randa arma	19 ΨΗΛΟ ΠΙΚΙ
20 vela cuchillo	20 vela di taglio	20 vela latina	20 yan yelken	20 ΛΑΤΙΝΙ
21 vela cuadra, redonda	21 vela quadra	21 pano redondo	21 kare yelken, kabasorta, arma yelkeni	21 ΤΕΤΡΑΓΩΝΟ ΠΑΝΙ
22 génova dos, génova de trabajo	22 fiocco normale	22 estai	22 normal yelken	22 ΦΛΟΚΟΣ
23 puño de driza	23 penna	23 punho da pena	23 yelken başlığı, başlık köşesi	23 ΚΟΡΥΦΗ - ΤΖΟΥΝΤΑ

ENGLISH	FRANÇAIS	DEUTSCH	NEDERLANDS	DANSK
5 THE BOAT	**5 LE BATEAU**	**5 DAS BOOT**	**5 DE BOOT, HET SCHIP**	**5 BÅDEN**
Rigging & sails	**Gréement et voiles**	**Rigg und Segel**	**Tuigage en zeilen**	**Rigning og sejl**
Sails	*Voiles*	*Segel*	*Zeilen*	*Sejl*
24 luff	24 guindant, envergure	24 Vorliek	24 voorlijk	24 mastelig
25 tack	25 point d'amure	25 Hals	25 hals	25 hals
26 foot	26 bordure	26 Unterliek	26 onderlijk, voetlijk	26 underlig
27 clew	27 point d'écoute	27 Schothorn	27 schoothoek, -hoorn	27 skødebarm
28 leech	28 chute	28 Achterliek	28 achterlijk	28 agterlig
29 leechline	29 hale-bas de chute	29 Regulierleine	29 achterlijktrimlijn	29 trimline
30 roach	30 rond, arrondi	30 Rundung des Achterlieks	30 gilling	30 bugt på storsejlets agterlig
31 headboard	31 planche de tête	31 Kopfbrett	31 zeilplankje	31 flynder
32 bolt rope	32 ralingue	32 Liektau	32 lijketouw	32 liget
33 tabling	33 doublage, gaine	33 Doppelung	33 dubbeling	33 forstærkning
34 batten pocket	34 étui ou gaine de latte	34 Lattentasche	34 zeillatzak	34 sejllomme
35 reef point	35 garcette	35 Reffbändsel	35 knuttel	35 rebeline
36 cringle	36 anneau, patte	36 Legel	36 grommer, kousje	36 kovs
37 luff wire	37 ralingue d'acier	37 Drahtvorliek	37 staaldraad voorlijk	37 wire-forlig
38 peak	38 pic, empointure	38 Piek	38 piek	38 pikken (gaffelrig)
39 throat	39 gorge	39 Klau	39 klauw	39 kværken
40 mast hoop	40 cercle de mât	40 Mastring, Legel	40 hoepel	40 mastering
41 horse	41 barre d'écoute	41 Leitwagen	41 overloop	41 løjbom
42 fully battened	42 voile lattée entièrement	42 durchgelattet	42 met doorlopende zeillatten	42 gennemgående sejlpinde
43 lazyjacks	43 lazy jacks	43 Lazy Jacks	43 lazyjacks	43 lazy jacks
Sailmaker	*Voilier*	*Segelmacher*	*Zeilmaker*	*Sejlmager*
1 weight of canvas	1 poids de la toile	1 Tuchstärke	1 gewicht van het doek	1 dugvægt
2 area	2 surface	2 Segelfläche	2 oppervlak	2 areal

ESPAÑOL	ITALIANO	PORTUGUÊS	TÜRKÇE	ΕΛΛΗΝΙΚΑ
5 EL BARCO	**5 LA BARCA**	**5 DO BARCO**	**5 TEKNE**	**5 ΤΟ ΣΚΑΦΟΣ**
Jarcias y velas	**Attrezzatura e vele**	**Massame e velas**	**Arma ve yelkenler**	**ΑΡΜΑΤΩΣΙΑ & ΠΑΝΙΑ**
Velas	*Vele*	*Velas*	*Yelkenler*	*ΠΑΝΙΑ*
24 gratil	24 caduta prodiera, inferitura	24 testa	24 orsa kenarı	24 ΓΡΑΝΤΙ
25 puño de amura	25 angolo di mura	25 punho da amura	25 önköşe, karula köşesi	25 ΠΟΔΑΡΙ
26 pujamen	26 bordame	26 esteira	26 alt kenar, alt yaka	26 ΠΟΔΙΑ
27 puño de escota	27 bugna	27 punho da escota	27 iskota köşesi	27 ΠΟΡΤΟΥΖΙ
28 baluma	28 balumina	28 valuma	28 güngörmez kenarı	28 ΑΕΤΟΣ
29 ánima	29 tirante della balumina, meolo	29 linha da valuma	29 güngörmez salvosu	29 ΣΧΟΙΝΙ ΑΕΤΟΥ (ΚΡΥΦΟ)
30 alunamiento	30 allunamento	30 curvatura convexa da valuma	30 kelebek, sehim	30 ΚΑΜΠΥΛΗ ΑΕΤΟΥ
31 tabla de gratil	31 tavoletta	31 refôrço triangular do punho da pena	31 yelken başlığı takviye ağacı laması	31 ΕΝΙΣΧΥΣΗ ΚΟΡΥΦΗΣ
32 relinga	32 ralinga, gratile	32 tralha	32 gradin halatı	32 ΚΡΥΦΟ
33 vaina	33 guaina	33 forras de refôrço	33 gradin uçkurluğu	33 ΣΤΡΙΦΩΜΑ
34 bolsa del sable	34 guaina della stecca	34 bôlsa da régua	34 balena cebi	34 ΘΗΚΗΣ ΜΠΑΛΕΝΑΣ
35 tomadores de rizo	35 mano di terzarolo	35 rizes	35 camadan kalçeti, kamçısı	35 ΣΗΜΕΙΑ ΜΟΥΔΑΣ
36 garrucho de cabo	36 brancarella, bosa	36 olhal	36 kamçı matafyonu	36 ΜΠΟΥΝΤΟΥΖΙ
37 relinga de envergue	37 ralinga (o gratile)	37 cabo da testa	37 tel gradin	37 ΓΡΑΝΤΙ-ΣΥΡΜΑΤΟΣΧΟΙΝΙ ΤΟΥ
38 pico	38 angolo di penna	38 pique	38 randa yelken giz köşesi	38 ΚΟΡΥΦΗ
39 puño de driza	39 gola	39 bôca	39 randa yelken karula köşesi	39 ΛΑΙΜΟΣ
40 zuncho	40 canestrello	40 aro	40 randa yelken direk halkası	40 ΚΟΛΛΙΕΣ
41 pie de gallo	41 trasto, barra di scotta	41 varão de escota	41 anayelken ıskotası güverte rayı	41 ΜΠΟΜΠΡΕΣΟ - ΜΠΑΛΚΟΝΙ
42 full batten	42 interamente steccata	42 réguas até ao mastro	42 tam balenalı	42 ΜΕ ΜΕΓΑΛΕΣ ΜΠΑΛΕΝΕΣ
43 lazy jacks	43 lazy jacks	43 lazy jacks	43 lazy jaks	43 ΣΚΟΙΝΙΑ ΠΟΥ ΚΡΑΤΑΝΕ ΤΗΝ ΜΑΙΣΤΡΑ ΔΙΠΛΩΜΕΝΗ ΣΤΟ ΜΑΙΝΑ
Velero	*Velaio*	*Veleiro*	*Yelken yapımcısı*	*ΙΣΤΙΟΡΡΑΠΤΗΣ*
1 peso de la lona	1 peso della tela	1 espessura da lona	1 bez ağırlığı	1 ΒΑΡΟΣ ΤΟΥ ΠΑΝΙΟΥ
2 area	2 superficie	2 área	2 alan, yüzey	2 ΕΠΙΦΑΝΕΙΑ

85

5 THE BOAT | 5 LE BATEAU | 5 DAS BOOT | 5 DE BOOT, HET SCHIP | 5 BÅDEN

Rigging & sails | Gréement et voiles | Rigg und Segel | Tuigage en zeilen | Rigning og sejl

ENGLISH	FRANÇAIS	DEUTSCH	NEDERLANDS	DANSK
Sailmaker	**Voilier**	**Segelmacher**	**Zeilmaker**	**Sejlmager**
3 flat	3 plate	3 flach geschnitten	3 vlak	3 flad
4 full, belly	4 creuse, le creux	4 bauchig geschnitten, Bauch	4 bol, buikig	4 stor bugt, pose
5 stretch a sail	5 roder, faire une voile	5 ein Segel ausstraken	5 een zeil rekken	5 strække et sejl
6 chafe	6 ragage, usure	6 schamfelen	6 schavielen	6 skamfiling
7 mildew	7 moisissure	7 Stockflecken	7 weer in het zeil	7 jordslået
8 seam	8 couture, lé	8 Naht	8 naad	8 søm
9 panel	9 panneau	9 gedoppeltes segeltuch	9 stuk zeildoek	9 bane
10 patch	10 rapiécer	10 flicken	10 lap	10 lap
11 restitch	11 recoudre	11 Nähte nachnähen	11 overstikken	11 sy efter
12 mend	12 réparer	12 ausbessern, reparieren	12 repareren	12 reparere
13 baggywrinkle	13 fourrage, gaine de hauban	13 Tausendfuß	13 lus-platting	13 skamfilings-gods
14 sail tiers, gaskets	14 rabans	14 Zeisinge	14 zeilbanden	14 sejsinger
15 sailbag	15 sac à voile	15 Segelsack	15 zeilzak	15 sejlpose
16 ultraviolet	16 ultraviolet	16 ultraviolett	16 ultraviolet	16 ultraviolet
17 sacrificial strip/ sunshade	17 bande anti UV	17 Sonnenschutzstreifen am Achterliek einer Rollfock	17 zonbeschermingsstrook	17 solskygge
Wire rope	**Fil, câble d'acier**	**Drahttauwerk**	**Staaldraadkabel**	**Stålwire**
1 strand	1 toron	1 Kardeel, Ducht	1 streng, kardeel	1 kordel
2 core	2 âme	2 Seele	2 hart, kern	2 hjerte
3 flexible	3 souple	3 biegsam	3 flexibel, soepel	3 bøjelig
4 stretch	4 élasticité	4 recken, Reck	4 rek	4 strække
5 shrink	5 rétrécissement	5 einlaufen	5 krimp	5 krympe
6 breaking strain	6 charge de rupture	6 Bruchlast	6 breekspanning	6 brudgrænse
7 the coil	7 glène	7 Tauwerksrolle	7 rol	7 kvejl
8 kink	8 coque	8 Kink	8 kink, slag	8 kinke
9 circumference	9 circonférence	9 Umfang	9 omtrek	9 omkreds
10 diameter	10 diamètre	10 Durchmesser	10 diameter	10 diameter
11 swaged fittings	11 embout serti	11 Endbeschlag	11 aangewalste kabel	11 endebeslag, presset på

ESPAÑOL	ITALIANO	PORTUGUÊS	TÜRKÇE	ΕΛΛΗΝΙΚΑ
5 EL BARCO	**5 LA BARCA**	**5 DO BARCO**	**5 TEKNE**	**5 ΤΟ ΣΚΑΦΟΣ**
Jarcias y velas	**Attrezzatura e vele**	**Massame e velas**	**Arma ve yelkenler**	**ΑΡΜΑΤΩΣΙΑ & ΠΑΝΙΑ**
Velero	*Velaio*	*Veleiro*	*Yelken yapımcısı*	*ΙΣΤΙΟΡΡΑΠΤΗΣ*
3 vela plana	3 piatta o magra	3 plana, sem saco	3 torsuz	3 ΣΤΕΓΝΟ
4 bolso, papo	4 grassa, pancia	4 vela cheia, com saco	4 torlu, tor	4 ΓΕΜΑΤΟ
5 estirar una vela	5 stirare una vela	5 esticar uma vela	5 yelken rodajı, yelken yapmak	5 ΦΟΡΜΑΡΩ ΤΑ ΠΑΝΙΑ
6 rozar	6 logoramento	6 desgaste do velame	6 sürtünmeden dolayı yıpranma	6 ΤΡΙΜΜΕΝΟ - ΤΡΙΨΙΜΟ ΠΑΝΙΟΥ
7 moho	7 muffa	7 garruncho	7 küf	7 ΜΟΥΦΛΑ
8 costura	8 cucire	8 bainha	8 yelken dikişi	8 ΡΑΦΗ
9 panel/veso	9 ferzo	9 pano	9 yaprak	9 ΦΥΛΛΟ ΠΑΝΙΟΥ
10 reforzar	10 rattoppare	10 remendar	10 yama	10 ΜΠΑΛΩΜΑ
11 recoser	11 ricucire	11 recoser	11 tamir dikişi	11 ΞΑΝΑΡΑΒΩ
12 reparar	12 rammendare	12 consertar	12 tamir	12 ΔΙΟΡΘΩΝΩ
13 pallete	13 filacci	13 coxim de enxárcia	13 kedi ayağı, kedi bıyığı	13 ΖΑΡΩΜΕΝΟ - ΞΕΧΥΛΩΜΕΝΟ
14 tomadores	14 gerli	14 bichas	14 yelken sargı bağları	14 ΕΝΙΣΧΥΣΕΙΣ
15 saco de vela	15 sacco da vela	15 saco das velas	15 yelken torbası	15 ΣΑΚΟΣ ΠΑΝΙΟΥ
16 ultravioleta	16 ultravioletto	16 ultravioleta	16 morötesi/ultraviyole ışını	16 ΥΠΕΡΙΩΔΕΙΣ
17 banda de protección UV	17 banda di protezione UV	17 faixa não recuperável	17 rüzgara dayanıklı güneşlik astarı	17 ΠΡΟΣΤΑΤΕΥΤΙΚΗ ΤΑΙΝΙΑ
Cable	*Cavi metallici*	*Cabo de aço*	*Tel halat*	*ΣΥΡΜΑΤΟΣΧΟΙΝΟ*
1 cordón	1 trefolo	1 cordão	1 tel halat kolu	1 ΚΛΩΝΟΣ
2 alma	2 anima	2 madre	2 tel halat göbeği	2 ΚΑΡΔΙΑ
3 flexible	3 flessibile	3 flexível	3 esnek tel halat	3 ΕΥΚΑΜΠΤΟ
4 estirar	4 stiramento	4 alongamento, esticar	4 elastikiyet	4 ΤΕΝΤΩΝΩ
5 encoger	5 restringimento	5 encolher	5 büzülme, çekme	5 ΜΑΖΕΥΩ
6 carga de rotura	6 carico di rottura	6 carga de rotura	6 kopma yükü	6 ΑΝΤΟΧΗ ΣΤΟ ΣΠΑΣΙΜΟ
7 muela de cabo	7 matassa, rotolo	7 pandeiro	7 halat rodası	7 ΓΥΡΟΣ - ΝΤΟΥΚΑ
8 coca	8 cocca	8 coca	8 volta	8 ΒΕΡΙΝΑ
9 mena	9 circonferenza	9 perímetro	9 halatın çevresi	9 ΠΕΡΙΦΕΡΕΙΑ
10 diámetro	10 diametro	10 diâmetro	10 çap	10 ΔΙΑΜΕΤΡΟΣ
11 efectos estampados	11 capicorda ricalcati	11 ferragem especial para ligar os cabos de aço sem costura	11 terminal	11 ΣΤΡΑΒΩΜΕΝΕΣ ΑΚΡΕΣ

ENGLISH	FRANÇAIS	DEUTSCH	NEDERLANDS	DANSK
5 THE BOAT	**5 LE BATEAU**	**5 DAS BOOT**	**5 DE BOOT, HET SCHIP**	**5 BÅDEN**

Rigging & sails	**Gréement et voiles**	**Rigg und Segel**	**Tuigage en zeilen**	**Rigning og sejl**
Ropes & materials	*Cordages et matériaux*	*Leinen und ihr Material*	*Touwwerk en materialen*	*Tovværk og materialer*
1 pennant, pendant	1 itague, pantoire	1 Schmeerreep	1 smeerreep	1 stander
2 lacing	2 transfilage	2 Reihleine	2 marllijn	2 lidseline
3 warp	3 amarre, grelin, aussière, haussière	3 Festmacher	3 landvast, meertouw, tros	3 varpetrosse
4 spring	4 garde montante	4 Spring	4 spring, scheertouw	4 spring
5 painter	5 bosse de canot	5 Fangleine	5 vanglijn, werplijn	5 fangline
6 marline	6 merlin	6 Marlleine	6 marlijn	6 merling
7 cod line	7 quarantenier, ligne	7 Hüsing	7 dunne lijn	7 stikline
8 braided	8 coton tressé	8 geflochtenes Baumwolltauwerk	8 gevlochten	8 flettet line
9 whipping twine	9 fil à surlier	9 Takelgarn	9 takelgaren	9 taklegarn
10 yarn	10 lusin, fil	10 Garn	10 garen	10 garn
11 tarred	11 goudronné	11 geteert	11 geteerd	11 tjæret
12 3-strand laid	12 cordage à 3 torons	12 dreikardeelig	12 3-kardeels geslagen	12 treslået
13 nylon (polyamide)	13 nylon (polyamide)	13 Nylon (Polyamid)	13 nylon (polyamide)	13 nylon (polyamid)
14 Terylene™, Dacron™ (polyester)	14 Terylène™, Dacron™ (polyester)	14 Terylen™, Dacron™ (Polyester)	14 Terylene™, Dacron™ (polyester)	14 Terylene™, Dacron™ (polyester)
15 Propathene™ (polypropylene)	15 Propathène™ (polypropylène)	15 Propathene™ (Polypropylen)	15 Propatheen™ (polypropyleen)	15 Polyprolylen™
16 Kevlar™ (polyaramid)	16 Kevlar™ (aramide)	16 Kevlar™ (Polyaramid)	16 Kevlar™ (polyamide)	16 Kevlar™
17 cotton	17 coton	17 Baumwolle	17 katoen	17 bomuld
18 Italian hemp	18 chanvre d'Italie	18 Hanf	18 hennep	18 hamp
19 sisal	19 sisal	19 Sisal	19 sisal	19 sisal
20 coir	20 coco	20 Kokos	20 kokostouw	20 kokos
21 manilla	21 manille, abaca	21 Manila	21 manillatouw	21 manilla
Splicing, knots, bends & hitches	*Epissures et nœuds*	*Spleiße, Knoten und Steke*	*Splitsen, knopen, bochten en steken*	*Splejsninger og knob*
1 eye splice	1 œil épissé	1 Augspleiß	1 oogsplits	1 øjesplejsning
2 long splice	2 épissure longue	2 Langspleiß	2 lange splits	2 langsplejsning

ESPAÑOL	ITALIANO	PORTUGUÊS	TÜRKÇE	ΕΛΛΗΝΙΚΑ
5 EL BARCO	**5 LA BARCA**	**5 DO BARCO**	**5 TEKNE**	**5 ΤΟ ΣΚΑΦΟΣ**
Jarcias y velas	**Attrezzatura e vele**	**Massame e velas**	**Arma ve yelkenler**	**ΑΡΜΑΤΩΣΙΑ & ΠΑΝΙΑ**
Cabulleria y materiales	*Cordami*	*Cabos e materiais*	*Halatlar & malzemeler*	*ΣΧΟΙΝΙΑ & ΥΛΙΚΑ*
1 amante	1 penzolo	1 chicote	1 camadan kalçeti	1 ΣΗΜΑΙΑ
2 envergue	2 laccio	2 armarilho	2 çapraz kordon bağlantı	2 ΛΗΓΑΔΟΥΡΑ
3 estacha, amarra	3 cavo da tonneggio	3 espia	3 demir halatı	3 ΑΓΚΥΡΟΣΧΟΙΝΟ
4 esprín	4 spring	4 regeiras, espringues	4 çapraz halatı, açmaz, spring	4 ΣΠΡΙΝΓΚ
5 boza	5 barbetta	5 boça	5 filika halatı/pariması	5 ΣΧΟΙΝΙ ΓΙΑ ΤΟ ΒΑΡΚΑΚΙ
6 merlin	6 merlino	6 merlim	6 mornel	6 ΔΙΚΛΩΝΟ ΣΧΟΙΝΑΚΙ
7 piola	7 lezzino, commando	7 linha de pesca	7 savlo, ip	7 ΤΡΙΚΛΩΝΗ ΤΖΙΒΑ
8 algodón trenzado	8 intrecciato	8 trançado de algodão	8 örgü halat	8 ΠΛΕΚΤΟ
9 piolilla	9 spago da impalmatura	9 cordame de pequeña bitola	9 piyan gırcalası	9 ΣΠΑΓΓΟΣ ΜΑΤΙΣΜΑΤΟΣ
10 meollar	10 filo	10 fibra	10 halat lifi	10 ΚΑΩΝΟΣ
11 alquitranado	11 catramato	11 alcatroado	11 ziftli halat	11 ΠΙΣΩΜΕΝΟ
12 cabo de tres cordones	12 a 3 legnoli	12 cabo de massa cochado	12 üç kollu halat	12 ΤΡΙΚΛΩΝΟ
13 nilón (poliamida)	13 nailon, nylon (poliamide)	13 nylon	13 naylon (polyamid)	13 ΝΑΥΛΟΝ - ΠΟΛΥΑΜΙΔΙΟ
14 Terylene™, Dacron™ (poliester)	14 Terital™ (poliestere)	14 Terylene™, Dacron™ (poliester)	14 Terilen™, Dacron™ (polyester)	14 ΝΤΑΚΡΟΝ - ΠΟΛΥΕΣΤΕΡΑΣ
15 Propatheno™ (polipropileno)	15 polipropilene	15 Propathene™ (polipropileno)	15 Polipropilen™	15 ΠΟΛΥΠΡΟΠΥΛΕΝΙΟ
16 Kevlar™ (poliamida)	16 Kevlar™ (poliaramide)	16 Kevlar™	16 Kevlar™	16 ΚΕΒΛΑΡ
17 algodón	17 cotone	17 algodão	17 pamuk	17 ΒΑΜΒΑΚΕΡΟ
18 cáñamo	18 canapa	18 linho italiano	18 İtalyan keteni halat	18 ΚΑΝΑΒΙΝΟ
19 sisal	19 sisal	19 sisal	19 sisal halat	19 ΣΙΖΑΛ
20 estopa	20 fibra di cocco	20 cairo	20 hindistan cevizi lifi	20 ΤΖΙΒΑ
21 abacá, manila	21 manila	21 cabo de manila	21 kendir halat, manila halatı	21 ΜΑΝΙΛΑ
Costuras y nudos	*Impiombature, nodi e colli*	*Uniões, nós e voltas*	*Dikişler, düğümler, volta ve bağlar*	*ΜΑΤΙΣΙΕΣ ΚΟΜΠΟΙ, ΤΣΑΚΙΣΤΕΣ ΘΗΛΕΙΕΣ*
1 gaza	1 gassa impiombata	1 mãozinha, costura de mão	1 kasa dikişi	1 ΓΛΑΣΑ
2 costura larga	2 impiombatura lunga	2 costura de laborar	2 uzun dikiş,kolbastı dikişi	2 ΜΑΚΡΥΑ ΜΑΤΙΣΙΑ

ENGLISH	FRANÇAIS	DEUTSCH	NEDERLANDS	DANSK
5 THE BOAT	**5 LE BATEAU**	**5 DAS BOOT**	**5 DE BOOT, HET SCHIP**	**5 BÅDEN**
Rigging & sails	**Gréement et voiles**	**Rigg und Segel**	**Tuigage en zeilen**	**Rigning og sejl**
Splicing, knots, bends & hitches	*Epissures et nœuds*	*Spleiße, Knoten und Steke*	*Splitsen, knopen, bochten en steken*	*Splejsninger og knob*
3 short splice	3 épissure courte, carrée	3 Kurzspleiß	3 korte splits	3 kortsplejsning
4 parcel	4 limander	4 schmarten	4 smarten	4 smerting
5 serve	5 fourrer	5 kleeden, bekleiden	5 kleden	5 klædning
6 whip	6 surlier	6 takeln	6 takelen	6 takling
7 lashing	7 saisine	7 Lasching	7 seizing, bindsel	7 bændsel
8 reef knot	8 nœud plat	8 Kreuzknoten	8 platte knoop	8 råbåndsknob
9 figure of eight	9 nœud en huit, en lacs	9 Achtknoten	9 achtknoop	9 flamsk knob
10 bowline	10 nœud de chaise	10 Palstek	10 paalsteek	10 pælestik
11 fisherman's bend	11 nœud de grappin	11 Roringstek	11 werpankersteek	11 baghånds knob
12 double sheet bend	12 nœud d'écoute double	12 doppelter Schotstek	12 dubbele schootsteek	12 dobbelt flagstik
13 clove hitch	13 demi-clés à capeler	13 Webleinstek	13 mastworp, weeflijnsteek	13 dobbelt halvstik
14 rolling hitch	14 nœud de bois, de fouet	14 Stopperstek	14 mastworp met voorslag	14 stopperstik
15 round turn and two half hitches	15 tour mort et deux demi-clés	15 Rundtörn mit zwei halben Schlägen	15 rondtorn met twee halve steken	15 rundtørn med to halvstik
On deck	**Sur le pont**	**An Deck**	**Aan dek**	**På dækket**
Deck gear	*Accastillage de pont*	*Decksausrüstung*	*Dekuitrusting*	*Udstyr på dækket*
1 pulpit	1 balcon avant	1 Bugkorb	1 preekstoel	1 prædikestol
2 stern pulpit, pushpit	2 balcon arrière	2 Heckkorb	2 hekstoel	2 agterpulpit
3 guardrail, lifeline	3 filière, garde-corps	3 Seereling	3 zeereling	3 rundliste, livline
4 stanchion	4 chandelier	4 Relingsstütze	4 scepter, relingsteun	4 scepter
5 samson post, bitts	5 bitte d'amarrage	5 Beting, Poller	5 voorbolder	5 samson post
6 ventilator	6 dorade, manche à air	6 Lüfter	6 ventilator	6 ventilator
7 porthole	7 hublot	7 Bullauge	7 patrijspoort	7 koøje
8 fender	8 défense, pare-battage	8 Fender	8 fender, stootkussen	8 fender
9 bowfender, noseband	9 défense d'étrave	9 Bugfender	9 neuswaring, boegfender	9 stævnbeslag

ESPAÑOL	ITALIANO	PORTUGUÊS	TÜRKÇE	ΕΛΛΗΝΙΚΑ
5 EL BARCO	**5 LA BARCA**	**5 DO BARCO**	**5 TEKNE**	**5 ΤΟ ΣΚΑΦΟΣ**
Jarcias y velas	**Attrezzatu e vele**	**Massame e velas**	**Arma ve yelkenler**	**ΑΡΜΑΤΩΣΙΑ & ΠΑΝΙΑ**
Costuras y nudos	*Impiombature, nodi e colli*	*Uniões, nós e voltas*	*Dikişler, düğümler, volta ve bağlar*	*ΜΑΤΙΣΙΕΣ ΚΟΜΠΟΙ, ΤΣΑΚΙΣΤΕΣ ΘΗΛΕΙΕΣ*
3 costura redonda	3 impiombatura corta	3 costura redonda	3 kısa dikiş	3 ΜΙΚΡΗ ΜΑΤΙΣΙΑ
4 precintar	4 bendare	4 precintar	4 badarna etmek	4 ΦΑΣΙΝΑΡΩ ΣΚΟΙΝΙ
5 aforrar	5 fasciare	5 forrar	5 façuna	5 ΠΑΤΡΟΝΑΡΩ ΣΚΟΙΝΙ
6 falcacear	6 impalmare	6 falcassar	6 basit piyan	6 ΜΑΤΙΖΩ
7 ligada	7 rizza	7 amarrar	7 gırcala ile façuna	7 ΔΕΝΩ-ΣΧΟΙΝΑΚΙ ΔΕΣΙΜΑΤΟΣ
8 nudo llano o de rizo	8 nodo piano	8 nó direito	8 camadan bağı	8 ΣΤΑΥΡΟΚΟΜΠΟΣ
9 nudo de 8	9 nodo Savoia	9 nó de trempe	9 kropi bağı	9 ΟΚΤΑΡΙ
10 as de guía	10 gassa d'amante	10 lais de guia pelo chicote	10 izbarço bağı	10 ΚΑΝΘΛΙΤΣΑ
11 cote y ballestrinque	11 gruppo d'ancorotto	11 volta de anête	11 anele bağı, balıkçı bağı	11 ΨΑΛΙΔΙΑ
12 vuelta de escota doble	12 gruppo doppio di scotta	12 nó de escota dobrado	12 çifte ıskota bağı	12 ΔΙΠΛΗ ΨΑΛΙΔΙΑ
13 ballestrinque, cote doble	13 nodo parlato	13 volta de fiél	13 kazık bağı	13 ΚΑΝΘΛΙΑ
14 doble vuelta mordida	14 nodo parlato doppio	14 volta de tomadouro	14 beden bağı, mezevoltalı kazık bağı	14 ΟΥΡΟΔΕΣΜΟΣ
15 vuelta redonda y dos cotes	15 un giro e due mezzi colli	15 volta redonda e cotes	15 kolona bağı, dülger bağı	15 ΤΣΑΚΙΣΤΗ
En cubierta	**Sul ponte**	**No convés**	**Güvertede**	**ΣΤΟ ΚΑΤΑΣΤΡΩΜΑ**
Accessorios de cubierta	*Attrezzature di coperta*	*Aparelhagem do convés*	*Güverte donanımı*	*ΕΞΟΠΛΙΣΜΟΣ ΚΑΤΑΣΤΡΩΜΑΤΟΣ*
1 púlpito	1 pulpito (di prua)	1 guarda proeiro	1 pulpit	1 ΔΕΛΦΙΝΙΕΡΑ
2 púlpito de popa	2 balcone	2 varandim	2 kıç pulpit, puşpit	2 ΠΡΥΜΝΙΟ ΚΑΓΚΕΛΛΟ
3 pasamano	3 battagliola, tientibene	3 balaustrada	3 vardavela punteli	3 ΡΕΛΙΑ
4 candelero	4 candeliere	4 balaústre	4 vardavela dikmesi	4 ΚΟΛΩΝΑΚΙ
5 bitón	5 monachetto, bitte	5 abita	5 bita	5 ΚΕΝΤΡΙΚΗ ΔΕΣΤΡΑ
6 ventilador	6 presa d'aria	6 ventilador	6 manika	6 ΑΕΡΑΓΩΓΟΣ
7 portillo	7 oblò	7 vigia	7 lumbuz	7 ΦΙΛΙΣΤΡΙΝΙ
8 defensa	8 parabordo	8 defensa, molhelha	8 usturmaça	8 ΜΠΑΛΟΝΙ
9 defensa de proa	9 parabordo di prua	9 barra da roda de proa	9 pruva usturmaçası	9 ΜΠΑΛΟΝΙ ΠΛΩΡΗΣ

ENGLISH	FRANÇAIS	DEUTSCH	NEDERLANDS	DANSK
5 THE BOAT	**5 LE BATEAU**	**5 DAS BOOT**	**5 DE BOOT, HET SCHIP**	**5 BÅDEN**
On deck	**Sur le pont**	**An Deck**	**Aan dek**	**På dækket**
Deck gear	*Accastillage de pont*	*Decksausrüstung*	*Dekuitrusting*	*Udstyr på dækket*
10 boathook	10 gaffe	10 Bootshaken	10 bootshaak, pikhaak	10 bådshage
11 davits	11 porte-manteau, bossoir	11 Davits	11 davits	11 davider
12 ladder	12 échelle	12 Leiter	12 ladder, trap	12 leider
13 sail cover	13 prélart, taud, bâche	13 Segelkleid	13 zeilkleed	13 sejlpresenning
14 awning	14 tente	14 Plane Markise	14 zonnetent	14 solsejl
15 bimini top	15 bimini	15 Sonnensegel	15 boven kuip gespannen zonnescherm	15 presenning
16 windscoop	16 manche à air	16 Windhutze	16 zeildoek windhapper	16 udluftningspose
17 sprayhood	17 capote	17 Sprayhood,Niedergangs persenning	17 buiskap	17 sprayhood
18 dodger	18 brise-vent	18 Spritzpersenning, Kleedjes	18 spatscherm	18 læsejl
19 tarpaulin	19 bâche, taud, prélart	19 Persenning	19 presenning	19 presenning
20 bucket	20 seau	20 Pütz	20 emmer	20 pøs
21 mop	21 vadrouille, faubert	21 Dweil	21 dekzwabber	21 svaber
22 scrubbing brush	22 brosse à récurer	22 Schrubber	22 boender	22 skurebørste
23 wheel	23 roue	23 Steuerrad	23 stuurrad	23 rat
24 steering wires	24 drosses	24 Ruderleitung	24 stuurlijnen	24 styre-wire
25 oilskins	25 cirés	25 Olzeug	25 oliegoed	25 olietøj
26 sou'wester	26 suroît	26 Südwester	26 zuidwester	26 sydvest
27 toerail	27 rail de fargue	27 Fußleiste	27 voetrail	27 skandæksliste
28 cleat	28 taquet	28 Klampe	28 klamp, klem, kikker	28 klampe
29 fairlead	29 chaumard	29 Lippe, Leitöse	29 geleideblok	29 klys
30 bow-roller	30 roulette d'étrave	30 Bugrolle	30 boegrol	30 stævnrulle
31 hawse	31 écubier	31 Klüse	31 kluis	31 klys
32 dorade vent	32 manche à air	32 Dorade-Lüfter	32 dekventilator dorade	32 doradeventil
33 cove locker	33 coffre	33 kleine seitliche Ablage imCockpit/ Schwalbennest	33 ingebouwd open kastje in kuip	33 aflukke

ESPAÑOL	ITALIANO	PORTUGUÊS	TÜRKÇE	ΕΛΛΗΝΙΚΑ
5 EL BARCO	**5 LA BARCA**	**5 DO BARCO**	**5 TEKNE**	**5 ΤΟ ΣΚΑΦΟΣ**
En cubierta	**Sul ponte**	**No convés**	**Güvertede**	**ΣΤΟ ΚΑΤΑΣΤΡΩΜΑ**
Accessorios de cubierta	*Attrezzature di coperta*	*Aparelhagem do convés*	*Güverte donanımı*	*ΕΞΟΠΛΙΣΜΟΣ ΚΑΤΑΣΤΡΩΜΑΤΟΣ*
10 bichero	10 gaffa (o mezzomarinaio)	10 croque	10 kanca, filika kancası	10 ΓΑΝΤΖΟΣ
11 pescante	11 gruette	11 turcos	11 mataforalar	11 ΚΑΠΟΝΙΑ
12 escala	12 scaletta	12 escada	12 iskele	12 ΣΚΑΛΑ
13 funda	13 copriranda, cagnaro	13 capa da vela	13 yelken kalepesi	13 ΚΑΛΥΜΑ ΠΑΝΙΟΥ
14 toldo	14 tenda parasole	14 toldo	14 güneş tentesi, tente	14 ΤΕΝΤΑ (ΜΠΑΛΝΤΑΝΙΚΟ)
15 toldilla	15 tendalino	15 toldo	15 sabit havuzluk tentesi	15 ΤΕΝΤΑ ΚΟΚΠΙΤ
16 cono de aire	16 monaca	16 manga de ventilação	16 bez manika	16 ΟΥΙΝΤΣΚΟΥΠ
17 capota	17 capottina	17 guarda patrão	17 serpinti körüğü	17 ΣΠΡΕΥΧΟΥΝΤ
18 baldera	18 paramare	18 sanefas	18 vardasilo	18 ΠΑΡΑΠΕΤΟ
19 encerado	19 telone	19 capa	19 branda örtü, branda	19 ΚΑΡΑΒΟΠΑΝΟ
20 balde	20 bugliolo	20 balde	20 kova	20 ΚΟΥΒΑΣ
21 lampazo	21 redazza	21 lambaz	21 mop	21 ΣΦΟΥΓΓΑΡΙΣΤΡΑ
22 escoba de fregar	22 frettazzo	22 escôva	22 fırça	22 ΒΟΥΡΤΣΑ
23 rueda del timón	23 ruota (del timone)	23 roda do leme	23 dümen dolabı	23 ΡΟΔΑ
24 guardín	24 frenelli (del timone)	24 gualdropes	24 dümen telleri	24 ΣΥΡΜΑΤΟΣΧΟΙΝΑ ΠΗΔΑΛΙΟΥ
25 chubasquero, ropa de agua	25 cerata	25 oleados	25 muşambalar, yağmurluk	25 ΝΙΤΣΕΡΑΔΕΣ
26 montera impermeable	26 cappello di cerata, sudovest	26 sueste	26 lodos, güneybatı rüzgârı	26 ΚΑΠΕΛΛΟ ΘΥΕΛΛΗΣ (ΚΟΥΚΟΣ)
27 regala	27 falchetta	27 amurada inferior	27 küpeşte, toerail	27 ΤΟΡΕΛΙ
28 cornamusa	28 galloccia	28 mordedor	28 koç boynuzu	28 ΚΟΤΣΑΝΕΛΛΟ/ΔΕΣΤΡΑ
29 pasacabos	29 passacavi, passascotte	29 entrada de antena	29 kurtağzı	29 ΜΑΤΙ
30 puntera de proa	30 musone	30 enrolador de retranca	30 pruva makarası	30 ΚΑΡΟΥΛΙ ΤΗΣ ΠΛΩΡΗΣ
31 escobén	31 cubia	31 escovém	31 loça	31 ΠΑΛΑΜΑΡΙ
32 Toma de aire con caja dorada	32 presa d'aria	32 ventilador	32 dorade tipi (su girmez) manika	32 ΕΞΑΕΡΙΣΤΗΡΑΣ
33 cofre	33 bastingaggio	33 paiol embutido/armário	33 höcre	33 ΜΠΑΛΑΟΥΡΟ

ENGLISH	FRANÇAIS	DEUTSCH	NEDERLANDS	DANSK
5 THE BOAT	**5 LE BATEAU**	**5 DAS BOOT**	**5 DE BOOT, HET SCHIP**	**5 BÅDEN**
On deck	**Sur le pont**	**An Deck**	**Aan dek**	**På dækket**
Deck gear	*Accastillage de pont*	*Decksausrüstung*	*Dekuitrusting*	*Udstyr på dækket*
34 lazarette	34 lazarette	34 kleiner Stauraum im Achterschiff	34 achterdekluik	34 sygelukaf
35 jackstay	35 ligne de vie	35 Jackstag	35 veiligheidslijn	35 jackstag
36 deck eye	36 anneau de pont	36 Decksauge	36 dekoog	36 øje
37 grab rail	37 main courante	37 Handläufer	37 handreling	37 håndliste
38 washboards	38 panneaux de descente	38 Waschbord	38 ventilerende kajuitafsluiting	38 skvætbord
39 sheet traveller	39 chariot d'écoute	39 Schotwagen, Schotrutscher	39 schoottraveller, overloop	39 slæde
40 hatch	40 panneau	40 Luke	40 luik	40 luge
41 vane, self-steering	41 girouette de régulateur d'allure	41 Windruder	41 windvaan, zelf-sturend	41 fane, vinge på selvstyrer
42 boarding ladder	42 échelle d'embarquement	42 Jakobsleiter	42 zwemtrap	42 landgang
Winches & windlass	*Treuils et guindeau*	*Winde, Ankerspill*	*Winches en lieren*	*Spil, ankerspil*
1 barrel	1 poupée	1 Trommel	1 trommel	1 spilkop
2 pawl	2 cliquet d'arrêt	2 Pall	2 pal	2 pal
3 winch handle	3 levier	3 Kurbel	3 zwengel	3 spilhåndtag
4 windlass, capstan	4 guindeau, cabestan	4 Ankerwinde, Ankerspill, Gangspill	4 kaapstander, ankerlier	4 spil
5 warping drum	5 poupée	5 Spillkopf	5 verhaalkop	5 ankerspil
6 gipsy	6 barbotin	6 Barbotin-Ring	6 kettingschijf	6 kædehjul
7 crank handle	7 manivelle	7 Kurbel	7 zwengel	7 spilhåndtag
8 spindle	8 mèche	8 Achse, Welle	8 spil	8 aksel
9 brake	9 frein	9 Bremse	9 rem	9 bremse
10 ratchet	10 rochet	10 Pallkranz, Sperrad	10 ratelsleutel, -hefboom	10 palring
11 footswitch	11 interrupteur de pied	11 Fußschalter	11 voetschakelaar	11 fodkontakt

ESPAÑOL	ITALIANO	PORTUGUÊS	TÜRKÇE	ΕΛΛΗΝΙΚΑ
5 EL BARCO	**5 LA BARCA**	**5 DO BARCO**	**5 TEKNE**	**5 ΤΟ ΣΚΑΦΟΣ**
En cubierta	**Sul ponte**	**No convés**	**Güvertede**	**ΣΤΟ ΚΑΤΑΣΤΡΩΜΑ**
Accessorios de cubierta	*Attrezzature di coperta*	*Aparelhagem do convés*	*Güverte donanımı*	*ΕΞΟΠΛΙΣΜΟΣ ΚΑΤΑΣΤΡΩΜΑΤΟΣ*
34 lazareto	34 interponte	34 lazareto	34 kıç ambar, kıç erzak ambarı	34 ΛΑΖΑΡΕΤΤΟ
35 guia de vida	35 fighiera	35 linha de segurança	35 emniyet kemeri bağlantı halatı	35 ΜΠΑΛΑΝΤΣΙΝΙ
36 pasacabo	36 osteriggio, occhio di bue	36 alboi	36 güverte mapası	36 ΟΚΙΟ
37 pasamano	37 mancorrente	37 corrimão	37 vardavela canhalatı	37 ΧΕΙΡΟΛΑΒΗ
38 tablas de la puerta de entrada	38 tambuccio	38 tampo de escotilha	38 tekne giriş kapısı	38 ΠΛΑΙΝΕΣ ΥΠΕΡΥΨΩΣΕΙΣ ΚΟΥΒΕΡΤΑΣ
39 escotera	39 carrello della scotta	39 calha de escota	39 iskota rayı arabası	39 ΒΑΓΟΝΕΤΤΑ ΣΚΟΤΑΣ
40 escotilla	40 boccaporto	40 escotilha	40 kaporta	40 ΧΑΤΣ - ΚΟΥΒΟΥΣΙ
41 veleta de piloto automatico	41 timone a vento	41 girouette/piloto aut. de vento	41 rüzgar dümeni	41 ΑΥΤΟΜΑΤΟΣ ΠΙΛΟΤΟΣ (ΑΝΕΜΟΥ)
42 escala de baño	42 passerella	42 escada de embarque	42 borda iskelesi	42 ΣΚΑΛΑ ΕΠΙΒΙΒΑΣΕΕΩΣ - ΠΑΣΑΡΕΛΑ
Winche, chigre	*Verricelli e argano*	*Molinetes e guinchos*	*Vinçler ve demir ırgatı*	*ΒΙΝΤΖΙΡΕΛΑ ΚΑΙ ΕΡΓΑΤΗΣ*
1 tambor	1 tamburo	1 saia	1 vinç tamburu	1 ΤΥΜΠΑΝΟ
2 linguete, pal	2 nottolino	2 linguete	2 tırnak	2 ΚΑΣΤΑΝΙΑ
3 palanca del winche	3 maniglia del verricello	3 alavanca, manivela	3 vinç kolu	3 ΜΑΝΕΛΛΑ
4 molinete, chigre, cabrestante	4 argano	4 molinete do ferro, cabrestante	4 demir ırgatı	4 ΕΡΓΑΤΗΣ
5 tambor	5 tamburo per tonneggio	5 saia, tambor	5 ırgat fenerliği	5 ΤΥΜΠΑΝΟ ΕΡΓΑΤΗ
6 tamborete	6 barbotin	6 gola	6 ırgat kalavetası	6 ΣΚΡΟΦΑ
7 maquinilla	7 maniglia	7 manivela	7 manivela kolu	7 ΛΕΒΙΕΣ ΕΡΓΑΤΗ
8 mecha	8 fusto	8 eixo, peão	8 dingil	8 ΚΑΤΑΚΟΡΥΦΟΣ ΑΞΟΝΑΣ ΕΡΓΑΤΗ
9 freno	9 freno	9 travão	9 fren, ırgat freni	9 ΦΡΕΝΟ
10 molinete	10 cricco	10 roquete	10 dişli	10 ΚΑΣΤΑΝΙΑ
11 pulsador de pie	11 comando a pedale	11 interruptor de pé	11 ayak şalteri	11 ΠΟΔΟΔΙΑΚΟΠΤΗΣ

ENGLISH	FRANÇAIS	DEUTSCH	NEDERLANDS	DANSK
5 THE BOAT	**5 LE BATEAU**	**5 DAS BOOT**	**5 DE BOOT, HET SCHIP**	**5 BÅDEN**
On deck	**Sur le pont**	**An Deck**	**Aan dek**	**På dækket**
Anchor	*Ancre*	*Anker*	*Anker*	*Anker*
1 bower anchor	1 ancre de bossoir	1 Buganker	1 boeganker	1 sværdanker
2 kedge	2 ancre à jet	2 Warpanker, Reserveanker	2 werpanker, hulpanker	2 varpanker
3 fisherman's anchor	3 ancre à jas	3 Stockanker	3 stokanker	3 stokanker
4 stock	4 jas	4 Stock	4 stok	4 ankerstok
5 shank	5 verge	5 Schaft	5 schacht	5 ankerlæg
6 flukes	6 pattes	6 Flunken	6 vloeien	6 flige
7 ring	7 organeau	7 Ring	7 roering	7 ring
8 CQR or plough anchor	8 CQR, ou ancre charrue	8 Pflugscharanker	8 CQR of ploegschaar-anker	8 plovanker, CQR
9 Danforth™	9 ancre à bascule	9 Danfortanker™	9 Danforth™ (anker)	9 Danforth™ anker
10 sea anchor	10 ancre flottante	10 Seeanker, Treibanker	10 drijfanker, zeeanker	10 drivanker
11 anchor warp	11 aussière, câblot	11 Ankertrosse	11 ankertros	11 ankertrosse
12 chain, cable	12 chaîne ou câble d'ancre	12 Ankerkette	12 ketting, kabel	12 kæde, trosse
13 link	13 maille, maillon	13 Kettenglied	13 schalm	13 kædeled
14 stud-link	14 maille à étai	14 Stegkette	14 damketting	14 stopkæde
15 navel pipe	15 écubler de pont	15 Kettenklüse	15 kettingkoker	15 kædebrønd
16 anchor buoy	16 bouée de corps-mort	16 Ankerboje	16 ankerboei	16 ankerbøje
17 tripping line	17 orin, lève-nez	17 Bojereep	17 neuringlijn	17 bøjereb
18 calibrated	18 calibre	18 kalibriert	18 gekalibreerd, geijkt	18 inddelt
Bilge pump	*Pompe de cale*	*Lenzpumpe*	*Lenspomp*	*Lænsepumper*
1 centrifugal pump	1 pompe centrifuge	1 Zentrifugalpumpe, Kreiselpumpe	1 centrifugaalpomp	1 centrifugalpumpe
2 diaphragm pump	2 pompe à diaphragme	2 Membranpumpe	2 membraanpomp	2 membranpumpe
3 semi-rotary pump	3 pompe semi-rotative	3 Flügelpumpe	3 vleugelpomp	3 nikke-pumpe
4 double-action pump	4 pompe à double effet	4 doppeltwirkende Pumpe	4 dubbel werkende pomp	4 dobbeltvirkende pumpe
5 self-priming pump	5 pompe auto-amorçante	5 selbstansaugende Pumpe	5 zelf aanzuigende pomp	5 selvansugende pumpe
6 capacity	6 capacité, débit	6 Leistungsfähigkeit	6 capaciteit	6 kapacitet
7 plunger	7 piston, plongeur	7 Kolben	7 plunjer	7 pumpestempel

ESPAÑOL	ITALIANO	PORTUGUÊS	TÜRKÇE	ΕΛΛΗΝΙΚΑ
5 EL BARCO	**5 LA BARCA**	**5 DO BARCO**	**5 TEKNE**	**5 ΤΟ ΣΚΑΦΟΣ**
En cubierta	**Sul ponte**	**No convés**	**Güvertede**	**ΣΤΟ ΚΑΤΑΣΤΡΩΜΑ**
Ancla	*Ancora*	*Ancora/ferro*	*Demir/çapa*	*ΑΓΚΥΡΑ*
1 ancla principal	1 àncora di prora	1 ferro de amura, de leva	1 baş/pruva demiri	1 ΚΥΡΙΑ ΑΓΚΥΡΑ
2 anclote	2 ancorotto	2 ancorote	2 tonoz demiri	2 ΣΑΛΠΑΦΟΥΝΤΑ
3 ancla de cepo	3 grappino	3 âncora com cêpo	3 balıkçı demiri	3 ΝΑΥΑΡΧΕΙΟ
4 cepo	4 ceppo	4 cêpo do ferro	4 demir çiposu	4 ΚΟΡΜΟΣ
5 caña	5 fuso	5 haste do ferro	5 demir bedeni	5 ΜΠΡΑΤΣΟ
6 uñas	6 marre	6 unhas do ferro	6 demir tırnakları	6 ΔΟΝΤΙΑ
7 arganeo	7 cicala	7 anete do ferro	7 demir anelesi	7 ΚΡΙΚΟΣ
8 CQR/Arado	8 àncora CQR, àncora a vomere	8 tipo CQR, de charrua	8 CQR veya sapan demir	8 ΥΝΙ ΣΗΚΙΟΥΑΡ
9 Danforth™	9 àncora Danforth™	9 tipo Danforth™	9 Danforth™ demiri	9 ΝΤΑΝΦΟΡΘ
10 ancla flotante	10 àncora galleggiante	10 âncora flutuante	10 fırtına demiri	10 ΠΛΩΤΗ ΑΓΚΥΡΑ
11 amarra del ancla	11 cavo di tonneggio	11 espia do ferro	11 demir halatı (tel)	11 ΑΓΚΥΡΟΣΚΟΙΝΟ
12 cadena, cable del ancla	12 catena, cavo	12 amarra	12 demir zinciri, demir tel halatı	12 ΑΛΥΣΣΙΔΑ
13 eslabón	13 maglia	13 elo	13 zincir baklası	13 ΚΡΙΚΟΣ ΑΛΥΣΣΙΔΑΣ
14 eslabón de contrete	14 maglia con traversino	14 elo com estai	14 lokmalı zincir	14 ΚΑΛΕΝΑ ΜΕ Θ
15 escobén	15 pozzo della catena	15 gateira	15 güverte zincir loçası	15 ΑΦΑΛΟΣ
16 boyarín del orinque	16 gavitello	16 bóia do arinque	16 demir şamandırası	16 ΣΗΜΑΔΟΥΡΑ ΑΓΚΥΡΟΒΟΛΙΑΣ
17 orinque	17 grippia	17 arinque	17 demir kurtarma halatı	17 ΚΛΕΦΤΗΣ
18 calibrada	18 calibrato	18 calibrado	18 kalibre zincir	18 ΒΑΘΜΟΛΟΓΗΜΕΝΗ
Bombas de achique	*Pompa di sentina*	*Bomba de esgoto*	*Sintine pompası*	*ΑΝΤΛΙΑ ΣΕΝΤΙΝΑΣ*
1 bomba centrifuga	1 pompa centrifuga	1 bomba centrífuga	1 santrifuj pompa	1 ΦΥΓΟΚΕΝΤΡΙΚΗ ΑΝΤΛΙΑ
2 bomba de diafragma	2 pompa a membrana	2 bomba de diafragma	2 diyaframlı pompa	2 ΑΝΤΛΙΑ ΔΙΑΦΡΑΓΜΑΤΟΣ
3 bomba de palanca	3 pompa semi-rotativa	3 bomba de relógio	3 kurbağa pompa	3 ΗΜΙΠΕΡΙΣΤΡΟΦΙΚΗ ΑΝΤΛΙΑ
4 bomba de doble efecto	4 pompa a doppio effetto	4 bomba de efeito duplo	4 emme-basma pompa	4 ΑΝΤΛΙΑ ΔΙΠΛΗΣ ΕΝΕΡΓΕΙΑΣ
5 bomba de cebado automático	5 pompa auto-innescante	5 bomba de ferrar automáticamente	5 kendi dolan pompa	5 ΑΥΤΟΠΛΗΡΟΥΜΕΝΗ ΑΝΤΛΙΑ
6 capacidad	6 portata	6 capacidade, débito	6 kapasite, debi	6 ΧΩΡΗΤΙΚΟΤΗΣ
7 émbolo	7 stantuffo	7 êmbolo	7 tulumba pistonu, çalpara	7 ΤΑΠΑ

ENGLISH	FRANÇAIS	DEUTSCH	NEDERLANDS	DANSK
5 THE BOAT	**5 LE BATEAU**	**5 DAS BOOT**	**5 DE BOOT, HET SCHIP**	**5 BÅDEN**
On deck	**Sur le pont**	**An Deck**	**Aan dek**	**På dækket**

ENGLISH	FRANÇAIS	DEUTSCH	NEDERLANDS	DANSK
Bilge pump	*Pompe de cale*	*Lenzpumpe*	*Lenspomp*	*Lænsepumper*
8 valve	8 soupape	8 Ventil	8 klep	8 ventil
9 washer	9 cuir, joint	9 Dichtungsscheibe	9 leertje	9 spændskive
10 impeller	10 rotor	10 Kreisel	10 impeller	10 impeller, vinge
11 suction pipe	11 tuyau d'aspiration	11 Ansaugrohr	11 zuigpijp	11 sugerør
12 strum box	12 crépine	12 Saugkorb	12 zuigkorf	12 sugekurv

Bosun's bag & chandlery stores	**Trousse du contremaître et articles de marine**	**Werkzeuge des Bootsmanns**	**Kabelgat**	**Bådsmandsgrej**
1 serving mallet	1 mailloche à fourrer	1 Kleedkeule	1 kleedkuil	1 klækølle
2 marline spike	2 épissoir	2 Marlspieker	2 marlspijker	2 merlespiger
3 caulking iron	3 fer ou ciseau de calfat	3 Kalfateisen	3 breeuw-, kalfaatijzer	3 kalfatrejern
4 bosun's chair	4 chaise de gabier	4 Bootsmannsstuhl	4 bootsmansstoel	4 bådsmandsstol
5 sailmaker's palm	5 paumelle	5 Segelhandschuh	5 zeilplaat	5 sejlmagerhandske
6 needle and thread	6 aiguille et fil à voile	6 Nadel und Garn	6 zeilnaald en zeilgaren	6 nål & tråd
7 adhesive	7 colle	7 Leim, Klebstoff	7 lijm	7 klæbemiddel, tape
8 insulating tape	8 ruban isolant, Chatterton	8 Isolierband	8 isolatieband	8 isolerbånd
9 knife	9 couteau	9 Mesiser	9 mes	9 kniv
10 whipping twine	10 fil à surlier	10 Takelgarn	10 takelgaren	10 taklegarn
11 sail patch	11 rapiècage de voile	11 Segelflicken	11 stukje reparatie-zeildoek	11 lap
12 cleat	12 taquet	12 Klampe	12 klamp, kikker	12 klampe
13 jam cleat	13 taquet coinceur, coinceur d'écoute	13 Curryklemme, Schotklemme	13 schootklem	13 clamcleat, aflaster
14 mooring bitts	14 bitte d'amarrage	14 Poller	14 beting	14 fortøjningspullert
15 belaying pin	15 cabillot	15 Beleg-, Koffeynagel	15 korvijnagel	15 kofilnagle

ESPAÑOL	ITALIANO	PORTUGUÊS	TÜRKÇE	ΕΛΛΗΝΙΚΑ
5 EL BARCO	**5 LA BARCA**	**5 DO BARCO**	**5 TEKNE**	**5 ΤΟ ΣΚΑΦΟΣ**
En cubierta	**Sul ponte**	**No convés**	**Güvertede**	**ΣΤΟ ΚΑΤΑΣΤΡΩΜΑ**
Bombas de achique 8 válvula 9 arandela 10 impelente 11 tubo de aspiración 12 alcachofa	***Pompa di sentina*** 8 valvola 9 rondella 10 girante 11 tubo d'aspirazione 12 succhiarola	***Bomba de esgoto*** 8 válvula 9 anel 10 impulsor 11 tubo de aspiração 12 caixa de lôdo	***Sintine pompası*** 8 supap 9 conta 10 impeller/pompa pervanesi 11 emme borusu 12 süzgeç	*ΑΝΤΛΙΑ ΣΕΝΤΙΝΑΣ* 8 ΒΑΛΒΙΔΑ 9 ΡΟΔΕΛΛΑ 10 ΙΜΠΕΛΛΕΡ 11 ΣΩΛΗΝΑ ΑΝΑΡΟΦΗΣΗΣ 12 ΠΟΤΗΡΙ - ΤΡΥΠΗΤΟ
Maleta de contramaestre y pertrechos	**Borsa e provviste del nostromo**	**Paiol do mestre e ferragem de embarcações**	**Porsun çantası ve malzemesi**	**ΕΡΓΑΛΕΙΑ ΚΑΙ ΥΛΙΚΑ ΣΚΑΦΟΥΣ**
1 maceta de aforrar 2 pasador 3 hierro de calafatear 4 guindola 5 rempujo 6 aguja e hilo de velas, filástica 7 adhesivo, pegamento 8 cinta aislante 9 cuchillo 10 filástica para falca-caer 11 remiendo de vela 12 cornamusa 13 barbeta 14 bitas 15 cabilla	1 mazzuolo per fasciature 2 caviglia da impiombature 3 presello per calafaggio 4 bansigo 5 guardamano 6 ago e spago 7 adesivo 8 nastro isolante 9 coltello 10 spago da impalmature 11 toppa della vela 12 galloccia 13 strozzascotte 14 bitte d'ormeggio 15 caviglia	1 macete de forrar 2 espicha 3 ferro de calafate 4 balso de carpinteiro 5 repucho 6 agulha e linha 7 adesivo 8 fita isoladora 9 faca/canivete 10 cordel de chicote 11 remendo da vela 12 cunho 13 mordente para escota 14 abita 15 malagueta	1 façuna maçunası/ façuna tokmağı 2 halat kavelası 3 kalafatçı demiri/ tokmağı 4 porsun salıncağı/ İskemlesi 5 yelkenci yüksüğü 6 iğne ve iplik 7 zamk 8 izole edici, bant 9 çakı 10 piyan çakısı 11 yelken yaması 12 koç boynuzu 13 kıstırmalı koç boynuzu/jam kilit 14 bağlama babası 15 kavilya	1 ΜΑΤΣΟΛΑ 2 ΚΑΒΙΛΛΙΑ 3 ΕΡΓΑΛΕΙΟ ΚΑΛΑΦΑΤΙΣΜΑΤΟΣ 4 ΚΑΝΤΗΛΙΤΣΑ 5 ΠΑΛΑΜΗ 6 ΒΕΛΟΝΑ ΚΑΙ ΚΛΩΣΤΗ 7 ΚΟΛΛΑ 8 ΜΟΝΩΤΙΚΗ ΤΑΙΝΙΑ 9 ΜΑΧΑΙΡΙ 10 ΣΠΑΓΓΟΣ ΜΑΤΙΣΜΑΤΟΣ 11 ΜΠΑΛΩΜΑ ΓΙΑ ΠΑΝΙ 12 ΚΟΤΣΑΝΕΛΛΟ 13 ΔΑΓΚΑΝΑΡΙ ΑΣΦΑΛΕΙΑΣ 14 ΜΠΑΜΠΑΔΕΣ 15 ΔΕΣΤΡΑ ΝΤΟΥΚΑΡΙΣΜΑΤΟΣ ΣΧΟΙΝΙΩΝ

ENGLISH	FRANÇAIS	DEUTSCH	NEDERLANDS	DANSK
5 THE BOAT	**5 LE BATEAU**	**5 DAS BOOT**	**5 DE BOOT, HET SCHIP**	**5 BÅDEN**
Bosun's bag & chandlery stores	**Trousse du contremaître et articles de marine**	**Werkzeuge des Bootsmanns**	**Kabelgat**	**Bådsmandsgrej**
16 fairlead	16 chaumard	16 Lippe, Verholklüse	16 verhaalklem	16 klyds
17 roller fairlead	17 chaumard à réa	17 Rollenklampe	17 verhaalklem met rol	17 klyds med rulle
18 sheet lead	18 filoire d'écoute	18 Leitöse	18 leioog	18 skødeviser
19 adjustable sheet lead	19 filoire d'écoute réglable	19 verstellbare Leitöse	19 verstelbaar leioog	19 indstillelig skødeviser
20 swivelling sheet lead	20 filoire à émerillon	20 drehbare Leitöse	20 wartelleioog	20 skødeviser med svirvel
21 eye bolt	21 piton de filière	21 Augbolzen	21 oogbout	21 øjebolt
22 block	22 poulie	22 Block	22 blok	22 blok
23 sheave	23 réa	23 Scheibe	23 schijf	23 skive
24 single block	24 poulie simple	24 einscheibiger Block	24 eenschijfsblok	24 enkeltblok
25 double block	25 poulie double	25 zweischeibiger Block	25 tweeschijfsblok	25 dobbeltblok
26 with becket	26 à ringot, à œil	26 mit Hundsvott	26 met hondsvot	26 med hundsvot
27 fiddle block	27 poulie violon	27 Violinblock	27 vioolblok	27 violinblok
28 shackle and pin	28 manille et vis, manille et clavette	28 Schäkel und Bolzen	28 sluiting met bout	28 sjækkel og bolt
29 D shackle	29 manille droite	29 U Schäkel	29 D-sluiting	29 'D'-sjækkel
30 harp shackle	30 manille violon	30 Bügelschäkel	30 harpsluiting	30 harpesjækkel
31 snap shackle	31 mousqueton à ressort	31 Schnapp-, Patentschäkel	31 patentsluiting	31 tryksjækkel
32 swivel	32 émerillon	32 Wirbel	32 wartel	32 svirvel
33 thimble	33 cosse	33 Kausch	33 kous	33 kovs
34 wire rope or bulldog grip	34 serre-câble à étrier	34 Seilklemme	34 staaldraadklem	34 wirelås
35 hank	35 mousqueton	35 Stagreiter	35 musketonhaak, knipleuver	35 fokkehage
36 jubilee clip	36 collier de serrage	36 Schlauchklemme,	36 slangklem	36 slangebinder
37 snatch block	37 poulie ourrante	37 Klappblock	37 voetblok, kinnebaks-blok	37 snap-blok
38 sail slider	38 coulisseau	38 Rutscher	38 glijleuver	38 sejlslæde
39 carabineer clip	39 mousqueton	39 Karabinerhaken	39 karabijnsluiting	39 karabinhage
40 rope clutch	40 bloqueur/coinceur	40 Kammklemme	40 touwklem	40 frølår
41 split pin	41 goupille fendue	41 Splint	41 splitpen	41 split
42 captive pin	42 goupille Mecanindus	42 Bolzen eines Schlüsselschäkels, Sicherheitsbolzen	42 borgpen	42 splitbolt

ESPAÑOL	ITALIANO	PORTUGUÊS	TÜRKÇE	ΕΛΛΗΝΙΚΑ
5 EL BARCO	**5 LA BARCA**	**5 DO BARCO**	**5 TEKNE**	**5 ΤΟ ΣΚΑΦΟΣ**
Maleta de contra maestre y pertrechos	**Borsa e provviste del nostromo**	**Paiol do mestre e ferragem de embarcações**	**Porsun çantası ve malzemesi**	**ΕΡΓΑΛΕΙΑ ΚΑΙ ΥΛΙΚΑ ΣΚΑΦΟΥΣ**
16 galápago, guía	16 passacavi	16 castanha	16 kurtağzı	16 ΜΑΤΙ
17 galápago de rolete	17 passacavi a rulli	17 tamanca	17 bastikalı kurtağzı	17 ΟΔΗΓΟΣ ΜΕ ΚΑΡΟΥΛΙ (ΑΓΚΥΡΑΣ)
18 escotera	18 passascotte	18 guia de escota	18 iskota köprüsü	18 ΟΔΗΓΟΣ ΣΚΟΤΑΣ
19 escotera regulable	19 passascotte regolabile	19 guia de escota ajustável	19 ayarlı ıskota köprü arabası	19 ΡΥΘΜΙΖΟΜΕΝΟΣ ΟΔΗΓΟΣ ΣΚΟΤΑΣ
20 escotera giratoria	20 passascotte girevole	20 guia de escota de tornél	20 hareketli ıskota köprüsü	20 ΠΕΡΙΣΤΡΕΦΟΜΕΝΟΣ ΟΔΗΓΟΣ ΣΚΟΤΑΣ
21 cáncamo de argolla	21 golfare	21 olhal de trapas	21 sabit mapa	21 ΜΑΠΑ
22 motón	22 bozzello	22 moitão	22 makara	22 ΡΑΟΥΛΟ
23 roldana	23 puleggia	23 roldana	23 makara dili	23 ΣΤΡΙΦΤΑΡΙ
24 motón sencillo, single	24 bozzello semplice	24 moitão singelo, simples	24 tek dilli makara	24 ΜΟΝΟ ΡΑΟΥΛΟ
25 motón doble	25 bozzello doppio	25 cadernal	25 çift dilli makara	25 ΔΙΠΛΟ ΡΑΟΥΛΟ
26 con manzanillo	26 con stroppo	26 moitão alçeado	26 kamçılı makara	26 ΜΕ ΣΧΟΙΝΑΚΙ
27 motón de briol	27 bozzello a violino	27 polé	27 makara rule/ikiz makara	27 ΡΑΟΥΛΟ ΜΕ ΔΑΓΚΑΝΑΡΙ
28 grillete y pasador o perno	28 grillo e perno	28 manilha e cavirão	28 kilit ve harbisi	28 ΝΑΥΤΙΚΟ ΚΛΕΙΔΙ
29 grillete en D	29 grillo a D	29 manilha direita	29 düz kilit	29 ΚΛΕΙΔΙ ΣΕ ΣΧΗΜΑ D
30 grillete de mucho oio	30 grillo a omega	30 manilha de ferradura de borracha	30 yan kilit	30 ΚΛΕΙΔΙ ΩΜΕΓΑ
31 grillete de enganche	31 moschettone	31 manilha de mola	31 yaylı kilit	31 ΚΛΕΙΔΙ ΜΕ ΚΟΥΜΠΙ
32 giratorio	32 girella, mulinello	32 tornél	32 fırdöndü	32 ΣΤΡΙΦΤΑΡΙ
33 guardacabo	33 redancia	33 sapatilho	33 radansa	33 ΔΑΧΤΥΛΗΘΡΑ
34 trinca de cable	34 morsetto	34 grampas	34 tel kıstırmacı	34 ΣΥΡΜΑΤΟΣΧΟΙΝΟ
35 garrucho, mosquetón	35 garroccio, canestrello	35 garruncho	35 yelken kancası	35 ΣΚΥΛΑΚΙ
36 abrazadera	36 fascetta a vite	36 abraçadeira ajustável	36 kelepçe	36 ΚΟΤΣΑΝΕΛΟ
37 pasteca	37 pastecca	37 moitão do conves	37 karnıyarık bastika	37 ΜΠΑΣΤΕΚΑ ΜΕ ΚΟΥΜΠΙ
38 corredera	38 garroccio scorrevole	38 slider	38 yelken gradin arabası/yelken arabası	38 ΓΚΛΙΣΙΕΡΑ
39 musqueton	39 moschettone a molla	39 grampo carabineiro	39 yaylı kanca	39 ΚΟΤΣΑΝΕΛΟ
40 mordaza	40 serracava	40 roldana do cabo	40 halat kıstırmacı	40 ΔΑΓΚΑΝΑ - ΦΡΕΝΟ
41 chaveta de seguridad	41 coppiglia	41 troço de abrir	41 toplu iğne	41 ΤΣΙΒΙ
42 pasador imperdible	42 perno prigioniero	42 pino captivo	42 çengelli iğne	42 ΠΕΙΡΟΣ

ENGLISH	FRANÇAIS	DEUTSCH	NEDERLANDS	DANSK
5 THE BOAT	**5 LE BATEAU**	**5 DAS BOOT**	**5 DE BOOT, HET SCHIP**	**5 BÅDEN**
Carpenter's toolbag	**Trousse à outils de menuisier**	**Werkzeuge des Zimmermanns**	**Timmermansuitrusting**	**Værktøj**
1 saw	1 scie	1 Säge	1 zaag	1 sav
2 plane	2 rabot	2 Hobel	2 schaaf	2 høvl
3 chisel	3 ciseau à bois	3 Meißel	3 beitel	3 mejsel
4 brace and bits	4 vilebrequin et mèches	4 Brustleier mit Einsätzen	4 booromslag en boren	4 svingbor og sneglebor
5 vice	5 étau	5 Schraubstock	5 bankschroef	5 skruestik
6 hammer	6 marteau	6 Hammer	6 hamer	6 hammer
7 screwdriver	7 tournevis	7 Schraubendreher	7 schroevedraaier	7 skruetrækker
8 hand drill and bits	8 chignolle à main avec forets	8 Drillbohrer und Bohrer	8 handboor en boren	8 håndbor og drilbor
9 hacksaw	9 scie à métaux	9 Metallsäge	9 metaalzaag	9 nedstryger
10 file	10 lime	10 Feile	10 vijl	10 fil
11 wire cutters	11 pinces coupantes	11 Drahtschere	11 draadschaar	11 wiresaks
12 rule	12 règle	12 Lineal	12 meetlat	12 tommestok
13 square	13 équerre	13 Winkel	13 winkelhaak	13 vinkel
14 spokeshave	14 racloire, vastringue	14 Ziehklinge	14 spookschaaf	14 bugthøvl
15 pliers	15 pinces	15 Drahtzange	15 buig-, vouwtang	15 tang
16 bradawl	16 poinçon	16 Nagelbohrer	16 els, priem	16 platbor
17 gimlet	17 vrille	17 Frittbohrer	17 splitsboor	17 vridbor
18 punch	18 chasse-clou	18 Dorn	18 pons	18 dorn
19 carborundum stone	19 pierre à aiguiser, à afflûter	19 Karborund-Abziehstein	19 carborundumsteen	19 slibesten
20 crosshead screwdriver	20 tournevis 'crosshead'	20 Kreuzschlitz-schraubendreher	20 kruiskop-schroevedraaier	20 kryds-skruetrækker
21 G clamp	21 serre-joint	21 Schraubzwinge	21 lijmtang	21 skruetvinge
Below deck	**Sous le pont**	**Unter Deck**	**Onderdeks**	**Under dæk**
Domestic items & plumbing	*Equipement d'intérieur et tuyauterie*	*Wohnraum und Rohrleitungen*	*Huishoudelijke zaken en sanitair*	*Kahytsudstyr, VVS*
1 mattress	1 matelas	1 Matratze	1 matras	1 madras
2 cushion	2 coussin	2 Sitzkissen, Polster	2 zitkussen[s]	2 pude(r)
3 pillow and case	3 oreiller et taie	3 Kopfkissen und Bezug	3 kussen en kussensloop	3 hovedpude, pudevår
4 sleeping bag	4 sac de couchage	4 Schlafsack	4 slaapzak	4 sovepose

ESPAÑOL	ITALIANO	PORTUGUÊS	TÜRKÇE	ΕΛΛΗΝΙΚΑ
5 EL BARCO	**5 LA BARCA**	**5 DO BARCO**	**5 TEKNE**	**5 ΤΟ ΣΚΑΦΟΣ**
Maleta de herramientas de carpintero	**Utensili da falegname**	**Caixa de carpinteiro**	**Marangoz aletleri**	**ΕΡΓΑΛΕΙΑ ΞΥΛΟΥΡΓΟΥ**
1 sierra	1 sega	1 serra	1 bıçkı/testere	1 ΠΡΙΟΝΙ
2 cepillo	2 pialla	2 plaina	2 rende	2 ΠΛΑΝΗ
3 formón	3 scalpello	3 cinzel, escôpro	3 keski	3 ΣΚΑΡΠΕΛΟ
4 berbiquí y broca	4 menarola e punte	4 arco de pua e brocas	4 matkap ve uçları	4 ΤΡΥΠΑΝΙΑ
5 mordaza	5 morsa	5 tôrno, prensa	5 mengene	5 ΣΦΙΚΤΗΡΑΣ
6 martillo	6 martello	6 martelo	6 çekiç	6 ΣΦΥΡΙ
7 destornillador	7 cacciavite	7 chave de parafuso	7 tornavida	7 ΚΑΤΣΑΒΙΔΙ
8 taladro y broca	8 trapano a mano e punte	8 berbequim manual e brocas	8 elmatkabı ve uçları	8 ΧΕΙΡΟΔΡΑΠΑΝΟ ΚΑΙ ΜΥΤΕΣ
9 serrucho	9 seghetto	9 serrote para metal	9 demir testeresi	9 ΣΙΔΗΡΟΠΡΙΟΝΟ
10 lima	10 lima	10 lima	10 eğe	10 ΛΙΜΑ
11 cortafrio	11 cesoie	11 alicate para cortar arame	11 tel kesici pense	11 ΚΟΦΤΗΣ ΣΥΡΜΑΤΟΣ
12 regla	12 righello	12 régua	12 cetvel	12 ΧΑΡΑΚΑΣ
13 escuadra	13 squadra	13 esquadro	13 gönye	13 ΟΡΘΟΓΩΝΙΟ
14 cabilla	14 pialletto a due manici	14 cortchet	14 sistre	14 ΦΑΛΤΣΕΤΤΑ
15 alicates	15 pinze	15 alicate	15 pens	15 ΤΑΝΑΛΙΑ
16 barrena	16 punteruolo	16 buril	16 zımba	16 ΤΡΥΠΑΝΙ -
17 barrenita	17 succhiello	17 verruma	17 burgu	17 ΤΡΥΠΑΝΙ
18 punzón	18 punzone	18 punção, furador	18 punta	18 ΤΡΥΠΗΤΗΡΙ
19 carborundo	19 pietra smeriglio	19 pedra de esmeril de carborundum	19 biley taşı	19 ΑΚΟΝΙ
20 destornillador para tornillos cruciforme	20 cacciavite a croce	20 chave philips	20 yıldız tornavida	20 ΣΤΑΥΡΟΚΑΤΣΑΒΙΔΟ
21 gato	21 morsetto a C	21 grampo G	21 işkence	21 ΜΙΚΡΟΣ ΣΦΙΚΤΗΡΑΣ
Bajo cubierta	**Sotto coperta**	**Abaixo do convés**	**Güverte altında**	**ΜΕΣΑ ΣΤΟ ΣΚΑΦΟΣ**
Menaje y fontaneria	*Casalinghi e idraulica*	*Artigos domésticos e esgotos*	*İç donanım & su tesisatı*	*ΟΙΚΟΣΚΕΥΗ & ΥΔΡΑΥΛΙΚΑ*
1 colchón	1 materasso	1 colchão	1 şilte	1 ΣΤΡΩΜΑ
2 cojínes	2 cuscino	2 almofadas	2 yastık	2 ΜΑΞΙΛΑΡΙ
3 almohada y funda	3 cuscino e federa	3 almofada e fronha	3 uyku yastığı ve kılıfı	3 ΜΑΞΙΛΑΡΙ & ΜΑΞΙΛΑΡΟΘΗΚΗ
4 saco de dormir	4 sacco a pelo	4 saco de dormir	4 uyku tulumu	4 ΥΠΝΟΣΑΚΟΣ

ENGLISH	FRANÇAIS	DEUTSCH	NEDERLANDS	DANSK
5 THE BOAT	**5 LE BATEAU**	**5 DAS BOOT**	**5 DE BOOT, HET SCHIP**	**5 BÅDEN**
Below deck	**Sous le pont**	**Unter Deck**	**Onderdeks**	**Under dæk**
Domestic items & plumbing	*Equipement d'intérieur et tuyauterie*	*Wohnraum und Rohrleitungen*	*Huishoudelijke zaken en sanitair*	*Kahytsudstyr, VVS*
5 sheet	5 drap	5 Bettlaken	5 laken	5 lagen
6 blanket	6 couverture	6 Decke	6 deken	6 tæppe
7 leeboard	7 planche ou toile de roulis	7 Kojenbrett, Kojensegel	7 kooiplank	7 køjebræt
8 WC, heads	8 WC, toilettes	8 Pumpklosett, Toilette	8 WC, toilet	8 toilet
9 non-return, valve	9 soupape de retenue	9 Rückschlagventil	9 terugslagklep	9 kontraventil
10 flap valve	10 soupape à clapet	10 Schwenkhahn	10 tuimelklep	10 klapventil
11 discharge piping	11 tuyau de débit	11 Abflußrohr	11 afvoerpijp	11 afløbsrør
12 seacock	12 vanne	12 Seeventil	12 buitenboordkraan	12 søventil
13 lavatory paper	13 papier hygiénique	13 Toilettenpapier	13 toiletpapier	13 toiletpapir
14 washbasin	14 lavabo	14 Waschbecken	14 wasbak, waskom	14 håndvask
15 towel	15 serviette	15 Handtuch	15 handdoek	15 håndklæde
16 soap	16 savon	16 Seife	16 zeep	16 sæbe
17 lock and key	17 serrure et clef	17 Schloß und Schlüssel	17 slot en sleutel	17 lås og nøgle
18 hinge	18 charnière	18 Scharnier	18 scharnier	18 hængsel
19 ashtray	19 cendrier	19 Aschbecher	19 asbak	19 askebæger
20 knife and fork	20 couteau et fourchette	20 Messer und Gabel	20 mes en vork	20 kniv og gaffel
21 spoon	21 cuillère	21 Löffel	21 lepel	21 ske
22 cup and saucer	22 tasse et soucoupe	22 Tasse und Untertasse	22 kop en schotel	22 kop og underkop
23 plate	23 assiette	23 Teller	23 bord	23 tallerken
24 glass	24 verre	24 Glas	24 glas	24 glas
25 mug	25 quart	25 Becher	25 mok, kroes	25 krus
26 bowl	26 bol	26 Schale	26 schaal	26 skål
27 duvet	27 couette	27 Steppdecke, Bettbezug	27 dekbed	27 duvet
28 pump	28 pompe	28 Pumpe	28 pomp	28 pumpe
29 seal	29 joint étanche	29 Verschluß	29 afdichting	29 pakning
30 holding tank	30 réservoir de rétention	30 Rückhaltetank	30 vuilwatertank	30 lagertank
31 shower	31 douche	31 Dusche	31 douche	31 bruser
32 shower tray	32 bac de douche	32 Duschwanne	32 douchebak	32 bruserbakke
33 leeboard/leecloth	33 planche/toile anti-roulis	33 Leebrett/Leesegel	33 slingerkleed kooiplank	33 klæde

ESPAÑOL	ITALIANO	PORTUGUÊS	TÜRKÇE	ΕΛΛΗΝΙΚΑ
5 EL BARCO	**5 LA BARCA**	**5 DO BARCO**	**5 TEKNE**	**5 ΤΟ ΣΚΑΦΟΣ**
Bajo cubierta	**Sotto coperta**	**Abaixo do convés**	**Güverte altında**	**ΜΕΣΑ ΣΤΟ ΣΚΑΦΟΣ**
Menaje y fontaneria	*Casalinghi e idraulica*	*Artigos domésticos e esgotos*	*İç donanım & su tesisatı*	*ΟΙΚΟΣΚΕΥΗ ΚΑΙ ΥΔΡΑΥΛΙΚΑ*
5 sábana	5 lenzuolo	5 lençol	5 yatak çarşafı	5 ΣΕΝΤΟΝΙ
6 manta, frazada	6 coperta	6 cobertor	6 battaniye	6 ΚΟΥΒΕΡΤΑ
7 gualdera	7 tavola anti-rollio	7 resguardo do beliche	7 yalpalık	7 ΠΛΑΤΗ ΣΑΝΙΔΑ ΚΟΥΚΕΤΤΑΣ
8 WC, sanitario	8 WC, locale igienico, cesso	8 WC, retrete	8 tuvalet	8 ΤΟΥΑΛΛΕΤΕΣ
9 válvula de retención	9 valvola di ritegno	9 válvula sem retôrno	9 cek valf	9 ΒΑΛΒΙΔΑ ΜΗ ΕΠΙΣΤΡΟΦΗΣ
10 válvula de charnela	10 valvola a cerniera	10 válvula de portinhola	10 klapeli valf	10 ΒΑΛΒΙΔΑ ΜΕ ΚΛΑΠΕΤΤΟ
11 tubo de descarga	11 scarichi a mare	11 tubo de descarga	11 boşaltma borusu	11 ΣΩΛΗΝΩΣΕΙΣ ΕΚΕΝΩΣΕΩΣ
12 llave de paso	12 presa d'acqua dal mare	12 torneira de segurança	12 deniz suyu valfı/ kinistin	12 ΒΑΝΑ ΘΑΛΑΣΣΗΣ
13 papel higiénico	13 carta igienica	13 papél higiénico	13 tuvalet kağıdı	13 ΧΑΡΤΙ ΥΓΕΙΑΣ
14 lavabo	14 lavandino	14 lavatório	14 lavabo	14 ΝΙΠΤΗΡΑΣ
15 toalla	15 asciugamano	15 toalha	15 havlu	15 ΠΕΤΣΕΤΑ
16 jabón	16 sapone	16 sabonete	16 sabun	16 ΣΑΠΟΥΝΙ
17 cerradura y llave	17 serratura e chiave	17 fechadura e chave	17 kilit ve anahtar	17 ΚΛΕΙΔΑΡΙΑ & ΚΛΕΙΔΙ
18 charnela, bisagra	18 cerniera	18 dobradiça	18 menteşe	18 ΜΕΝΤΕΣΕΣ
19 cenicero	19 posacenere	19 cinzeiro	19 küllük, kültablası	19 ΣΤΑΧΤΟΔΟΧΕΙΟ
20 cuchilla y tenedor	20 coltello e forchetta	20 faca e garfo	20 bıçak ve çatal	20 ΜΑΧΑΙΡΙ ΚΑΙ ΠΗΡΟΥΝΙ
21 cuchara	21 cucchiaio	21 colher	21 kaşık	21 ΚΟΥΤΑΛΙ
22 taza y platillo	22 tazza e piattino	22 chávena e pires	22 kâse ve sosluk	22 ΦΛΥΤΖΑΝΙ ΚΑΙ ΠΙΑΤΑΚΙ
23 plato	23 piatto	23 prato	23 tabak	23 ΠΙΑΤΟ
24 vaso	24 bicchiere	24 copo	24 bardak	24 ΠΟΤΗΡΙ
25 pote	25 boccale	25 caneca	25 maşrapa/kupa	25 ΦΛΥΤΖΑΝΙ / ΚΟΥΠΑ
26 tazón	26 ciotola	26 tigela	26 kâse/çanak	26 ΠΙΑΤΟ ΣΟΥΠΑΣ / ΜΠΩΛ
27 edredon	27 piumino	27 edredon	27 kuştüyü	27 ΠΑΠΛΩΜΑ
28 bomba	28 pompa	28 bomba	28 pompa/tulumba	28 ΑΝΤΛΙΑ
29 cierre hermético	29 guarnizione	29 selo	29 conta	29 ΦΛΑΝΤΖΑ
30 deposito de aguas sucias	30 serbatoio	30 depósito de reserva de esgotos	30 rezervuar	30 ΤΑΝΚΙ ΑΠΟΒΛΗΤΩΝ
31 ducha	31 doccia	31 duche	31 duş	31 ΝΤΟΥΣ
32 plato de ducha	32 piatto della doccia	32 bacia do duche	32 duş tavası	32 ΝΤΟΥΣΙΕΡΑ
33 balderas, lona de escora	33 tavola antirollio/tela antirollio	33 orça	33 yalpalık	33 ΣΑΝΙΔΑ/ΥΦΑΣΜΑ ΑΣΦΑΛΕΙΑΣ ΣΤΗΝ ΚΟΥΚΕΤΑ

ENGLISH	FRANÇAIS	DEUTSCH	NEDERLANDS	DANSK
5 THE BOAT	**5 LE BATEAU**	**5 DAS BOOT**	**5 DE BOOT, HET SCHIP**	**5 BÅDEN**
Below deck	**Sous le pont**	**Unter Deck**	**Onderdeks**	**Under dæk**
Domestic items & plumbing	*Equipement d'intérieur et tuyauterie*	*Wohnraum und Rohrleitungen*	*Huishoudelijke zaken en sanitair*	*Kahytsudstyr, VVS*
34 calorifier	34 échangeur de chaleur	34 Wärmespender	34 verwarming	34 varmeanlæg
35 cabin heater	35 appareil de chauffage de cabine	35 Kajütheizung	35 kajuitverwarming	35 varmeapparat
36 catalytic	36 catalytique	36 Katalytofen	36 katalytisch	36 katalytisk
37 flue/chimney	37 conduite/cheminée	37 Rauchrohr	37 rookkanaal, schoorsteen	37 skorsten
38 duct	38 gaine	38 Kanal	38 kanaal, buis, leiding	38 kanal, rør
Galley	*Cuisine*	*Kombüse*	*Kombuis*	*Kabys*
1 pressure stove	1 réchaud à pétrole	1 Petroleumkocher	1 petroleumstel	1 tryk-komfur
2 pressure gauge	2 jauge de pression	2 Manometer	2 drukmeter	2 trykmåler
3 self-pricking	3 à déboucheur	3 automatische Düsenreinigung, selbstreinigend	3 automatische doorsteekinrichting	3 selvrensende
4 pricker	4 déboucheur	4 Pricker	4 doorsteekdraadje	4 rensenål
5 methylated spirits	5 alcool à brûler	5 Brennspiritus	5 spiritus	5 kogesprit
6 gas stove	6 réchaud à gaz	6 Propangaskocher, Gasherd	6 gasstel	6 gasovn
7 gas cylinder	7 bouteille	7 Gasflasche	7 gasfles	7 gasflaske
8 gimbals	8 à la Cardan	8 kardanische Aufhängung	8 cardanische ophanging	8 kardansk ophæng
9 sink	9 évier	9 Abwaschbecken	9 gootsteen	9 vask
10 plug	10 bouchon	10 Stöpsel	10 stop	10 prop
11 tap	11 robinet	11 Hahn	11 kraan	11 hane
12 washer	12 joint	12 Dichtungsring	12 leertje	12 pakning, skive
13 washing-up liquid	13 détergent	13 Abwaschmittel	13 afwasmiddel	13 opvaskemiddel
14 frying pan	14 poêle à frire	14 Bratpfanne	14 braadpan	14 stegepande
15 saucepan	15 casserole, poêlon	15 Kochtopf	15 steelpan	15 kasserolle
16 pressure cooker	16 casserole à pression, cocotte-minute	16 Schnellkochtopf	16 drukpan, snelkookpan	16 trykkoger
17 kettle	17 bouilloire	17 Kessel	17 ketel	17 kedel
18 tin/can	18 boîte en fer	18 Dose	18 blik	18 dåse
19 tin opener	19 ouvre-boîtes	19 Dosenöffner	19 blikopener	19 dåseåbner

ESPAÑOL	ITALIANO	PORTUGUÊS	TÜRKÇE	ΕΛΛΗΝΙΚΑ
5 EL BARCO	**5 LA BARCA**	**5 DO BARCO**	**5 TEKNE**	**5 ΤΟ ΣΚΑΦΟΣ**
Bajo cubierta	**Sotto coperta**	**Abaixo do convés**	**Güverte altında**	**ΜΕΣΑ ΣΤΟ ΣΚΑΦΟΣ**
Menaje y fontaneria	*Casalinghi e idraulica*	*Artigos domésticos e esgotos*	*İç donanım & su tesisatı*	*ΟΙΚΟΣΚΕΥΗ ΚΑΙ ΥΔΡΑΥΛΙΚΑ*
34 calorífero	34 scalda-acqua	34 calorífico	34 kalorifer	34 ΚΑΛΟΡΙΦΕΡ
35 calentador de cabina	35 calorifero in cabina	35 aquecedor	35 kamara ısıtıcısı/soba	35 ΘΕΡΜΑΣΤΡΑ ΚΑΜΠΙΝΑΣ
36 catalítico	36 catalitico	36 catalítico	36 katalitik	36 ΚΑΤΑΛΥΤΙΚΟΣ
37 tubo/chimenea	37 canna fumaria	37 chaminé	37 baca	37 ΚΑΠΝΟΔΟΧΟΣ
38 conducto	38 condotto	38 canalização	38 boru/hava borusu	38 ΑΕΡΑΓΩΓΟΣ
Fogón	*Cambusa*	*Cozinha de bordo*	*Kuzine, galey*	*ΚΟΥΖΙΝΑ*
1 cocina de petróleo	1 fornello a pressione	1 fogão de pressão	1 petrol ocağı	1 ΓΚΑΖΙΕΡΑ - ΦΟΥΡΝΟΣ
2 manómetro	2 manometro	2 manómetro de pressão	2 basınç göstergesi	2 ΜΑΝΟΜΕΤΡΟ
3 auto-limpiador	3 autopulitore	3 espevitador automático	3 basınca kendiliğinden yanan, otomatik yanan, ateşleyici	3 ΚΛΕΙΝΕΙ ΜΕ ΚΑΒΙΛΙΑ ΜΟΝΟ ΤΟΥ
4 punzón del quemador	4 scovolatore	4 agulha	4 ateşleyici	4 ΚΑΒΙΛΙΑ - ΓΛΩΣΙΔΙ
5 alcohol desnatural-izado	5 alcool denaturato	5 alcool para queimar	5 ispirto/yakılacak ispirto	5 ΜΕΘΥΛΟΠΝΕΥΜΑ
6 cocina de gas	6 stufa a gas	6 fogão a gás	6 gaz ocağı (LPG vs)	6 ΚΟΥΖΙΝΑ ΥΓΡΑΕΡΙΟΥ
7 cilindro, carga de gas	7 bombola di gas	7 cilindro, bidão do gás	7 gaz tüpü	7 ΦΙΑΛΗ ΥΓΡΑΕΡΙΟΥ
8 balancera, cardan	8 càrdano	8 suspensão cardan	8 yalpa çemberleri/ yalpalık	8 ΣΤΗΡΙΓΜΑΤΑ ΦΟΥΡΝΟΥ - ΑΝΤΙΖΥΓΙΑ
9 fregadero	9 lavello	9 lava-loiça	9 evye	9 ΝΕΡΟΧΥΤΗΣ
10 tapón	10 tappo	10 bujão, tampa	10 tıkaç, tıpa	10 ΤΑΠΑ ΝΕΡΟΧΥΤΗ
11 grifo	11 rubinetto	11 torneira	11 musluk	11 ΒΡΥΣΗ
12 arandela	12 guarnizione	12 anel, válvula da torneira	12 conta	12 ΠΛΥΝΤΗΡΙΟ
13 detergente	13 detersivo	13 detergente liquido para lavar a loiça	13 deterjan	13 ΥΓΡΟ ΠΛΥΣΙΜΑΤΟΣ
14 sartén	14 padella	14 frigideira	14 tava	14 ΤΗΓΑΝΙ
15 cacerola, cazo	15 tegame	15 panela	15 tencere	15 ΚΑΤΣΑΡΟΛΑ
16 olla de presión	16 pentola a pressione	16 panela de pressão	16 düdüklü tencere	16 ΧΥΤΡΑ ΤΑΧΥΤΗΤΟΣ
17 caldero	17 bricco	17 chaleira	17 çaydanlık	17 ΤΣΑΓΙΕΡΑ
18 lata/bote	18 lattina	18 lata	18 kutu, konserve	18 ΚΟΝΣΕΡΒΑ
19 abrelatas	19 apriscatole	19 abre-latas	19 kutu açacağı	19 ΑΝΟΙΚΤΗΡΙ ΚΟΝΣΕΡΒΑΣ

ENGLISH	FRANÇAIS	DEUTSCH	NEDERLANDS	DANSK
5 THE BOAT	**5 LE BATEAU**	**5 DAS BOOT**	**5 DE BOOT, HET SCHIP**	**5 BÅDEN**
Below deck	**Sous le pont**	**Unter Deck**	**Onderdeks**	**Under dæk**
Galley	*Cuisine*	*Kombüse*	*Kombuis*	*Kabys*
20 bottle	20 bouteille	20 Flasche	20 fles	20 flaske
21 corkscrew	21 tire-bouchon	21 Korkenzieher	21 kurketrekker	21 proptrækker
22 matches	22 allumettes	22 Streichhölzer	22 lucifers	22 tændstikker
23 salt	23 sel	23 Salz	23 zout	23 salt
24 pepper	24 poivre	24 Pfeffer	24 peper	24 peber
25 mustard	25 moutarde	25 Senf	25 mosterd	25 sennep
26 water	26 eau	26 Wasser	26 water	26 vand
27 jerrycan	27 jerrycan/bidon	27 Brennstoffkanister	27 jerrycan	27 dunk
28 seawater pump	28 pompe à eau de mer	28 Seewasserpumpe	28 buitenboordpomp	28 saltvandspumpe
29 gas alarm	29 alarme anti-gaz	29 Gasmelder	29 gasalarm	29 gasalarm
30 fire blanket	30 couverture anti-feu	30 Feuerlöschdecke	30 brand-afdekdeken	30 brandtæppe
31 grill pan	31 plat à grill	31 Bratpfanne	31 braadpan	31 grillpande
32 gas burner	32 brûleur à gaz	32 Gasbrenner	32 gasbrander	32 gasblus
33 oven	33 four	33 Backofen	33 oven	33 ovn
34 pressure	34 pression	34 Druck	34 druk	34 tryk
Interior lighting	*Eclairage intérieur*	*Innenbeleuchtung*	*Binnenverlichting*	*Belysning*
1 candle	1 bougie	1 Kerze	1 kaars	1 stearinlys
2 paraffin lamp	2 lampe à pétrole	2 Petroleumlampe	2 petroleumlamp	2 petroleumslampe
3 chimney	3 verre	3 Zylinder	3 lampeglas	3 lampeglas
4 vaporizing lamp, Tilley	4 lampe à pression	4 Petroleumdrucklampe	4 petroleumgaslamp	4 Optimus lampe
5 mantle	5 manchon	5 Glühstrumpf	5 kousje	5 glødenet
6 electric torch	6 torche électrique	6 Taschenlampe, Stablampe	6 zaklantaarn	6 lommelygte
7 dry battery	7 pile sèche	7 Trockenbatterie	7 batterij	7 tørbatteri
8 bulb	8 ampoule	8 Glühlampe	8 lamp	8 elektrisk pære
9 wick	9 mèche	9 Docht	9 kousje voor gaslamp	9 væge
10 nightlights	10 veilleuses	10 Nachtleuchten	10 nachtverlichting	10 natbelysning

ESPAÑOL	ITALIANO	PORTUGUÊS	TÜRKÇE	ΕΛΛΗΝΙΚΑ
5 EL BARCO	**5 LA BARCA**	**5 DO BARCO**	**5 TEKNE**	**5 ΤΟ ΣΚΑΦΟΣ**

Bajo cubierta	**Sotto coperta**	**Abaixo do convés**	**Güverte Altında**	**ΜΕΣΑ ΣΤΟ ΣΚΑΦΟΣ**
Fogón	***Cambusa***	***Cozinha de bordo***	***Kuzine, galey***	*ΚΟΥΖΙΝΑ*
20 botella	20 bottiglia	20 garrafa	20 şişe	20 ΜΠΟΥΚΑΛΙ
21 sacacorchos	21 cavatappi	21 saca-rolhas	21 tirbuşon	21 ΤΙΡΜΠΟΥΣΟΝ
22 cerillas	22 fiammiferi	22 fósforos	22 kibrit	22 ΣΠΙΡΤΑ
23 sal	23 sale	23 sal	23 tuz	23 ΑΛΑΤΙ
24 pimienta	24 pepe	24 pimenta	24 karabiber	24 ΠΙΠΕΡΙ
25 mostaza	25 mostarda	25 mustarda	25 hardal	25 ΜΟΥΣΤΑΡΔΑ
26 agua	26 acqua	26 àgua	26 su	26 ΝΕΡΟ
27 lata	27 tanica	27 depósito/jerrican	27 bidon	27 ΚΑΝΙΣΤΡΟ
28 bomba de agua de mar	28 pompa per acqua di mare	28 bomba de àgua salgada	28 deniz suyu pompası	28 ΑΝΤΛΙΑ ΘΑΛΑΣΣΗΣ
29 alarme de gas	29 allarme anti-gas	29 alarme de gás	29 gaz kaçağı alarmı	29 ΣΥΝΑΓΕΡΜΟΣ ΥΓΡΑΕΡΙΟΥ
30 manta ignifugas	30 coperta antincendio	30 pano incombustivel	30 yangın battaniyesi/alev battaniyesi	30 ΠΥΡΟΣΒΕΣΤΙΚΗ ΚΟΥΒΕΡΤΑ
31 parrilla	31 griglia	31 grelhadeira	31 izgara	31 ΠΛΑΚΑ ΨΗΣΙΜΑΤΟΣ
32 mechero de gas	32 bruciatore a gas	32 queimador	32 brülör/gaz beki	32 ΜΑΤΙ ΓΚΑΖΙΟΥ
33 horno	33 forno	33 forno	33 fırın	33 ΦΟΥΡΝΟΣ
34 presión	34 pressione	34 pressão	34 basınç	34 ΠΙΕΣΗ
Alumbrado interior	***Illuminazione interna***	***Iluminação interior***	***Işıklandırma***	*ΕΣΩΤΕΡΙΚΟΣ ΦΩΤΙΣΜΟΣ*
1 vela	1 candela	1 vela	1 mum	1 ΚΕΡΙ
2 lámpara de petróleo	2 lampada a petrolio	2 candieiro de petróleo	2 petrol lambası	2 ΛΑΜΠΑ ΠΕΤΡΕΛΑΙΟΥ
3 mambrú, tubo de chimenea	3 vetro (di lampada a petrolio)	3 vidro ou chaminé	3 lamba şişesi	3 ΚΑΠΝΟΔΟΧΟΣ / ΓΥΑΛΙ ΛΑΜΠΑΣ
4 lámpara de vapor	4 lampada a vapori di petrolio	4 candieiro de pressão	4 lüks lambası, tilley	4 ΛΟΥΞ
5 camisa	5 reticella	5 camisa	5 manşon, lüks lambası gömleği	5 ΑΜΙΑΝΤΟΣ
6 linterna	6 torcia elettrica	6 lanterna eléctrica portátil	6 pilli el feneri	6 ΦΑΚΟΣ
7 pila seca	7 batteria a secco	7 pilha sêca	7 kuru pil	7 ΜΠΑΤΑΡΙΑ
8 bombilla	8 lampadina	8 lâmpada	8 ampul	8 ΛΑΜΠΑΚΙ
9 mecha	9 stoppino	9 pavio	9 fitil	9 ΦΙΤΙΛΙ
10 lamparilla	10 luci notturne	10 luzes nocturnas	10 gece ışıkları	10 ΦΩΤΑ ΝΥΧΤΟΣ

ENGLISH	FRANÇAIS	DEUTSCH	NEDERLANDS	DANSK
5 THE BOAT	**5 LE BATEAU**	**5 DAS BOOT**	**5 DE BOOT, HET SCHIP**	**5 BÅDEN**
Dinghy, tender	**Annexe, youyou**	**Beiboot**	**Bijboot**	**Jolle**
1 oar, scull, sweep	1 aviron, rame, godille	1 Riemen	1 roeiriem	1 åre, vrikkeåre, styreåre
2 rowlock	2 dame de nage	2 Dolle, Zepter, Rundsel	2 dol	2 åregaffel
3 painter	3 bosse	3 Fangleine	3 vanglijn	3 fangline
4 fender	4 bourrelet, boudin	4 Wieling	4 fender, kabelaring	4 fender
5 bow or nose fender	5 défense d'étrave	5 Maus, Bugfender	5 leguaan, boegfender	5 stævnfender
6 bottom boards	6 plancher	6 Bodenbretter	6 buikdenning	6 bundbrædder
7 gunwale	7 plat-bord	7 Dollbord	7 dolboord	7 lønning
8 thwart	8 banc	8 Ducht	8 doft	8 tofte
9 to scull	9 godiller	9 wriggen	9 wrikken	9 at vrikke
10 to tow	10 remorquer	10 schleppen	10 slepen	10 at slæbe
11 to row	11 nager, ramer	11 pullen, rudern	11 roeien	11 at ro
12 outboard bracket	12 support de hors-bord	12 Außenborderhalterung	12 console voor buitenboordmotor	12 påhængsmotorbeslag
13 inflatable	13 pneumatique	13 aufblasbar	13 opblaasbaar	13 gummibåd, oppustelig
14 rigid	14 rigide	14 steif	14 hard, stijf	14 fast
15 pram	15 prame	15 Prahm	15 praam	15 pram
Flags	**Pavillons**	**Flaggen**	**Vlaggen**	**Flag**
1 ensign	1 pavillon	1 Nationalflagge	1 natievlag	1 nationalflag
2 burgee	2 guidon	2 Clubstander	2 clubstandaard	2 stander
3 pennant	3 flamme	3 Wimpel	3 wimpel	3 vimpel
4 racing flag	4 pavillon de course	4 Rennflagge	4 wedstrijdvlag	4 kapsejladsflag, ejerstander
5 courtesy ensign	5 pavillon de courtoisie, pavillon du pays visité	5 Gastflagge	5 gastvlag	5 høflighedsflag
6 flagstaff	6 mât de pavillon	6 Flaggenstock	6 vlaggestok	6 flagspil
7 burgee stick	7 digon, hampe de fanion	7 Standerstock	7 trommelstok	7 standerspil
8 to dress ship overall	8 envoyer le grand pavois	8 Flaggengala, über die Toppen flaggen	8 pavoiseren	8 flage over top
9 to dip the ensign	9 saluer	9 dippen	9 groeten met de vlag	9 kippe med flaget
10 half mast	10 en berne	10 halbstock	10 halfstok	10 flage på halv

ESPAÑOL	ITALIANO	PORTUGUÊS	TÜRKÇE	ΕΛΛΗΝΙΚΑ
5 EL BARCO	**5 LA BARCA**	**5 DO BARCO**	**5 TEKNE**	**5 ΤΟ ΣΚΑΦΟΣ**
Chinchorro, bote	**Battellino, tender**	**Côco, escaler**	**Dingi, bot**	**ΒΑΡΚΑΚΙ**
1 remo, remo de singar, espadilla	1 remo, bratto	1 remo	1 kürek, boyna küreği	1 ΚΟΥΠΙ
2 tolete, horquilla	2 scalmo	2 forqueta	2 ayıskarmoz	2 ΣΚΑΡΜΟΣ
3 boza	3 barbetta	3 boça	3 pruva halatı	3 ΣΧΟΙΝΙ
4 defensa	4 parabordo	4 defensa, molhelha	4 usturmaça	4 ΜΠΑΛΟΝΙ
5 defensa de proa	5 parabordo di prua	5 molhelha da prôa	5 pruva usturmaçası	5 ΜΠΑΛΟΝΙ ΠΛΩΡΗΣ
6 cuartel, enjaretado	6 pagliolo	6 paneiros	6 farşlar	6 ΠΑΤΩΜΑ ΒΑΡΚΑΣ
7 borda, regala	7 capodibanda, parapetto	7 alcatrate, borda	7 küpeşte, filika küpeştesi	7 ΚΟΥΠΑΣΤΗ
8 bancada	8 banco	8 banco, bancada	8 oturak	8 ΕΓΚΑΡΣΙΟ ΚΑΘΙΣΜΑ
9 singar	9 brattare	9 remar á gingar	9 boyna küreğiyle yürütmek	9 ΚΩΠΗΛΑΤΩ
10 remolcar	10 rimorchiare	10 rebocar	10 yedek çekme	10 ΡΥΜΟΥΛΚΩ
11 bogar, remar	11 remare, vogare	11 remar	11 kürek çekmek	11 ΚΩΠΗΛΑΤΩ
12 soporte para motor fueraborda	12 staffa per fuoribordo	12 polé de borda fora	12 takma motor braketi	12 ΒΑΣΗ ΕΞΩΛΕΜΒΙΑΣ
13 bote neumático	13 gonfiabile	13 inflável	13 şişme	13 ΦΟΥΣΚΩΤΗ
14 rigido	14 rigido	14 rígido	14 sert	14 ΑΚΑΜΠΤΗ
15 chinchorro	15 pram	15 carrinho	15 pram	15 ΒΑΡΚΙ
Banderas	**Bandiere**	**Bandeiras**	**Bayraklar**	**ΣΗΜΑΙΕΣ**
1 pabellón	1 bandiera	1 bandeira nacional	1 ulusal bayrak	1 ΣΗΜΑΙΑ ΕΘΝΙΚΗ
2 grímpola	2 guidone	2 galhardete	2 flama, üç köşeli	2 ΕΠΙΣΕΙΩΝ ΟΜΙΛΟΥ
3 gallardete	3 fiamma, pennello	3 flâmula	3 flama	3 ΕΠΙΣΕΙΩΝ ΙΔΙΟΚΤΗΤΗ
4 grimpolón	4 bandiera da regata	4 galhardete de regata	4 yarış bayrağı	4 ΕΠΙΣΕΙΩΝ ΑΓΩΝΩΝ
5 bandera de cortesía, pabellón extranjero	5 bandiera di cortesia	5 bandeira de cortesia	5 nezaket bayrağı, ziyaret olunan ülke bayrağı	5 ΣΗΜΑΙΑ ΕΠΙΣΚΕΠΤΟΜΕΝΗΣ ΧΩΡΑΣ
6 asta de bandera	6 asta della bandiera	6 pau de bandeira	6 bayrak gönderi	6 ΚΟΝΤΑΡΙ ΣΗΜΑΙΑΣ
7 asta de grimpola	7 asta del guidone	7 pau do galhardete	7 gidon çubuğu	7 ΚΟΝΤΑΡΙ ΕΠΙΣΕΙΟΝΤΟΣ
8 engalanar el buque	8 pavesare la nave	8 embandeirar em arco	8 bayrak donanması	8 ΣΗΜΑΙΟΣΤΟΛΙΣΜΟΣ
9 guindamaina, saludar con la bandera	9 ammainare la bandiera	9 arriar a bandeira nacional para cumprimentar	9 bayrakla selâmlama	9 ΑΝΕΒΟΚΑΤΕΒΑΖΩ ΤΗΝ ΣΗΜΑΙΑ
10 a media asta	10 a mezz'asta	10 meia-haste	10 mezestre	10 ΜΕΣΙΣΤΙΑ

ENGLISH	FRANÇAIS	DEUTSCH	NEDERLANDS	DANSK
6 THE ENGINE	**6 LE MOTEUR**	**6 MASCHINE**	**6 DE MOTOR**	**6 MOTOREN**
Engine type & description	**Type de moteur et description**	**Maschinentyp und Beschreibung**	**Motortype en beschrijving**	**Motortype og beskrivelse**
1 two-stroke	1 à deux temps	1 Zweitakt	1 tweetakt	1 totakt
2 four-stroke	2 à quatre temps	2 Viertakt	2 viertakt	2 firetakt
3 petrol engine	3 moteur à essence	3 Benzinmotor	3 benzinemotor	3 benzinmotor
4 diesel engine	4 moteur diesel	4 Dieselmotor	4 dieselmotor	4 dieselmotor
5 engine serial number	5 numéro de série du moteur	5 Motorenseriennummer	5 motor-serienummer	5 serienummer
6 engine model number	6 numéro de modèle du moteur	6 Maschinentypnummer	6 motor-typenummer	6 modelnummer
7 number of cylinders	7 nombre de cylindres	7 Zylinderzahl	7 cilinderaantal	7 cylinderantal
8 cubic capacity	8 cylindrée	8 Zylinderinhalt	8 cilinderinhoud	8 slagvolumen
9 horsepower	9 cheval-vapeur	9 Pferdestärke	9 paardekracht	9 hestekræfter
Diesel engines	**Moteurs diesel**	**Dieselmotoren**	**Dieselmotoren**	**Dieselmotorer**
Parts	*Eléments de moteur diesel*	*Dieselmotorbauteile*	*Onderdelen*	*Maskininstallationen*
1 engine bed, seating	1 chaise, base du moteur	1 Motorfundament	1 fundatie	1 maskinfundament
2 mounting	2 console de suspension	2 Aufhängungskonsole	2 motorsteun	2 beslag
3 shims	3 épaisseurs	3 Unterlegscheibe	3 vulring	3 mellemlæg
4 throttle	4 accélérateur	4 Füllungshebel für Einspritzpumpe	4 brandstof-regelaar	4 gashåndtag
5 control cable	5 câble de contrôle	5 Bedienungsseil	5 morsekabel	5 kontrolkabel
6 gearbox	6 boîte de vitesses	6 Getriebekasten	6 tandwielkast	6 gearkasse
7 clutch	7 embrayage	7 Kupplung	7 koppeling	7 kobling
8 cylinder head	8 culasse	8 Zylinderkopf	8 cilinderkop	8 topstykke
9 cylinder block	9 bloc-cylindres	9 Zylinderblock	9 cilinderblok	9 cylinderblok
10 cylinder	10 cylindre	10 Zylinder	10 cilinder	10 cylinder
11 piston	11 piston	11 Kolben	11 zuiger	11 stempel
12 camshaft	12 arbre à came	12 Nockenwelle	12 nokkenas	12 knastaksel
13 pushrod	13 tige du culbuteur	13 Stoßstange	13 klepstoterstang	13 ventilløfter
14 rocker arm	14 culbuteur	14 Kipphebel	14 tuimelaar	14 vippearm
15 inlet valve	15 soupape d'admission	15 Einlaßventil	15 inlaatklep	15 indsugningsventil
16 exhaust valve	16 soupape d'échappement	16 Auslaßventil	16 uitlaatklep	16 udblæsningsventil

ESPAÑOL	ITALIANO	PORTUGUÊS	TÜRKÇE	ΕΛΛΗΝΙΚΑ
6 EL MOTOR	**6 IL MOTORE**	**6 DO MOTOR**	**6 MOTOR**	**6 ΜΗΧΑΝΗ**
Tipo de motor y descripción	**Tipo e descrizione del motore**	**Tipo do motor e descrição**	**Motor tipi & tanımı**	**ΤΥΠΟΣ & ΠΕΡΙΓΡΑΦΗ**
1 dos tiempos 2 cuatro tiempos 3 motor de gasolina 4 motor diesel 5 número de serie del motor 6 número de modelo del motor 7 número de cilindros 8 cilindrada 9 caballos de vapor CV	1 due tempi 2 quattro tempi 3 motore a benzina 4 motore diesel 5 numero di matricola del motore 6 numero di modello del motore 7 numero di cilindri 8 cilindrata 9 potenza	1 de dois tempos 2 de quatro tempos 3 motor a gasolina 4 motor diesel 5 número do motor 6 número do modelo do motor 7 número de cilindros 8 cilindrada 9 cavalos força	1 iki zamanlı 2 dört zamanlı 3 benzinli motor 4 dizel motor 5 motor seri numarası 6 motor model numarası 7 silindir adedi 8 silindir hacmi 9 beygir gücü	1 ΔΙΧΡΟΝΗ 2 ΤΕΤΡΑΧΡΟΝΗ 3 ΒΕΝΖΙΝΟΜΗΧΑΝΗ 4 ΠΕΤΡΕΛΑΙΟΜΗΧΑΝΗ 5 ΑΡΙΘΜΟΣ ΠΛΑΙΣΙΟΥ ΜΗΧΑΝΗΣ 6 ΑΡΙΘΜΟΣ ΜΟΝΤΕΛΟΥ ΜΗΧΑΝΗΣ 7 ΑΡΙΘΜΟΣ ΚΥΛΙΝΔΡΩΝ 8 ΚΥΒΙΣΜΟΣ 9 ΙΠΠΟΔΥΝΑΜΗ
Motores diesel	**Motori diesel**	**Motores diesel**	**Dizel motorlar**	**ΠΕΤΡΕΛΑΙΟΜΗΧΑΝΕΣ**
Partes de motores diesel 1 bancada, polin 2 soporte 3 suplemento 4 regulador 5 cable de control 6 caja de cambio 7 embrague 8 culata 9 bloque de cilindros 10 cilindro 11 émbolo 12 árbol de levas 13 varilla de distribución 14 balancin 15 válvula de admisión 16 válvula de escape	*Parti del motore diesel* 1 basamento del motore 2 supporto 3 spessori 4 acceleratore 5 cavetto di comando 6 cambio 7 frizione 8 testata 9 blocco cilindri 10 cilindro 11 pistone 12 alberino a camme 13 asta di comando del bilanciere 14 bilanciere 15 valvola d'aspirazione 16 valvola di scarico	*Peças dos motores diesel* 1 fixe do motor 2 suporte dos mancais 3 calços 4 acelarador 5 cabo de control 6 caixa de velocidades 7 embraiagem 8 cabeça do motor 9 bloco do motor 10 cilindro 11 pistão, êmbolo 12 árvore de cames 13 haste de comando do balancim 14 balancim 15 válvula de admissão 16 válvula de escape	*Dizel motor parçaları* 1 motor yatağı 2 motor kulağı 3 motor kulak pulları 4 gaz 5 Kumanda teli 6 Şanzıman, vites kutusu 7 kavrama 8 silindir kapağı 9 silindir bloku 10 silindir 11 piston 12 eksantrik mili 13 itme çubuğu 14 sallanma düzeni kolu 15 giriş supapı 16 egzost supapı	*ΜΕΡΗ* 1 ΒΑΣΗ ΜΗΧΑΝΗΣ 2 ΕΔΡΑΝΑ 3 ΣΦΗΝΕΣ ΖΥΓΟΣΤΑΘΜΙΣΗΣ 4 ΓΚΑΖΙΑ 5 ΝΤΙΖΑ ΧΕΙΡΙΣΜΟΥ 6 ΚΙΒΩΤΙΟ ΤΑΧΥΤΗΤΩΝ 7 ΣΥΜΠΛΕΚΤΗΣ 8 ΚΑΠΑΚΙ ΚΥΛΙΝΔΡΩΝ (ΜΗΧΑΝΗΣ) 9 ΣΩΜΑ ΜΗΧΑΝΗΣ 10 ΚΥΛΙΝΔΡΟΣ 11 ΠΙΣΤΟΝΙ 12 ΕΚΚΕΝΤΡΟΦΟΡΟΣ 13 ΒΑΛΒΙΔΑ 14 ΠΙΑΝΟΛΑ 15 ΒΑΛΒΙΔΑ ΕΙΣΑΓΩΓΗΣ 16 ΒΑΛΒΙΔΑ ΕΞΑΓΩΓΗΣ

ENGLISH	FRANÇAIS	DEUTSCH	NEDERLANDS	DANSK
6 THE ENGINE	**6 LE MOTEUR**	**6 MASCHINE**	**6 DE MOTOR**	**6 MOTOREN**
Diesel engines	**Moteurs diesel**	**Dieselmotoren**	**Diesel motoren**	**Dieselmotorer**
Parts	*Eléments de moteur diesel*	*Dieselmotorbauteile*	*Onderdelen*	*Maskininstallationen*
17 valve spring	17 ressort de soupape	17 Ventilfeder	17 klepveer	17 ventilfjeder
18 valve seat	18 siège de soupape	18 Ventilsitz	18 klepzitting	18 ventilsæde
19 valve guide	19 guide de soupape	19 Ventilführung	19 klepgeleider	19 ventilstyr
20 injection pump	20 pompe à injection	20 Einspritzpumpe	20 injectiepomp	20 insprøjtningspumpe
21 decompressor	21 décompresseur	21 Dekompressions-einrichtung	21 decompressor	21 dekompressor
22 crankcase	22 carter	22 Kurbelgehäuse	22 carter	22 krumtaphus
23 crankshaft	23 vilebrequin	23 Kurbelwelle	23 krukas	23 krumtapaksel
24 flywheel	24 volant	24 Schwungrad	24 vliegwiel	24 svinghjul
25 sump	25 carter à huile	25 Ölwanne	25 oliecarter	25 bundkar
26 dipstick	26 jauge d'huile	26 Ölmeßstab	26 oliepeilstok	26 målepind-olie
27 oil-filler cap	27 bouchon	27 Öleinfüllverschluß	27 olievuldop	27 hætte til oliepåfyldning
28 oil filter	28 filtre à huile	28 Ölfilter	28 oliefilter	28 oliefilter
29 oil drain	29 vidange d'huile	29 Ölablaß	29 olieaftap	29 olieprop
30 oil pump	30 pompe à huile	30 Ölpumpe	30 oliepomp	30 oliepumpe
31 air intake	31 prise d'air	31 Lufteinlaß	31 luchtinlaat	31 luftindtag
32 air filter	32 filtre à air	32 Luftfilter	32 luchtfilter	32 luftfilter
33 seacock	33 vanne	33 Seeventil	33 buitenboordkraan	33 søventil
34 water strainer	34 filtre à eau	34 Wasserfilter	34 waterfilter	34 vandfilter
35 raw water	35 eau brute	35 Seewasser	35 hard water	35 søvand
36 fresh water	36 eau douce	36 Süßwasser	36 zoet water	36 ferskvand
37 water pump	37 pompe à eau	37 Wasserpumpe	37 waterpomp	37 vandpumpe
38 header tank	38 collecteur de réservoir	38 Ausgleichstank	38 koelwater-druktank	38 fødetank
39 water filler cap	39 bouchon de prise d'eau	39 Wasserfüllstutzen	39 watervuldop	39 vandpåfyldning
40 waterjacket	40 chemise d'eau	40 Wassermantel	40 koelmantel	40 kølekapper
41 heat exchanger	41 échangeur thermique	41 Wärmetauscher	41 warmtewisselaar	41 varmeveksler
42 exhaust	42 tuyau d'échappement	42 Auspuffrohr	42 uitlaat	42 udblæsningsrør
43 silencer	43 silencieux	43 Schalldämpfer	43 geluiddemper, knalpot	43 lydpotte
44 starter motor	44 démarreur	44 Anlasser	44 startmotor	44 startmotor
45 solenoid	45 solénoide	45 Magnetspule	45 spoel	45 solenoide

ESPAÑOL	ITALIANO	PORTUGUÊS	TÜRKÇE	ΕΛΛΗΝΙΚΑ
6 EL MOTOR	**6 IL MOTORE**	**6 DO MOTOR**	**6 MOTOR**	**6 ΜΗΧΑΝΗ**
Motores diesel	**Motori diesel**	**Motores diesel**	**Dizel motorlar**	**ΠΕΤΡΕΛΑΙΟΜΗΧΑΝΕΣ**
Partes de motores diesel	*Parti del motore diesel*	*Peças dos motores diesel*	*Dizel motor parçaları*	*ΜΕΡΗ*
17 muelle de válvula	17 molla di valvola	17 mola de válvula	17 supap yayı	17 ΕΛΑΤΗΡΙΑ ΒΑΛΒΙΔΑΣ
18 asiento	18 sede di valvola	18 sede de válvula	18 supap yedeği	18 ΕΔΡΑΝΟ ΒΑΛΒΙΔΑΣ
19 guia	19 guida di valvola	19 guia de válvula	19 supap kılavuzu	19 ΟΔΗΓΟΣ ΒΑΛΒΙΔΑΣ
20 bomba de inyección	20 pompa d'iniezione	20 bomba de injecção	20 enjeksiyon pompası	20 ΑΝΤΛΙΑ ΨΕΚΑΣΜΟΥ
21 descompresor	21 decompressore	21 descompressor	21 dekompresyon vanası	21 ΑΠΟΣΥΜΠΙΕΣΤΗΣ
22 cárter	22 carter	22 carter	22 karter	22 ΚΑΡΤΕΡ
23 cigüeñal	23 albero a gomiti	23 cambota	23 krank mili, şaftı	23 ΜΑΝΙΒΕΛΛΑ
24 volante	24 volano	24 volante	24 volan	24 ΦΤΕΡΩΤΗ
25 cárter de aceite	25 coppa (dell'olio)	25 carter do óleo	25 yağ karteri	25 ΚΑΡΤΕΡ
26 varilla de sondar	26 astina del livello	26 vareta	26 yağ seviye çubuğu	26 ΔΕΙΚΤΗΣ ΛΑΔΙΟΥ
27 tapa de tanque de aceite	27 tappo del bocchettone dell'olio	27 tampa de entrada de óleo	27 yağ doldurma kapağı	27 ΚΑΠΑΚΙ ΦΙΛΤΡΟΥ ΛΑΔΙΩΝ
28 filtro de aceite	28 filtro dell'olio	28 filtro de óleo	28 yağ filtresi	28 ΦΙΛΤΡΟ ΛΑΔΙΟΥ
29 grifo de purga de aceite	29 drenaggio dell'olio	29 dreno do óleo	29 yağ boşaltma tapası	29 ΕΞΑΓΩΓΗ ΛΑΔΙΟΥ
30 bomba de aceite	30 pompa dell'olio	30 bomba de óleo	30 yağ pompası	30 ΑΝΤΛΙΑ ΛΑΔΙΟΥ
31 admisión de aire	31 presa d'aria	31 tomada de ar	31 hava girişi	31 ΕΙΣΑΓΩΓΗ ΑΕΡΑ
32 filtro de aire	32 filtro aria	32 filtro de água	32 hava filtresi	32 ΦΙΛΤΡΟ ΑΕΡΑ
33 grifo de fondo	33 presa d'acqua a mare	33 válvula de fundo	33 deniz suyu vanası/ Kinistin valfı	33 ΒΑΝΑ ΘΑΛΑΣΣΗΣ
34 filtro de agua	34 filtro dell'acqua	34 filtro	34 su süzgeci	34 ΦΙΛΤΡΟ (ΠΛΕΓΜΑ) ΝΕΡΟΥ ΘΑΛΑΣΣΗΣ
35 agua de mar	35 acqua sporca	35 água natural	35 deniz (göl) suyu	35 ΘΑΛΑΣΣΙΝΟ ΝΕΡΟ
36 agua dulce	36 acqua dolce	36 água doce	36 tatlı su	36 ΦΡΕΣΚΟ ΝΕΡΟ
37 bomba de agua	37 pompa dell'acqua	37 bomba de água	37 su pompası	37 ΑΝΤΛΙΑ ΝΕΡΟΥ
38 deposito de expansión	38 serbatoio collettore	38 depósito superior	38 makina su deposu	38 ΔΟΧΕΙΟ ΣΤΑΘΜΗΣ
39 tapon para rellenar agua	39 tappo bocchettone dell'acqua	39 tampão de enchimento de água	39 su doldurma tapası	39 ΚΑΠΑΚΙ ΓΙΑ ΣΥΜΠΛΗΡΩΜΑ ΝΕΡΟΥ
40 camisa	40 camicia d'acqua	40 camisa de água	40 suceketi	40 ΥΔΡΟΧΙΤΩΝΙΟ
41 intercambiador de calor	41 scambiatore di calore	41 permutador de calor	41 ısı eşanjörü	41 ΕΝΑΛΛΑΚΤΗΣ ΘΕΡΜΟΤΗΤΟΣ
42 tubo de escape	42 scappamento	42 tubo de escape	42 egzost	42 ΕΞΑΤΜΗΣΗ
43 silencioso	43 silenziatore	43 silencioso	43 susturucu	43 ΣΙΓΑΣΤΗΡΑΣ
44 motor de arranque	44 motorino d'avviamento	44 motor de arranque	44 marş motoru	44 ΜΙΖΑ
45 solenoide	45 solenoide	45 bobine	45 sarmal bobin	45 ΣΩΛΗΝΟΕΙΔΕΣ

ENGLISH	FRANÇAIS	DEUTSCH	NEDERLANDS	DANSK
6 THE ENGINE	**6 LE MOTEUR**	**6 MASCHINE**	**6 DE MOTOR**	**6 MOTOREN**
Diesel engines	**Moteurs diesel**	**Dieselmotoren**	**Dieselmotoren**	**Dieselmotorer**
Parts	*Eléments de moteur diesel*	*Dieselmotorbauteile*	*Onderdelen*	*Maskininstallationen*
46 starting handle	46 manivelle	46 Anlaßkurbel	46 startknop	46 starthåndtag
47 alternator	47 alternateur	47 Wechselstromgenerator	47 wisselstroomdynamo	47 omskifter
48 fuel filter	48 filtre à carburant	48 Brennstoffilter	48 brandstoffilter	48 brændstoffilter
49 glow plug	49 bougie incandescente	49 Glühkerze	49 gloeispiraal	49 glødestift
50 turbocharger	50 turbocompresseur	50 Turbolader	50 turbolader	50 turbocharger
Fuel supply	*Alimentation de carburant*	*Brennstoffversorgung*	*Brandstoftoevoer*	*Brændstofsystemet*
1 lift pump	1 pompe élévatoire	1 Förderpumpe	1 opvoerpomp	1 fødepumpe
2 fuel filter	2 filtre à carburant	2 Brennstoffilter	2 brandstoffilter	2 brændstoffilter
3 water-separating filter	3 séparateur d'eau	3 Wasserabscheider	3 waterseparatiefilter	3 vandudskillelsesfilter
4 injector	4 injecteur	4 Einspritzer	4 verstuiver, inspuiter	4 injector
5 nozzle	5 gicleur	5 Düse	5 verstuiver, sproeier	5 strålerør
6 to bleed	6 purger	6 entlüften	6 ontluchten	6 at udlufte
7 fuel tank	7 réservoir de carburant	7 Brennstofftank	7 brandstoftank	7 brændstoftank
8 jerrycan	8 jerrycan/bidon	8 Brennstoffkanister	8 jerrycan	8 dunk
9 funnel	9 entonnoir	9 Trichter	9 schoorsteen	9 tragt
Gearbox	*Boîte de vitesses/inverseur-réducteur*	*Getriebe*	*Tandwielkast*	*Gearkasse*
1 reverse and reduction	1 marche arrière et réduction	1 Umkehr- und Reduktionsgetriebe	1 achteruit en reductie	1 bak- & reduktionsgear
2 output shaft	2 arbre secondaire	2 Abtriebswelle	2 uitgaande aandrijfas	2 udgående aksel
3 input shaft	3 arbre primaire	3 Antriebswelle	3 inkomende aandrijfas	3 indgående aksel
4 dipstick	4 jauge d'huile	4 Meßstab	4 peilstok	4 målepind
5 control cable	5 cable de contrôle	5 Bedienungsseil	5 bedieningskabel	5 kontrolkabel

ESPAÑOL	ITALIANO	PORTUGUÊS	TÜRKÇE	ΕΛΛΗΝΙΚΑ
6 EL MOTOR	**6 IL MOTORE**	**6 DO MOTOR**	**6 MOTOR**	**6 ΜΗΧΑΝΗ**

Motores diesel	**Motori diesel**	**Motores diesel**	**Dizel motorlar**	**ΠΕΤΡΕΛΑΙΟΜΗΧΑΝΕΣ**
Partes de motores diesel 46 manivela de arranque 47 alternador 48 filtro de combustible 49 bujia de precalentamiento 50 turbocompresor	***Parti del motore diesel*** 46 manopola d'avviamento 47 alternatore 48 filtro carburante 49 candeletta 50 turbocompressore	***Peças dos motores diesel*** 46 manivela de arranque 47 alternador 48 filtro de gasóleo 49 bujão incandescente 50 compressor turbo	***Dizel motor parçaları*** 46 çalıştırma kolu 47 alternatör 48 yakıt filtresi 49 ısıtma bujisi 50 türbo kompresör	*ΜΕΡΗ* 46 ΜΑΝΙΒΕΛΛΑ 47 ΕΝΑΛΛΑΚΤΗΣ 48 ΦΙΛΤΡΟ ΚΑΥΣΙΜΟΥ 49 ΠΡΟΘΕΡΜΑΝΤΗΡΑΣ 50 ΤΟΥΡΜΠΟ
Suministro de combustible 1 bomba aspirante 2 filtro de combustible 3 separador 4 inyector 5 pulverizador 6 purgar 7 tanque de combustible 8 lata 9 embudo	***Rifornimento carburante*** 1 pompa a spostamento diretto 2 filtro del carburante 3 filtro separatore dell'acqua 4 iniettore 5 ugello 6 spurgare 7 serbatoio del carburante 8 tanica 9 imbuto	***Fornecimento de gasóleo*** 1 bomba de elevação 2 filtro de óleo 3 filtro de separação da àgua 4 injector 5 bocal 6 pingar 7 tanque de combustível 8 deposito/jerrican 9 funil	***Yakıt ikmali*** 1 yakıt pompası 2 yakıt filtresi 3 su ayırıcı filtre 4 enjektör 5 nozül 6 havasını almak 7 yakıt tankı 8 bidon 9 baca	*ΤΡΟΦΟΔΟΣΙΑ ΚΑΥΣΙΜΟΥ* 1 ΑΝΤΛΙΑ ΑΝΥΨΩΣΕΩΣ 2 ΦΙΛΤΡΟ ΚΑΥΣΙΜΟΥ 3 ΝΕΡΟΠΑΓΙΔΑ 4 ΨΕΚΑΣΤΗΣ 5 ΜΠΕΚ 6 ΕΞΑΕΡΩΝΩ 7 ΤΑΝΚΙ ΚΑΥΣΙΜΟΥ 8 ΚΑΝΙΣΤΡΟ 9 ΧΩΝΙ
Caja de cambio 1 inversor-reductor 2 árbol motor 3 árbol primario 4 varilla del nivel de aceite 5 cable de mando	***Scatola del cambio*** 1 inversione e riduzione 2 albero d'uscita 3 albero d'entrata 4 astina del livello 5 cavetto di comando	***Caixa de velocidades*** 1 inverter e reduzir 2 veio 3 veio 4 vareta 5 cabo de controle	***Şanjman/dişli kutusu*** 1 geri ve hız düşürücü/geri ve redüksiyon 2 çıkış şaftı 3 giriş şaftı 4 yağ seviye çubuğu 5 kumanda	*ΚΙΒΩΤΙΟ ΤΑΧΥΤΗΤΩΝ* 1 ΡΕΒΕΡΣΑ & ΜΕΙΩΤΗΡΑΣ 2 ΑΞΟΝΑΣ ΜΕΤΑΔΟΣΗΣ 3 ΑΞΟΝΑΣ ΜΗΧΑΝΗΣ 4 ΔΕΙΚΤΗΣ ΛΙΠΑΝΤΙΚΟΥ 5 ΝΤΙΖΑ ΧΕΙΡΙΣΜΟΥ

ENGLISH	FRANÇAIS	DEUTSCH	NEDERLANDS	DANSK
6 THE ENGINE	**6 LE MOTEUR**	**6 MASCHINE**	**6 DE MOTOR**	**6 MOTOREN**
Diesel engines	**Moteurs diesel**	**Dieselmotoren**	**Dieselmotoren**	**Dieselmotorer**
Instruments & controls	*Instruments et contrôles*	*Instrumente & Bedienungen*	*Instrumenten en besturingen*	*Instrumenter*
1 temperature gauge	1 thermomètre	1 Thermometer	1 temperatuurmeter	1 kølevandstermometer
2 oil-pressure gauge	2 manomètre d'huile	2 Öldruckmesser	2 oliedrukmeter	2 olietryksmåler
3 ammeter	3 ampèremètre	3 Amperemeter	3 ampèremeter	3 amperemeter
4 fuel gauge	4 jauge de combustible	4 Tankanzeige	4 brandstofmeter	4 brændstofmåler
5 tachometer	5 compte-tours	5 Drehzahlmesser	5 toerenteller	5 tachometer
6 water gauge	6 jauge d'eau	6 Wasserstandsanzeiger	6 watermeter	6 måleinstrument, vand
7 manifold pressure gauge	7 indicateur de pression d'admission	7 Mehrfachdruckmesser, Manometer	7 spruitstukdrukmeter	7 måleinstrument, manifold-tryk
8 warning light	8 lampe-témoin	8 Warnlicht	8 waarschuwingslampje	8 advarselslys
9 audible alarm	9 alarme sonore	9 akustischer Alarm	9 geluidsalarm	9 lydalarm
10 battery state indicator	10 indicateur de niveau de batterie	10 Batteriezustands-anzeiger	10 accuconditiemeter	10 batterimåler
11 starter switch	11 bouton de démarrage	11 Startschalter	11 startschakelaar	11 startkontakt
12 decompressor (stop)	12 décompresseur (arrêt)	12 Dekompressions-einrichtung	12 stopkabel, decompressor	12 stopknap
13 throttle	13 accélérateur, commande des gaz	13 Drosselventil	13 gashandel	13 gashåndtag
14 clutch	14 embrayage	14 Kupplung	14 koppeling	14 kobling
15 gear shift	15 levier de vitesse	15 Schalthebel	15 versnellingshandel	15 gearskift
16 control cable (Morse type)	16 câble de contrôle (type Morse)	16 Bedienungsseil (Typ Morse)	16 bedieningskabel (Morse)	16 kontrolkabel (Morse)

ESPAÑOL	ITALIANO	PORTUGUÊS	TÜRKÇE	ΕΛΛΗΝΙΚΑ
6 EL MOTOR	**6 IL MOTORE**	**6 DO MOTOR**	**6 MOTOR**	**6 ΜΗΧΑΝΗ**
Motores diesel	**Motori diesel**	**Motores diesel**	**Dizel motorlar**	**ΠΕΤΡΕΛΑΙΟΜΗΧΑΝΕΣ**
Instrumentos y mandos	*Strumenti e comandi*	*Instrumentos e controles*	*Aygıtlar & göstergeler*	*ΟΡΓΑΝΑ & ΕΛΕΓΧΟΙ*
1 termómetro	1 termometro	1 termómetro	1 termometre, Isı göstergesi	1 ΔΕΙΚΤΗΣ ΘΕΡΜΟΚΡΑΣΙΑΣ
2 manómetro de aceite	2 indicatore di pressione olio	2 manómetro de óleo	2 yağ basınç göstergesi	2 ΔΕΙΚΤΗΣ ΠΙΕΣΕΘΣ ΛΑΔΙΟΥ
3 amperímetro	3 amperometro	3 amperimetro	3 ampermetre	3 ΑΜΠΕΙΡΟΜΕΤΡΟ
4 manómetro de combustible	4 indicatore del carburante	4 indicador de combustivel	4 yakıt göstergesi	4 ΔΕΙΚΤΗΣ ΚΑΥΣΙΜΩΝ
5 taquímetro	5 tachimetro	5 conta rotações	5 takometre/devir göstergesi	5 ΤΑΧΥΜΕΤΡΟ
6 indicador de nivel de agua	6 indicatore di livello acqua	6 medidor de água	6 su göstergesi/ termometre	6 ΔΕΙΚΤΗΣ ΝΕΡΟΥ
7 indicador de presión del colector de escape	7 manometro del collettore	7 manómetro de pressão do colector	7 manifold basınç göstergesi	7 ΔΕΙΚΤΗΣ ΠΙΕΣΗΣ ΚΑΥΣΙΜΟΥ
8 señal visible de alarme	8 lampadina spia	8 luz de alarme	8 ikaz ışığı	8 ΠΡΟΕΙΔΟΠΟΙΗΤΙΚΗ ΛΥΧΝΙΑ
9 señal sonora de alarme	9 allarme sonoro	9 alarme sonoro	9 sesli alarm	9 ΗΧΗΤΙΚΟΣ ΣΥΝΑΓΕΡΜΟΣ
10 indicador de carga de batería	10 indicatore di carica batteria	10 indicador do estado da bateria	10 akü durumu göstergesi	10 ΔΕΙΚΤΗΣ ΚΑΤΑΣΤΑΣΗΣ ΜΠΑΤΑΡΙΑΣ
11 interruptor de arranque	11 comando d'avviamento	11 botão de arranque	11 marş düğmesi	11 ΔΙΑΚΟΠΤΗΣ ΕΚΚΙΝΗΣΕΩΣ
12 descompresor (stop)	12 decompressore	12 descompressor (parar)	12 dekompresyon (stop)	12 ΑΠΟΣΥΜΠΙΕΣΤΗΣ (ΣΤΟΠ)
13 acelerador	13 acceleratore	13 acelerador	13 gaz kolu	13 ΓΚΑΖΙΑ
14 embrague	14 frizione	14 embraiagem	14 kavrama	14 ΣΥΜΠΛΕΚΤΗΣ
15 palanca de cambios	15 cambio	15 alavanca de mudanças	15 vites değiştirme	15 ΑΛΛΑΓΗ ΤΑΧΥΤΗΤΩΝ (ΛΕΒΙΕΣ)
16 cable tipo Morse	16 cavetto di comando (tipo Morse)	16 cabo de controle (tipo morse)	16 kumanda teli (Morse tipi)	16 ΝΤΙΖΑ ΕΛΕΓΧΟΥ ΤΥΠΟΥ ΜΟΡΣ

ENGLISH	FRANÇAIS	DEUTSCH	NEDERLANDS	DANSK
6 THE ENGINE	**6 LE MOTEUR**	**6 MASCHINE**	**6 DE MOTOR**	**6 MOTOREN**
Petrol engines/outboards	**Moteurs à essence/ hors-bord**	**Benzinmotoren/ Außenbordmotoren**	**Benzinemotoren/ buitenboordmotoren**	**Benzinmotorer/ påhængsmotorer**
1 fuel tank	1 réservoir de combustible	1 Brennstofftank	1 brandstoftank	1 brændstoftank
2 fuel pump	2 pompe à combustible	2 Brennstoffpumpe	2 brandstofpomp	2 brændstofpumpe
3 air filter	3 filtre à air	3 Luftfilter	3 luchtfilter	3 luftfilter
4 carburettor	4 carburateur	4 Vergaser	4 carburateur	4 karburator
5 float chamber	5 cuve du flotteur	5 Schwimmerkammer	5 vlotterkamer	5 svømmehus
6 needle valve	6 pointeau	6 Nadelventil	6 vlotternaald	6 nåleventil
7 main jet	7 gicleur principal	7 Hauptdüse	7 hoofdsproeier	7 hovedstrålespids
8 slow-running jet	8 gicleur de ralenti	8 Leerlaufdüse	8 stationaire sproeier	8 tomgangsdyse
9 throttle, butterfly	9 papillon des gaz	9 Drosselklappe	9 smoorklep	9 gasspjæld, gashåndtag
10 mixture rich/lean	10 mélange, riche/pauvre	10 Gemisch, reich/mager	10 mengsel rijk/arm	10 blanding fed/mager
11 to adjust	11 régler	11 einstellen	11 afstellen	11 justere, indstille
12 sparking plug	12 bougie	12 Zündkerze	12 bougie	12 tændrør
13 to spark	13 faire une étincelle	13 Funken geben	13 vonken	13 gnistre
14 to fire	14 s'allumer	14 zünden	14 starten, aanslaan	14 tænde
15 ignition	15 ignition	15 Zündung	15 contact	15 tænding
16 points	16 vis platinées	16 Unterbrecherkontakt	16 contactpuntjes	16 spidser
17 magneto	17 magnéto	17 Magnetzünder	17 magneet	17 magneto
18 2-stroke	18 deux temps	18 zweitakt	18 tweetact	18 totakts
19 4-stroke	19 quatre temps	19 viertakt	19 viertakt	19 firetakts
20 choke	20 starter	20 Schoker, Anlaßhilfe	20 choke	20 choke
21 pull rope	21 cordelette de démarrage	21 Zugseil	21 trekkoord	21 startsnor
22 twist-grip throttle	22 poignée de commande	22 Drehgriffgashebel	22 gasgever op handvat	22 gashåndtag, vridbart
23 fuel tap	23 robinet de carburant	23 Brennstoffhahn	23 brandstofkraan	23 brændstofhane
24 gap	24 écartement	24 Elektrodenabstand	24 opening	24 åbning
25 condenser	25 condensateur	25 Kondensator	25 condensator	25 kondensator
26 distributor	26 delco	26 Verteiler	26 verdeler	26 fordeler
27 coil	27 bobine	27 Spule	27 spoel	27 tændspole

ESPAÑOL	ITALIANO	PORTUGUÊS	TÜRKÇE	ΕΛΛΗΝΙΚΑ
6 EL MOTOR	**6 IL MOTORE**	**6 DO MOTOR**	**6 MOTOR**	**6 ΜΗΧΑΝΗ**
Motores de gasolina/ fuerabordas	**Motori a benzina / fuoribordo**	**Motores a gasolina/ fora de borda**	**Benzinli, motorlar/takma motorlar**	**ΒΕΝΖΙΝΟΜΗΧΑΝΕΣ / ΕΞΩΛΕΜΒΙΕΣ**
1 tanque de combustible	1 serbatoio del carburante	1 depósito de combustivel	1 yakıt tankı	1 ΔΟΧΕΙΟ ΒΕΝΖΙΝΗΣ
2 bomba de alimentación	2 pompa del carburante	2 bomba de combustivel	2 yakıt pompası	2 ΑΝΤΛΙΑ ΒΕΝΖΙΝΗΣ
3 filtro de aire	3 filtro dell'aria	3 filtro de ar	3 hava filtresi	3 ΦΙΛΤΡΟ ΑΕΡΟΣ
4 carburador	4 carburatore	4 carburador	4 karbüratör	4 ΚΑΡΜΠΥΡΑΤΕΡ
5 cámara del flotador	5 vaschetta	5 câmara do flutador	5 şamandıra kabı	5 ΦΛΟΤΤΕΡ
6 válvula de aguja	6 valvola a spillo	6 válvula de nivel	6 karbüratör iğneciği	6 ΒΕΛΟΝΟΕΙΔΗΣ ΒΑΛΒΙΔΑ
7 surtidor principal	7 ugello principale	7 gicleur do máximo	7 ana meme	7 ΨΕΚΑΣΜΟΣ ΥΨΗΛΗΣ
8 surtidor de ralentí	8 ugello del minimo	8 gicleur do relantie	8 rölanti memesi	8 ΨΕΚΑΣΜΟΣ ΧΑΜΗΛΗΣ
9 mariposa	9 acceleratore	9 borboleta	9 gaz kelebeği	9 ΠΕΤΑΛΟΥΔΑ
10 mezcla, rica/pobre	10 miscela ricca, magra	10 mistura, rica/pobre	10 karışım, zengin/fakir	10 ΜΙΓΜΑ ΠΛΟΥΣΙΟ/ΦΤΩΧΟ
11 ajustar, reglar	11 regolare	11 para ajustar	11 ayar etmek	11 ΡΥΘΜΙΖΩ
12 bujía	12 candela	12 vela	12 buji	12 ΜΠΟΥΖΙ
13 echar chispas	13 far la scintilla	13 faiscar	13 çakmak, kıvılcım oluşturmak	13 ΣΠΙΝΘΗΡΙΖΩ
14 encender	14 accendersi	14 acender	14 ateşlemek	14 ΑΡΠΑΖΩ
15 encendido	15 accensione	15 ignição	15 yakmak, yakış	15 ΑΝΑΦΛΕΞΗ
16 contactos	16 puntine	16 pontos	16 platin	16 ΣΗΜΕΙΑ
17 magneto	17 magneto	17 magneto	17 manyeto	17 ΜΑΝΙΑΤΟ
18 dos tiempos	18 2 tempi	18 2 tempos	18 iki zámanlı	18 ΔΙΧΡΟΝΟ
19 cuatro tiempos	19 4 tempi	19 4 tempos	19 dört zamanlı	19 ΤΕΤΡΑΧΡΟΝΟ
20 el starter	20 valvola dell'aria	20 fechar o ar	20 jigle	20 ΑΕΡΑΣ
21 cabo de arranque	21 cavetto d'avviamento	21 puxar o cabo	21 çekme halatları/ çalıştırma halatı	21 ΣΧΟΙΝΑΚΙ ΕΚΚΙΝΗΣΗΣ
22 acelerador de puño	22 acceleratore a manopola	22 acelarador de punho	22 gaz kumandası kolda	22 ΓΚΑΖΙΑ ΣΤΗ ΛΑΓΟΥΔΕΡΑ
23 grifo del depósito de combustible	23 rubinetto del carburante	23 tampa de depósito	23 yakıt musluğu	23 ΤΑΠΑ ΒΕΝΖΙΝΗΣ
24 juego	24 distanza tra gli elettrodi	24 abertura	24 açıklık	24 ΑΠΟΣΤΑΣΗ
25 condensador	25 condensatore	25 condensador	25 kondansatör	25 ΣΥΜΠΥΚΝΩΤΗΣ
26 distribuidor	26 distributore	26 distribuidor	26 distribütör	26 ΝΤΙΣΤΡΙΜΠΥΤΕΡ
27 bobina	27 bobina	27 bobina	27 bobin	27 ΠΕΡΙΕΛΙΞΗ

ENGLISH	FRANÇAIS	DEUTSCH	NEDERLANDS	DANSK
6 THE ENGINE	**6 LE MOTEUR**	**6 MASCHINE**	**6 DE MOTOR**	**6 MOTOREN**
Engineering components	**Pièces mécaniques**	**Maschinenelemente**	**Technische onderdelen**	**Tilbehør**
1 screw	1 vis	1 Schraube	1 schroef	1 skrue
2 bolt	2 boulon	2 Bolzen	2 bout	2 bolt
3 nut	3 écrou	3 Mutter	3 moer	3 møtrik
4 locknut	4 contre-écrou	4 Gegen-, Sicherungsmutter	4 borgmoer	4 kontramøtrik
5 wing nut	5 vis papillon	5 Flügelmutter	5 vleugelmoer	5 fløjmøtrik
6 washer	6 rondelle	6 Unterlegsscheibe	6 ring	6 spændeskive
7 spring washer	7 rondelle élastique	7 Federring	7 veerring	7 fjederskive
8 spindle	8 broche	8 Spindel, Achse	8 spil	8 spindel
9 shaft	9 arbre	9 Welle	9 as	9 aksel
10 spring	10 ressort	10 Feder	10 veer	10 fjeder
11 lever	11 levier	11 Hebel	11 hefboom	11 vægtstang
12 bush	12 bague, buselure	12 Buchse	12 bus	12 bøsning
13 bearing	13 palier	13 Lager	13 lager	13 leje
14 ball bearing	14 roulement à billes	14 Kugellager	14 kogellager	14 kugleleje
15 split pin	15 goupille fendue	15 Splint	15 splitpen	15 split
16 gasket	16 garniture, joint	16 Dichtung	16 pakking	16 pakning
17 spacer	17 anneau d'écartement	17 Abstandsring	17 afstandsring	17 afstandsstykke
18 gear wheel	18 pignon	18 Zahnrad	18 tandwiel	18 tandhjul
19 belt	19 courroie	19 Riemen	19 riem	19 drivrem
20 pulley	20 poulie	20 Riemenscheibe	20 riemschijf	20 remskive
21 drain tap	21 robinet de vidange	21 Ablaßhahn	21 aftapkraan	21 tappehane
22 grease cup	22 pot de graissage	22 Schmierkopf	22 vetpot	22 fedtkop
23 self-tapping	23 vis Parker	23 selbstschneidend	23 zelftappend	23 selvtappende
24 V-belt	24 courroie trapézoidale	24 Keilriemen	24 V-snaar	24 kilerem
25 stainless steel	25 acier inoxidable	25 Edelstahl	25 roestvij staal (RVS)	25 rustfrit stål
26 mild steel	26 acier doux	26 Baustahl	26 vloeistaal, smeltijzer	26 stål
27 copper	27 cuivre rouge	27 Kupfer	27 koper	27 kobber
28 brass	28 cuivre jaune	28 Messing	28 brons, messing	28 messing
29 nylon	29 nylon	29 Nylon	29 nylon	29 nylon
30 grub screw	30 vís sans tête	30 Madenschraube	30 stífttap	30 grub skrue
31 O ring	31 joint torique	31 O-ring	31 O-ring	31 O ring

ESPAÑOL	ITALIANO	PORTUGUÊS	TÜRKÇE	ΕΛΛΗΝΙΚΑ
6 EL MOTOR	**6 IL MOTORE**	**6 DO MOTOR**	**6 MOTOR**	**6 ΜΗΧΑΝΗ**
Piezas de maquinaria	**Parti meccaniche**	**Componentes**	**Motor parçaları**	**ΜΗΧΑΝΟΛΟΓΙΚΑ ΕΞΑΡΤΗΜΑΤΑ**
1 tornillo	1 vite	1 parafuso	1 vida	1 ΒΙΔΑ
2 perno	2 bullone	2 parafuso de porca	2 cıvata	2 ΜΠΟΥΛΟΝΙ
3 tuerca	3 dado	3 porca	3 somun	3 ΠΑΞΙΜΑΔΙ
4 contratuerca	4 controdado	4 contraporca	4 kontra somun	4 ΠΑΞΙΜΑΔΙ ΑΣΦΑΛΕΙΑΣ
5 tuerca de orejas	5 galletto	5 porca de orelhas	5 kelebek somun	5 ΠΕΤΑΛΟΥΔΑ
6 arandela	6 rondella, rosetta	6 anilha	6 roleda, pul	6 ΡΟΔΕΛΛΑ
7 arandela de muelle	7 rondella elastica	7 anilha de mola	7 yaylı roleda	7 ΓΚΡΟΒΕΡ
8 eje	8 fuso, alberino	8 fuso	8 yatak, spindel	8 ΑΤΡΑΚΤΟΣ
9 eje, árbol	9 asse, albero	9 veio	9 şaft	9 ΑΞΟΝΑΣ
10 resorte, muelle	10 molla	10 mola	10 yay	10 ΕΛΑΤΗΡΙΟ
11 palanca	11 leva	11 alavanca	11 levye	11 ΛΕΒΙΕΣ
12 buje, casquillo	12 boccola	12 casquilho	12 yüksük	12 ΑΝΤΙΤΡΙΒΙΚΟΣ ΔΑΚΤΥΛΙΟΣ
13 cojinete	13 cuscinetto	13 chumaceira	13 yatak	13 ΚΟΥΖΙΝΕΤΟ
14 cojinete de bolas	14 cuscinetto a sfere	14 rolamento de esferas	14 bilyalı rulman	14 ΡΟΥΛΕΜΑΝ
15 pasador abierto, chaveta	15 coppiglia	15 troço	15 catal pin, kopilya	15 ΤΣΙΒΙ
16 empaquetadura junta	16 guarnizione	16 junta	16 conta	16 ΦΛΑΝΤΖΑ
17 anillo de distancia	17 distanziale	17 espaçador	17 arama halkası	17 ΔΙΑΧΩΡΙΣΤΗΣ
18 piñón, rueda dentada	18 ingranaggio	18 engrenagem	18 Pinyon, dişli	18 ΟΔΟΝΤΟΤΟΣ ΤΡΟΧΟΣ
19 correa	19 cinghia	19 correia	19 kayış	19 ΙΜΑΝΤΑΣ
20 polea	20 puleggia	20 roldana	20 mákara, kasnak	20 ΤΡΟΧΑΛΙΑ
21 válvula de drenage	21 rubinetto di drenaggio	21 torneira de drenagem	21 boşaltma musluğu	21 ΕΞΑΓΩΓΗ
22 engrasador	22 ingrassatore	22 copo de lubrificação	22 gresörluk	22 ΛΙΠΑΝΤΗΡ
23 autorroscante	23 autofilettante	23 autocolante	23 sac vidası	23 ΒΙΔΑ ΠΟΥ ΠΙΑΝΕΙ ΧΩΡΙΣ ΠΑΞΙΜΑΔΙ
24 correa de transmission en V	24 cinghia trapezoidale	24 correia em V	24 V-kayışı	24 ΙΜΑΝΤΑΣ ΤΡΙΓΩΝΙΚΟΣ
25 acero inoxidable	25 acciaio inossidabile	25 aço inoxidável	25 paslanmaz çelik	25 ΑΝΟΞΕΙΔΩΤΟ ΑΤΣΑΛΙ
26 acero dulce	26 acciaio dolce	26 aço maneável/ferro maneável	26 yumuşak çelik, yumuşak sac	26 ΑΠΛΟ ΑΤΣΑΛΙ
27 cobre	27 rame	27 cobre	27 bakır	27 ΧΑΛΚΙΝΟ
28 latón	28 ottone	28 bronze	28 sarı	28 ΜΠΡΟΥΤΖΙΝΟ
29 nilón	29 nylon, nailon	29 nylon	29 nylon	29 ΝΑΥΛΟΝ
30 tornillo sin cabeza	30 brugola	30 parafuso sem cabeça	30 sabitleme vidası	30 ΒΙΔΑ ΑΣΦΑΛΕΙΑΣ
31 arandela de goma	31 O ring	31 O ring	31 O ring	31 ΔΑΚΤΥΛΙΔΙ ΛΑΣΤΙΧΕΝΙΟ

ENGLISH	FRANÇAIS	DEUTSCH	NEDERLANDS	DANSK
6 THE ENGINE	**6 LE MOTEUR**	**6 MASCHINE**	**6 DE MOTOR**	**6 MOTOREN**
Engineering checks & repairs	**Vérifications et réparations mécaniques**	**Motorwartung und Reparatur**	**Technische controle en reparaties**	**Check og reparationer**
1 broken	1 cassé	1 gebrochen	1 gebroken	1 knækket
2 damaged	2 endommagé	2 beschädigt	2 beschadigd	2 beskadiget
3 worn	3 usé	3 abgenutzt	3 versleten	3 slidt
4 pitted	4 piqué	4 angefressen	4 ingevreten	4 tilsodet
5 blocked	5 bouché, bloqué	5 verstopft	5 geblokkeerd	5 blokeret
6 loose	6 desserré	6 lose	6 los	6 løs
7 to stall	7 caler	7 abwürgen	7 afslaan, vastlopen	7 at gå i stå
8 to leak	8 fuir, s'échapper	8 lecken	8 lekken	8 at lække
9 to oil	9 huiler, lubrifier	9 ölen	9 oliën, smeren	9 at smøre
10 to grease	10 graisser	10 schmieren	10 invetten	10 at smøre med fedt
11 to change the oil	11 faire la vidange d'huile	11 das Öl wechseln	11 de olie verversen	11 at skifte olie
12 to charge the battery	12 charger la batterie	12 Batterie aufladen	12 de accu laden	12 oplade batteri
13 to top up the battery	13 remplir la batterie	13 Batterie auffüllen	13 de accu bijvullen	13 fylde batteriet op
14 to overhaul	14 revision, mettre à neuf	14 überholen	14 reviseren, overhalen	14 at efterse
15 to test	15 vérifier	15 prüfen	15 testen	15 at prøve
16 to adjust	16 régler	16 einstellen	16 afstellen	16 indstille
17 to clean	17 nettoyer	17 reinigen	17 schoonmaken	17 at rense
18 to tighten	18 serrer, bloquer	18 anziehen	18 aandraaien	18 at stramme
19 to loosen	19 desserrer, libérer	19 nachlassen, lockern	19 losmaken, losdraaien	19 at løsne
20 to decarbonize	20 décalaminer	20 entkohlen	20 ontkolen	20 afkokse
21 to grind in valves	21 roder ou rectifier les soupapes	21 Ventile einschleifen	21 klep inslijpen	21 slibe ventiler
22 to bleed	22 purger d'air	22 entlüften	22 ontluchten	22 udlufte
23 to reline	23 regarnir	23 machschleifen, instandsetzen	23 uitlijnen	23 rette/line op
24 burnt	24 brûlé	24 verbrannt	24 verbrand	24 brændt
25 to check	25 vérifier	25 prüfen	25 controleren	25 kontrollere
26 to drain	26 vidanger	26 ablassen	26 aftappen	26 at tømme
27 temperature	27 température	27 Temperatur	27 temperatuur	27 temperatur
28 revolutions	28 tours	28 Umdrehungen	28 omwentelingen	28 omdrejninger
29 low	29 bas/basse	29 niedrig	29 laag	29 lav
30 high	30 élevé/élevée	30 hoch	30 hoog	30 høj
31 torque	31 couple	31 Drehmoment	31 koppel	31 drejningsmoment

ESPAÑOL	ITALIANO	PORTUGUÊS	TÜRKÇE	ΕΛΛΗΝΙΚΑ
6 EL MOTOR	**6 IL MOTORE**	**6 DO MOTOR**	**6 MOTOR**	**6 ΜΗΧΑΝΗ**
Revisiones y reparaciónes mecánicas	**Controlli e riparazioni del motorista**	**Testes e reparações**	**Motor kontrolleri ve tamirler**	**ΜΗΧΑΝΟΛΟΓΙΚΟΙ ΕΛΕΓΧΟΙ & ΕΠΙΣΚΕΥΕΣ**
1 roto	1 rotto	1 partido	1 kırık	1 ΣΠΑΣΜΕΝΟ
2 averiado	2 danneggiato	2 danificado	2 hasarlı	2 ΧΑΛΑΣΜΕΝΟ
3 gastado	3 usurato, consumato	3 gasto	3 eskimiş	3 ΦΘΑΡΜΕΝΟ
4 picado	4 vaiolato	4 picado	4 karıncalanmış	4 ΟΞΕΙΔΩΜΕΝΗ
5 obstruido	5 bloccato	5 obstruído	5 bloke/tıkalı	5 ΒΟΥΛΩΜΕΝΟ
6 flojo	6 lento	6 solto	6 gevşek	6 ΧΑΛΑΡΟ
7 detenerse	7 fermarsi	7 afogar, parar	7 sıkışmak/stop etmek	7 ΧΑΝΕΙ
8 gotear	8 perdere	8 perder líquido, verter	8 sızma	8 ΤΡΕΧΕΙ
9 lubricar	9 lubrificare	9 meter óleo	9 yağlamak	9 ΛΑΔΩΝΩ
10 engrasar	10 ingrassare	10 lubrificar	10 greslemek	10 ΓΡΑΣΑΡΩ
11 cambiar el aceite	11 cambiare l'olio	11 mudar o óleo	11 yağ değiştirmek	11 ΑΛΛΑΖΩ ΛΑΔΙΑ
12 cargar la batería	12 caricare la batteria	12 carregar bateria	12 bataryayı şarj etmek	12 ΦΟΡΤΙΖΩ ΤΗΝ ΜΠΑΤΑΡΙΑ
13 rellenar la batería	13 rabboccare la batteria	13 atestar bateria	13 bataryayı tam doldurmak	13 ΣΥΜΠΛΗΡΩΝΩ ΤΗΝ ΜΠΑΤΑΡΙΑ
14 revisiòn	14 revisionare	14 fazer revisão	14 revizyon, yenilemek	14 ΕΠΙΣΚΕΥΑΖΩ
15 probar	15 controllare	15 ensaiar	15 kontrol etmek	15 ΔΟΚΙΜΑΖΩ
16 ajustar, regular	16 regolare	16 regular	16 ayar etmek	16 ΡΥΘΜΙΖΩ
17 limpiar	17 pulire	17 limpar	17 temizlemek	17 ΚΑΘΑΡΙΖΩ
18 apretar	18 stringere	18 apertar	18 sıkmak	18 ΣΦΙΞΙΜΟ
19 aflojar	19 allentare	19 desapertar	19 gevşetmek, boşaltmak	19 ΛΑΣΚΑΡΙΣΜΑ
20 descarbonizar	20 disincrostare	20 descarbonisar	20 karbonu gidermek	20 ΞΕΚΑΠΝΙΣΜΑ
21 esmerilar las válvulas	21 smerigliare le valvole	21 rodar ou rectificar válvulas	21 supapları rektifiye etmek	21 ΤΡΙΨΙΜΟ ΒΑΛΒΙΔΩΝ
22 purgar	22 spurgare	22 sangrar	22 havasını almek	22 ΕΞΑΕΡΩΣΗ
23 renovar los forros	23 sostituire i ferodi	23 calçar de novo	23 balata yenilemek	23 ΕΥΘΥΓΡΑΜΜΙΣΗ
24 quemado	24 bruciato	24 queimado	24 yanmış	24 ΚΑΜΜΕΝΟΣ
25 revisar	25 verificare	25 verificar	25 kontrol etmek	25 ΕΛΕΓΧΟΣ
26 purgar	26 svuotare	26 drenagem	26 boşaltmak, suyunu boşaltmak	26 ΑΔΕΙΑΣΜΑ
27 temperatura	27 temperatura	27 temperatura	27 ısı	27 ΘΕΡΜΟΚΡΑΣΙΑ
28 revoluciones	28 giri	28 rotações	28 torna, devir, tur	28 ΣΤΡΟΦΕΣ
29 baja	29 basso	29 baixo	29 al çak	29 ΧΑΜΗΛΟ
30 alta	30 alto	30 alto	30 yüksek	30 ΥΨΗΛΟ
31 fuerza de torsión	31 coppia	31 aperto	31 burkulma emsali	31 ΡΟΠΗ

ENGLISH	FRANÇAIS	DEUTSCH	NEDERLANDS	DANSK
6 THE ENGINE	**6 LE MOTEUR**	**6 MASCHINE**	**6 DE MOTOR**	**6 MOTOREN**
Engineering checks & repairs	**Vérifications et réparations mécaniques**	**Motorwartung und Reparatur**	**Technische controle en reparaties**	**Check og reparationer**
32 friction 33 suction 34 pressure 35 combustion 36 compression	32 friction 33 aspiration 34 pression 35 combustion 36 compression	32 Reibung 33 Ansaugung 34 Druck 35 Verbrennung 36 Verdichtung	32 wrijving/frictie 33 zuiging 34 druk 35 verbranding 36 compressie	32 friktion 33 sug 34 tryk 35 forbrænding 36 kompression
Engine problems	**Problèmes de moteur**	**Maschinenprobleme**	**Motorproblemen**	**Motorproblemer**
1 will not start	1 ne démarre pas	1 startet nicht	1 start niet	1 vil ikke starte
2 flat battery	2 batterie à plat	2 erschöpfte Batterie	2 lege accu	2 batteriet er fladt
3 smoke	3 fumée	3 Rauch	3 rook	3 røg
4 black	4 noire	4 schwarz	4 zwart	4 sort
5 white	5 blanche	5 weiß	5 wit	5 hvid
6 blue	6 bleue	6 blau	6 blauw	6 blå
7 misfire	7 avoir des ratés d'allumage	7 Fehlzündung	7 niet aanslaan	7 tænder ikke
8 to idle unevenly	8 avoir un ralenti irrégulier	8 unregelmäßig laufen	8 stationair onregelmatig draaien	8 går ujævnt
9 to knock	9 cliqueter	9 klopfen	9 kloppen, tikken	9 banke
10 to overheat	10 surchauffer	10 überhitzen	10 te warm worden	10 overophedet
11 to lose power	11 perdre de la puissance	11 Leistung verlieren	11 vermogen verliezen	11 taber kraft
12 low oil pressure	12 pression d'huile basse	12 niedriger Öldruck	12 lage oliedruk	12 lavt olietryk
13 rising oil level	13 niveau d'huile en hausse	13 steigender Ölstand	13 oplopend oliepeil	13 stigende oliestand
14 to burn oil	14 consommer de l'huile	14 Öl verbrennen	14 olie gebruiken, olie verbranden	14 brænder olie
15 no fuel	15 manque de carburant	15 kein Brennstoff	15 geen brandstof	15 ingen brændstof
16 dirty fuel	16 carburant sale	16 verunreinigter Brennstoff	16 vuile brandstof	16 skidt i brændstoffet
17 air in fuel	17 air dans le carburant	17 Luft im Brennstoff	17 lucht in de brandstofleiding	17 luft i brændstoffet
18 water in fuel	18 eau dans le carburant	18 Wasser im Brennstoff	18 water in de brandstof	18 vand i brændstoffet
19 bacteria in fuel	19 bactéries dans le carburant	19 Bakterien im Brennstoff	19 bacteriën in de brandstof	19 bakterier i brændstoffet

ESPAÑOL	ITALIANO	PORTUGUÊS	TÜRKÇE	ΕΛΛΗΝΙΚΑ
6 EL MOTOR	**6 IL MOTORE**	**6 DO MOTOR**	**6 MOTOR**	**6 ΜΗΧΑΝΗ**
Revisiones y reparaciónes mecánicas	**Controlli e riparazioni del motorista**	**Testes e reparações**	**Motor kontrolleri ve tamirler**	**ΜΗΧΑΝΟΛΟΓΙΚΟΙ ΕΛΕΓΧΟΙ & ΕΠΙΣΚΕΥΕΣ**
32 fricción	32 attrito	32 fricção	32 sürtünme	32 ΤΡΙΒΗ
33 aspiración	33 aspirazione	33 aspiração	33 emme	33 ΑΝΑΡΡΟΦΗΣΗ
34 presión	34 pressione	34 pressão	34 basınç	34 ΠΙΕΣΗ
35 combustión	35 combustione	35 combustão	35 patlama	35 ΚΑΥΣΗ
36 compresión	36 compressione	36 compressão	36 sıkıştırma, kompresyon	36 ΣΥΜΠΙΕΣΗ
Problemas de motor	**Problemi al motore**	**Problemas do motor**	**Motor sorunları**	**ΠΡΟΒΛΗΜΑΤΑ ΜΗΧΑΝΗΣ**
1 fallo de arranque	1 non parte	1 não pega	1 çalışmıyor	1 ΔΕΝ ΞΕΚΙΝΑΕΙ
2 batería a cero	2 batteria scarica	2 bateria em baixo	2 batarya boş	2 ΑΔΕΙΑ ΜΠΑΤΑΡΙΑ
3 humo	3 fumo	3 fumo	3 duman	3 ΚΑΠΝΟΣ
4 negro	4 nero	4 preto	4 kara, siyah	4 ΜΑΥΡΟΣ
5 blanco	5 bianco	5 branco	5 beyaz	5 ΑΣΠΡΟΣ
6 azul	6 blu, azzurro	6 azul	6 mavi	6 ΜΠΛΕ
7 fallo de encendido	7 perdere colpi	7 ignição dificiente	7 çalışmıyor, ateşlemiyor	7 ΡΑΤΑΡΕΙ
8 ralenti no regulado	8 essere irregolare al minimo	8 funcionando de maneira irregular	8 rölantisi bozuk	8 ΑΝΩΜΑΛΟ ΡΑΛΑΝΤΙ
9 hacer explosiones	9 battere in testa	9 bater	9 vuruntu, darbelemek	9 ΚΤΥΠΑΕΙ
10 sobrecalentar	10 surriscaldare	10 sobreaquecer	10 fazla ısınma	10 ΥΠΕΡΘΕΡΜΑΙΝΕΤΑΙ
11 perder fuerza	11 perdere potenza	11 perder a potência	11 güç kaybetmek	11 ΧΑΝΕΙ ΙΣΧΥ
12 presion de aceite baja	12 bassa pressione dell'olio	12 baixa pressão de óleo	12 düşük yağ basıncı	12 ΧΑΜΗΛΗ ΠΙΕΣΗ ΛΑΔΙΟΥ
13 aumento de nivel de aceite	13 livello olio in aumento	13 subida do nível do óleo	13 yağ seviyesi yükseliyor	13 ΑΝΕΒΑΙΝΕΙ Η ΣΤΑΘΜΗ ΛΑΔΙΟΥ
14 quemar aceite	14 bruciare olio	14 a queimar, óleo	14 yağ yakmak	14 ΚΑΙΕΙ ΛΑΔΙ
15 falta de combustible	15 a secco di carburante	15 sem combustivel	15 yakıt yok, yakıt gelmiyor	15 ΟΧΙ ΚΑΥΣΙΜΑ
16 combustible sucio	16 carburante sporco	16 gasóleo sujo	16 pis yakıt	16 ΒΡΩΜΙΚΑ ΚΑΥΣΙΜΑ
17 aire en el combustible	17 aria nel carburante	17 ar no gasóleo	17 yakıtta hava	17 ΑΕΡΑΣ ΣΤΑ ΚΑΥΣΙΜΑ
18 agua en el combustible	18 acqua nel carburante	18 àgua no gasóleo	18 yakıtta su bulunması	18 ΝΕΡΟ ΣΤΑ ΚΑΥΣΙΜΑ
19 bacterias en el combustible	19 batteri nel carburante	19 bacterias no gasóleo	19 yakıtta bakteri	19 ΜΙΚΡΟΒΙΑ ΣΤΑ ΚΑΥΣΙΜΑ

ENGLISH	FRANÇAIS	DEUTSCH	NEDERLANDS	DANSK
6 THE ENGINE	**6 LE MOTEUR**	**6 MASCHINE**	**6 DE MOTOR**	**6 MOTOREN**
Engineer's stores	**Provisions de mécanicien**	**Vorräte des Maschinisten**	**Technisch magazijn**	**Reservedele**
1 petrol	1 essence	1 Benzin	1 benzine	1 benzin
2 paraffin/kerosene	2 kérosène, pétrole	2 Petroleum	2 petroleum/kerosine	2 petroleum
3 diesel oil	3 gas-oil, mazout	3 Dieselöl	3 dieselolie	3 dieselolie
4 engine oil	4 huile	4 Schmieröl	4 motorolie	4 motorolie
5 grease	5 graisse	5 Fett	5 vet	5 fedt
6 distilled water	6 eau distillée	6 destilliertes Wasser	6 gedestileerd water	6 destilleret vand
7 hydraulic fluid	7 liquide hydraulique	7 Hydrauliköl	7 hydraulische vloeistof	7 hydraulikvædske
8 antifreeze	8 anti-gel	8 Frostschutzmittel	8 antivries	8 frostvædske
9 methylated spirits	9 alcool à brûler	9 Brennspiritus	9 methylalcohol	9 denatureret sprit
10 filter element	10 éléments de filtre	10 Filter	10 filterelement	10 filterindsats
11 gasket	11 joint	11 Packung, Dichtung	11 pakking	11 pakning
12 anode	12 anode	12 Anode	12 anode	12 anode
13 jubilee clip	13 collier BC	13 Schlauchklemme	13 slangklem	13 slangebinder
14 adhesive tape	14 ruban adhésif/ chatterton	14 Klebestreifen	14 plakband	14 tape
15 hose	15 tuyau	15 Schlauch	15 slang	15 slange
16 drive belt	16 courroie d'entrainement	16 Treibriemen	16 aandrijfriem	16 drivrem
17 impeller	17 roue à ailettes	17 Impeller	17 impeller, waaier	17 impeller
18 diaphragm	18 diaphragme	18 Membrane	18 membraan	18 membran
19 thermostat	19 thermostat	19 Thermostat	19 thermostaat	19 termostat
20 sensor	20 détecteur	20 Fühler	20 voeler, sensor	20 føler
21 O ring	21 joint torique	21 O-Ring	21 O-ring	21 O-ring

ESPAÑOL	ITALIANO	PORTUGUÊS	TÜRKÇE	ΕΛΛΗΝΙΚΑ
6 EL MOTOR	**6 IL MOTORE**	**6 DO MOTOR**	**6 MOTOR**	**6 ΜΗΧΑΝΗ**
Suministros de maquinista	**Scorte del motorista**	**Lojas de motores/oficinas**	**Motorcu malzemesi**	**ΑΝΤΑΛΛΑΚΤΙΚΑ ΜΗΧΑΝΗΣ**
1 gasolina	1 benzina	1 gasolina	1 benzin	1 ΒΕΝΖΙΝΗ
2 petróleo/keroseno	2 petrolio/kerosene	2 petróleo	2 gazyağı/kerosen	2 ΚΗΡΟΖΙΝΗ
3 gasoil	3 gasolio	3 gasóleo	3 motorin	3 ΠΕΤΡΕΛΑΙΟ
4 aceite de motor	4 olio lubrificante	4 óleo de motor	4 motor yağı	4 ΛΑΔΙ ΜΗΧΑΝΗΣ
5 grasa	5 grasso	5 massa	5 gres yağı	5 ΓΡΑΣΣΟ
6 agua destilada	6 acqua distillata	6 água destilada	6 damıtık su	6 ΑΠΕΣΤΑΓΜΕΝΟ ΝΕΡΟ
7 aceite hidráulico	7 olio idraulico	7 óleo para sistema hidráulico	7 hidrolik yağı	7 ΥΓΡΟ ΥΔΡΑΥΛΙΚΩΝ
8 anticongelante	8 antigelo	8 anti-congelante	8 antifriz	8 ΑΝΤΙΨΥΚΤΙΚΟ
9 alcohol desnatural-izada	9 alcool denaturato	9 alcool metílico	9 alkol, ispirto	9 ΑΛΚΟΟΛΕΣ
10 elemento de filtro	10 elemento del filtro	10 filtro	10 filtre elemanı	10 ΦΙΛΤΡΟ
11 empaquetadura	11 guarnizione	11 anilha	11 conta	11 ΠΑΡΕΜΒΥΣΜΑ
12 ánodo	12 anodo	12 ânodo	12 tutya	12 ΑΝΟΔΙΟ
13 abrazadera	13 fascetta a vite	13 abraçadeira ajustável	13 kelepçe	13 ΑΓΚΙΣΤΡΟ
14 cinta aislante	14 nastro adesivo	14 fitá adesiva	14 yapışkan bant	14 ΑΥΤΟΚΟΛΛΗΤΗ ΤΑΙΝΙΑ
15 manguera	15 tubo flessibile	15 tubo	15 hortum	15 ΣΩΛΗΝΑΣ
16 correa de transmisión	16 cinghia di trasmissione	16 correia	16 transmisyon kayışı	16 ΙΜΑΝΤΑΣ ΚΙΝΗΣΗΣ
17 impulsor	17 girante	17 impeler	17 impeller/tulumba pervanesi	17 ΙΜΠΕΛΕΡ
18 diafragma	18 membrana	18 diafragma	18 diyafram	18 ΔΙΑΦΡΑΓΜΑ
19 termostato	19 termostato	19 termostato	19 termostat	19 ΘΕΡΜΟΣΤΑΤΗΣ
20 sensor	20 sensore	20 sensor	20 müşir	20 ΑΙΣΘΗΤΗΡΑΣ (ΣΕΝΣΟΡΑΣ)
21 arandela de goma	21 O ring	21 O ring	21 O ring	21 ΔΑΚΤΥΛΙΟΣ-ΚΟΥΛΟΥΡΙ

ENGLISH	FRANÇAIS	DEUTSCH	NEDERLANDS	DANSK
6 THE ENGINE	**6 LE MOTEUR**	**6 MASCHINE**	**6 DE MOTOR**	**6 MOTOREN**
Engineer's toolbox	**Boîte à outils de mécanicien**	**Werkzeuge des Maschinisten**	**Monteursgereedschappen**	**Værktøjskasse**
1 grease gun	1 pompe de graissage	1 Fettpresse	1 vetpomp	1 fedtsprøjte
2 oil can	2 burette à huile	2 Ölkanne	2 oliekan	2 smørekande
3 feeler gauge	3 calibre à lames (d'epaisseur)	3 Meßfühler	3 voelermaat	3 føler
4 wrench	4 clef à molettes	4 Schraubenschlüssel	4 schroefsleutel	4 skruenøgle
5 mole wrench	5 pince-étau	5 verstellbarer Maulschlüssel	5 engelse sleutel	5 skiftenøgle
6 stilson wrench	6 clef à pipes	6 Rohrzange	6 verstelbare (stilson) sleutel	6 stilsonnøgle
7 pliers	7 pinces	7 Zange	7 buigtang	7 tang
8 bolt cutters	8 coupe-boulon	8 Bolzenschneider	8 staaldraad-kniptang	8 boltsaks
9 open spanner	9 clef	9 Maulschlüssel	9 steeksleutel	9 gaffelnøgle
10 ring spanner	10 clef fermée	10 Ringschlüssel	10 ringsleutel	10 ringnøgle
11 box spanner	11 clef à douille	11 Steckschlüssel	11 dopsleutel	11 topnøgle
12 Allen key	12 clef Allen	12 Innensechskantschlüssel Imbusschlüssel	12 imbussleutel	12 Allen-nøgle
13 screwdriver	13 tournevis	13 Schraubendreher	13 schroevedraaier	13 skruetrækker
14 crosshead screwdriver	14 tournevis cruciforme	14 Kreuzschlitz-schraubendreher	14 kruiskop-schroevedraaier	14 stjerneskruetrækker
15 hammer	15 marteau	15 Hammer	15 hamer	15 hammer
16 vice	16 étau	16 Schraubstock	16 bankschroef	16 skruestik
17 soldering iron	17 fer à souder	17 Lötkolben	17 soldeerbout	17 loddekolbe
18 funnel with filter	18 entonnoir à filtre	18 Trichter mit Filter	18 schoorsteen met filter	18 tragt med filter

ESPAÑOL	ITALIANO	PORTUGUÊS	TÜRKÇE	ΕΛΛΗΝΙΚΑ
6 EL MOTOR	**6 IL MOTORE**	**6 DO MOTOR**	**6 MOTOR**	**6 ΜΗΧΑΝΗ**
Maleta de herramientas de maquinista	**Attrezzi del motorista**	**Caixa de ferramentas**	**Motorcu alet kutusu**	**ΕΡΓΑΛΕΙΑ ΜΗΧΑΝΙΚΟΥ**
1 engrasador a presión	1 ingrassatore	1 pistola de lubrificação	1 gres tabancası	1 ΓΡΑΣΣΑΔΟΡΟΣ
2 aceitera	2 oliatore	2 lata de óleo	2 yağ tenekesi	2 ΚΟΥΤΙ ΛΑΔΙ
3 calibres de huelgo	3 spessimetro	3 canivete de folgas	3 platin ayar çakısı	3 ΦΙΛΕΡΑΚΙ (ΒΑΛΒΙΔΩΝ ΡΥΘΜΙΣΗ)
4 llave inglesa	4 chiave	4 chave inglesa	4 somun	4 ΓΑΛΛΙΚΟ ΚΛΕΙΔΙ
5 alicates de presión	5 pinza autobloccante	5 chave inglesa de garras ajustáveis	5 iki ağızlı anahtar	5 ΑΥΞΟΜΕΙΟΥΜΕΝΟ-ΓΕΡΜΑΝΙΚΟ
6 llave stilson	6 chiave stringitubi	6 chave de tubos de garras ajustáveis	6 ayarlı anahtar	6 ΣΩΛΗΝΟΚΑΒΟΥΡΑΣ
7 alicates	7 pinze	7 alicate	7 pense	7 ΠΕΝΣΑ
8 cizalla de pernos	8 tagliabulloni	8 corta-cavilhas	8 cıvata keskisi, çapraz keski	8 ΚΟΦΤΗΣ
9 llave plana fija de boca	9 chiave a forchetta	9 chave inglesa de bocas abertas	9 açık anahtar	9 ΑΝΟΙΧΤΟ ΚΛΕΙΔΙ
10 llave de estrella	10 chiave poligonale	10 chave de anel	10 yıldız anahtar	10 ΔΑΚΤΥΛΙΟΕΙΔΕΣ ΚΛΕΙΔΙ
11 llave de tubo	11 chiave a tubo	11 chave de caixa	11 boru anahtar	11 ΓΟΥΒΩΤΟ ΚΛΕΙΔΙ
12 llave allen	12 chiave Allen, chiave per viti a sede esagonale	12 chave de Allen	12 allen anahtar	12 ΑΛΕΝ ΚΛΕΙΔΙ
13 destornillador	13 cacciavite	13 chave de fendas	13 tornavida	13 ΚΑΤΣΑΒΙΔΙ
14 destornillador para tornillos cruciforme	14 cacciavite con testa a croce	14 chave philips	14 yıldız tornavida	14 ΣΤΑΥΡΟΚΑΤΣΑΒΙΔΟ
15 martillo	15 martello	15 martelo	15 çekiç	15 ΣΦΥΡΙ
16 mordaza	16 morsa	16 tôrno, prensa	16 mengene	16 ΜΕΓΓΕΝΗ
17 soldador	17 saldatore	17 ferro de soldar	17 havya	17 ΚΟΛΛΗΤΗΡΙ
18 embudo con filtro	18 imbuto con filtro	18 funil com filtro	18 filtreli huni	18 ΧΩΝΙ ΜΕ ΦΙΛΤΡΟ

ENGLISH	FRANÇAIS	DEUTSCH	NEDERLANDS	DANSK
7 DRIVE SYSTEM	**7 SYSTEME DE PROPULSION**	**7 ANTRIEBSSYSTEM**	**7 AANDRIJFSYSTEEM**	**7 SKRUEINSTALLATION**
1 propeller, screw	1 hélice	1 Propeller, Schraube	1 schroef	1 propel/skrue
2 blade	2 pale	2 Flügel	2 schroefblad	2 blad
3 pitch	3 pas	3 Steigung	3 spoed	3 stigning
4 feathering propeller	4 hélice pouvant être mise en drapeau	4 Faltpropeller	4 klapschroef	4 sammenklappelig skrue
5 variable-pitch propeller	5 hélice à pas variable	5 Verstellpropeller	5 verstelbare schroef	5 vridbar skrue
6 right-handed	6 pas à droite	6 rechtsdrehend	6 rechts draaiend	6 højregang
7 left-handed	7 pas à gauche	7 linksdrehend	7 links draaiend	7 venstregang
8 stern tube	8 tube d'étambot	8 Stevenrohr	8 schroefaskoker	8 stævnrør
9 stern gland	9 presse-étoupe de tube d'étambot	9 Stevenrohrverschluß	9 schroefasgland	9 fedtkop
10 stuffing box	10 presse-étoupe	10 Stopfbuchse	10 pakkingbus	10 opbevaringskasse
11 propeller shaft	11 arbre d'hélice	11 Propellerwelle	11 schroefas	11 skrueaksel
12 flexible coupling	12 accouplement flexible	12 flexible Kupplung	12 flexibele koppeling	12 flexkobling
13 driven shaft	13 arbre entrainé	13 angetriebene Welle	13 doorboorde aandrijfas	13 drivaksel
14 P bracket	14 support d'hélice	14 Wellenlagerbock	14 schroefassteunlager	14 P bracket
15 cutless bearing	15 bague hydrolube	15 ungeteiltes Lager	15 buslager	15 leje
16 rope cutter	16 coupe-câbles	16 Leinenschneider	16 draadsnijder bij de schroef	16 kniv
17 key	17 clavette	17 Paßfeder für Wellennut	17 sleutel	17 nøgle

ESPAÑOL	ITALIANO	PORTUGUÊS	TÜRKÇE	ΕΛΛΗΝΙΚΑ
7 SISTEMA PROPULSORA	**7 SISTEMA DI PROPULSIONE**	**7 SISTEMA DE CONDUÇÃO**	**7 YÜRÜTME SİSTEMİ**	**7 ΣΥΣΤΗΜΑ ΠΡΟΩΘΗΣΗΣ**
1 hélice	1 elica	1 hélice	1 pervane	1 ΠΡΟΠΕΛΛΑ
2 pala	2 pala	2 lámina	2 kanat, pervane kanadı	2 ΦΤΕΡΟ
3 paso de la hélice	3 passo	3 passo	3 pitch	3 ΒΗΜΑ
4 hélice de palas movibles	4 elica con pale in bandiera	4 hélice com passo egulável	4 katlanan pervane	4 ΠΤΥΣΣΟΜΕΝΗ ΠΡΟΠΕΛΛΑ
5 hélice de paso variable	5 elica a passo variabile	5 hélice com passo variável	5 pitch kontrollü pervane	5 ΠΡΟΠΕΛΛΑ ΜΕΤΑΒΛΗΤΟΥ ΒΗΜΑΤΟΣ
6 paso a la derecha	6 destro	6 direito	6 sağa devirli	6 ΔΕΞΙΟΣΤΡΟΦΗ
7 paso a la izquierda	7 sinistro	7 esquerdo	7 şola devirli	7 ΑΡΙΣΤΕΡΟΣΤΡΟΦΗ
8 bocina	8 astuccio (dell'albero portaelica)	8 manga do veio	8 şaft kovanı	8 ΧΩΝΙ
9 prensa-estopa de la bocina	9 premistoppa	9 bucim	9 şaft kovanı, salmastra gleni	9 ΜΠΟΥΣΑ
10 prensa-estopa de la bocina	10 premibaderna	10 calxa do bucim, empanque	10 salmastra kutusu	10 ΣΤΥΠΙΟΘΛΙΠΤΗΣ
11 eje/árbol de la hélice	11 albero dell'elica	11 veio do hélice	11 pervane şaftı, şaft	11 ΑΞΟΝΑΣ ΠΡΟΠΕΛΛΑΣ
12 acoplamiento flexible	12 giunto flessibile	12 acopulamento flexível	12 elastiki kaplin	12 ΕΥΛΥΓΙΣΤΗ ΕΝΩΣΗ
13 el árbol motor	13 albero condotto	13 velo motor	13 makina şaft kaplini	13 ΑΞΟΝΑΣ
14 soporte del eje de la hélice	14 staffa dell'elica	14 poleé em P	14 braket, şaft kaplini	14 Π-ΜΠΡΑΤΣΟ
15 casquillo	15 cuscinetto premistoppa	15 mancal do cutelo	15 yatak, şaft yatağı	15 ΤΟΞΟΕΙΔΕΣ ΡΟΥΛΕΜΑΝ
16 cortacables de la hélice	16 lama taglialenze	16 corta-cabos	16 halat kesme mahmuzu	16 ΚΟΦΤΗΣ ΣΚΟΙΝΙΟΥ
17 chaveta	17 chiavetta	17 chave	17 anahtar, kilit anahtarı	17 ΚΛΕΙΔΙ

ENGLISH	FRANÇAIS	DEUTSCH	NEDERLANDS	DANSK
8 STEERING SYSTEM	**8 APPAREILS A GOUVERNER**	**8 STEUERUNGSANLAGE**	**8 STUUR SYSTEEM**	**8 STYRESYSTEM**
1 wheel	1 barre à roue	1 Steuerrad	1 stuurwiel	1 rat
2 tiller	2 barre franche	2 Pinne	2 helmstok	2 rorpind
3 rudder	3 gouvernail/safran	3 Ruder	3 roer	3 ror
4 balanced rudder	4 gouvernail compensé	4 Balanceruder	4 balansroer	4 balanceror
5 spade rudder	5 safran à pelle	5 Spatenruder	5 plaatroer	5 spaderor
6 gudgeon	6 fémelot	6 Lagerzapfen	6 penborg	6 rorløkke
7 pintle	7 aiguillot	7 Fingerling	7 vingerling	7 tap
8 rudderstock	8 mèche	8 Ruderschaft	8 roerkoning	8 rorstamme
9 stuffing box	9 presse-étoupe	9 Stopfbuchse	9 pakkingbus	9 kasse
10 quadrant	10 quadrant	10 Quadrant	10 kwadrant	10 kvadrant
11 rod steering	11 direction par biellettes	11 Gestägesteuerung	11 stuurgerei d.m.v stuurstangen	11 styrestænger
12 rack-and-pinion	12 crémaillère et pignon	12 Zahnstange mit Ritzel	12 tandwielaandrijving	12 drev
13 worm-drive	13 transmission par vis sans fin	13 Schneckenantrieb	13 wormaandrijving	13 snekkedrev
14 ball bearing	14 roulement à billes	14 Kugellager	14 kogellager	14 kugleleje
15 bevel	15 biseau	15 Kegelrad, Schmiege	15 conisch, afgeschuind	15 spidshjul
16 chain-drive	16 transmission par chaîne	16 Kettenantrieb	16 kettingaandrijving	16 kædedrev
17 sprocket	17 pignon de chaîne	17 Zahnrad	17 tand van tandwiel	17 kædehjul
18 cable steering	18 direction par câbles	18 Seilzugsteuerung	18 kabelbesturing	18 styreliner
19 hydraulic	19 hydraulique	19 Hydraulik	19 hydraulisch	19 hydraulisk
20 hydraulic ram/piston	20 piston hydraulique	20 Hydraulikkolben	20 hydraulische cilinder/zuiger	20 hydraulisk stempel
21 universal joint	21 cardan	21 Kreuzgelenk	21 universele aansluiting	21 universalled
22 self-steering	22 pilote automatique	22 Selbststeuer	22 zelfsturend	22 selvstyrende
23 windvane	23 girouette	23 Windfahne	23 windvaan	23 vindfáne/sejl

ESPAÑOL	ITALIANO	PORTUGUÊS	TÜRKÇE	ΕΛΛΗΝΙΚΑ
8 SISTEMA DE GOBIERNO	**8 SISTEMA DI GOVERNO**	**8 SISTEMA DE GOVERNO DO BARCO**	**8 DÜMEN SİSTEMİ**	**8 ΣΥΣΤΗΜΑ ΔΙΕΥΘΥΝΣΗΣ**
1 rueda del timón	1 ruota	1 roda do leme	1 dümen dolabı	1 ΡΟΔΑ
2 barra del timón	2 barra (del timone)	2 cana do leme	2 yeke	2 ΛΑΓΟΥΔΕΡΑ
3 pala del timón	3 timone	3 leme	3 dümen	3 ΤΙΜΟΝΙ
4 timón compensado	4 timone bilanciato	4 leme compensado	4 mütevazin/balanslı dümen/dengeşik dümen	4 ΙΣΟΡΡΟΠΟ ΠΗΔΑΛΙΟ
5 timón eliptica	5 timone a pala	5 leme em pá	5 pala dümen	5 ΡΕΣΠΕΤΟ ΠΗΔΑΛΙΟ
6 hembra	6 femminella	6 cavilha/perno	6 dümen dişi iğneciği	6 ΠΕΙΡΟΣ-ΓΟΜΦΟΣ ΠΗΔΑΛΙΟΥ
7 macho	7 agugliotto	7 macaho do leme	7 dümen erkek iğneciği	7 ΒΕΛΟΝΙ
8 mecha del timón	8 asta del timone	8 cabo do leme	8 dümen anası, dümen mili	8 ΑΞΟΝΑΣ ΠΗΔΑΛΙΟΥ
9 prensa-estopa	9 premibaderna	9 calxa do bucim, empanque	9 dümen kovanı, salmastra gleni	9 ΣΤΥΠΙΟΘΛΙΠΤΗΣ
10 sector del timón	10 quadrante	10 quadrante dos gualdropes	10 dümen kadranı	10 ΤΟΞΟ ΤΟΥ ΠΗΔΑΛΙΟΥ
11 sistema de gobierno por varillas	11 trasmissione a biella	11 transmissão de barra	11 rotlu dümen takımı	11 ΜΟΧΛΟΤΙΜΟΝΟ
12 piñón y cremallera	12 pignone e cremagliera	12 cremalheira e seu carreto	12 dişlikol ve fener dişli	12 ΚΡΕΜΑΓΕΡΑ
13 transmisión por tornillo sin fin	13 trasmissione a vite senza fine	13 transmissão por sem fim e coroa	13 sonsuz dişlili dümen takımı	13 ΚΙΝΗΣΗ ΜΕ ΑΤΕΡΜΟΝΑ
14 rodamiento a bolas	14 cuscinetto a sfere	14 rolamento de resferras	14 rulman	14 ΡΟΥΛΕΜΑΝ (ΕΝΣΦΑΙΡΟ)
15 bisel	15 bisello	15 chanfro	15 eğim	15 ΚΩΝΙΚΗ ΕΜΠΛΟΚΗ
16 transmisión por cadena	16 trasmissione a catena	16 transmissão percurrente	16 zincir aktarmalı dümen sistemi	16 ΚΙΝΗΣΗ ΜΕ ΑΛΥΣΙΔΑ
17 rueda dentada	17 rocchetto	17 dente de roda	17 zincir dişlisi, sproket	17 ΟΔΟΝΤΩΤΟΣ ΤΡΟΧΟΣ ΑΛΥΣΣΙΔΑΣ
18 sistema de gobierno por cables	18 timone a catena	18 gualdrope	18 telli dümen aktarma sistemi	18 ΤΙΜΟΝΙ ΜΕ ΣΥΡΜΑΤΟΣΧΟΙΝΑ
19 hidráulico	19 idraulica	19 hidraulico	19 hidrolik	19 ΥΔΡΑΥΛΙΚΟ (ΤΙΜΟΝΙ)
20 pistón hidráulico	20 pistone idraulico	20 macaco hidraulico	20 hidrolik ram/piston	20 ΥΔΡΑΥΛΙΚΟ ΩΣΤΗΡΙΟ/ ΠΙΣΤΟΝΙ
21 articulación, cardano	21 cardano	21 junta universal	21 istavroz kaplin	21 ΕΛΕΥΘΕΡΗ ΑΡΘΡΩΣΗ
22 piloto automático	22 ad autogoverno	22 leme automático	22 otomatik pilot	22 ΑΥΤΟΟΔΗΓΟΥΜΕΝΟ
23 veleta	23 pala a vento	23 leme automático de vento	23 rüzgar dümeni	23 ΑΝΕΜΟΤΙΜΟΝΟ

ENGLISH	FRANÇAIS	DEUTSCH	NEDERLANDS	DANSK
8 STEERING SYSTEM	**8 APPAREILS A GOUVERNER**	**8 STEUERUNGSANLAGE**	**8 STUUR SYSTEEM**	**8 STYRESYSTEM**
24 trim-tab	24 flaps	24 Trimmklappe, Trimmruderblatt	24 trimvlak	24 trimanordning
25 ratchet	25 roue à cliquet	25 Sperrkranz, Sperrklinke	25 pal	25 pal
26 autopilot	26 pilote automatique	26 Autopilot	26 automatische piloot	26 autopilot
27 belt drive	27 transmission par courroie	27 Riemenantrieb	27 riemaandrijving	27 remtræk
28 rotary drive	28 transmission rotative	28 Rotationsantrieb	28 roterende aandrijving	28 drejetræk
29 linear drive	29 transmission linéaire	29 Linearantrieb	29 lineaire aandrijving	29 linetræk

ESPAÑOL	ITALIANO	PORTUGUÊS	TÜRKÇE	ΕΛΛΗΝΙΚΑ
8 SISTEMA DE GOBIERNO	**8 SISTEMA DI GOVERNO**	**8 SISTEMA DE GOVERNO DO BARCO**	**8 DÜMEN SİSTEMİ**	**8 ΣΥΣΤΗΜΑ ΔΙΕΥΘΥΝΣΗΣ**
24 flaps	24 trimmer	24 compensador	24 trım-tab	24 ΦΛΑΠΣ
25 trinquete	25 cricco	25 linguete	25 cırcır dişli	25 ΚΑΣΤΑΝΙΑ
26 piloto automático	26 autopilota	26 piloto automático	26 otopilot	26 ΑΥΤΟΜΑΤΟΣ ΠΙΛΟΤΟΣ (ΠΥΞΙΔΑΣ)
27 transmisión por correa	27 trasmissione a cinghia	27 correia de transmissão	27 kayışlı aktarma	27 ΚΙΝΗΣΗ ΜΕ ΙΜΑΝΤΑ
28 fuerza giratoria	28 trasmissione rotativa	28 transmissão rotativa	28 döner aktarma	28 ΠΕΡΙΣΤΡΟΦΙΚΗ ΜΕΤΑΔΟΣΗ
29 fuerza lineal	29 trasmissione lineare	29 transmissão linear	29 doğrusal aktarma	29 ΓΡΑΜΜΙΚΗ ΜΕΤΑΔΟΣΗ

ENGLISH	FRANÇAIS	DEUTSCH	NEDERLANDS	DANSK
9 REFRIGERATION	**9 REFRIGERATION**	**9 KÜHLSYSTEM**	**9 KOELING**	**9 KØLEANLÆG**
1 compressor	1 compresseur	1 Kompressor	1 compressor	1 kompressor
2 magnetic clutch	2 embrayage magnétique	2 Magnetkupplung	2 magneetkoppeling	2 magnetisk kobling
3 condenser	3 condensateur	3 Kondensator	3 condensator	3 kondensator
4 heat exchanger	4 échangeur thermique	4 Wärmetauscher	4 warmtewisselaar	4 varmeveksler
5 receiver/filter/drier	5 récepteur filtre/sècheur	5 Sammler/Filter/Trockner	5 filter/droger	5 modtager/filter/tørreanordning
6 accumulator	6 accumulateur	6 Druckspeicher	6 verzamelaar	6 akkumulator
7 liquid line	7 tuyau à liquide	7 Kondensatleitung	7 vloeistofleiding	7 vædskestand
8 expansion valve	8 soupape d'expansion	8 Verdamperventil	8 expansieventiel	8 ekspansionsventil
9 evaporator/holding plate	9 évaporateur	9 Verdamperplatte	9 verdamper	9 fordamper
10 thermostat	10 thermostat	10 Thermostat	10 thermostaat	10 termostat
11 capillary tube	11 tube capillaire	11 Kapillarrohr	11 haarbuisje	11 kapillarrør
12 sensing bulb	12 ampoule-témoin	12 Meßfühler	12 voeler	12 følerør
13 suction line	13 tuyau d'aspiration	13 Saugleitung	13 zuigleiding	13 føderør
14 discharge line	14 tuyau de débit	14 Ausflußleitung	14 aftapleiding	14 afløbsrør
15 high pressure cut-out	15 interrupteur de haute pression	15 Hochdruckabschaltung	15 hogedrukstop	15 højtryksafbryder
16 low pressure cut-out	16 interrupteur de basse pression	16 Niederdruckabschaltung	16 lagedrukstop	16 lavtryksafbryder
17 hose	17 tuyau	17 Schlauch	17 slang	17 slange
18 sight glass	18 verre de débit visible	18 Schauglas	18 kijkglas	18 kighul
19 air	19 air	19 Luft	19 lucht	19 luft
20 refrigerant	20 réfrigérant	20 Kühlmittel	20 koelmiddel	20 kølevædske
21 to purge	21 purger	21 durchspülen, reinigen	21 zuiveren, leegmaken	21 at rense
22 to charge	22 charger	22 auffüllen	22 opladen, laden	22 at lade
23 to crack open a valve	23 ouvrir une vanne un tout petit peu	23 ein Ventil aufreißen	23 ventiel open laten springen	23 at sprænge en ventil
24 to leak	24 fuir	24 lecken	24 lekken	24 at lække
25 to seal	25 rendre étanche	25 abdichten	25 afdichten	25 at tætne

ESPAÑOL	ITALIANO	PORTUGUÊS	TÜRKÇE	ΕΛΛΗΝΙΚΑ
9 REFRIGERACION	**9 REFRIGERAZIONE**	**9 REFRIGERAÇÃO**	**9 SOĞUTMA**	**9 ΨΥΚΤΙΚΟ ΣΥΣΤΗΜΑ**
1 compresor	1 compressore	1 compressor	1 kompresör	1 ΣΥΜΠΙΕΣΤΗΣ
2 embrague magnético	2 frizione magnetica	2 válvula magnética	2 manyetik kavrama	2 ΜΑΓΝΗΤΙΚΟΣ ΣΥΜΠΛΕΚΤΗΣ
3 condensador	3 condensatore	3 condensador	3 kondensatör	3 ΣΥΜΠΥΚΝΩΤΗΣ
4 intercambiador de calor	4 scambiatore di calore	4 permutador de calor	4 ısı eşanjörö	4 ΕΝΑΛΛΑΚΤΗΣ ΘΕΡΜΟΤΗΤΑΣ
5 receptora/ filtro/secadora	5 serbatoio/filtro/ essiccatore	5 filtro/secador	5 sıvı kabı/filtre/kurutucu	5 ΔΕΚΤΗΣ/ΦΙΛΤΡΟ/ ΞΗΡΑΝΤΗΡΑΣ
6 acumulador	6 accumulatore	6 acumulador	6 toplayıcı	6 ΣΥΣΣΩΡΕΥΤΗΣ
7 tubo de alimentación	7 tubo del liquido	7 circuito de líquidos	7 sıvı borusu	7 ΣΩΛΗΝΑΣ ΥΓΡΟΥ
8 válvula de expansion	8 valvola d'espansione	8 válvula de expansão	8 genleşme valfi	8 ΒΑΛΒΙΔΑ ΕΚΤΟΝΩΣΕΩΣ
9 evaporador/placa acumuladora	9 evaporatore/piastra d'appoggio	9 evaporador	9 evaporatör	9 ΕΞΑΕΡΩΤΗΣ (ΠΙΑΣΤΡΑ)
10 termostato	10 termostato	10 termostato	10 termostat	10 ΘΕΡΜΟΣΤΑΤΗΣ
11 tubo capilar	11 tubo capillare	11 tubo capilar	11 kılcal boru	11 ΤΡΙΧΟΕΙΔΗΣ ΣΩΛΗΝΑΣ
12 sensor de termostato	12 sonda a bulbo	12 sensor	12 müşir	12 ΑΙΣΘΗΤΗΡΑΣ
13 tubo de aspiración	13 tubo d'aspirazione	13 tubo de aspiração	13 emme borusu	13 ΓΡΑΜΜΗ ΑΝΑΡΡΟΦΗΣΕΩΣ
14 tubo de descarga	14 tubo di scarico	14 tubo de descarga	14 atma (deşarj) borusu	14 ΓΡΑΜΜΗ ΕΚΤΟΝΩΣΕΩΣ
15 interruptor de alta presión	15 interruttore di pressione massima	15 corte da alta pressão	15 yüksek basınç kesicisi	15 ΔΙΑΚΟΠΗ ΥΨΗΛΗΣ ΠΙΕΣΕΩΣ
16 interruptor de baja presión	16 interruttore di pressione minima	16 corte da baixa pressão	16 alçak basınç kesicisi	16 ΔΙΑΚΟΠΗ ΧΑΜΗΛΗΣ ΠΙΕΣΕΩΣ
17 manguera	17 tubo flessibile	17 tubo de borracha	17 hortum	17 ΣΩΛΗΝΑΣ (ΚΟΛΛΑΡΟ)
18 tubo de vidrio de nivel	18 spia di condensa	18 vizor	18 gözetleme camı	18 ΠΑΡΑΘΥΡΑΚΙ
19 aire	19 aria	19 ar	19 hava	19 ΑΕΡΑΣ
20 refrigerante	20 refrigerante	20 refrigerante	20 soğutucu	20 ΨΥΚΤΙΚΟ
21 purgar	21 spurgare	21 purgar	21 temizleme, boşaltma	21 ΚΑΘΑΡΙΖΩ
22 cargar	22 caricare	22 carregar	22 doldurmak	22 ΦΟΡΤΙΖΩ
23 abrir una válvula muy poco	23 socchiudere una valvola	23 abrir uma válvula por rachas	23 vanayı biraz açmak	23 ΛΑΣΚΑΡΩ ΛΙΓΟ ΒΑΛΒΙΔΑ
24 perder	24 perdere	24 pingar	24 sızmak, sızdırmak	24 ΔΙΑΡΡΟΗ
25 sellar	25 sigillare	25 vedar	25 sızıntıyı kesmek	25 ΣΤΕΓΑΝΟΠΟΙΗΣΗ

ENGLISH	FRANÇAIS	DEUTSCH	NEDERLANDS	DANSK
10 ELECTRICS & ELECTRONICS	**10 APPAREILS ELECTRIQUES ET ELECTRONIQUES**	**10 ELEKTROTECHNIK UND ELEKTRONIK**	**10 ELEKTRICITEIT EN ELEKTRONICA**	**10 ELEKTRICITET OG ELEKTRONIK**
Electricity supply & distribution	**Alimentation et distribution d'électricité**	**Elektrische Versorgung und Verteilung**	**Elektriciteitsvoorziening en verdeling**	**Forsyning og fordeling af elektricitet**
1 shore power	1 courant de terre	1 Stromversorgung von Land	1 walstroom	1 elforsyning fra land
2 alternating current/AC	2 courant alternatif	2 Wechselstrom	2 wisselstroom, wisselspanning, AC	2 vekselstrøm
3 direct current/DC	3 courant continu	3 Gleichstrom	3 gelijkstroom, gelijkspanning, DC	3 jævnstrøm
4 voltage	4 tension	4 Spannung	4 spanning	4 spænding
5 line	5 ligne	5 Leitung	5 leiding	5 ledning
6 neutral	6 neutre	6 Nulleiter	6 neutraal	6 nul
7 earth	7 terre	7 Erde	7 aarde	7 jord
8 battery	8 batterie	8 Batterie	8 accu, batterij	8 batteri
9 amp/hours capacity	9 capacité ampères/heures	9 Ampere/Stunden Kapazität	9 ampèreuur-capaciteit	9 kapacitet i amp-timer
10 lead-acid	10 batterie électrolyte	10 Bleiakkumulator	10 accuzuur	10 batterisyre
11 nickel cadmium	11 nickel cadmium	11 Nickel-Kadmium-Akkumulator	11 nikkel-cadmium	11 nikkel-kadmium
12 dry battery	12 pile sèche	12 Trockenbatterie	12 droge batterij, droge accu	12 tørbatteri
13 alkaline	13 alkalin	13 Nickel-Eisen-Akkumulator	13 alkaline	13 alkaline
14 zinc carbon	14 zinc carbon	14 Zink-Kohlenstoff-Batterie	14 zinkkoolstof, zinkcarbon	14 zink-karbonat
15 mercury	15 mercure	15 Quecksilber	15 kwik	15 kviksølv
16 lithium	16 lithium	16 Lithium	16 lithium	16 lithium
17 silver oxide	17 oxide d'argent	17 Silberoxyd	17 zilveroxyde	17 sølvoxid
18 positive terminal	18 borne positive	18 Plus-Pol	18 positieve poolklem	18 positiv pol
19 negative terminal	19 borne négative	19 Minus-Pol	19 negatieve poolklem	19 negativ pol
20 alternator	20 alternateur	20 Wechselstromgenerator	20 generator	20 vekselstrømsgenerator
21 carbon brush	21 balai de carbone	21 Kohlebürsten	21 koolborstel	21 kulbørste
22 dynamo	22 dynamo	22 Gleichstromgenerator	22 dynamo	22 dynamo
23 commutator	23 commutateur	23 Polumwandler	23 collector, stroomwisselaar	23 omskifter
24 generator	24 génératrice	24 Erzeuger	24 generator	24 generator
25 wind generator	25 éolienne	25 Windgenerator	25 windgenerator	25 vindmotor

ESPAÑOL	ITALIANO	PORTUGUÊS	TÜRKÇE	ΕΛΛΗΝΙΚΑ
10 SISTEMAS ELECTRICOS Y ELECTRONICOS	**10 ELETTRICITA E ELETTRONICA**	**10 SISTEMAS ELECTRICO E ELECTRÓNICO**	**10 ELEKTRİK & ELEKTRONİKLER**	**10 ΗΛΕΚΤΡΙΚΑ ΚΑΙ ΗΛΕΚΤΡΟΝΙΚΑ**
Suministro de electricidad y distribución	**Alimentazione e distribuzione d'elettricità**	**Fonte de energia e distribuição**	**Elektrik ikmal ve dağılımı**	**ΗΛΕΚΤΡΙΚΗ ΤΡΟΦΟΔΟΣΙΑ ΚΑΙ ΔΙΑΝΟΜΗ**
1 corriente de tierra	1 energia da terra	1 alimentação de terra	1 kıyı ceryanı	1 ΡΕΥΜΑ ΑΠΟ ΣΤΕΡΙΑ
2 corriente alterna	2 corrente alternata/c.a.	2 corrente alterna	2 alternatif akım/AC	2 ΕΝΑΛΛΑΣΣΟΜΕΝΟ ΡΕΥΜΑ
3 corriente continua	3 corrente continua/c.c.	3 corrente contínua	3 doğru akım	3 ΣΥΝΕΧΕΣ ΡΕΥΜΑ
4 voltaje	4 tensione	4 voltagem	4 voltaj	4 ΤΑΣΙΣ (ΒΟΛΤ)
5 conductor	5 linea	5 cabo electrico	5 hat, elektrik hattı	5 ΓΡΑΜΜΗ
6 neutral	6 neutro	6 neutro	6 nötr	6 ΟΥΔΕΤΕΡΟ
7 masa. tierra	7 terra	7 terra	7 toprak	7 ΓΕΙΩΣΗ
8 batería	8 batteria	8 bateria	8 batarya, akümülator	8 ΜΠΑΤΑΡΙΑ
9 capacida en amperíos/hora	9 capacità in amperore	9 amperes hora/ capacidade	9 amper/saat kapasitesi	9 ΙΣΧΥΣ ΣΕ ΑΜΠΕΡΩΡΙΑ
10 plomo-ácido	10 al piombo	10 acido-chumbo	10 kurşun-asit batarya	10 ΜΟΛΥΒΔΟΥ ΟΞΕΟΣ
11 níquel-cadmio	11 al nichel-cadmio	11 niquel-cadmio	11 nikel-kadmiyum	11 ΝΙΚΕΛΙΟΥ ΚΑΔΜΙΟΥ
12 pila seca	12 batteria a secco	12 bateria seca	12 kuru akü	12 ΜΠΑΤΑΡΙΑ ΧΩΡΙΣ ΥΓΡΑ
13 alcalino	13 alcalina	13 alcalino	13 alkali	13 ΑΛΚΑΛΙΚΗ
14 carbono-cinc	14 allo zinco-carbonio	14 zinco carbono	14 çinko-karbon	14 ΨΕΥΔΑΡΓΥΡΟΥ ΑΝΘΡΑΚΑ
15 mercurio	15 al mercurio	15 mercurio	15 cıva	15 ΥΔΡΑΡΓΥΡΟΥ
16 litio	16 al litio	16 lítio	16 lityum	16 ΛΙΘΙΟΥ
17 oxido de plata	17 all'ossido d'argento	17 oxido de prata	17 gümüş oksit	17 ΟΞΕΙΔΙΟΥ ΤΟΥ ΑΡΓΥΡΟΥ
18 borna positiva	18 terminale positivo	18 polo positivo	18 artı uç	18 ΘΕΤΙΚΟΣ ΑΚΡΟΔΕΚΤΗΣ
19 borna negativa	19 terminale negativo	19 polo negativo	19 eksi uç	19 ΑΡΝΗΤΙΚΟΣ ΑΚΡΟΔΕΚΤΗΣ
20 alternador	20 alternatore	20 alternador	20 alternatör	20 ΑΛΤΕΡΝΕΙΤΟΡ
21 escobilla de carbón	21 spazzola di carbonio	21 escova de carvão	21 karbon fırça	21 ΨΗΚΤΡΑ ΑΝΘΡΑΚΑ
22 dinamo	22 dinamo	22 dinâmo	22 dinamo	22 ΔΥΝΑΜΟ
23 conmutador	23 commutatore	23 comutador	23 komütatör, cereyan anahtarı	23 ΣΥΛΛΕΚΤΗΣ
24 dinamo, generador	24 generatore	24 gerador	24 jeneratör	24 ΓΕΝΝΗΤΡΙΑ
25 generador de viento	25 generatore a vento	25 gerador de vento	25 rüzgar jeneratörö	25 ΓΕΝΝΗΤΡΙΑ ΑΝΕΜΟΥ

ENGLISH	FRANÇAIS	DEUTSCH	NEDERLANDS	DANSK
10 ELECTRICS & ELECTRONICS	**10 APPAREILS ELECTRIQUES**	**10 ELEKTROTECHNIK UND ELEKTRONIK**	**10 ELEKTRICITEIT EN ELEKTRONICA**	**10 ELEKTRICITET & ELEKTRONIK**
Electricity supply & distribution	**Alimentation et distribution d'électricité**	**Elektrische Versorgung und Verteilung**	**Elektriciteitsvoorziening en verdeling**	**Forsyning og fordeling af elektricitet**
26 solar panel/cell	26 paneau solaire/pile	26 Solarzellen	26 zonnepaneel/cel	26 solpanel/solcelle
27 battery charger	27 chargeur de batterie	27 Batterieladegerät	27 acculader, gelijkrichter	27 ladeapparat
28 voltage regulator	28 régulateur de tension	28 Spannungsregler	28 spanningsregelaar	28 spændingsregulator
29 current controller/battery manager	29 régulateur de courant	29 Stromregler	29 laadautomaat	29 strømregulator
30 isolating diode	30 diode d'isolement	30 Trenndiode	30 sperdiode	30 isolationsdiode
31 relay	31 relai	31 Relais	31 relais	31 relæ
32 coil	32 bobine	32 Spule	32 spoel	32 induktionsspole
33 solenoid	33 solénoïde	33 Magnetspule	33 draadspoel	33 solenoide
34 power lead	34 câble de courant	34 Hauptstromleitung	34 vermogensaansluiting	34 strømkabel
35 live	35 sous tension	35 stromführend	35 onder spanning	35 strømførende
36 switch	36 interrupteur	36 Schalter	36 schakelaar	36 kontakt
37 insulation	37 isolement	37 Isolierung	37 isolatie	37 isolation
38 cable	38 câble	38 Kabel	38 kabel	38 ledning
39 flexible	39 souple	39 flexibel	39 flexibel	39 bøjelig
40 coaxial	40 coaxial	40 koaxial	40 coax	40 koaxial
41 load	41 charge	41 Last, Stromverbrauch	41 belasting	41 lade
42 resistance	42 résistance	42 Widerstand	42 weerstand	42 modstand
43 impedance	43 impédance	43 Scheinwiderstand	43 impedantie	43 impedans
44 junction box	44 boîte de raccordement	44 Klemmkasten	44 lasdoos, aansluitkast	44 samlekasse
45 fuse	45 fusible	45 Sicherung	45 zekering	45 sikring
46 fuse box	46 boîtier à fusible	46 Sicherungskasten	46 zekeringkast	46 sikringskasse
47 circuit breaker	47 disjoncteur	47 Ausschalter	47 hoofdzekering	47 strømafbryder
48 distribution panel	48 tableau de distribution	48 Verteilertafel	48 verdelerpaneel	48 fordelertavle
49 transformer	49 transformateur	49 Transformator	49 transformator	49 transformator
50 inverter	50 onduleur	50 Wechselrichter	50 inverter	50 omformer
51 ammeter	51 ampèremètre	51 Amperemeter	51 ampèremeter	51 amperemeter
52 voltmeter	52 voltmètre	52 Voltmeter	52 voltmeter	52 voltmeter

ESPAÑOL	ITALIANO	PORTUGUÊS	TÜRKÇE	ΕΛΛΗΝΙΚΑ
10 SISTEMAS ELECTRICOS	**10 ELETTRICITA E ELETTRONICA**	**10 SISTEMAS ELECTRICO E ELECTRÓNICO**	**10 ELEKTRİK & ELEKTRONİKLER**	**10 ΗΛΕΚΤΡΙΚΑ ΚΑΙ ΗΛΕΚΤΡΟΝΙΚΑ**
Suministro de electricidad y distribución	**Alimentazione e distribuzione d'elettricità**	**Fonte de energia e distribuição**	**Elektrik ikmal ve dağılımı**	**ΗΛΕΚΤΡΙΚΗ ΤΡΟΦΟΛΟΣΙΑ ΚΑΙ ΔΙΑΝΟΜΗ**
26 placa solar	26 pannello/cella solare	26 painel solar	26 güneş enerjisi panosu	26 ΓΕΝΝΗΤΡΙΑ ΗΛΙΑΚΗ
27 cargador de batería	27 caricabatteria	27 carregador de bateria	27 akü şarj aygıtı, redresör	27 ΦΟΡΤΩΤΗΣ ΜΠΑΤΑΡΙΑΣ
28 regulador de tensión	28 regolatore di tensione	28 regulador de voltagem	28 voltaj regülatörü	28 ΡΥΘΜΙΣΤΗΣ ΤΑΣΕΩΣ
29 regulador de corriente	29 regolatore di corrente/ salvabatteria	29 controlador de corrente/ interruptor de baterias	29 akım düzenleyicisi/akü ayarlayıcısı, konjektör	29 ΕΛΕΓΚΤΗΣ ΡΕΥΜΑΤΟΣ/ ΑΥΤΟΜΑΤΟΣ ΜΠΑΤΑΡΙΑ
30 diodo aislante	30 diodo di disaccoppiamento	30 díodo	30 yalıtım/izolasyon diyotu	30 ΔΙΟΔΟΣ ΑΠΟΜΟΝΩΣΗΣ
31 relé	31 relé	31 relé	31 röle	31 ΑΣΦΑΛΕΙΑ
32 bobina	32 bobina	32 bobine	32 bobin	32 ΠΗΝΙΟ
33 solenoide	33 solenoide	33 solenoide	33 solenoid	33 ΣΩΛΗΝΟΕΙΔΗΣ
34 cable de fuerza	34 cavo di potenza	34 fio da energia	34 faz hattı	34 ΓΡΑΜΜΗ ΡΕΥΜΑΤΟΣ
35 activo	35 sotto tensione	35 positivo	35 faz	35 ΖΩΝΤΑΝΟ - ΕΝΕΡΓΟΠΟΙΗΜΕΝΟ
36 interruptor	36 interruttore	36 interruptor	36 akım anahtarı	36 ΔΙΑΚΟΠΤΗΣ
37 aislamiento	37 isolamento	37 isolamento	37 yalıtım	37 ΜΟΝΩΣΗ
38 cable	38 cavo	38 cabo	38 kablo	38 ΚΑΛΩΔΙΟ
39 flexible	39 flessibile	39 flexível	39 elastiki	39 ΕΥΚΑΜΠΤΟ
40 coaxial	40 coassiale	40 coaxial	40 koaxial	40 ΟΜΟΑΞΟΝΙΚΟΣ
41 carga	41 carico	41 carregar	41 yük	41 ΦΟΡΤΙΟ
42 resistencia	42 resistenza	42 resistência	42 rezistans/mukavemet	42 ΑΝΤΙΣΤΑΣΗ
43 impedancia	43 impedenza	43 impedância	43 empedans	43 ΔΙΑΚΟΠΗ
44 caja de distribución	44 scatola di giunzione	44 caixa de ligação	44 kofra, kofra kutusu	44 ΚΙΒΩΤΙΟ ΕΝΩΣΕΩΝ ΔΙΚΤΥΟΥ
45 fusible	45 fusibile	45 fusível	45 sigorta	45 ΑΣΦΑΛΕΙΑ
46 caja de fusibles	46 scatola dei fusibili	46 caixa de fusíveis	46 sigorta kutusu	46 ΑΣΦΑΛΕΙΟΘΗΚΗ
47 disyuntor, cortacir-cuitos	47 interruttore	47 interruptor	47 akım kesici	47 ΑΣΦΑΛΕΙΑ
48 tablero de distribu-ción	48 quadro di distribuzione	48 painél de distribuição	48 dağıtım tablosu	48 ΔΙΑΝΟΜΕΑΣ
49 transformador	49 trasformatore	49 transformador	49 transformatör	49 ΜΕΤΑΣΧΗΜΑΤΙΣΤΗΣ
50 invertador	50 invertitore	50 inversor	50 inverter	50 ΜΕΤΑΤΡΟΠΕΑΣ
51 amperímetro	51 amperometro	51 amperímetro	51 ampermetre	51 ΑΜΠΕΡΟΜΕΤΡΟ
52 voltímetro	52 voltmetro	52 voltímetro	52 voltmetre	52 ΒΟΛΤΟΜΕΤΡΟ

ENGLISH	FRANÇAIS	DEUTSCH	NEDERLANDS	DANSK
10 ELECTRICS & ELECTRONICS	**10 APPAREILS ELECTRIQUES**	**10 ELEKTROTECHNIK UND ELEKTRONIK**	**10 ELEKTRICITEIT EN ELEKTRONICA**	**10 ELEKTRICITET & ELEKTRONIK**
Electrical & electronic equipment	**Appareils électriques et électroniques**	**Elektrische und elektronische Ausrüstung**	**Elektrische en elektronische installaties**	**Elektrisk og elektronisk udstyr**
Lights	*Feux*	*Lichter*	*Verlichting*	*Lys/lanterner*
1 navigation lights	1 feux de navigation/de route/de position	1 Positionslichter	1 navigatieverlichting	1 navigationslys
2 bi-colour	2 bicolore	2 zweifarbig	2 tweekleuren	2 tofarvet
3 tri-colour	3 tricolore	3 dreifarbig	3 driekleuren	3 trefarvet
4 green	4 vert	4 grün	4 groen	4 grøn
5 red	5 rouge	5 rot	5 rood	5 rød
6 white	6 blanc	6 weiß	6 wit	6 hvid
7 masthead light	7 feu de tête de mât	7 Toplicht	7 toplicht	7 toplys
8 steaming light	8 feu de route	8 Dampferlicht	8 stoomlicht	8 sidelanterner
9 stern light	9 feu arrière/de poupe	9 Hecklicht	9 heklicht	9 agterlanterne
10 anchor light/riding light	10 feu de mouillage	10 Ankerlicht	10 ankerlicht	10 ankerlanterne
11 searchlight/spotlight	11 projecteur/spot	11 Scheinwerfer	11 zoeklicht	11 søgelys/spotlight
12 bulb	12 ampoule	12 Glühbirne	12 lamp	12 pære
Radio	*Radio*	*Funkanlage, Radio*	*Radio*	*Radio*
1 aerial/antenna	1 antenne	1 Antenne	1 antenne	1 antenne
2 stub aerial	2 antenne courte	2 Stabantenne	2 staafantenne	2 kort antenne
3 whip aerial	3 antenne fouet	3 Peitschenantenne	3 sprietantenne	3 piskeantenne
4 live aerial	4 antenne sous tension	4 Betriebsantenne	4 actieve antenne	4 aktiv antenne
5 insulated backstay	5 pataras isolé	5 isoliertes Achterstag	5 geiisoleerd achterstag	5 isoleret agterstag
6 ferrite rod	6 barreau de ferrite	6 Ferritstab	6 ferriet-staafantenne	6 ferrit-antenne
7 loop aerial	7 antenne-cadre	7 Rahmenantenne	7 raamantenne	7 pejleantenne
8 emergency aerial	8 antenne de secours	8 Hilfsantenne	8 noodantenne	8 nødantenne
9 VHF	9 VHF	9 UKW, Ultrakurzwelle	9 VHF, marifoon	9 VHF
10 medium frequency/MF	10 ondes moyennes	10 Mittelwelle	10 middengolf	10 mellembølge/MF
11 short wave	11 ondes courtes	11 Kurzwelle	11 kortegolf	11 kortbølge
12 single sideband/SSB	12 BLU	12 Einseitenband	12 enkelzijdsband, SSB	12 single sideband/SSB
13 lower sideband/LSB	13 BLU inférieure	13 unteres Seitenband	13 onderzijdsband	13 lower sideband/LSB

ESPAÑOL	ITALIANO	PORTUGUÊS	TÜRKÇE	ΕΛΛΗΝΙΚΑ
10 SISTEMAS ELECTRICOS	**10 ELETTRICITA E ELETTRONICA**	**10 SISTEMAS ELECTRICO E ELECTRÓNICO**	**10 ELEKTRİK & ELEKTRONİKLER**	**10 ΗΛΕΚΤΡΙΚΑ ΚΑΙ ΗΛΕΚΤΡΟΝΙΚΑ**
Equipamiento eléctrico y electrónico	**Apparecchi elettrici e elettronici**	**Equipamentos electrico e electrónico**	**Elektrik ve elektronik ekipman**	**ΗΛΕΚΤΡΙΚΟΣ ΚΑΙ ΗΛΕΚΤΡΟΝΙΚΟΣ ΕΞΟΠΛΙΣΜΟΣ**
Luces	*Fanali, luci*	*Luzes*	*Işıklar/fenerler*	*ΦΩΤΑ*
1 luces de navegación	1 luci di navigazione	1 luzes de navegação	1 seyir fenerleri	1 ΦΩΤΑ ΝΑΥΣΙΠΛΟΙΑΣ
2 bicolor	2 bicolore	2 bicolor	2 iki renkli	2 ΔΙΧΡΩΜΟ
3 tricolor	3 tricolore	3 tricolor	3 üç renkli	3 ΤΡΙΧΡΩΜΟ
4 verde	4 verde	4 verde	4 yeşil	4 ΠΡΑΣΙΝΟ
5 rojo	5 rosso	5 encarnado	5 kırmızı	5 ΚΟΚΚΙΝΟ
6 blanco	6 bianco	6 branco	6 beyaz	6 ΑΣΠΡΟ
7 luz de tope todo horizonte	7 luce in testa d'albero	7 luz do mastro	7 direkbaşı feneri	7 ΦΩΣ ΑΓΚΥΡΟΒΟΛΙΑΣ
8 luz de tope	8 luce di navigazione a motore	8 luz de navegação a motor	8 silyon feneri	8 ΦΩΣ ΜΗΧΑΝΟΚΙΝΗΣΗΣ
9 luz de alcance, de popa	9 luce di poppa	9 farol de caça ou popa	9 pupa feneri	9 ΦΩΣ ΚΟΡΩΝΗΣ (ΠΡΥΜΝΗΣ)
10 luz de fondeado	10 luce di fonda	10 luz de barco fundeado	10 demir feneri	10 ΦΩΣ ΑΓΚΥΡΟΒΟΛΙΑΣ
11 proyector	11 proiettore/spot	11 projector	11 projektör	11 ΠΡΟΒΟΛΕΑΣ
12 bombilla	12 lampadina	12 lâmpada	12 ampul	12 ΛΑΜΠΑ
Radio	*Radio*	*Rádio*	*Radyo/telsiz*	*ΠΟΜΠΟΙ*
1 antena	1 antenna	1 antena aerea no rádio	1 anten	1 ΚΕΡΑΙΑ
2 antena de pora	2 antenna corta a tronco	2 antena curta	2 kısa anten	2 ΣΚΛΗΡΗ ΚΕΡΑΙΑ
3 antena látigo	3 antenna flessibile	3 antena em chicote	3 kamçı anten	3 ΜΑΣΤΙΓΙΟ ΚΕΡΑΙΑ
4 antena en emisión	4 antenna sotto tensione	4 antena ligada á corrente	4 cereyanlı anten	4 ΕΝΕΡΓΟΣ ΚΕΡΑΙΑ
5 backstay aislado	5 paterazzo isolato	5 backstay isolado	5 yalıtımlı kıçıstralya	5 ΜΟΝΩΜΕΝΟΣ ΕΠΙΤΟΝΟΣ
6 varilla de ferrite	6 antenna di ferrite	6 antena de ferrite	6 ferrit çubuk	6 ΚΕΡΑΙΑ ΦΕΡΙΤΗ
7 antena de cuadro	7 antenna a telaio	7 quadro	7 çember anten	7 ΣΤΡΟΓΓΥΛΗ ΚΕΡΑΙΑ
8 antena de emergencia	8 antenna d'emergenza	8 antena de emergência	8 yedek anten	8 ΚΕΡΑΙΑ
9 VHF	9 VHF	9 VHF	9 VHF/çok yüksek frekans	9 ΒΙ-ΕΙΤΣ-ΕΦ
10 onda media	10 frequenze medie	10 MF	10 MF/orta frekans	10 ΜΕΣΑΙΑ ΣΥΧΝΟΤΗΤΑ
11 onda corta	11 onde corte	11 ondas curtas	11 kısa dalga	11 ΒΡΑΧΕΑ ΚΥΜΑΤΑ
12 banda lateral	12 banda singola/SSB	12 SSB	12 SSB dalga	12 ΕΣ-ΕΣ-ΜΠΙ
13 banda lateral inferior	13 banda inferiore/LSB	13 LSB	13 LSB dalga	13 ΕΛ-ΕΣ-ΜΠΙ

ENGLISH	FRANÇAIS	DEUTSCH	NEDERLANDS	DANSK
10 ELECTRICS & ELECTRONICS	**10 APPAREILS ELECTRIQUES**	**10 ELEKTROTECHNIK UND ELEKTRONIK**	**10 ELEKTRICITEIT EN ELEKTRONICA**	**10 ELEKTRICITET & ELEKTRONIK**
Electrical & electronic equipment	**Appareils électriques et électroniques**	**Elektrische und elektronische Ausrüstung**	**Elektrische en elektronische installaties**	**Elektrisk og elektronisk udstyr**
Radio	*Radio*	*Funkanlage, Radio*	*Radio*	*Radio*
14 upper sideband/USB	14 BLU supérieure	14 oberes Seitenband	14 bovenzijdsband	14 upper sideband/USB
15 to receive	15 recevoir	15 empfangen	15 ontvangen	15 at modtage
16 to transmit	16 émettre	16 senden	16 zenden	16 at sende
17 transceiver	17 émetteur-récepteur	17 Sende-Empfänger	17 zendontvanger	17 modtager
18 microphone	18 microphone	18 Mikrofon	18 microfoon	18 mikrofon
19 loudspeaker	19 haut-parleur	19 Lautsprecher	19 luidspreker	19 højttaler
20 headphones	20 écouteurs	20 Kopfhörer	20 koptelefoon	20 høretelefoner
21 amplifier	21 amplificateur	21 Verstärker	21 versterker	21 forstærker
22 radiotelephone	22 radiotéléphone	22 Sprechfunk	22 radiotelefoon	22 radiotelefon
23 single channel	23 monocanal	23 Einkanal	23 simplex	23 enkelttale
24 dual channel	24 double canal	24 Zweikanal	24 duplex	24 modtale
25 call sign	25 indicatif	25 Rufzeichen	25 roepnaam	25 kaldesignel
26 channel	26 canal	26 Kanal, Sprechweg	26 kanaal	26 kanal
27 'over'	27 'à vous'	27 'over'	27 'over'	27 'over'
28 gain	28 gain	28 Verstärkungsgrad	28 gain	28 styrke
29 squelch	29 réglage silencieux	29 Rauschsperre	29 squelch	29 squelch
30 Navtex	30 Navtex	30 nautische Warnung über Telex	30 navtex	30 navtex
31 Weatherfax	31 fax météo	31 Wetterfax	31 weerkaartenschrijver	31 vejrfax
Navigation instruments	*Instruments de navigation*	*Navigationsinstrumente*	*Navigatie-instrumenten*	*Instrumenter*
1 binnacle compass	1 compas sur fût	1 Gehäusekompaß	1 kompas in kompashuis	1 kompas med nathus
2 fluxgate compass	2 compas électronique	2 Fluxgatekompaß	2 fluxgatekompas	2 kompas
3 handbearing compass	3 compas de relèvement	3 Handpeilkompaß	3 handpeilkompas	3 håndpejlekompas
4 autopilot	4 pilote automatique	4 Selbststeueranlage	4 autopiloot	4 autopilot/selvstyrer
5 boat heading	5 cap	5 Kursrichtung	5 scheepskoers	5 kurs

ESPAÑOL	ITALIANO	PORTUGUÊS	TÜRKÇE	ΕΛΛΗΝΙΚΑ
10 SISTEMAS ELECTRICOS	**10 ELETTRICITA E ELETTRONICA**	**10 SISTEMAS ELECTRICO E ELECTRÓNICO**	**10 ELEKTRİK & ELEKTRONİKLER**	**10 ΗΛΕΚΤΡΙΚΑ ΚΑΙ ΗΛΕΚΤΡΟΝΙΚΑ**
Equipamiento eléctrico y electrónico	**Apparecchi elettrici e elettronici**	**Equipamentos electrico e electrónico**	**Elektrik ve elektronik ekipman**	**ΗΛΕΚΤΡΙΚΟΣ ΚΑΙ ΗΛΕΚΤΡΟΝΙΚΟΣ ΕΞΟΠΛΙΣΜΟΣ**

ESPAÑOL	ITALIANO	PORTUGUÊS	TÜRKÇE	ΕΛΛΗΝΙΚΑ
Radio	*Radio*	*Rádio*	*Radyo/telsiz*	*ΠΟΜΠΟΙ*
14 banda lateral superior	14 banda superiore/USB	14 USB	14 USB dalga	14 ΓΙΟΥ-ΕΣ-ΜΠΙ
15 recibir	15 ricevere	15 receber	15 almak	15 ΛΗΨΗ
16 transmitir	16 trasmettere	16 transmitir	16 yayınlamak/telsizle mesaj geçmek	16 ΕΚΠΟΜΠΗ
17 transmisor-receptor	17 ricetrasmettitore	17 transreceptor	17 verici/transmitör	17 ΠΟΜΠΟΔΕΚΤΗΣ
18 micrófono	18 microfono	18 microfone	18 mikrofon	18 ΜΙΚΡΟΦΩΝΟ
19 altavoz	19 autoparlante	19 autofalante	19 hoparlör	19 ΜΕΤΑΦΩΝΟ
20 auricular	20 cuffia	20 auscultadores	20 kulaklık	20 ΑΚΟΥΣΤΙΚΑ
21 amplificador	21 amplificatore	21 amplificador	21 amplifikatör/yükseltici	21 ΕΝΙΣΧΥΤΗΣ
22 radioteléfono	22 radiotelefono	22 rádiotelefone	22 radyotelefon cihazı	22 ΡΑΔΙΟΤΗΛΕΦΩΝΟ
23 canal sencillo	23 canale singolo	23 canal único	23 tek kanal	23 ΜΟΝΟΥ ΚΑΝΑΛΙΟΥ
24 canal doble	24 canale doppio	24 dois canais	24 çift kanal	24 ΔΙΠΛΟΥ ΚΑΝΑΛΙΟΥ
25 señal de llamada	25 nominativo	25 indicativo de chamada	25 telsiz çağırı işareti	25 ΔΙΑΚΡΙΤΙΚΑ (ΣΤΑΘΜΟΥ)
26 canal	26 canale	26 canal	26 kanal	26 ΚΑΝΑΛΙ
27 'cambio'	27 'cambio'	27 escuto	27 tamam, bitti	27 ΟΒΕΡ
28 ganancia	28 guadagno	28 ganho	28 ses ayarı	28 ΙΣΧΥΣ
29 sintonia fina	29 squelch	29 squelch	29 bastırıcı	29 ΣΚΟΥΕΛΤΣ
30 Navtex	30 navtex	30 Navtex	30 navtex	30 ΝΑΒΤΕΞ
31 Weatherfax	31 fax meteo	31 Weatherfax	31 weatherfax	31 ΦΑΞ ΔΕΛΤΙΟ ΚΑΙΡΟΥ (ΟΥΕΔΕΡΦΛΞ)
Instrumentos de navegación	*Strumenti di navigazione*	*Instrumentos*	*Seyir göstergeleri*	*ΟΡΓΑΝΑ ΝΑΥΣΙΠΛΟΙΑΣ*
1 compás de bitacora	1 bussola a chiesuola	1 agulha de bitácula	1 kürsülü pusla/miyar pusla	1 ΣΤΑΘΕΡΗ ΠΥΞΙΔΑ
2 fluxgate, compás electrónico	2 bussola fluxgate	2 fluxgate	2 fluxgate puslu	2 ΗΛΕΚΤΡΟΝΙΚΗ ΠΥΞΙΔΑ
3 compás de marcaciones	3 bussola da rilevamento	3 agulha de marcar	3 elkerteriz puslası	3 ΠΥΞΙΔΑ ΧΕΙΡΟΣ
4 piloto automático	4 autopilota	4 piloto automático	4 otopilot, otomatik dümen	4 ΑΥΤΟΜΑΤΟΣ ΠΙΛΟΤΟΣ
5 con proa a ...	5 prora della barca	5 proa	5 tekne pruvasının yönü	5 ΚΑΤΕΥΘΥΝΣΗ ΠΛΟΙΟΥ

ENGLISH	FRANÇAIS	DEUTSCH	NEDERLANDS	DANSK
10 ELECTRICS & ELECTRONICS	**10 APPAREILS ÉLECTRIQUES**	**10 ELEKTROTECHNIK UND ELEKTRONIK**	**10 ELEKTRICITEIT EN ELEKTRONICA**	**10 ELEKTRICITET & ELEKTRONIK**
Electrical & electronic equipment	**Appareils électriques et électroniques**	**Elektrische und elektronische Ausrüstung**	**Elektrische en elektronische installaties**	**Elektrisk og elektronisk udstyr**
Navigation instruments	*Instruments de navigation*	*Navigationsinstrumente*	*Navigatie-instrumenten*	*Instrumenter*
6 Decca Yacht Navigator™/DYN	6 Decca™	6 Decca™-Navigator	6 Decca™ navigator	6 Decca Yacht Navigator™/DYN
7 Loran C	7 Loran	7 Loran C	7 Loran C	7 Loran C
8 transit satellite	8 satellite de transit	8 umlaufender Satellit	8 positii gevende satelliet	8 transmissionssatellit
9 Global Positioning System/GPS	9 GPS	9 erdgebundenes Positionierungssystem/ GPS-System	9 Global Positioning System/GPS	9 Global Positioning System/GPS
10 computer	10 ordinateur	10 Computer	10 computer	10 computer
11 modem	11 modem	11 Modem	11 modem	11 modem
12 printer	12 imprimante	12 Drucker	12 printer	12 printer
13 electronic plotter	13 marqueur électronique	13 Plotter	13 plotter	13 elektronisk plotter
14 waypoint	14 waypoint	14 Wegepunkt	14 waypoint	14 waypoint
15 radio direction finder/RDF	15 gonio	15 Funkpeiler	15 radiorichtingzoeker	15 radiopejler
16 null	16 secteur d'extinction	16 Null, nicht vorhanden	16 ongeldig, nulwaarde	16 nul
17 depth/echo sounder	17 sondeur	17 Echolot	17 echolood	17 ekkolod
18 fishfinder	18 sondeur à poissons	18 Fischsucher	18 viszoeker	18 fiskelod
19 log	19 loch	19 Log	19 log	19 log
20 boatspeed	20 vitesse du bateau	20 Bootsgeschwindigkeit	20 scheepssnelheid, vaart	20 fart gennem vandet
21 distance	21 distance	21 Distanz, Abstand	21 afstand	21 distance
22 impeller	22 roue à ailettes	22 Impeller	22 waaier, impeller	22 impeller/rotor
23 propeller	23 hélice	23 Propeller	23 propeller, schroef	23 skrue/propel
24 paddle wheel	24 roue à aubes	24 Schaufelrad	24 scheprad	24 skovlhjul
25 wind speed	25 vitesse du vent	25 Windgeschwindigkeit	25 windsnelheid	25 vindhastighed
26 wind direction	26 direction du vent	26 Windrichtung	26 windrichting	26 vindretning
27 radar scanner	27 antenne radar	27 Radar-Antenne	27 radarscanner	27 radarscanner
28 radar screen	28 écran de radar	28 Radar-Schirm	28 radarscherm	28 radarskærm
29 radar detector	29 récepteur radar d'alarme	29 Radar-Warner	29 radardetector	29 plotter

ESPAÑOL	ITALIANO	PORTUGUÊS	TÜRKÇE	ΕΛΛΗΝΙΚΑ
10 SISTEMAS ELECTRICOS	**10 ELETTRICITA E ELETTRONICA**	**10 SISTEMAS ELECTRICO E ELECTRÓNICO**	**10 ELEKTRİK & ELEKTRÓNIKLER**	**10 ΗΛΕΚΤΡΙΚΑ ΚΑΙ ΗΛΕΚΤΡΟΝΙΚΑ**
Equipamiento eléctrico y electrónico	**Apparecchi elettrici e elettronici**	**Equipamentos electrico e electrónico**	**Elektrik ve elektronik ekipman**	**ΗΛΕΚΤΡΙΚΟΣ ΚΑΙ ΗΛΕΚΤΡΟΝΙΚΟΣ ΕΞΟΠΛΙΣΜΟΣ**
Instrumentos de navegación	*Strumenti di navigazione*	*Instrumentos*	*Seyir göstergeleri*	*ΟΡΓΑΝΑ ΝΑΥΣΙΠΛΟΙΑΣ*
6 Decca™	6 Decca Yacht Navigator™/DYN	6 Decca Yacht Navigator™/ DYN	6 Decca™	6 ΝΤΕΚΑ™
7 Loran C	7 Loran C	7 Loran C	7 Loran C	7 ΛΟΡΑΝ
8 satelite de transito	8 satellite in transito	8 passagem de satélite	8 transit uydu	8 ΣΑΤΕΛΙΤΗΣ
9 GPS	9 Global Positioning System/GPS	9 GPS	9 GPS	9 ΤΖΙ-ΠΙ-ΕΣ
10 computadora	10 computer	10 computador	10 bilgisayar	10 ΚΟΜΠΙΟΥΤΕΡ
11 modem	11 modem	11 modem	11 modem	11 ΜΟΝΤΕΜ
12 impresora	12 stampante	12 impressora	12 printer	12 ΠΡΙΝΤΕΡ (ΕΚΤΥΠΩΤΗΣ)
13 plotter	13 plotter elettronico	13 plotter	13 elektronik plotlama aygıtı	13 ΗΛΕΚΤΡΟΝΙΚΟ ΠΛΟΤΕΡ ΑΠΟΤΥΠΩΣΗΣ
14 waypoint	14 waypoint	14 waypoint	14 rota değiştirme yeri	14 ΠΡΟΟΡΙΣΜΟΣ
15 gonio	15 radiogoniometro	15 rádio goniómetro	15 telsiz kerteriz/RDF	15 ΡΑΔΙΟΓΩΝΙΟΜΕΤΡΟ
16 nulo	16 zero	16 nulo	16 sıfır	16 ΜΗΔΕΝ
17 sondador acústico	17 ecoscandaglio	17 sonda	17 iskandil/ekolu iskandil	17 ΒΥΘΟΜΕΤΡΟ
18 fishfinder	18 ecoscandaglio da pesca	18 sonda para peixe	18 balık bulucu	18 ΑΝΙΧΝΕΥΤΗΣ ΨΑΡΙΩΝ
19 corredera	19 log, solcometro	19 odómetro	19 parakete/hız ölçücü	19 ΔΡΟΜΟΜΕΤΡΟ
20 velocidad del barco	20 velocità della barca	20 velocidade do barco	20 tekne hızı	20 ΤΑΧΥΤΗΤΑ ΣΚΑΦΟΥΣ
21 distancia	21 distanza	21 distância	21 mesafe/uzaklık	21 ΑΠΟΣΤΑΣΗ
22 impulsor	22 girante	22 roda de pás do odómetro	22 parakete pervanesi	22 ΙΜΠΕΛΕΡ
23 hélice	23 elica	23 hélice do odómetro	23 pervane	23 ΠΡΟΠΕΛΛΑΚΙ
24 rueda de paletas	24 ruota a pale	24 roda de pás	24 çark	24 ΤΡΟΧΟΣ
25 velocidad del viento	25 velocità del vento	25 velocidade do vento	25 rüzgar hızı	25 ΤΑΧΥΤΗΤΑ ΑΝΕΜΟΥ
26 direccion del viento	26 direzione del vento	26 direcção do vento	26 rüzgar yönü	26 ΔΙΕΥΘΥΝΣΗ ΑΝΕΜΟΥ
27 antena de radar	27 radar a scansione	27 scanner	27 radar anteni	27 ΣΑΡΩΤΗΣ ΡΑΝΤΑΡ - ΚΕΡΑΙΑ
28 pantalla de radar	28 schermo radar	28 PPI	28 radar ekranı	28 ΟΘΟΝΗ ΡΑΝΤΑΡ
29 detector de radar	29 radar detector	29 detector de radar	29 radar bulucu	29 ΑΝΙΧΝΕΥΤΗΣ ΡΑΝΤΑΡ

ENGLISH	FRANÇAIS	DEUTSCH	NEDERLANDS	DANSK
10 ELECTRICS & ELECTRONICS	**10 APPAREILS ELECTRIQUES**	**10 ELEKTROTECHNIK UND ELEKTRONIK**	**10 ELECTRICITEIT EN ELECTRONICA**	**10 ELEKTRICITET & ELEKTRONIK**
Electrical & electronic equipment	**Appareils électriques et électroniques**	**Elektrische und elektronische Ausrüstung**	**Electrische en electronische instalaties**	**Elektrisk og elektronisk udstyr**
Navigation instruments	*Instruments de navigation*	*Navigationsinstrumente*	*Navigatie-instrumenten*	*Instrumenter*
30 radar reflector	30 réflecteur radar	30 Radar-Reflektor	30 radarreflector	30 radarreflekter
31 emergency position indicating radio beacon/EPIRB	31 EPIRB/balise de détresse	31 Seenotfunkboje/EPIRB	31 EPIRB	31 emergency position indicating radio beacon/ EPIRB
32 search and rescue (SAR) transponder	32 SAR	32 Seenotfunkboje	32 search and rescue baken	32 eftersøgning-sapperatur/SAR
Terms	*Termes*	*Fachausdrücke*	*Uitdrukkingen*	*Benævnelser*
1 interface	1 interface	1 Interface	1 interface	1 interface
2 sender	2 transmetteur	2 Sender, Geber	2 zender	2 sender
3 transducer	3 transducteur	3 Wandler	3 overdrager/transducer	3 transducer
4 repeater	4 répétiteur	4 Verstärker	4 repeater	4 repeater
5 microprocessor	5 microprocesseur	5 Mikroprozessor	5 microprocessor	5 mikroprocessor
6 printed circuit board	6 plaque de circuit imprimé	6 Platine	6 printplaat	6 printplade
7 analogue	7 analogue	7 analog	7 analoog	7 analog
8 digital	8 digital	8 digital	8 digitaal	8 digital
9 to calibrate	9 calibrer	9 kalibrieren	9 kalibreren	9 at indstille
10 keyboard/keypad	10 clavier	10 Tastatur	10 toetsenbord	10 tastatur
11 heat sink	11 dissipateur thermique	11 Kühlkörper	11 koelplaat	11 køleanordning
12 cathode ray tube	12 tube à rayons cathodiques	12 Braun'sche Röhre	12 kathodestraalbuis	12 katoderør
13 light emitting diode/LED	13 diode électronumiscente DEL	13 Leuchtdiode/LED	13 lichtgevende diode/LED	13 lysdiode
14 discharge tube (neon/xenon)	14 tube à décharge (néon/xénon)	14 Gasentladungsröhre	14 gasontladingsbuis	14 udgangsrør (neon/xenon)
15 liquid crystal display/LCD	15 afficheur à cristaux liquides	15 Flüssigkristallanzeige/LCD	15 LCD-scherm	15 skærmbillede i flydende krystal

ESPAÑOL	ITALIANO	PORTUGUÊS	TÜRKÇE	ΕΛΛΗΝΙΚΑ
10 SISTEMAS ELECTRICOS	**10 ELETTRICITA E ELETTRONICA**	**10 SISTEMAS ELECTRICO E ELECTRÓNICO**	**10 ELEKTRİK & ELEKTRONİKLER**	**10 ΗΛΕΚΤΡΙΚΑ ΚΑΙ ΗΛΕΚΤΡΟΝΙΚΑ**
Equipamiento eléctrico y electrónico	**Apparecchi elettrici e elettronici**	**Equipamentos electrico e electrónico**	**Elektrik ve elektronik ekipman**	**ΗΛΕΚΤΡΙΚΟΣ ΚΑΙ ΗΛΕΚΤΡΟΝΙΚΟΣ ΕΞΟΠΛΙΣΜΟΣ**
Instrumentos de navegación	*Strumenti di navigazione*	*Instrumentos*	*Seyir göstergeleri*	*ΟΡΓΑΝΑ ΝΑΥΣΙΠΛΟΙΑΣ*
30 reflector de radar	30 riflettore radar	30 reflector de radar	30 radar yansıtıcısı/radar reflektörü	30 ΑΝΑΚΛΑΣΤΗΡΑΣ ΡΑΝΤΑΡ
31 radio baliza para localización de sinistros	31 EPIRB/radiomeda indicatrice di posizione d'emergenza	31 EPIRB	31 acil durumda konum belirleyici radyo bıkın/ÉPIRB	31 ΕΠΙΡΜΠ
32 transpondador de busca y salvamenta	32 trasponditore di ricerca e salvataggio (SAR)	32 EPIRB com communicação	32 SAR aygıtı arama ve kurtarma transponderi	32 ΠΟΜΠΟΔΕΚΤΗΣ ΔΙΑΣΩΣΗΣ
Terminos	*Termini*	*Termos*	*Terimler*	*ΟΡΟΛΟΓΙΑ*
1 interface	1 interfaccia	1 interface	1 interface/birleştirici	1 ΣΥΝΔΕΣΗ - ΙΝΤΕΡΦΕΗΣ
2 transmisor	2 trasmettitore	2 emissora	2 gönderici/sender	2 ΠΟΜΠΟΣ
3 transductor	3 trasduttore	3 transdutor	3 enerji iletme sistemi	3 ΠΟΜΠΟΔΕΚΤΗΣ
4 repetidor	4 ripetitore	4 repetidor	4 tekrarlayıcı	4 ΕΠΑΝΑΛΗΠΤΗΣ
5 microprocésador	5 microprocessore	5 microprocessador	5 mikro işlemci/ mikroprosesör	5 ΜΙΚΡΟΕΠΕΞΕΡΓΑΣΤΗΣ
6 placa circuito impreso	6 scheda a circuito stampato	6 circuito impresso	6 baskılı devre	6 ΚΑΡΤΑ ΤΥΠΩΜΕΝΟΥ ΚΥΚΛΩΜΑΤΟΣ
7 análogo	7 analogico	7 análogo	7 analog	7 ΑΝΑΛΟΓΙΚΟ
8 digital	8 digitale	8 digital	8 dijital	8 ΨΗΦΙΑΚΟ
9 calibrar	9 tarare	9 calibrar	9 ayarlamak/kalibre etmek	9 ΡΥΘΜΙΣΗ
10 teclado	10 tastiera/tastierino	10 teclado	10 klavye	10 ΠΛΗΚΤΡΟΛΟΓΙΟ
11 varistor, thiristor	11 dissipatore di calore	11 dissipador de calor	11 ısı dağıtıcı	11 ΛΕΚΑΝΗ ΘΕΡΜΟΤΗΤΑΣ
12 tubo de rayos catódicos	12 tubo a raggi catodici	12 tubo de raio catódicos	12 katot lambası	12 ΚΑΘΟΔΙΚΟΣ ΣΩΛΗΝΑΣ
13 diodo emisor de luz	13 diodo fotoemettitore/ LED	13 LED	13 ışık neşredici diyot/LED	13 ΔΙΟΔΟΣ ΕΚΠΟΜΠΗΣ ΦΩΤΟΣ
14 lampara xenon	14 tubo a scarica (neon/ xenon)	14 tubo de neon	14 neon lambası	14 ΣΩΛΗΝΑΣ ΕΚΦΟΡΤΙΣΗΣ (ΝΕΟΝ/ΞΕΝΟΝ)
15 display cristal liquido	15 display a cristalli liquidi/LCD	15 cristal liquido	15 likit kristal gösterge/LCD	15 ΕΝΔΕΙΞΗ ΜΕ ΥΓΡΟΥΣ ΚΡΥΣΤΑΛΛΟΥΣ

ENGLISH	FRANÇAIS	DEUTSCH	NEDERLANDS	DANSK
10 ELECTRICS & ELECTRONICS	**10 APPAREILS ELECTRIQUES**	**10 ELEKTROTECHNIK UND ELEKTRONIK**	**10 ELEKTRICITEIT EN ELEKTRONICA**	**10 ELEKTRICITET & ELEKTRONIK**
Electrician's toolbag	**Trousse à outils d'électricien**	**Werkzeuge des Elektrikers**	**Elektriciensgereedschap**	**Elektrikerværktøj**
1 soldering iron 2 multimeter 3 mains tester 4 cable cutter 5 cable stripper 6 crimping pliers 7 insulating tape	1 fer à souder 2 multimètre 3 vérificateur de secteur 4 coupe-câbles 5 dénudeur de câble 6 pince à sertir 7 chatterton	1 Lötkolben 2 Multimeter 3 Netzprüfer, Polprüfer 4 Kabelschneider 5 Abisolierzange 6 Kerbzange 7 Isolierband	1 soldeerbout 2 multimeter 3 spanningzoeker 4 draadtang, kniptang 5 striptang 6 krimptang 7 isolatieband	1 loddekolbe 2 måleinstrument 3 polsøger 4 skævbider 5 afisolertang 6 kabelskotang 7 isolerbånd
Electrician's stores	**Provisions d'électricien**	**Elektrolager**	**Elektriciensvoorraad**	**Elektriske reservedele**
1 light bulb 2 fluorescent tube 3 cable clip 4 crimp connector 5 fuse 6 plug 7 socket 8 knob 9 grommet 10 multicore solder	1 ampoule 2 tube fluorescent 3 lyre 4 cosse 5 fusible 6 prise de courant 7 prise de courant mural 8 bouton 9 passe-fil 10 soudure à noyau multiple	1 Glühbirne 2 Leuchtstoffröhre 3 Kabelschelle 4 Kabelschuh 5 Sicherung 6 Stecker 7 Steckdose 8 Knopf 9 Kabeldurchführung 10 Lötdraht	1 lamp 2 TL-buis 3 kabelklem 4 krimp-connector, kabelschoen 5 zekering 6 plug, stekker 7 stopcontact, voetje 8 knop 9 doorvoer 10 soldeer	1 pære/lampe 2 lysstofrør 3 kabelclips 4 samlemuffe 5 sikring 6 prop 7 fatning 8 dup 9 ring/øje 10 loddetin
Electrical & electronic problems	**Problèmes électriques et électroniques**	**Elektrische und elektronische Problemen**	**Elektrische en elektronische problemen**	**Elektriske og elektroniske problemer**
1 broken 2 burnt out 3 corroded	1 ne fonctionne pas 2 grille 3 corrode	1 unterbrochen 2 ausgebrannt 3 korrodiert	1 gebroken 2 verbrand 3 gecorrodeerd	1 gået i stykker 2 brændt af 3 irret

ESPAÑOL	ITALIANO	PORTUGUÊS	TÜRKÇE	ΕΛΛΗΝΙΚΑ
10 SISTEMAS ELECTRICOS	**10 ELETTRICITA E ELETTRONICA**	**10 SISTEMAS ELECTRICO E ELECTRÓNICO**	**10 ELEKTRİK & ELEKTRONİKLER**	**10 ΗΛΕΚΤΡΙΚΑ ΚΑΙ ΗΛΕΚΤΡΟΝΙΚΑ**
Maleta de herramientas de electricista	**Borsa dell'elettricista**	**Caixa de electricista**	**Elektrikçinin alet kutusu**	**ΕΡΓΑΛΕΙΑ ΗΛΕΚΤΡΟΛΟΓΟΥ**
1 soldador eléctrico 2 multimetro 3 comprobador de tensión 4 alicates para cortar 5 alicates pelacables 6 tenazas conectoras 7 cinta aislante	1 saldatore 2 multimetro 3 voltmetro di rete 4 pinza tagliacavi 5 pinza spelafili 6 pinza a crimpare 7 nastro isolante	1 ferro de soldar 2 multímetro 3 aparelho de testes 4 corta arame 5 descarnador 6 alicate de terminais 7 fita isoladora	1 havya 2 multimetre 3 faz kalemi 4 kablo kesici 5 kablo sıyırıcı 6 pense 7 izole bant/yalıtıcı bant	1 ΚΟΛΛΗΤΗΡΙ 2 ΠΟΛΥΜΕΤΡΟ 3 ΕΛΕΓΧΟΣ ΚΥΡΙΑΣ ΠΑΡΟΧΗΣ 4 ΚΟΦΤΗΣ ΚΑΛΩΔΙΩΝ 5 ΓΥΜΝΩΤΗΣ ΚΑΛΩΔΙΩΝ 6 ΠΕΝΣΑ 7 ΜΟΝΩΤΙΚΗ ΤΑΙΝΙΑ
Suministros de electricista	**Scorte dell'elettricista**	**Loja de artigos electricos**	**Elektrikçi/malzemesi**	**ΥΛΙΚΑ ΗΛΕΚΤΡΟΛΟΓΟΥ**
1 bombilla 2 tubo fluorescente 3 grapo de plastico 4 terminal faston 5 fusible 6 enchufe macho 7 enchufe hembra 8 boton 9 prensa-estopa 10 estano con resina	1 lampadina 2 lampada fluorescente 3 fermacavo 4 connettore a crimpare, connettore rapido 5 fusibile 6 spina 7 presa 8 manopola 9 occhiello metallico 10 lega per saldare con fondente	1 lâmpada 2 tubo fluorescente 3 terminal 4 terminal 5 fusível 6 ficha 7 tomada 8 botão 9 olhal 10 solda de várias cores	1 ampul 2 floresan lamba 3 kablo tesbit klipi 4 kablo başı, klemens 5 sigorta 6 elektrik fişi 7 priz 8 elektrik düğmesi 9 lastik kablo koruyucusu 10 pastalı lehim	1 ΛΑΜΠΑ – ΛΑΜΠΤΗΡΑΣ 2 ΛΑΜΠΑ ΦΘΟΡΙΟΥ 3 ΑΚΡΟΔΕΚΤΗΣ 4 ΕΝΩΣΗ 5 ΑΣΦΑΛΕΙΑ 6 ΑΡΣΕΝΙΚΗ ΠΡΙΖΑ 7 ΘΗΛΥΚΗ ΠΡΙΖΑ 8 ΚΟΥΜΠΙ 9 ΔΑΚΤΥΛΙΟΣ 10 ΠΟΛΥΠΗΡΥΝΟ ΚΟΛΛΗΤΗΡΙ
Problemas eléctricos y electrónicos	**Problemi elettrici e elettronici**	**Problemas electricos e electrónicos**	**Elektrik ve elektronik problemler**	**ΗΛΕΚΤΡΙΚΑ ΚΑΙ ΗΛΕΚΤΡΟΝΙΚΑ ΠΡΟΒΛΗΜΑΤΑ**
1 roto 2 quemado 3 coroído	1 rotto 2 bruciato 3 corroso	1 partido 2 queimado 3 corroído	1 bozuk 2 yanmış, yanık 3 paslanmış	1 ΣΠΑΣΜΕΝΑ 2 ΚΑΜΜΕΝΟ 3 ΔΙΑΒΡΩΜΕΝΟ

ENGLISH	FRANÇAIS	DEUTSCH	NEDERLANDS	DANSK
10 ELECTRICS & ELECTRONICS	**10 APPAREILS ELECTRIQUES**	**10 ELEKTROTECHNIK UND ELEKTRONIK**	**10 ELEKTRICITEIT EN ELEKTRONICA**	**10 ELEKTRICITET & ELEKTRONIK**
Electrical & electronic problems	**Problèmes électriques et électroniques**	**Elektrische und elektronische Probleme**	**Elektrische en elektronische problemen**	**Elektriske og elektroniske problemer**
4 discharged	4 à plat	4 entladen	4 ontladen, leeg	4 afladet
5 erratic	5 irrégulier	5 fehlerhaft	5 ontregeld, grillig	5 fejlagtig
6 to explode	6 exploser	6 explodieren	6 exploderen, ontploffen	6 at eksplodere
7 intermittent fault	7 faute intermittente	7 zeitweiliger Fehler	7 intermitterende fout	7 periodisk fejl
8 leak	8 fuite	8 Fehlerstrom	8 lek	8 læk
9 loose connection	9 connection lâche	9 lose Verbindung	9 losse verbinding	9 løs forbindelse
10 no display	10 manque d'image	10 keine Anzeige	10 geen beeld	10 ingen visning
11 no power	11 panne d'énergie	11 kein Strom	11 geen spanning, geen voeding	11 ingen strøm
12 no response	12 pas de réaction	12 keine Reaktion	12 geen reactie	12 ingen reaktion
13 weak response	13 réaction faible	13 schwache Reaktion	13 zwakke reactie	13 svag reaktion
14 to overheat	14 surchauffer	14 überhitzen	14 oververhitten	14 overophedet
15 short circuit	15 court-circuit	15 Kurzschluß	15 kortsluiting	15 kortsluttet
16 to smell bad	16 sentir mauvais	16 schlecht riechen	16 stinken	16 lugter brændt

ESPAÑOL	ITALIANO	PORTUGUÊS	TÜRKÇE	ΕΛΛΗΝΙΚΑ
10 SISTEMAS ELECTRICOS	**10 ELETTRICITA E ELETTRONICA**	**10 SISTEMAS ELECTRICO E ELECTRÓNICO**	**10 ELEKTRİK & ELEKTRONİKLER**	**10 ΗΛΕΚΤΡΙΚΑ ΚΑΙ ΗΛΕΚΤΡΟΝΙΚΑ**
Problemas eléctricos y electrónicos	**Problemi elettrici e elettronici**	**Problemas electricos e electrónicos**	**Elektrik ve elektronik problemler**	**ΗΛΕΚΤΡΙΚΑ ΚΑΙ ΗΛΕΚΤΡΟΝΙΚΑ ΠΡΟΒΛΗΜΑΤΑ**
4 descargado	4 scarico	4 descarregado	4 boşalmış	4 ΑΔΕΙΑΣΜΕΝΟΣ
5 errático	5 erratico	5 errático	5 yanıltıcı, tutarsız	5 ΔΙΑΚΟΠΤΟΜΕΝΟΣ
6 estallar	6 esplodere	6 prestes a explodir	6 patlamak	6 ΕΚΡΗΞΗ
7 defecto intermitente	7 guasto intermittente	7 falhas intermitentes	7 fasılalı hata	7 ΔΙΑΚΟΠΤΟΜΕΝΟ ΠΡΟΒΛΗΜΑ (ΖΗΜΙΑ)
8 resistencia de escape	8 perdita	8 pingar	8 sızıntı	8 ΔΙΑΡΡΟΗ
9 conexión floja	9 collegamento allentato	9 perde contacto	9 gevşek bağlantı	9 ΛΑΣΚΑ ΕΠΑΦΗ
10 no indica	10 non c'è display;	10 sem mostrador	10 göstergede bir şey yok	10 ΟΧΙ ΕΝΔΕΙΞΗ
11 sin fuerza	11 non c'è potenza	11 sem corrente	11 akım yok/güç (cereyan) yok	11 ΟΧΙ ΙΣΧΥΣ
12 sin respuesta	12 non c'è risposta	12 sem resposta	12 cevap yok	12 ΟΧΙ ΑΝΤΑΠΟΚΡΙΣΗ
13 respuesta debil	13 risposta debole	13 resposta muito fraca	13 cevap zayıf	13 ΑΔΥΝΑΤΗ ΑΝΤΑΠΟΚΡΙΣΗ
14 sobrecalentar	14 surriscaldarsi	14 aquecimento	14 ısınma/fazla ısınma	14 ΥΠΕΡΘΕΡΜΑΝΣΗ
15 corto cicuito	15 cortocircuito	15 curtocircuito	15 kısa devre	15 ΒΡΑΧΥΚΥΚΛΩΜΑ
16 oler mal	16 aver cattivo odore	16 mau cheiro	16 kötü kokmak	16 ΑΣΧΗΜΗ ΜΥΡΩΔΙΑ

ENGLISH	FRANÇAIS	DEUTSCH	NEDERLANDS	DANSK
11 IN THE SHIPYARD	**11 AU CHANTIER**	**11 AUF DER SCHIFFSWERFT**	**11 OP DE SCHEEPSWERF**	**11 PÅ VÆRFT**
Maintenance	**Entretien**	**Instandhaltung**	**Onderhoud**	**Vedligeholdelse**
1 scrub the bottom	1 nettoyer la carène à la brosse	1 das Unterwasserschiff reinigen	1 onderwaterschip schoonmaken	1 at skrubbe bunden
2 draw the keelbolts	2 enlever ou sortir les boulons de quille	2 die Kielbolzen heraus-schlagen	2 kielbouten trekken	2 at trække kølboltene
3 caulk the seams	3 calfater les coutures	3 die Nähte kalfatern	3 de naden breeuwen	3 at kalfatre nåderne
4 overhaul	4 revision	4 überholen	4 overhalen, reviseren	4 at efterse
5 strengthen	5 renforcer	5 verstärken	5 versterken	5 forstærke
6 replace	6 remplacer	6 erneuern	6 vervangen	6 forny
7 make watertight	7 étancher, rendre étanche	7 wasserdicht machen	7 waterdicht maken	7 gøre vandtæt
8 stop a leak	8 aveugler une voie d'eau	8 Leck abdichten	8 een lek dichten	8 stoppe en lækage
9 check	9 contrôler	9 kontrollieren, nachsehen	9 controleren	9 at efterse
10 pressure wash	10 lavage-pression	10 Hochdruckreinigung	10 hogedruk-reiniging	10 trykspuling
11 osmosis	11 osmose	11 Osmose	11 osmose	11 osmose
12 wicking	12 hydrophilage	12 Eindringen von Wasser in das Laminat	12 vocht doorgevend	12 polstring
13 polish	13 lustrer	13 Politur	13 poetsmiddel	13 polere
14 blister	14 cloque	14 Blasen	14 blaar	14 blærer
Painting	**Peinture**	**Anstrich**	**Schilderwerk**	**Malerarbejde**
1 burn off	1 brûler	1 abbrennen	1 afbranden	1 brænde af
2 rub down	2 poncer	2 schleifen	2 schuren	2 slibe ned
3 stop	3 enduire	3 spachteln	3 plamuren	3 spartle
4 primer	4 couche d'impression	4 Grundanstrich	4 primer, grondverf	4 grundmaling
5 undercoat	5 sous-couche	5 Vorstreichfarbe	5 grondlaag	5 understrygning
6 enamel paint	6 émail	6 Glanzanstrich	6 glansverf	6 emaljemaling
7 varnish	7 vernis	7 Lack	7 vernis, lak	7 lak
8 antifouling paint	8 peinture antisalissante ou antifouling	8 anwuchsverhütende Farbe	8 aangroeiwerende verf	8 bundmaling
9 hard	9 dur	9 hart	9 hard	9 hård

ESPAÑOL	ITALIANO	PORTUGUÊS	TÜRKÇE	ΕΛΛΗΝΙΚΑ
11 EN EL ASTILLERO	**11 IN CANTIERE**	**11 NO ESTALEIRO**	**11 TERSANEDE**	**11 ΣΤΟ ΚΑΡΝΑΓΙΟ**
Astillero, mantenimiento	**Manutenzione**	**Manutenção**	**Bakım**	**ΣΥΝΤΗΡΗΣΗ**
1 limpiar fondos	1 pulire la carena	1 escovar, limpar o fundo	1 karinayı fırçalamak	1 ΤΡΙΨΙΜΟ ΥΦΑΛΩΝ
2 sacar los pernos de la quilla	2 levare i bulloni di chiglia	2 retirar cavilhas do patilhão	2 omurga cıvatalarını sökmek	2 ΒΓΑΖΩ ΤΙΣ ΤΖΑΒΕΤΕΣ
3 calafatear las costuras	3 calafatare i comenti	3 calafetar as baínhas	3 armuzları kalafat etmek	3 ΚΑΛΑΦΑΤΙΖΩ ΕΝΩΣΕΙΣ
4 recorrer, revisar	4 revisionare	4 fazer revisão, rever	4 revizyon, genel bakım	4 ΓΕΝΙΚΗ ΕΠΙΣΚΕΥΗ
5 reforzar	5 rinforzare	5 reforçar	5 takviye, sağlamlaştırma	5 ΕΝΙΣΧΥΣΗ
6 reemplazar	6 sostituire	6 substituir, repôr	6 değiştirme	6 ΑΝΤΙΚΑΤΑΣΤΑΣΗ
7 hacer estanco	7 rendere stagno	7 tornar estanque	7 sızdırmaz hale getirmaek	7 ΣΤΕΓΑΝΟΠΟΙΗΣΗ
8 taponar	8 chiudere una falla	8 tapar uma entrada de água	8 suyunu kesmek, su yerini tamir etmek	8 ΣΤΑΜΑΤΑΩ ΔΙΑΡΡΟΗ
9 comprobar	9 controllare	9 verificar	9 kontrol etmek	9 ΕΛΕΓΧΟΣ
10 limpieza a presión	10 lavaggio a pressione	10 lavagem à pressão	10 tazyikli suyla yıkamak	10 ΥΔΡΟΒΟΛΗ
11 osmosis	11 osmosi	11 osmose	11 ozmos	11 ΟΣΜΩΣΗ
12 wicking	12 verniciatura a stoppino	12 colocar mechas	12 fitillenme	12 ΦΥΤΙΛΙΑΖΩ
13 pulir	13 lucidare	13 polir	13 parlatma	13 ΓΥΑΛΙΣΜΑ
14 ampolla	14 bolla	14 com bolhas	14 kabarcık	14 ΦΟΥΣΚΑΛΑ
Pintado	**Pittura**	**Pintura**	**Boya**	**ΒΑΨΙΜΟ**
1 quemar con soplete	1 bruciare via (la pittura)	1 queimar	1 boyayı yakmak	1 ΚΑΙΩ
2 lijar	2 raschiare	2 passar à lixa	2 zımparalamak	2 ΤΡΙΒΩ
3 boza, estopor	3 stuccare	3 encher	3 durdurmak	3 ΣΤΑΜΑΤΩ
4 imprimación	4 prima mano	4 primário	4 primer, astar katı	4 ΑΣΤΑΡΙ
5 primera mano de pintura	5 mano di fondo	5 aparelho	5 astar boya	5 ΚΑΤΩ ΣΤΡΩΜΑ
6 pintura de esmalte	6 smalto	6 tinta de esmalte	6 yağlı boya, parlak boya	6 ΣΜΑΛΤΟΧΡΩΜΑ
7 barniz	7 vernice	7 verniz	7 vernik	7 ΒΕΡΝΙΚΙ
8 pintura de patente, anti-incrustante	8 vernice antivegetativa	8 tinta anti-vegetativa	8 zehirli boya, anti-fouling	8 ΜΟΡΑΒΙΑ
9 duro	9 dura	9 forte	9 sert	9 ΣΚΛΗΡΟΣ

ENGLISH	FRANÇAIS	DEUTSCH	NEDERLANDS	DANSK
11 IN THE SHIPYARD	**11 AU CHANTIER**	**11 AUF DER SCHIFFSWERFT**	**11 OP DE SCHEEPSWERF**	**11 PÅ VÆRFT**
Painting	**Peinture**	**Anstrich**	**Schilderwerk**	**Malerarbejde**
10 self-polishing	10 auto-lustrant	10 selbst glättend	10 zelfslijpend	10 selv-polerende
11 eroding	11 qui s'écaille	11 anfressen	11 wegvretend	11 tæring/slid
12 copper	12 cuivre	12 Kupfer	12 koper (rood)	12 kobber
13 copolymer	13 copolymer	13 Antifoulingfarbe	13 copolymeer	13 copolymer
14 boot-topping	14 bande de flottaison	14 Wasserpaß-Farbe	14 waterlijnverf	14 vandliniemaling
15 non-slip deck paint	15 peinture anti-dérapante	15 rutsch- und trittfester Decksanstrich	15 antislipverf	15 skridsikker dæksmaling
16 stripper, paint remover	16 décapant	16 Abbeizer	16 afbijtmiddel	16 farvefjerner
17 blow lamp	17 lampe à souder	17 Lötlampe	17 afbrander, stripper	17 blæselampe
18 paintbrush	18 pinceau	18 Pinsel	18 verfkwast	18 pensel
19 scraper	19 grattoir	19 Schraper	19 schraper	19 skrabejern
20 sandpaper	20 papier de verre	20 Sandpapier	20 schuurpapier	20 sandpapir
21 sandblast	21 sabler	21 sandgestrahlt	21 zandstralen	21 sandblæse
22 peel	22 peler	22 abblättern	22 afschillen	22 skalle
23 gel coat	23 gel-coat	23 Gelcoat	23 gelcoat	23 gelcoat
24 polish	24 lustrer	24 Politur	24 poetsmiddel	24 voks/polish
25 epoxy	25 époxy	25 Epoxyd	25 epoxy, kunsthars	25 epoxy
26 paint roller	26 rouleau à peinture	26 Farbrolle	26 verfroller	26 malerulle
27 spray	27 peindre au pistolet	27 Spritzen	27 verfspuiter	27 spray
28 white spirit	28 white-spirit	28 Spiritus	28 verdunner	28 denatureret sprit
Laying up	**Désarmement**	**Auflegen**	**Opleggen**	**Lægge op**
1 haul out	1 tirer à terre, au sec	1 an Land holen	1 uit het water halen, droogzetten	1 tage på land
2 winter storage	2 hivernage	2 Winterlager	2 winterberging	2 vinteropbevaring
3 under cover	3 sous abri	3 abgedeckt, in einer Halle	3 afgedekt, onderdak	3 under tag
4 mud berth	4 en vasière	4 im Schlick liegen	4 ligplaats in het slik	4 vinterplads i mudder

ESPAÑOL	ITALIANO	PORTUGUÊS	TÜRKÇE	ΕΛΛΗΝΙΚΑ
11 EN EL ASTILLERO	**11 IN CANTIERE**	**11 NO ESTALEIRO**	**11 TERSANEDE**	**11 ΣΤΟ ΚΑΡΝΑΓΙΟ**
Pintado	**Pittura**	**Pintura**	**Boya**	**ΒΑΨΙΜΟ**
10 auto pulimentado	10 autolucidante	10 auto-polimento	10 kendi kendini parlatan	10 ΑΥΤΟΓΥΑΛΙΖΟΜΕΝΟ
11 erosionando	11 erosione	11 erodido	11 erozyonlu	11 ΔΙΑΒΡΩΤΙΚΟ
12 cobre	12 rame	12 cobre	12 bakır	12 ΧΑΛΚΟΣ
13 copolimer	13 copolimero	13 copolimer	13 kopolimer	13 ΣΥΜΠΟΛΥΜΕΡΕΣ
14 pintura de la flotación	14 anticorrosiva	14 boot-topping, tinta para faixa da linha de água	14 faça boyası	14 ΒΑΨΙΜΟ ΙΣΑΛΟΥ
15 pintura antideslizante	15 vernice antisdrucciolevole per ponte	15 tinta anti escorregante para convez	15 kaymaz güverte boyası	15 ΑΝΤΙΓΛΥΣΤΡΙΚΟ ΧΡΩΜΑ
16 decapan	16 sverniciatore	16 decapante	16 boya sökücü	16 ΡΙΜΟΥΒΕΡ
17 soplete	17 lampada a saldare	17 maçarico	17 kaynaklama lambası	17 ΚΑΜΙΝΕΤΟ
18 brocha	18 pennello	18 pincel, brocha	18 boya fırçası	18 ΠΙΝΕΛΟ
19 rasqueta	19 raschietto	19 raspa	19 raspa	19 ΞΥΣΤΡΑ
20 papel de lija	20 cartavetro	20 lixa	20 zımpara kâğıdı	20 ΓΥΑΛΟΧΑΡΤΟ
21 chorro de arena	21 sabbiatura	21 lixa de àgua	21 kum raspası	21 ΑΜΜΟΒΟΛΗ
22 pelar	22 spelatura	22 decapar	22 soymak, kazımak	22 ΞΕΦΛΟΥΔΙΖΩ
23 gel coat	23 gelcoat	23 gelcoat	23 jelkot	23 ΤΖΕΛ ΚΟΤ
24 pulir	24 polish	24 pulir	24 parlatıcı, poliş	24 ΓΥΑΛΙΣΜΑ
25 epoxy	25 epossi	25 epoxi	25 epoksi	25 ΕΠΟΞΙΚΟΣ
26 rodillo de pintar	26 rullo per pittura	26 rolo	26 boya rulosu	26 ΡΟΛΛΟ
27 spray	27 spruzzo	27 pintura à pistola	27 sprey boya	27 ΣΠΡΕΥ
28 aguarras	28 acquaragia	28 diluente	28 alkol	28 ΛΕΥΚΟ ΟΙΝΟΠΝΕΥΜΑ
Desarmar	**Disarmo**	**Colocar em seco**	**Tekneyi kapatma**	**ΑΠΟΘΕΣΗ ΣΚΑΦΟΥΣ**
1 varar	1 tirare in secco	1 alar, encalhar	1 karaya çekmek	1 ΑΝΕΛΚΥΣΗ
2 invernada	2 rimessaggio invernale	2 encalhar para o inverno	2 kışlama	2 ΧΕΙΜΕΡΙΝΗ ΠΑΡΑΜΟΝΗ
3 sombrajo	3 al coperto	3 pôr em barracão	3 kapalı yerde	3 ΣΚΕΠΑΣΜΕΝΟ
4 cama de fango	4 posto in secco (di barca)	4 encalhar no lôdo	4 çamura yatırmak	4 ΑΓΚΥΡΟΒΟΛΙΟ ΣΕ ΛΑΣΠΗ

159

ENGLISH	FRANÇAIS	DEUTSCH	NEDERLANDS	DANSK
11 IN THE SHIPYARD	**11 AU CHANTIER**	**11 AUF DER SCHIFFSWERFT**	**11 OP DE SCHEEPSWERF**	**11 PÅ VÆRFT**
Laying up	**Désarmement**	**Auflegen**	**Opleggen**	**Lægge op**
5 unstep the mast	5 démâter	5 den Mast herausnehmen	5 de mast afnemen	5 tage masten ud
6 cradle	6 ber, berceau	6 Slippwagen, Verladebock	6 wieg	6 vugge
7 to fit out	7 armer	7 ausrüsten, instandsetzen	7 uitrusten	7 udruste/klargøre
8 step the mast	8 mâter	8 den Mast einsetzen	8 mast plaatsen	8 rejse masten
9 to launch	9 mettre à l'eau	9 zu Wasser lassen	9 te water laten	9 at søsætte
10 legs	10 béquilles	10 seitliche Stützen für ein Boot beim Trockenfallen	10 poten	10 ben
11 slip	11 cale	11 Slipanlage	11 helling	11 bedding
12 crane	12 grue	12 Kran	12 kraan	12 kran
13 hoist	13 grue	13 Hebevorrichtung	13 kraan	13 at hejse
14 lift	14 grue	14 Lift	14 botenlift	14 at løfte
15 hard standing	15 aire de mise à sec en dur	15 fester Untergrund	15 op een harde ondergrond	15 stå hårdt
16 sling	16 élingue	16 Gurt	16 hijsband	16 strop
17 ladder	17 échelle	17 Leiter	17 ladder, trap	17 stige

ESPAÑOL	ITALIANO	PORTUGUÊS	TÜRKÇE	ΕΛΛΗΝΙΚΑ
11 EN EL ASTILLERO	**11 IN CANTIERE**	**11 NO ESTALEIRO**	**11 TERSANEDE**	**11 ΣΤΟ ΚΑΡΝΑΓΙΟ**
Desarmar	**Disarmo**	**Colocar em seco**	**Tekneyi kapatma**	**ΑΠΟΘΕΣΗ ΣΚΑΦΟΥΣ**
5 abatir el palo	5 disalberare	5 desmontar o mastro	5 direği sökmek	5 ΞΑΛΜΠΟΥΡΩΜΑ
6 cuna, calzo	6 vaso, invasatura	6 berço	6 beşik, kızak	6 ΚΑΒΑΛΕΤΟ
7 alistar	7 armare	7 armar	7 donatma	7 ΑΡΜΑΤΩΝΩ
8 arbolar el palo	8 alberare	8 montar, armar o mastro	8 direği dikmek	8 ΑΛΜΠΟΥΡΩΜΑ
9 botar, lanzar al agua	9 varare	9 desencalhar, pôr na água	9 denize indirmek	9 ΚΑΘΕΛΚΥΣΗ
10 escoras	10 puntelli, trampoli	10 escovas	10 dikmeleri	10 ΥΠΟΣΤΗΡΙΓΜΑΤΑ
11 varadero	11 scivolo	11 rampa de cais/deslize	11 kızak rampası	11 ΓΛΥΣΤΡΑ
12 grua	12 gru	12 guindaste	12 kreyn, vinç	12 ΓΕΡΑΝΟΣ
13 montacargas	13 issare	13 içar	13 kaldırmak	13 ΑΝΥΨΩΝΩ
14 travelift	14 sollevare	14 içar	14 kaldırmak	14 ΣΗΚΩΝΩ
15 varadero	15 suolo duro	15 estaleiro permanente	15 çekek alanı	15 ΣΤΕΡΕΩΜΕΝΟ
16 eslinga	16 braga	16 fundas	16 kayış	16 ΣΑΜΠΑΝΙ
17 escala	17 scala	17 escada	17 merdiven, iskele	17 ΣΚΑΛΑ

ENGLISH	FRANÇAIS	DEUTSCH	NEDERLANDS	DANSK
12 AT SEA	**12 EN MER**	**12 AUF SEE**	**12 OP ZEE**	**12 TIL SØS**
Sailing terms	**Termes de navigation à voile**	**Seemännische Ausdrücke**	**Scheepvaart-uitdrukkingen**	**Sejlsportsudtryk**
Points of sailing	*Les allures*	*Kurse zum Wind*	*Koersen*	*Sejlads*
1 head wind	1 vent debout	1 Gegenwind	1 wind tegen	1 modvind
2 head-to-wind	2 nez dans le vent	2 in den Wind	2 recht in de wind	2 vindret
3 the tack	3 bordée, bord	3 Schlag, Überstaggehen	3 slag	3 stagvending
4 port tack	4 bâbord amures	4 Steuerbordbug	4 slag over bakboord	4 bagbords halse
5 starboard tack	5 tribord amures	5 Backbordbug	5 slag over stuurboord	5 styrbords halse
6 to beat	6 tirer des bords, louvoyer	6 kreuzen	6 laveren, kruisen	6 at krydse
7 to go about	7 virer au vent	7 über Stag gehen, wenden	7 overstag gaan	7 at vende
8 'ready about'	8 'Paré à virer'	8 'Klar zum Wenden'	8 'Klaar om te wenden'	8 'klar at vende'
9 'lee-oh'	9 'Envoyez'	9 'Ree'	9 'Ree'	9 'læ'
10 close-hauled	10 au plus près	10 hoch am Wind	10 hoog aan de wind	10 kloshalet
11 on the wind	11 au près	11 am Wind, beim Wind	11 bij de wind	11 bidevind
12 full and by	12 au près bon plein	12 voll und bei	12 vol en bij, onder vol zeil	12 rumskøds
13 wind abeam	13 vent de travers, de côté	13 halber Wind	13 wind dwars, halve wind	13 vinden tværs
14 reaching	14 largue	14 raumschots	14 ruimschoots zeilen	14 slør
15 wind free	15 vent arrière ou portant	15 raumer Wind	15 ruime wind	15 fri vind
16 wind on the quarter	16 vent de la hanche, largue	16 Backstagsbrise	16 bakstagswind	16 vinden agten for tværs
17 running	17 vent arrière	17 vor dem Wind	17 voor de wind zeilen	17 lænse
18 dead before the wind	18 plein vent arrière	18 platt vor dem Wind	18 pal voor de wind zeilen	18 med vinden ret agterind
19 run by the lee	19 sous le vent, sur la panne	19 vor dem Wind nach Lee segeln	19 binnen de wind zeilen	19 lige før man bommer
20 to gybe	20 empanner, gambeyer	20 halsen	20 gijpen, halzen	20 at bomme

ESPAÑOL	ITALIANO	PORTUGUÊS	TÜRKÇE	ΕΛΛΗΝΙΚΑ
12 EN EL MAR	**12 IN MARE**	**12 NO MAR**	**12 DENİZDE**	**12 ΣΤΗΝ ΘΑΛΑΣΣΑ**
Terminos de vela	**Termini nautici**	**Termos vélicos**	**Denizcilik terimleri**	**ΝΑΥΤΙΚΟΙ ΟΡΟΙ**
Mareaje	*Andature*	*Pontos onde velejar*	*Seyir yönleri*	*ΣΤΟΙΧΕΙΑ//ΤΡΟΠΟΙ ΙΣΤΙΟΠΛΟΙΑΣ*
1 viento de proa	1 vento di prua	1 vento de prôa	1 pruva rüzgârı, baş rüzgârı	1 ΑΝΕΜΟΣ ΚΑΤΑΠΛΩΡΑ
2 proa al viento	2 prua al vento	2 aproado ao vento	2 rüzgâr pruvada, rüzgâr yakada	2 ΠΛΩΡΗ ΠΑΝΩ ΣΤΟΝ ΕΝΑΜΟ
3 bordada	3 il bordo	3 o bordo	3 kontra-tramola	3 ΤΟ ΜΠΡΑΤΣΟ
4 amurado a babor	4 bordo con mure a sinistra	4 amuras a bombordo	4 iskele kontra - iskele tramola	4 ΑΡΙΣΤΕΡΗΝΕΜΟΣ
5 amurado a estribor	5 bordo con mure a dritta	5 amuras a estibordo	5 sancak kontra - sancak tramola	5 ΔΕΞΗΝΕΜΟΣ
6 barloventear, ceñir	6 bolinare	6 bolinar	6 volta seyri	6 ΤΑΞΙΔΕΥΩ ΜΕ ΤΑΚ
7 virar	7 virare di bordo	7 virar por de vante	7 tramola etmek	7 ΑΝΑΣΤΡΕΦΩ-ΚΑΝΩ ΤΑΚ
8 'listo para virar'	8 'Pronti a virare'	8 'claro a virar'	8 'tramolaya hazır ol'	8 ΕΤΟΙΜΟΙ ΓΙΑ ΤΑΚ
9 ¡vira!'	9 'Vira'	9 'vira'	9 'tramola' yekeyi rüzgâr altına almak	9 ΕΤΟΙΜΟΣ ΓΙΑ ΤΑΚ ΑΠΟ ΤΙΜΟΝΙΕΡΑ
10 ciñendo	10 di bolina stretta	10 bolina cerrada	10 borina, toka prasya seyir	10 ΟΡΤΣΑΡΙΣΤΟΣ
11 de bolina	11 al vento, controventro	11 bolinando	11 orsa seyri	11 ΠΑΝΩ ΣΤΟΝ ΑΝΕΜΟ
12 en viento	12 a gonfie vele	12 de bolina	12 tam orsa, geniş orsa	12 ΠΛΕΩ ΟΡΤΣΑ ΧΩΡΙΣ ΕΚΠΕΣΜΟ
13 viento de través	13 col vento al traverso (o a mezza nave)	13 vento pelo través	13 kemere rüzgarı	13 ΑΝΕΜΟΣ ΣΤΟ ΠΛΑΙ
14 a un largo	14 di lasco	14 a um largo	14 apazlama, laşkasına	14 ΠΛΑΓΙΟΔΡΟΜΩ
15 viento libre	15 a vento largo	15 vento aberto, largo	15 yürütücü rüzgâr	15 ΑΝΕΜΟΣ ΛΑΣΚΑΔΑ
16 viento de aleta	16 vento al giardinetto	16 vento pela alhêta	16 geniş apaz	16 ΑΝΕΜΟΣ ΔΕΥΤΕΡΟΠΡΥΜΑ
17 en popa	17 col vento in poppa	17 navegar com vento à pôpa	17 pupa	17 ΚΑΤΑΠΡΥΜΑ ΠΛΕΥΣΗ
18 en pura empopada	18 col vento in fil di ruota	18 à pôpa razada	18 rüzgârı iğnecikten alarak	18 ΑΝΕΜΟΣ ΚΑΤΑΠΡΥΜΑ
19 tomar por la lua	19 col vento al giardinetto	19 correr à pôpa com vento iá por sotavento	19 rüzgâr altına	19 ΤΑΞΙΔΕΥΩ ΥΠΗΝΕΜΑ - ΣΤΑΒΕΝΤΩΜΕΝΟΣ
20 trasluchar	20 strambare	20 cambar	20 kavança	20 ΥΠΟΣΤΡΕΦΩ (ΤΣΙΜΑ)

163

ENGLISH	FRANÇAIS	DEUTSCH	NEDERLANDS	DANSK
12 AT SEA	**12 EN MER**	**12 AUF SEE**	**12 OP ZEE**	**12 TIL SØS**
Sailing terms	**Termes de navigation à voile**	**Seemännische Ausdrücke**	**Scheepvaart-uitdrukkingen**	**Sejlsportsudtryk**
Points of sailing	*Les allures*	*Kurse zum Wind*	*Koersen*	*Sejlads*
21 accidental gybe	21 empannage involontaire, gambeyage accidentel	21 unfreiwilliges Halsen, giepen	21 onvrijwillige gijp	21 utilsigtet bomning
22 heading wind	22 le vent refuse	22 schralender Wind	22 schralende wind	22 vinden spidser
23 freeing wind	23 le vent adonne	23 raumender Wind	23 ruimer inkomende wind	23 vinden rummer
24 windward/leeward	24 au vent/sous le vent	24 luvwärts/leewärts	24 loefwaarts/lijwaarts	24 luv/læ
Setting sails	*Etablir les voiles*	*Segel setzen*	*Zeil zetten*	*At sætte sejl*
1 bend on the sails	1 enverguer les voiles	1 die Segel anschlagen	1 aanslaan van de zeilen	1 at slå sejl under
2 hank on the jib	2 endrailler le foc	2 die Stagreiter einpicken	2 het inpikken van de fok	2 at slå fokken under
3 put in the battens	3 enfiler les lattes	3 Segellatten einsetzen	3 zeillatten inzetten	3 at sætte sejlpinde i lommerne
4 pull out the foot	4 étarquer le point d'écoute	4 das Underliek ausholen	4 voetlijk strekken	4 strække underliget
5 reeve the sheets	5 passer les écoutes dans les margouillets	5 die Schoten einscheren	5 de schoten inscheren	5 skære skøderne i
6 tighten the topping lift	6 peser sur la balancine	6 andirken	6 kraanlijn doorzetten	6 totte bomdirken
7 hoist the sail	7 hisser, établir la voile	7 Segel vorheißen	7 zeil hijsen	7 hejse sejl
8 sweat up the halyard	8 étarquer la drisse	8 das Fall steif durchsetzen	8 de vallen doorzetten	8 at strække faldet
9 change a sail	9 changer une voile	9 ein Segel auswechseln	9 een zeil verwisselen	9 skifte sejl
10 to shackle on	10 emmailler, maniller	10 einschäkeln	10 met sluiting vastzetten	10 sjække fast
11 lower, hand a sail	11 amener, baisser ou rentrer une voile	11 ein Segel bergen	11 een zeil strijken, innemen	11 at bjærge et sejl
12 to furl	12 serrer, ferler	12 auftuchen, bändseln	12 opdoeken	12 rulle sammen
13 in stops	13 à envergures-cassantes ou bosses-cassantes	13 aufgetucht	13 opgestopt	13 i knæk
14 to set a preventer	14 mettre une retenue	14 ein Backstag setzen	14 borgen	14 at sætte et stop

ESPAÑOL	ITALIANO	PORTUGUÊS	TÜRKÇE	ΕΛΛΗΝΙΚΑ
12 EN EL MAR	**12 IN MARE**	**12 NO MAR**	**12 DENİZDE**	**12 ΣΤΗΝ ΘΑΛΑΣΣΑ**
Terminos de vela	**Termini nautici**	**Termos vélicos**	**Denizcilik terimleri**	**ΝΑΥΤΙΚΟΙ ΟΡΟΙ**
Mareaje	*Andature*	*Pontos onde velejar*	*Seyir yönleri*	*ΣΤΟΙΧΕΙΑ ΤΡΟΠΟΙ ΙΣΤΙΟΠΛΟΙΑΣ*
21 trasluchada involuntaria	21 strambata accidentale	21 cambar involuntáriamente	21 istenmeden kavança, arızı kavança	21 ΜΗ ΕΛΕΓΧΟΜΕΝΗ ΥΠΟΣΤΡΟΦΗ
22 escasear el viento	22 vento che rifiuta, scarseggia	22 vento que casseia	22 rüzgâr yakadan esiyor, borinanın üzerinden esiyor	22 ΦΑΤΣΑΡΕΙ Ο ΑΝΕΜΟΣ
23 alargarse el viento	23 vento che ridonda	23 vento que alarga	23 rüzgâr açtı, yürütücü oldu	23 ΣΙΓΟΝΤΑΡΕΙ Ο ΑΝΕΜΟΣ
24 barlovento/sotavento	24 sopravvento/ sottovento	24 barlavento/sotavento	24 rüzgâr üstü/rüzgâr altı	24 ΠΡΟΣΗΝΕΜΟ/ΥΠΗΝΕΜΟ
Dar la vela	*Alzare le vele*	*Preparação das velas*	*Yelken basmak*	*ΣΗΚΩΜΑ ΠΑΝΙΩΝ*
1 envergar las velas	1 inferire le vele	1 envergar os panos	1 yelkenleri donatmak	1 ΚΟΤΣΑΡΩ ΠΑΝΙΑ
2 envergar el foque	2 ingarrocciare il fiocco	2 envergar o estai	2 floku ıstralyaya kancalamak, floku donatmak	2 ΚΟΤΣΑΡΩ ΤΟΝ ΦΛΟΚΟ
3 colocar los sables	3 mettere le stecche	3 meter as réguas	3 batenleri yerleştirmek	3 ΒΑΖΩ ΜΠΑΝΕΛΛΕΣ
4 tesar el pujamen	4 tesare la bugna	4 esticar o punho da escota	4 alt yakayı germek	4 ΦΕΡΜΑΡΩ ΤΟ ΠΟΔΑΡΙ
5 guarnir las escotas	5 incocciare le scotte	5 gornir o cabo da escota	5 iskotaları donatmak	5 ΔΕΝΩ ΣΚΟΤΕΣ ΣΤΑ ΠΟΡΤΟΥΖΙΑ
6 tesar el amantillo	6 tesare l'amantiglio	6 esticar o amantilho	6 balançinayı doldurmak boşunu almak	6 ΦΕΡΜΑΡΩ ΤΟ ΤΟΠΙΝ ΛΙΦΤ
7 izar la vela	7 issare la vela	7 içar a vela	7 yelken basmak	7 ΣΗΚΩΝΩ ΤΟ ΠΑΝΙ
8 tesar bien la driza	8 mettere in forza la drizza	8 entesar a adriça	8 mandarın boşunu almak, mandarı kasmak	8 ΦΕΡΜΑΡΩ ΤΟ ΜΑΝΤΑΡΙ
9 cambiar una vela	9 cambiare una vela	9 mudar uma vela	9 bir yelkeni değiştirmek	9 ΑΛΛΑΓΗ ΠΑΝΙΟΥ
10 engrilletar	10 ammanigliare	10 emanilhar	10 kilit vurmak	10 ΒΑΖΩ ΚΛΕΙΔΙ
11 arriar una vela	11 ammainare una vela	11 arriar a vela	11 yelkeni mayna etmek	11 ΜΑΙΝΑΡΩ ΤΟ ΠΑΝΙ
12 aferrar	12 serrare	12 ferrar	12 sarmak	12 ΤΥΛΙΓΩ
13 enjuncar, enchorizar	13 giuncato	13 rafiar	13 yelken sarma kalçeteleri	13 ΜΕ ΚΟΝΤΡΟΛ
14 fijación de un guía retenida	14 montare una ritenuta	14 instalar um preventer	14 kıç ıstralyayı donatmak	14 ΒΑΖΩ ΠΡΙΒΕΝΤΕΡ

ENGLISH	FRANÇAIS	DEUTSCH	NEDERLANDS	DANSK
12 AT SEA	**12 EN MER**	**12 AUF SEE**	**12 OP ZEE**	**12 TIL SØS**
Sailing terms	**Termes de navigation à voile**	**Seemännische Ausdrücke**	**Scheepvaart-uitdrukkingen**	**Sejlsportsudtryk**
Sail trimming	*Régler, tendre les voiles*	*Segel trimmen*	*Zeiltrim*	*Sejltrim*
1 to sheet a sail	1 border les voiles	1 ein Segel schoten	1 de schoot van een zeil vastzetten	1 at skøde et sejl
2 to make fast, belay	2 amarrer; tourner ou frapper une amarre	2 festmachen, belegen	2 beleggen, vastmaken	2 at sætte fast
3 to ease out, pay out	3 choquer, filer, mollir	3 fieren, schricken, auffieren	3 vieren, uitvieren	3 at slække ud
4 to coil a rope	4 lover	4 ein Tau aufschießen	4 een touw opschieten	4 at kvejle op
5 to take a turn	5 frapper un tour, donner un tour	5 einen Rundtörn machen	5 een torn nemen	5 tage rundtørn
6 to haul in, harden	6 embraquer, haler; peser sur, souquer, border	6 dichholen	6 schoot doorzetten	6 hale hjem/totte
7 to cast off/let go	7 larguer, démarrer	7 loswerfen	7 loswerpen, losgooien	7 kaste los/lade gå
8 reef down	8 prendre un ris	8 reffen	8 een rif steken	8 rebe ned
9 to move the sheet traveller	9 déplacer le charriot d'écoute	9 den Schottraveller verschieben	9 de traveller verzetten	9 flytte en skødeviser
10 to flake out a rope	10 entasser une corde	10 eine Leine an Deck flach auslegen	10 opschieten	10 flade et reb ud
Under sail	*Sous voiles*	*Unter Segel*	*Onder zeil*	*Under sejl*
1 full, drawing	1 pleine, portante	1 vollstehend, ziehend	1 vol	1 sejlet står fuldt og trækker
2 lifting	2 faseyer	2 killen	2 killen	2 sejlet lever
3 aback	3 à contre	3 backstehen	3 bak	3 bakker
4 slatting	4 battante, fouettante	4 schlagen	4 klapperen	4 blafrer
5 to let fly	5 larguer	5 fliegen lassen	5 laten vieren	5 lade gå/flyve
6 to back the jib	6 contrebrasser, porter le foc au vent	6 Fock backhalten	6 fok bak houden	6 bakke fokken
7 wing-on-wing	7 en papillon	7 beidseits ausgefahrene Segel	7 met dubbele voorzeilen	7 spile forsejlene

ESPAÑOL	ITALIANO	PORTUGUÊS	TÜRKÇE	ΕΛΛΗΝΙΚΑ
12 EN EL MAR	**12 IN MARE**	**12 NO MAR**	**12 DENİZDE**	**12 ΣΤΗΝ ΘΑΛΑΣΣΑ**
Terminos de vela	**Termini nautici**	**Termos vélicos**	**Denizcilik terimleri**	**ΝΑΥΤΙΚΟΙ ΟΡΟΙ**
Marear las velas	*Regolare le vele*	*Afinação das velas*	*Yelken trimi/ayarı*	*ΤΡΙΜΑΡΙΣΜΑ ΠΑΝΙΩΝ*
1 cazar una vela	1 mettere le scotte a una vela	1 caçar a vela	1 yelken ıskotasını doldurmak	1 ΠΑΙΡΝΩ ΣΚΟΤΑ ΜΕΣΑ
2 amarrar	2 dar volta (a una cima), rizzare	2 amarrar, passar volta a um cunho	2 koçboynuzuna volta etmek	2 ΣΤΕΡΕΩΝΩ
3 amollar, filar	3 lascare (una vela), filare (una cima)	3 folgar a vela	3 iskotayı (halatı) kaçırmak	3 ΛΑΣΚΑΡΩ-ΑΦΗΝΩ
4 adujar un cabo	4 aduggliare una cima	4 colher um cabo	4 bir halatı roda etmek	4 ΝΤΟΥΚΙΑΖΩ ΣΚΟΙΝΙ
5 tomar una vuelta	5 prendere una volta	5 passar uma volta	5 bir volta almak	5 ΠΑΙΡΝΩ ΒΟΛΤΑ
6 cazar	6 cazzare, cazzare a ferro	6 caçar	6 boşunu almak, doldurmak	6 ΦΕΡΜΑΡΩ
7 largar	7 mollare	7 largar	7 laşka etmek, boş koymak	7 ΑΦΗΝΩ
8 tomar rizos	8 terzarolare	8 rizar	8 camadana vurmak	8 ΠΑΙΡΝΩ ΜΟΥΔΑ
9 mover el carro de escota	9 spostare il punto di scotta	9 mover o carrinho da escota	9 iskota güverte arabasının yerini değiştirmek	9 ΜΕΤΑΚΙΝΩ ΤΟ ΒΑΓΟΝΑΚΙ ΣΚΟΤΑΣ
10 cabo listo para largar	10 abbisciare (mettere in chiaro) una cima	10 desfiar/escarçar cabos	10 halat rodasını açmak	10 ΝΤΟΥΚΙΑΖΩ ΣΚΟΙΝΙ
A la vela	*Sotto vela*	*Velejando*	*Yelkenle seyir*	*ΙΣΤΙΟΠΛΕΟΝΤΑΣ*
1 llena, portando	1 piena, che porta	1 cheia, cheio, a puxar	1 yelken dolu, tam çekiyor	1 ΓΕΜΑΤΑ-ΤΡΑΒΑΝΕ
2 tocando	2 che si alza	2 encher por sotavento	2 yelken yapraklıyor	2 ΕΛΞΗ
3 en facha	3 a collo	3 aquartelado	3 terslemek	3 ΑΝΤΙΝΕΜΩΜΑ
4 flamear	4 che sbatte, che fileggia	4 bater pano	4 yapraklanma	4 ΠΑΙΞΙΜΟ-ΧΤΥΠΗΜΑ
5 arriar en banda	5 lasciar fileggiare	5 largar o pano	5 laşka etmek, yelkeni boşaltmak	5 ΑΦΗΝΩ ΤΕΛΕΙΩΣ ΤΟ ΠΑΝΙ
6 acuartelar el foque	6 mettere il fiocco a collo	6 aquartelar o estai	6 floku rüzgara tersten göstermek	6 ΣΙΑΡΩ ΤΟ ΦΛΟΚΟ
7 orejas de burro	7 a farfalla, a forbice	7 armar em borboleta	7 ayı bacağı	7 ΠΕΤΑΛΟΥΔΑ

ENGLISH	FRANÇAIS	DEUTSCH	NEDERLANDS	DANSK
12 AT SEA	**12 EN MER**	**12 AUF SEE**	**12 OP ZEE**	**12 TIL SØS**
Seamanship	**Sens marin**	**Seemannschaft**	**Zeemanschap**	**Sømandsskab**
Boat characteristics	***Caractéristiques du bateau***	***Schiffseigenschaften***	***Booteigenschappen***	***Bådens egenskaber***
1 seaworthy	1 marin, qui tient bien la mer	1 seetüchtig	1 zeewaardig	1 sødygtig
2 stability	2 stabilité	2 Stabilität	2 stabiliteit	2 stabilitet
3 to heel	3 giter	3 krängen, überliegen	3 hellen, overhellen	3 at krænge/smide til
4 stiff	4 raide à la toile	4 steif	4 stijf	4 rank
5 tender	5 gîtard	5 rank	5 slap	5 kilden
6 to point well	6 tenir bon cap	6 hoch am Wind segeln	6 hoog aan de wind zeilen	6 at holde højt
7 weather helm	7 être ardent	7 luvgierig	7 loefgierig	7 luvgerrig
8 lee helm	8 être mou	8 leegierig	8 lijgierig	8 lægerrig
9 to pitch	9 tanguer	9 einsetzen, stampfen	9 stampen	9 at stampe
10 to roll	10 rouler	10 rollen	10 rollen	10 at rulle
11 to yaw	11 faire des embardées	11 gieren	11 gieren	11 at gire
Helming	***A la barre***	***Rudergehen***	***Sturen***	***At styre***
1 helm	1 barre, gouvernail	1 Ruder	1 roer	1 ror
2 put up the helm	2 mettre la barre dessus	2 Ruder nach Luv	2 afhouden	2 styre højere
3 bear away	3 abattre, laisser arriver	3 abfallen	3 afhouden, afvallen	3 sejle afsted
4 sail fuller	4 abattre, venir sous le vent	4 voller segeln	4 voller zeilen	4 holde fulde sejl
5 put down the helm	5 mettre la barre dessous	5 Ruder nach Lee	5 oploeven	5 styre lavere
6 luff up	6 lofer	6 anluven	6 oploeven	6 luffe
7 to point higher	7 venir au vent, remonter	7 höher anliegen	7 hoger sturen	7 holde højere
8 pinching	8 finasser, faire trop bon cap	8 kneifen	8 knijpen	8 at knibe
9 to meet her	9 rencontrer	9 aufkommen	9 opvangen (wind)	9 støtte båden

ESPAÑOL	ITALIANO	PORTUGUÊS	TÜRKÇE	ΕΛΛΗΝΙΚΑ
12 EN EL MAR	**12 IN MARE**	**12 NO MAR**	**12 DENİZDE**	**12 ΣΤΗΝ ΘΑΛΑΣΣΑ**
Arte marinero	**Arte della navigazione**	**Arte de marinheiro**	**Denizcilik**	**ΝΑΥΤΟΣΥΝΗ**
Caracteristicas del barco	*Qualitá della barca*	*Caracteristicas do barco*	*Tekne nitelikleri*	*ΧΑΡΑΚΤΗΡΙΣΤΙΚΑ ΣΚΑΦΟΥΣ*
1 navegabilidad	1 marina, che tiene il mare	1 qualidades de mar	1 denizci tekne	1 ΑΞΙΟΠΛΟΟ
2 estabilidad	2 stabilità	2 estabilidade	2 denge	2 ΕΥΣΤΑΘΕΙΑ
3 escorar	3 sbandare	3 inclinar	3 yana yatma, bayılma	3 ΚΟΥΠΑΣΤΑΡΩ
4 duro	4 dura	4 com muita estabilidade	4 rüzgara bayılmiyor	4 ΚΟΥΠΑΣΤΑΡΕΙ ΔΥΣΚΟΛΑ
5 blando	5 cedevole	5 com pouca estabilidade	5 kolay bayılmak	5 ΚΟΥΠΑΣΤΑΡΕΙ ΕΥΚΟΛΑ
6 bolinero	6 boliniera	6 bolinar bem	6 iyi yol tutmak, rotadan kaçmamak	6 ΠΑΕΙ ΣΤΗΝ ΠΟΡΕΙΑ
7 ardiente	7 orziera	7 leme com tendência para orçar	7 orsaya kaçan, rüzgâr üstüne kaçan	7 ΠΟΔΙΖΕΙ ΤΟ ΤΙΜΟΝΙ
8 propenso a la arribada	8 puggiera	8 leme com tendência para arribar	8 bociye kaçan, rüzgâr altına kaçan	8 ΟΡΤΣΑΡΕΙ ΤΟ ΤΙΜΟΝΙ
9 cabecear, arfar	9 beccheggiare	9 balanço longitudinal	9 baş-kıç yapmak	9 ΣΚΑΜΠΑΝΕΥΑΣΜΑ
10 balancear	10 rollare	10 balanço transversal	10 yalpalamak, yalpaya düşmek	10 ΜΠΟΤΖΙ
11 guiñar	11 straorzare	11 guinar	11 rotadan âni sapmak	11 ΦΕΥΓΩ ΑΠΟ ΤΗΝ ΠΟΡΕΙΑ-ΕΚΤΡΕΠΟΜΑΙ
Gobernar	*Governare*	*Governar*	*Dümen tutmak*	*ΤΙΜΟΝΕΥΟΝΤΑΣ*
1 caña	1 timone	1 o lomo	1 dümen	1 ΤΙΜΟΝΙ
2 levantar la caña	2 mettere il timone alla puggia	2 lomo de oncontro	2 dümeni kırmak, dümeni üzerine tutmak	2 ΠΟΔΙΖΩ ΜΕ ΤΟ ΤΙΜΟΝΙ
3 arribar	3 poggiare	3 arribar	3 teknenin başını açmak, boci kaçmak	3 ΠΟΔΙΖΩ
4 marear la vela	4 abbattere	4 navegar mais arribado	4 rüzgâr altına kaçmak, bociye kaçmak	4 ΓΕΜΑΤΟ ΠΑΝΙ
5 meter la caña	5 mettere il timone all'orza	5 leme de ló	5 yekeyi rüzgâr altına basmak	5 ΟΡΤΣΑΡΩ ΜΕ ΤΟ ΤΙΜΟΝΙ
6 orzar	6 orzare	6 orçar	6 orsalamak	6 ΛΟΦΑΡΩ - ΑΝΕΒΑΙΝΩ ΣΤΗΝ ΕΓΓΥΤΑΤΗ
7 ceñir más	7 stringere di più	7 orçar mais	7 daha yüksek seyretmek	7 ΑΝΕΒΑΙΝΩ ΚΙ ΑΛΛΟ ΣΤΟΝ ΚΑΙΡΟ
8 orzar a fil de roda	8 stringere al limite	8 à trinca	8 orsada çok kasmak	8 ΜΠΙΤΖΑΡΩ
9 gobernar al encuentro	9 governare con anticipo	9 levar ao encontro	9 karşilamak	9 ΑΝΑΠΟΔΟ ΤΙΜΟΝΙ

ENGLISH	FRANÇAIS	DEUTSCH	NEDERLANDS	DANSK
12 AT SEA	**12 EN MER**	**12 AUF SEE**	**12 OP ZEE**	**12 TIL SØS**
Seamanship	**Sens marin**	**Seemannschaft**	**Zeemanschap**	**Sømandsskab**
Helming	*A la barre*	*Rudergehen*	*Sturen*	*At styre*
10 on course	10 maintenir le cap	10 auf Kurs	10 op koers	10 på kursen
11 off course	11 ne pas suivre la route	11 vom Kurs abgewichen	11 van koers	11 ude af kurs
12 alter course	12 changer de cap	12 Kurs ändern	12 koers veranderen	12 ændre kurs
13 to answer the helm	13 obéir à la barre	13 dem Ruder gehorchen	13 naar het roer luisteren	13 lystre roret
Under way	*En route*	*In Fahrt*	*Onderweg*	*Sejlads*
1 to have way	1 avoir de l'erre, lancée	1 Fahrt voraus machen	1 vaart hebben	1 at have styrefart
2 to make headway	2 avancer, filer	2 Fahrt über Grund machen	2 vooruit vaart lopen	2 at gå fremover
3 to stem the tide	3 remonter la marée	3 den Strom aussegeln	3 het tij doodzeilen	3 at stævne strømmen
4 becalmed	4 encalminé	4 bekalmt	4 door windstilte geplaagd	4 ligge i vindstille
5 to drift	5 dériver	5 treiben, abtreiben	5 afdrijven	5 at drive
6 sternway	6 culer	6 Achterausfahrt	6 achteruitvaren, deinzen	6 at sakke
7 bow wave	7 moustaches	7 Bugwelle	7 boeggolf	7 bovbølge
8 stern wave, wake, wash	8 lame de sillage, sillage	8 Heckwelle, Kielwasser	8 hekgolf, kielzog	8 hækbølge/kølvand
9 way enough	9 erre suffisante	9 genug Fahrt	9 genoeg vaart	9 fart nok
10 full ahead	10 en avant toute	10 volle Fahrt voraus	10 volle kracht vooruit	10 fuld kraft frem
11 slow astern	11 arrière lentement	11 langsame Fahrt zurück	11 langzaam achteruit	11 langsomt bak
12 lose way	12 perdre de l'erre, casser son erre	12 Fahrt verlieren	12 vaart verliezen	12 tabe fart
13 leeway	13 dérive	13 Abdrift	13 afdrijven	13 afdrift
Heavy weather	*Gros temps*	*Schweres Wetter*	*Zwaar weer*	*Hårdt vejr*
1 shorten sail	1 réduire la voile	1 Segel verkleinern	1 zeil minderen	1 mindske sejl
2 to reef down	2 prendre un ris	2 reffen	2 reven	2 at rebe
3 close reefed	3 au bas ris	3 dicht gerefft	3 dichtgereefd	3 klosrebet
4 shake out a reef	4 larguer un ris	4 ausreffen, Reffs auschütten	4 een rif uitnemen, uitreven	4 stikke et reb ud

ESPAÑOL	ITALIANO	PORTUGUÊS	TÜRKÇE	ΕΛΛΗΝΙΚΑ
12 EN EL MAR	**12 IN MARE**	**12 NO MAR**	**12 DENİZDE**	**12 ΣΤΗΝ ΘΑΛΑΣΣΑ**
Arte marinero	**Arte della navigazione**	**Arte de marinheiro**	**Denizcilik**	**ΝΑΥΤΟΣΥΝΗ**
Gobernar	*Governare*	*Governar*	*Dümen tutmak*	*ΤΙΜΟΝΕΥΟΝΤΑΣ*
10 a rumbo	10 in rotta	10 estar no rumo	10 rotada seyretmek	10 ΣΤΗΝ ΠΟΡΕΙΑ
11 fuera de rumbo	11 fuori rotta	11 estar fora do rumo	11 rota dışına çıkmak	11 ΕΚΤΟΣ ΠΟΡΕΙΑΣ
12 cambiar el rumbo	12 cambiare la rotta	12 alterar o rumo	12 rota değiştirmek	12 ΑΛΛΑΓΗ ΠΟΡΕΙΑΣ
13 responder bien al timón	13 rispondere al timone	13 obedecer ao leme	13 dümen dinlemek	13 ΤΟ ΠΛΟΙΟ ΑΚΟΥΕΙ ΣΤΟ ΤΙΜΟΝΙ
Navegando	*In navigazione*	*A caminho*	*Yolda*	*ΤΑΞΙΔΕΥΟΝΤΑΣ*
1 llevar camino, ir avante	1 avere abbrivio	1 ter andamento	1 bulunmak	1 ΕΧΩ ΔΡΟΜΟ
2 hacer camino	2 avanzare	2 ganhar andamento	2 ilerlemek, yol bulunmak	2 ΚΙΝΟΥΜΑΙ ΜΠΡΟΣ
3 vencer la marea	3 risalire la marea	3 vencer a corrente	3 akıntıda yükselmek	3 ΚΟΝΤΡΑΡΩ - ΤΟ ΡΕΥΜΑ ΚΑΙ ΠΡΟΧΩΡΩ
4 encalmado	4 abbonacciato	4 encalmado	4 rüzgârsız kalmak	4 ΚΑΡΑΝΤΙΑΣΜΕΝΟΣ
5 derivar	5 derivare	5 andar à deriva	5 akıntıya kapılmak	5 ΠΑΡΑΣΥΡΟΜΑΙ
6 navegar hacia atrás, ciar	6 abbrivio indietro	6 andamento a ré	6 geri gitmek, kaymak	6 ΕΚΠΙΠΤΩ ΠΡΟΣ ΤΑ ΠΙΣΩ
7 bigote	7 onda di prora	7 onda da prôa	7 pruva dalgası	7 ΚΥΜΑ ΠΛΩΡΗΣ
8 bigote de aleta	8 onda di poppa, scia	8 onda da pôpa, esteira	8 kıç dalgası, dümen suyu	8 ΑΠΟΝΕΡΟ
9 salida	9 abbrivio sufficiente	9 andamento suficiente	9 üzerinde yeterli yol bulunmak	9 ΑΡΚΕΤΟΣ ΔΡΟΜΟΣ
10 avante toda	10 avanti tutta	10 tôdo avante	10 tam yol ileri	10 ΠΡΟΣΩ ΟΛΟΤΑΧΩΣ
11 atrás despacio	11 indietro adagio	11 a ré devagar	11 ağıryol ileri	11 ΑΡΓΑ ΑΝΑΠΟΔΑ
12 perder marcha	12 perdere abbrivio	12 perder andamento	12 yoldan düşmek, yavaşlamak	12 ΧΑΝΩ ΔΡΟΜΟ
13 abatimiento	13 scarroccio	13 sotavento	13 rüzgâr altına düşmek	13 ΣΤΑΒΕΝΤΟ ΕΚΠΕΣΜΟΣ
Mal tiempo	*Cattivo tempo*	*Mau tempo*	*Kötü hava*	*ΚΑΚΟΚΑΙΡΙΑ*
1 reducir paño	1 ridurre le vele	1 reduzir o pano	1 yelken azaltmak	1 ΜΕΙΩΝΩ ΙΣΤΙΟΦΟΡΙΑ
2 tomar rizos	2 terzarolare	2 rizar	2 camadana vurmak	2 ΜΟΥΔΑΡΩ
3 llevar todos los rizos	3 terzarolato al massimo	3 muito rizado	3 alt sıra camadanı vurmak	3 ΑΜΠΑΣΟ ΜΟΥΔΑ
4 largar los rizos	4 togliere una mano di terzaroli	4 desrizar	4 bir camadanı sökmek	4 ΞΕΜΟΥΔΑΡΩ

171

ENGLISH	FRANÇAIS	DEUTSCH	NEDERLANDS	DANSK
12 AT SEA	**12 EN MER**	**12 AUF SEE**	**12 OP ZEE**	**12 TIL SØS**
Seamanship	**Sens marin**	**Seemannschaft**	**Zeemanschap**	**Sømandsskab**
Heavy weather	*Gros temps*	*Schweres Wetter*	*Zwaar weer*	*Hårdt vejr*
5 under bare poles	5 à sec de toile	5 vor Topp und Takel	5 voor top en takel	5 for riggen alene
6 stream a sea anchor	6 mouiller sur une ancre flottante	6 einen Treibanker ausbringen	6 een zeeanker uitbrengen	6 benytte et drivanker
7 stream a warp	7 filer une aussière en remorque	7 eine Trosse nachschleppen	7 een tros achteruit brengen	7 stikke et varp ud
8 strike the topmast	8 saluer un grain, rentrer le flèche	8 die Toppstenge streichen	8 de topmast strijken	8 stryge topmasten
9 heave-to	9 capeyer, mettre à la cape, prendre la cape	9 beiliegen, beidrehen	9 bijdraaien	9 ligge underdrejet
10 to lie a'hull	10 mettre à sec de voiles	10 das Boot dwars in der See treiben lassen, beiliegen	10 plat liggen	10 ligge uden sejl
11 ride out a storm	11 étaler une tempête	11 Sturm abreiten	11 een storm afrijden	11 ride en storm ud
12 blow out a sail	12 déchirer, perdre une voile	12 ein Segel fliegt aus den Lieken	12 een zeil uit het lijk waaien	12 skøre et sejl
13 ship a green sea	13 embarquer un paquet de mer	13 grünes Wasser übernehmen	13 een zee overnemen	13 tage en grøn sø ombord
14 weather bound	14 bloqué par le temps	14 eingeweht	14 door het weer opgehouden	14 indeblæst
15 to secure	15 arrimer	15 sichern	15 zeeklaar maken, sjorren	15 at sikre
16 to stow	16 ranger	16 stauen	16 stuwen	16 at stuve
17 to lash down	17 attacher	17 festlaschen	17 sjorren	17 at surre
Aground	*Echoué*	*Auf Grund sitzen*	*Aan de grond*	*Grundstødning*
1 high and dry	1 au sec	1 hoch und trocken	1 hoog en droog, droog vallen	1 gået på grund
2 to heel the boat	2 faire gîter le bateau	2 das Boot krängen	2 de boot krengen	2 at krænge båden
3 to refloat	3 dégager, deséchouer	3 wieder flottmachen	3 vlot brengen	3 at få båden let

172

ESPAÑOL	ITALIANO	PORTUGUÊS	TÜRKÇE	ΕΛΛΗΝΙΚΑ
12 EN EL MAR	**12 IN MARE**	**12 NO MAR**	**12 DENİZDE**	**12 ΣΤΗΝ ΘΑΛΑΣΣΑ**
Arte marinero	**Arte della navigazione**	**Arte de marinheiro**	**Denizcilik**	ΝΑΥΤΟΣΥΝΗ
Mal tiempo	***Cattivo tempo***	***Mau tempo***	***Kötü hava***	*ΚΑΚΟΚΑΙΡΙΑ*
5 a palo seco	5 ad albero secco	5 em árvore sêca	5 kuru direkle seyir	5 ΞΥΛΑΡΜΕΝΟΣ
6 largar un ancla flotante	6 filare un'ancora galleggiante	6 deitar a âncora flutuante	6 bir deniz demiri salmak	6 ΣΥΡΩ ΠΛΩΤΗ ΑΓΚΥΡΑ
7 largar una estacha por popa	7 filare un cavo di tonneggio	7 deitar ao mar um cabo a servir de âncora flutuante	7 yedekleme tel halatını göndermek	7 ΣΥΡΩ ΣΚΟΙΝΙ
8 calar el mastelero	8 sghindare l'alberetto	8 arriar o mastaréu	8 direkbaşı yelkenini mayna etmekle fırtınayı karşılamak	8 ΜΑΙΝΑΡΩ ΤΟ ΕΠΙΣΤΗΛΙΟ
9 fachear, capear	9 mettersi alla cappa	9 meter de capa	9 tekneyi fırtınada eylendirmek	9 ΤΡΑΒΕΡΣΩΝΩ
10 al pairo	10 stare in cappa secca	10 pairar	10 fırtınayı kuru direkle karşılamak	10 ΑΝΑΚΩΧΗ - ΑΛΛΑ ΚΑΠΑ ΞΥΛΑΡΜΕΝΟΣ
11 aguantar un mal tiempo	11 sostenere una burrasca	11 aguentar um temporal	11 fırtınayı göğüslemek	11 ΑΝΤΙΜΕΤΩΠΙΖΩ ΘΥΕΛΛΑ
12 rifar una vela	12 strappare una vela	12 desfazer uma vela	12 yelkeni yırtmak	12 ΣΚΙΖΕΤΑΙ ΠΑΝΙ
13 embarcar un golpe de mar	13 prendere un'incappellata	13 embarcar grande massa de água	13 dalganın güverteyi yalaması	13 ΚΑΤΑΚΛΥΖΟΜΑΙ ΑΠΟ ΜΕΓΑΛΟ ΚΥΜΑ
14 detenido por mal tiempo	14 trattenuto dal maltempo	14 abrigado, aguardando melhoria de tempo	14 hava nedeniyle limanı terk edemem	14 ΠΟΔΙΣΜΕΝΟΣ ΛΟΓΩ ΚΑΚΟΚΑΙΡΙΑΣ
15 amarrar	15 fissare	15 fixar em segurança	15 emniyete almak	15 ΣΙΓΟΥΡΕΥΩ
16 estibar	16 stivare	16 estivar	16 yerine yerleştirmek	16 ΑΠΟΘΗΚΕΥΩ
17 trincar, amarrar	17 rizzare	17 amarrar	17 denizbağı vurmak, bağlamak	17 ΔΕΝΩ
Varado, encallado	***In secca***	***Encalhar***	***Karaya oturmak***	*ΠΡΟΣΑΡΑΞΗ*
1 estar en seco	1 completamente in secca	1 ficar em sêco	1 tekneyi yatırmak	1 ΠΡΟΣΑΡΑΓΜΕΝΟ ΕΞΩ ΑΠΟ ΤΟ ΝΕΡΟ
2 tumbar, dar la banda	2 sbandare la barca	2 inclinar o barco	2 yana yatma, bayılma	2 ΚΟΥΠΑΣΤΑΡΩ ΤΟ ΣΚΑΦΟΣ
3 poner a flote	3 rimettere a galla	3 pôr a flutuar	3 tekneyi yüzdürmek	3 ΞΑΝΑΕΠΙΠΛΕΩ

173

ENGLISH	FRANÇAIS	DEUTSCH	NEDERLANDS	DANSK
13 NAVIGATION	**13 NAVIGATION**	**13 NAVIGATION**	**13 NAVIGATIE**	**13 NAVIGATION**
Equipment	**Equipement**	**Ausrüstung**	**Uitrusting**	**Udstyr**
Chart table	*Table à cartes*	*Kartentisch*	*Kaartentafel*	*Kortbord*
1 Pilot	1 Instructions Nautiques	1 Seehandbuch	1 zeemansgids, loods	1 lodsbog
2 Nautical Almanac	2 Almanach Nautique	2 Nautischer Almanach	2 nautische amanak	2 nautisk almanak
3 Tide Tables	3 Annuaire des Marées	3 Gezeitentafeln	3 getijtafels	3 tidevandstabeller
4 Tidal Stream Atlas	4 Atlas des Marées	4 Stromatlas	4 stroomatlas	4 tidevandsatlas
5 List of Lights	5 Livre des Phares	5 Leuchtfeuerverzeichnis	5 lichtenlijst	5 fyrliste
6 Notices to Mariners	6 Avis aux Navigateurs	6 Nachrichten für Seefahrer	6 bericht aan zeevarenden	6 efterretninger for søfarende
7 deviation table	7 courbe des déviations	7 Deviationstabelle	7 stuurtafel	7 deviationstabel
8 parallel ruler	8 règles parallèles	8 Parallellineal	8 paralleliniaal	8 parallellineal
9 protractor	9 rapporteur	9 Winkelmesser	9 gradenboog	9 transportør
10 triangular protractor	10 rapporteur triangulaire	10 Kursdreieck	10 driehoek	10 trekantet transportør
11 pencil	11 crayon	11 Bleistift	11 potlood	11 blyant
12 rubber	12 gomme	12 Radiergummi	12 gum, vlakgom	12 viskelæder
13 dividers	13 pointes sèches	13 Kartenzirkel	13 kaartpasser	13 passer
14 binoculars	14 jumelles	14 Fernglas, Doppelglas	14 kijker, verrekijker	14 kikkert
15 plotter	15 traceur	15 Plotter	15 plotter	15 plotter
Sextant	*Sextant*	*Sextant*	*Sextant*	*Sekstant*
1 horizon, index glass	1 petit, grand miroir	1 Horizont-, Indexspiegel	1 kimspiegel, grote spiegel	1 horizont, alidespejl
2 index error	2 erreur de l'alidade	2 Indexfehler	2 indexfout	2 indexfejl
3 index bar	3 alidade	3 Index	3 nonius	3 indeksen
4 shades	4 filtres	4 Schattengläser	4 gekleurde glazen	4 blændglas
5 micrometer drum	5 tambour micrométrique	5 Trommel	5 trommel	5 mikrometerskrue
6 arc	6 limbe	6 Gradbogen	6 boog	6 buen

ESPAÑOL	ITALIANO	PORTUGUÊS	TÜRKÇE	ΕΛΛΗΝΙΚΑ
13 NAVEGACION	**13 NAVIGAZIONE**	**13 NAVEGAÇÃO**	**13 NAVİGASYON**	**13 ΝΑΥΤΙΛΙΑ**
Equipamiento	**Attrezzature**	**Equipamento**	**Ekipman**	**ΕΞΟΠΛΙΣΜΟΣ**

Mesa de cartas	*Tavolo di carteggio*	*Mesa de cartas*	*Harita masası*	*ΤΡΑΠΕΖΙ ΧΑΡΤΩΝ*
1 Derrotero	1 Portolano	1 Pilôto, Roteiro da costa	1 Notik bilgiler, Kılavuz	1 ΠΙΛΟΤΟΣ
2 Almanaque Náutico	2 Effemeridi	2 Almanaque Náutico	2 Notik Almanak	2 ΝΑΥΤΙΚΟ ΗΜΕΡΟΛΟΓΙΟ
3 Tabla de Mareas	3 Tavole di marea	3 Tabela de Marés	3 Akıntılar Yıllığı	3 ΠΙΝΑΚΕΣ ΠΑΛΙΡΡΟΙΩΝ
4 Atlas de Mareas	4 Atlante delle correnti	4 Atlas de Marés	4 Akıntılar Atlası	4 ΑΤΛΑΣ ΠΑΛΙΡΡΟΙΑΚΩΝ ΡΕΥΜΑΤΩΝ
5 Cuaderno de Faros	5 Elenco dei fari	5 Lista de Faróis	5 Fenerler Kitabı	5 ΦΑΡΟΔΕΙΚΤΗΣ
6 Aviso a los Navegantes	6 Avvisi ai Naviganti	6 Avisos aos Navegantes	6 Denizcilere İlanlar	6 ΟΔΗΓΙΕΣ ΠΡΟΣ ΝΑΥΤΙΛΟΜΕΝΟΥΣ
7 table de desviós	7 tabella delle deviazioni	7 tábua de desvios	7 arızi sapma	7 ΠΙΝΑΚΙΔΙΟ ΠΑΡΕΚΤΡΟΠΩΝ
8 paralelas	8 parallele	8 régua de paralelas	8 paralel cetvel	8 ΔΙΠΑΡΑΛΛΗΛΟΣ
9 transportador	9 goniometro	9 transferidor	9 protaktor/raportör	9 ΜΟΙΡΟΓΝΩΜΟΝΙΟ
10 transportador triangular	10 squadretta	10 transferidor triangul	10 üçgenli raportör	10 ΤΡΙΓΩΝΙΚΟ ΜΟΙΡΟΓΝΩΜΟΝΙΟ
11 lapiz	11 matita	11 lápis	11 kurşun kalem	11 ΜΟΛΥΒΙ
12 goma	12 gomma	12 borracha	12 silgi	12 ΓΟΜΑ
13 compás de puntas	13 compasso	13 compasso de bicos	13 pergel	13 ΚΟΥΜΠΑΣΟ
14 gemelos, prismáticos	14 binocolo	14 binóculos	14 dürbün	14 ΚΥΑΛΙΑ
15 plotter/maquina de dabujar	15 plotter	15 ploter	15 mevki koyma aleti	15 ΑΠΟΤΥΠΩΤΗΣ ΠΟΡΕΙΑΣ
Sextante	*Sestante*	*Sextante*	*Sekstant*	*ΕΞΑΝΤΑΣ*
1 espejo pequeño, espejo grande	1 specchio piccolo, specchio grande	1 espelho pequeno, espelho grande	1 ufuk/index merceği	1 ΟΠΙΖΩΝ. ΜΕΓΑΛΟ ΚΑΤΟΠΤΡΟ ΕΞΑΝΤΑ
2 error de indice	2 errore d'indice	2 êrro de indice	2 endex hatası/alidad hatası	2 ΣΦΑΛΜΑ ΕΞΑΝΤΑ
3 alidade	3 alidada	3 barra do indice	3 sekstant gösterge kolu, uzade kolu	3 ΜΠΡΑΤΣΟ ΕΞΑΝΤΑ
4 vidrios de color	4 filtri	4 vidros corados	4 filtreler	4 ΦΙΛΤΡΑ-ΕΓΧΡΩΜΑ ΓΥΑΛΙΑ ΕΞΑΝΤΑ
5 tornillo micrométrico	5 tamburo micrometrico	5 micrómetro	5 mikrometre tamburu	5 ΜΙΚΡΟΜΕΤΡΙΚΟ ΤΥΜΠΑΝΟ
6 arco, limbo	6 lembo	6 limbo	6 ark	6 ΤΟΞΟ

ENGLISH	FRANÇAIS	DEUTSCH	NEDERLANDS	DANSK
13 NAVIGATION	**13 NAVIGATION**	**13 NAVIGATION**	**13 NAVIGATIE**	**13 NAVIGATION**
Equipment	**Equipement**	**Ausrüstung**	**Uitrusting**	**Udstyr**
Patent log	*Loch enregistreur, sillomètre*	*Patentlog*	*Patentlog*	*Patentlog*
1 rotator	1 hélice	1 Propeller	1 (log) vin	1 rotor
2 log line	2 ligne du loch	2 Logleine	2 loglijn	2 logline
3 register	3 enregistreur	3 Meßuhr	3 (log) klok	3 logur
4 record on the log	4 enregistrer	4 loggen	4 logaanwijzing	4 loggens visning
5 stream the log	5 mouiller le loch	5 das Log ausbringen	5 de log uitzetten	5 at sætte loggen
6 speed-variation indicator	6 speedomètre	6 Speedometer, Geschwindigkeitsmesser	6 snelheidsmeter	6 fartindikator
Compass	*Compas*	*Kompaß*	*Kompas*	*Kompas*
1 bowl	1 boîtier	1 Kessel	1 ketel	1 skål/kop
2 glass	2 verre	2 Glas	2 glas	2 glas
3 card, rose	3 rose des vents	3 Rose	3 (kompas) roos	3 kompasrose
4 lubber line	4 ligne de foi	4 Steuerstrich	4 zeilstreep	4 styrestreg
5 binnacle	5 habitacle	5 Kompaßhaus	5 nachthuis	5 nathus
6 grid steering compass	6 compas à grille	6 Gridkompaß, Gitterkompaß	6 stuurkompas met stuurringen	6 parallelstyrekompas
7 ring sight	7 alidade	7 Peildiopter	7 peiltoestel	7 pejlediopter
8 pelorus	8 taximètre	8 Peilscheibe	8 pelorus	8 pejleskive
9 hand bearing compass	9 compas de relèvement	9 Handpeilkompaß	9 handpeilkompas	9 håndpejlekompas
10 to swing a compass	10 établir la courbe de déviation	10 Deviationsbestimmung	10 vaststellen van de deviatie	10 deviationsbestemmelse
11 to adjust a compass	11 compenser un compas	11 kompensieren	11 compenseren	11 rette kompas
12 heeling error	12 déviation à la gîte	12 Krängungsfehler	12 hellingsfout	12 krængningsfejl
13 North (N); South (S)	13 Nord (N); Sud (S)	13 Nord (N); Süd (S)	13 noord (N), zuid (Z)	13 Nord (N); Syd (S)
14 East (E); West (W)	14 Est (E); Ouest (O)	14 Ost (E); West (W)	14 oost (O), west (W)	14 Øst (Ø); Vest (V)

ESPAÑOL	ITALIANO	PORTUGUÊS	TÜRKÇE	ΕΛΛΗΝΙΚΑ
13 NAVEGACION	**13 NAVIGAZIONE**	**13 NAVEGAÇÃO**	**13 NAVİGASYON**	**13 ΝΑΥΤΙΛΙΑ**
Equipamiento	**Attrezzature**	**Equipamento**	**Ekipman**	**ΕΞΟΠΛΙΣΜΟΣ**
Corredera	*Log, solcometro a elica*	*Odómetro*	*Patent parakete*	*ΔΡΟΜΟΜΕΤΡΟ*
1 hélice	1 elichetta	1 hélice	1 rotor/pervane	1 ΡΟΤΟΡΑΣ
2 cordel de la corredera	2 sagola del log	2 linha do odómetro	2 parakete salvosu	2 ΣΚΟΙΝΙ
3 registrador	3 contatore	3 contador	3 kontör, kaydedici	3 ΚΑΤΑΓΡΑΦΗ
4 registrar las millas	4 registrare sul log	4 registar no odómetro	4 parakete kaydı	4 ΕΝΔΕΙΞΗ ΣΤΗΝ ΠΑΡΚΕΤΑ
5 largar la corredera	5 filare il log	5 lançar o odómetro	5 parakateyi denize salmak	5 ΣΥΡΩ ΤΗΝ ΠΑΡΚΕΤΑ
6 indicador de velocidad	6 tachimetro	6 indicador de velocidade	6 hız değişim göstergesi	6 ΕΝΔΕΙΞΗ ΜΕΤΑΒΟΛΗΣ ΤΑΧΥΤΗΤΑΣ
Compás, aguja náutica	*Bussola*	*Agulha*	*Pusla*	*ΠΥΞΙΔΑ*
1 mortero	1 mortaio	1 morteiro	1 pusla taşı	1 ΛΕΚΑΝΗ ΠΥΞΙΔΑΣ
2 vidrio	2 vetro	2 tampa de vidro	2 pusla camı	2 ΓΥΑΛΙ
3 rosa	3 rosa dei venti	3 rosa dos ventos	3 pusla kardı, pusla gülü	3 ΑΝΕΜΟΛΟΓΙΟ
4 linea de fé	4 linea di fede	4 linha de fé	4 tekne baş-kıç hattı	4 ΓΡΑΜΜΗ ΠΥΞΙΔΑΣ
5 bitácora	5 chiesuola	5 bitácula	5 pusla kürsüsü, sehpası	5 ΠΥΞΙΔΟΘΗΚΗ, ΓΚΡΙΖΟΛΑ
6 Compás de gobernar	6 bussola con indicatore di rotta	6 agulha com indicador de rumo	6 rota göstericili dümenci puslası	6 ΗΛΕΚΤΡΟΝΙΚΗ ΠΥΞΙΔΑ
7 circulo de marcar	7 cerchio azimutale	7 quadrante graduado com aparelho de marcar	7 yuvarlak nişangah	7 ΔΙΟΠΤΡΑ ΠΥΞΙΔΑΣ
8 taximetro	8 peloro, grafometro	8 pelorus	8 kerteriz aleti	8 ΠΗΛΩΡΟΣ
9 aguja de marcar	9 bussola da rilevamento	9 agulha de marcar portátil	9 el kerteriz puslası	9 ΠΥΞΙΔΑ ΔΙΟΠΤΕΥΣΕΩΣ
10 hallar los desvios de la aguja	10 fare i giri di bussola	10 regular a agulha	10 arızi sapma eğrisini çizmek	10 ΣΤΡΟΦΗ ΠΥΞΙΔΑΣ
11 ajustar, compensar el compás	11 ritoccare la deviazione	11 regular, ajustar	11 pusla hatasını gidermek puslayı düzeltmek ayarlamak	11 ΡΥΘΜΙΣΗ ΠΥΞΙΔΑΣ
12 error de escora	12 errore di sbandamento	12 desvio devido à inclimação	12 meyil hatası	12 ΣΦΑΛΜΑ ΚΛΙΣΕΩΣ
13 Norte (N); Sur (S)	13 Nord (N); Sud (S)	13 Norte (N); Sul (S)	13 Kuzey (N), Güney (S)	13 ΒΟΡΡΑΣ - ΝΟΤΟΣ
14 Este, (E); Oeste (W)	14 Est (E); Ovest (O)	14 Este (E); Oeste (O ou W)	14 Doğu (E), Batı (W)	14 ΑΝΑΤΟΛΗ - ΔΥΣΗ

ENGLISH	FRANÇAIS	DEUTSCH	NEDERLANDS	DANSK
13 NAVIGATION	**13 NAVIGATION**	**13 NAVIGATION**	**13 NAVIGATIE**	**13 NAVIGATION**
Equipment	**Equipement**	**Ausrüstung**	**Uitrusting**	**Udstyr**
Compass 15 North-East (NE) 16 North-North-East (NNE) 17 North by East 18 point 19 degree	*Compas* 15 Nord-est (NE) 16 Nord-nord-est (NNE) 17 Nord quart nord-est (N4NE) 18 quart 19 degré	*Kompaß* 15 Nordost (NE) 16 Nordnordost (NNE) 17 Nord zu Ost (NNE) 18 Strich 19 Grad	*Kompas* 15 noordoost (NO) 16 noordnoordoost (NNO) 17 noord ten oosten 18 streek 19 graad	*Kompas* 15 Nordøst (NØ) 16 Nord-nordøst (NNØ) 17 Nord til Øst (N-Ø) 18 streg 19 grad
Sounding 1 lead 2 sounding pole 3 echo sounder	*Sonder* 1 plomb de sonde 2 barre de sonde 3 échosondeur	*Loten* 1 Lot 2 Peilstock 3 Echolot	*Dieptepeiling* 1 lood 2 slaggaard, peilboom 3 echolood	*Lodskud* 1 lod 2 målestage 3 ekkolod
Chartwork	**Navigation**	**Seekartenarbeit**	**Kaartpassen**	**Arbejde med søkort**
Charts 1 title 2 scale 3 latitude/longitude 4 meridian 5 minute 6 nautical mile 7 correction	*Cartes marines* 1 titre 2 échelle 3 latitude/longitude 4 méridien 5 minute 6 mille marin 7 correction	*Seekarten* 1 Titel 2 Maßstab 3 Breite/Länge 4 Meridian 5 Minute, Bogenminute 6 Seemeile 7 Berichtigung	*Zeekaarten* 1 titel 2 schaal 3 breedte/lengte 4 meridiaan 5 minuut 6 nautische mijl 7 correctie	*Søkort* 1 navn/benævnelse 2 skala 3 bredde/længde 4 meredian 5 minut 6 sømil 7 rettelse
Dangers 1 rock awash at the level of chart datum 2 rock which covers and uncovers, height above chart datum	*Dangers* 1 roche à fleur d'eau au niveau de zéro des cartes 2 roche, hauteur au-dessus du niveau de zéro des cartes	*Gefahren* 1 Fels in Höhe des Kartennulls 2 Fels trockenfallend, Höhe über KN	*Gevaren* 1 rots ligt op reductievlak 2 droogvallende rots, meethoogte boven het reductievlak	*Farer* 1 skær i vandskorpen 2 skvulpeskær, højde over kortdatum

ESPAÑOL	ITALIANO	PORTUGUÊS	TÜRKÇE	ΕΛΛΗΝΙΚΑ
13 NAVEGACION	**13 NAVIGAZIONE**	**13 NAVEGAÇÃO**	**13 NAVİGASYON**	**13 ΝΑΥΤΙΛΙΑ**
Equipamiento	**Attrezzature**	**Equipamento**	**Ekipman**	**ΕΞΟΠΛΙΣΜΟΣ**
Compás, aguja náutica 15 Nordeste (NE) 16 Nornordeste (NNE) 17 Norte cuarta al Este (N $1/4$ NE) 18 cuarta 19 grado	*Bussola* 15 Nord-Est (NE) 16 Nord-Nord-Est (NNE) 17 Nord una quarta a Est (N q E) 18 quarta 19 grado	*Agulha* 15 Nordeste (NE) 16 Nor-nordeste (NNE) 17 Norte quarta leste (N4NE) 18 quarta 19 grau	*Pusla* 15 Kuzey-doğu (NE) 16 Kuzey-Kuzey-Doğu (NNE) 17 Kuzey-Doğu 18 kerte 19 derece	*ΠΥΞΙΔΑ* 15 ΒΟΡΕΙΟΑΝΑΤΟΛΙΚΟΣ 16 ΒΟΡΕΙΟΣ - ΒΟΡΕΙΟΑΝΑΤΟΛΙΚΟΣ 17 ΑΠΟ ΒΟΡΡΑ ΠΡΟΣ ΝΟΤΟ 18 ΚΑΡΤΙΝΙ 19 ΜΟΙΡΑ
Sondear 1 escandallo, plomo 2 sonda de varilla 3 sonda acústica	*Scandagliare* 1 piombo 2 canna per scandagliare 3 ecoscandaglio	*Sonda* 1 sonda, prumo de mão 2 vara para sondagem 3 sondador acústica	*İskandil* 1 iskandil kurşunu 2 ekolu iskandil 3 ekolu iskandil	*ΒΥΘΟΜΕΤΡΗΣΗ* 1 ΣΚΑΝΤΑΓΙΟ 2 ΡΑΒΔΙ ΒΥΘΟΜΕΤΡΗΣΗΣ 3 ΒΥΘΟΜΕΤΡΟ
Trabajos de carta de navegación	**Carteggio**	**Cartear**	**Harita çalışması**	**ΕΡΓΑΣΙΕΣ ΕΠΙ ΧΑΡΤΟΥ**
Cartas náuticas 1 título 2 escala 3 latitud/longitud 4 meridiano 5 minuto 6 milla marítima 7 corrección	*Carte nautiche* 1 titolo 2 scala 3 latitudine/ longitudine 4 meridiano 5 minuto primo 6 miglio nautico 7 correzione	*Cartas hidrográficas* 1 titulo 2 escala 3 latitude/longitude 4 meridiano 5 minuto 6 milha marítima 7 correcção	*Deniz haritaları* 1 harita kitabesi 2 ölçek 3 enlem/boylam 4 meridyen 5 dakiká 6 deniz mili 7 düzeltme	*ΧΑΡΤΕΣ* 1 ΤΙΤΛΟΣ 2 ΚΛΙΜΑΚΑ 3 ΠΛΑΤΟΣ/ΜΗΚΟΣ 4 ΜΕΣΗΜΒΡΙΝΟΣ 5 ΠΡΩΤΟ ΤΗΣ ΜΟΙΡΑΣ 6 ΝΑΥΤΙΚΟ ΜΙΛΙ 7 ΔΙΟΡΘΩΣΗ
Peligros 1 piedra a flor de agua en marea escorada 2 piedra, altura sobre la bajamar escorada	*Pericoli* 1 scoglio a fior d'acqua a livello zero della carta 2 scoglio affiorante, altezza sopra il livello zero della carta	*Perigos* 1 rocha que aflora na baixa-mar 2 rocha, altura acima de baixa-mar	*Tehlikeler* 1 harita datum seviyesinde bulunan kaya 2 aralıklı olarak su altında kalan ve görünen kaya yüksek lik chart datumunun üzerinde	*ΚΙΝΔΥΝΟΙ* 1 ΒΡΑΧΟΣ ΑΠΟΚΑΛΥΠΤΟΜΕΝΟΣ 2 ΒΡΑΧΟΣ ΚΑΛΥΠΤΟΜΕΝΟΣ ΚΑΙ ΑΠΟΚΑΛΥΠΤΟΜΕΝΟΣ

179

ENGLISH	FRANÇAIS	DEUTSCH	NEDERLANDS	DANSK
13 NAVIGATION	**13 NAVIGATION**	**13 NAVIGATION**	**13 NAVIGATIE**	**13 NAVIGATION**
Chartwork	**Navigation**	**Seekartenarbeit**	**Kaartpassen**	**Arbejde med søkort**
Dangers	***Dangers***	***Gefahren***	***Gevaren***	***Farer***
3 sunken rock	3 roche submergée	3 Unterwasserklippe (Klp)	3 blinde klip	3 undervandsskær
4 wreck (Wk)	4 épave	4 Wrack (Wk)	4 wrak (Wk)	4 vrag
5 bank (Bk.)	5 banc (B¹)	5 Bank	5 bank (Bk)	5 banke (Bk)
6 shoal (Sh.)	6 haut fond (H¹ F¹)	6 Untiefe (Untf)	6 droogte, ondiepte	6 grund
7 reef (Rf.)	7 récif (R¹)	7 Riff (R)	7 rif	7 rev (Rf)
8 obstruction (Obstn)	8 obstruction (Obs)	8 Schiffahrtshindernis (se) (Sch-H)	8 obstructie, hindernis (Obstr)	8 hindring (Obsn)
9 overfalls, tide rips	9 remous et clapotis	9 Stromkabbelung	9 stroomrafelingen	9 strømsø
10 eddies	10 tourbillons	10 Stromwirbel	10 draaikolken	10 strømhvirvler
11 breakers (Br.)	11 brisants (Br)	11 Brandung (Brdg)	11 brekers, branding	11 brænding
12 seaweed, kelp	12 algues, herbes marines	12 Seetang, Seegras	12 zeewier	12 tang
13 dries (dr)	13 assèche	13 trockenfallend (trfall)	13 droogvallend	13 tørrer (Dr)
14 covers (cov)	14 couvre	14 bedeckt	14 onderlopend	14 overskylles (Cov)
15 uncovers (uncov)	15 découvre	15 unbedeckt	15 droogvallend	15 bliver synlig (Uncov)
16 limiting danger line	16 limite des dangers	16 Gefahrengrenze	16 gevaarlijn	16 ydergrænse for farelinie
17 isolated danger	17 danger isolé	17 einzeln liegende Gafahr	17 losliggend gevaar	17 isoleret hindring
Buoys & beacons	***Bouées et balises***	***Tonnen und Baken***	***Boeien en bakens***	***Sømærker***
1 cardinal system	1 système cardinal	1 Kardinalsystem	1 cardinaalstelsel	1 kardinalsystem
2 lateral system	2 système latéral	2 Lateralsystem	2 lateraalstelsel	2 sideafmærkning
3 light buoy	3 bouée lumineuse	3 Leuchttonne	3 lichtboei	3 lystønde
4 whistle buoy	4 bouée sonore à sifflet	4 Heultonne (Hl-Tn)	4 brulboei (Brul)	4 fløjtetønde
5 bell buoy	5 bouée sonore à cloche	5 Glockentonne (Gl-Tn)	5 belboei (Bel)	5 klokkebøje

ESPAÑOL	ITALIANO	PORTUGUÊS	TÜRKÇE	ΕΛΛΗΝΙΚΑ
13 NAVEGACION	**13 NAVIGAZIONE**	**13 NAVEGAÇÃO**	**13 NAVİGASYON**	**13 ΝΑΥΤΙΛΙΑ**
Trabajos de carta de navegación	**Carteggio**	**Cartear**	**Harita çalışması**	**ΕΡΓΑΣΙΕΣ ΕΠΙ ΧΑΡΤΟΥ**
Peligros	*Pericoli*	*Perigos*	*Tehlikeler*	*ΚΙΝΔΥΝΟΙ*
3 roca siempre cubierta	3 scoglio sommerso	3 rocha submersa	3 batık kaya	3 ΥΠΟΒΡΥΧΙΟΣ ΒΡΑΧΟΣ
4 naufragio (Nauf)	4 relitto	4 navio naufragado	4 gemi leşi, batık gemi	4 ΝΑΥΑΓΙΟ
5 banco (B⁽ᵒ⁾)	5 banco (Bco)	5 banco	5 bank	5 ΠΑΓΚΟΣ
6 bajo (B⁰)	6 secca	6 baixo	6 sığlık	6 ΡΗΧΑ
7 arrecife (Arrᵉ)	7 scogliera (Sc)	7 recife	7 kaya	7 ΥΦΑΛΟΣ
8 obstrucción (Obstⁿ)	8 ostacolo (Ost)	8 obstrução	8 engel	8 ΕΜΠΟΔΙΟ
9 escarceos, hileros	9 frangenti di marea	9 bailadeiras	9 dalgacıklar, akıntı çırpıntısı	9 ΑΝΑΒΡΑΣΜΟΣ. ΚΥΜΑΤΙΣΜΟΣ ΛΟΓΩ ΠΑΛΙΡΡΟΙΑΣ
10 remolinos	10 vortici	10 redemoínhos	10 anafor	10 ΔΙΝΕΣ
11 rompientes	11 frangenti	11 rebentação	11 kırılan dalgalar	11 ΣΠΑΣΙΜΟ ΤΗΣ ΘΑΛΑΣΣΑΣ. ΑΒΑΘΗ
12 algas, hierbas marinas	12 alghe	12 algas, sargaços	12 saz	12 ΦΥΚΙΑΔΑ
13 que vela en bajamar	13 affiora	13 fica em sêco	13 kurur	13 ΞΕΡΕΣ
14 cubre	14 si copre	14 cobre	14 örter, kapanır	14 ΚΑΛΥΠΤΕΤΑΙ
15 descubre	15 si scopre	15 descobre	15 örtmez kapanmaz	15 ΞΕΝΕΡΙΖΕΙ. ΑΠΟΚΑΛΥΠΤΕΤΑΙ
16 limite de peligro	16 limite dei pericoli	16 limite de perigo	16 tehlikeler sınırı	16 ΟΡΙΟΘΕΤΗΣΗ ΕΠΙΚΙΝΔΥΝΗΣ ΠΕΡΙΟΧΗΣ
17 peligro aislado	17 pericolo isolato	17 perigo isolado	17 yalın tehlike	17 ΜΕΜΟΝΩΜΕΝΟΣ ΚΙΝΔΥΝΟΣ
Boyas y balizas	*Boe e mede*	*Bóias e faróis*	*Şamandıralar ve bıkınlar*	*ΣΗΜΑΝΤΗΡΕΣ ΚΑΙ ΠΛΩΤΟΙ ΥΦΑΛΟΔΕΙΚΤΕΣ (ΑΛΕΩΡΙΑ)*
1 sistema cardinal	1 sistema cardinale	1 sistema cardeal	1 yönleç şamandıralama sistemi	1 ΑΡΙΘΜΗΤΙΚΟ ΣΥΣΤΗΜΑ
2 sistema lateral	2 sistema laterale	2 sistema lateral	2 yanlaç şamandıralama sistemi	2 ΠΛΕΥΡΙΚΟ ΣΥΣΤΗΜΑ
3 boya luminosa	3 boa luminosa	3 bóia luminosa	3 fener şamandırası	3 ΦΩΤΟΣΗΜΑΝΤΗΡΑΣ
4 boya de silbato	4 boa a fischio	4 bóia de apito	4 düdüklü şamandıra	4 ΣΗΜΑΝΤΗΡΑΣ ΣΥΡΙΓΜΩΝ
5 boya de campana	5 boa a campana	5 bóia de sino	5 çan şamandırası	5 ΚΩΔΩΝΟΣΗΜΑΝΤΗΡΑΣ

ENGLISH	FRANÇAIS	DEUTSCH	NEDERLANDS	DANSK
13 NAVIGATION	**13 NAVIGATION**	**13 NAVIGATION**	**13 NAVIGATIE**	**13 NAVIGATION**
Chartwork	**Navigation**	**Seekartenarbeit**	**Kaartpassen**	**Arbejde med søkort**
Buoys & beacons	***Bouées et balises***	***Tonnen und Baken***	***Boeien en bakens***	***Sømærker***
6 can buoy	6 bouée plate, cylindrique; cylindre	6 Stumpftonne	6 stompe boei	6 stumptønde
7 conical buoy	7 bouée conique, cône	7 Spitztonne	7 spitse boei	7 spidstønde
8 spherical buoy	8 bouée sphérique, disque	8 Kugeltonne	8 bolton	8 kuglebøje
9 spar buoy	9 bouée à espar	9 Spierentonne	9 sparboei	9 spirtønde
10 pillar buoy	10 bouée à fuseau	10 Bakentonne	10 torenboei	10 bøje med stage
11 barrel buoy	11 bouée tonne, tonne	11 Faßtonne	11 drum, ton	11 fadtønde
12 mid-channel buoy	12 bouée de milieu de chenal	12 Mittefahrwassertonne	12 midvaarwaterboei	12 midtfarvandsbøje
13 topmark	13 voyant	13 Toppzeichen	13 topteken	13 topbetegnelse
14 mooring buoy	14 coffre d'amarrage, corps-mort	14 Festmachetonne	14 meerboei	14 ankerbøje
15 fixed beacon	15 balise fixe	15 Bake	15 kopbaken	15 båke
16 floating beacon	16 balise flottante	16 Bakentonne	16 drijfbaken	16 flydende sømærke
17 perches	17 perches, pieux	17 Pricken	17 steekbakens	17 stage
18 chequered (cheq)	18 à damiers (dam)	18 gewürfelt	18 geblokt (Gb)	18 ternet (Cheq)
19 horizontal stripes (HS)	19 à bandes horizontales	19 waagerecht gestreift	19 horizontaal gestreept (HS)	19 vandrette striber (HS)
20 vertical stripes (VS)	20 à bandes verticales	20 senkrecht gestreift	20 verticaal gestreept	20 lodrette striber (VS)
21 Racon	21 Racon	21 Radarantwortbake	21 radarantwoordbaken	21 racon
22 Lanby	22 Lanby	22 Grobe automatisch arbeitende Tonne	22 grote automatische superboei, Lanby	22 Lanby

ESPAÑOL	ITALIANO	PORTUGUÊS	TÜRKÇE	ΕΛΛΗΝΙΚΑ
13 NAVEGACION	**13 NAVIGAZIONE**	**13 NAVEGAÇÃO**	**13 NAVİGASYON**	**13 ΝΑΥΤΙΛΙΑ**
Trabajos de carta de navegación	**Carteggio**	**Cartear**	**Harita çalışması**	**ΕΡΓΑΣΙΕΣ ΕΠΙ ΧΑΡΤΟΥ**
Boyas y balizas	*Boe e mede*	*Bóias e faróis*	*Şamandıralar ve bıkınlar*	*ΣΗΜΑΝΤΗΡΕΣ ΚΑΙ ΠΛΩΤΟΙ ΥΦΑΛΟΔΕΙΚΤΕΣ (ΑΛΕΩΡΙΑ)*
6 boya cilíndrica	6 boa cilindrica	6 bóia cilíndrica	6 silindrik şamandıra	6 ΚΥΛΙΝΔΙΡΚΟΣ ΣΗΜΑΝΤΗΡΑΣ
7 boya cónica	7 boa conica	7 bóia cónica	7 konik şamandıra	7 ΚΩΝΙΚΟΣ ΣΗΜΑΝΤΗΡΑΕ
8 boya esférica	8 boa sferica	8 bóia esférica	8 küresel şamandıra	8 ΣΦΑΙΡΙΚΟΣ ΣΗΜΑΝΤΗΡΑΣ
9 boya de espeque	9 boa ad asta	9 bóia de mastro	9 gönderli şamandıra	9 ΣΤΗΛΟΕΙΔΗΣ ΣΗΜΑΝΤΗΡΑΣ
10 boya de huso	10 boa a fuso	10 bóia de pilar	10 sütunlu şamandıra	10 ΠΑΣΣΑΛΟΣΗΜΑΝΤΗΡΑΣ
11 barril	11 boa a barile	11 bóia de barril	11 varil şamandıra	11 ΒΑΡΕΛΟΕΙΔΗΣ ΣΗΜΑΝΤΗΡΑΣ
12 boya de centro de canal	12 boa a centro canale	12 bóia de canal	12 kanal ortası şamandırası	12 ΤΣΑΜΑΔΟΥΡΑ ΣΤΟ ΜΕΣΟ ΤΟΥ ΚΑΝΑΛΙΟΥ
13 marca de tope	13 miraglio	13 alvo	13 şamandıra tepeliği	13 ΚΟΡΥΦΑΙΟΣΗΜΑ
14 boya de amarre, muerto	14 boa d'ormeggio, corpo morto	14 bóia de amarracão	14 bağlama şamandırası	14 ΤΣΑΜΑΔΟΥΡΑ
15 baliza fija	15 meda fissa	15 baliza fixa	15 baliz sabit bıkın	15 ΣΤΑΘΕΡΟΣ ΥΦΑΛΟΔΕΙΚΤΗΣ
16 baliza flotante	16 meda galleggiante	16 baliza flutuante	16 yüzer baliz, yüzer bıkın	16 ΠΛΩΤΟΣ ΥΦΑΛΟΔΕΙΚΤΗΣ
17 marca	17 pali	17 estaca	17 işaretleme kazıkları	17 ΠΑΣΣΑΛΟΣ ΠΟΥ ΔΕΙΚΝΕΙ ΡΗΧΑΔΕΣ
18 damero, a cuadros	18 a scacchi	18 aos quadrados (x)	18 damalı	18 ΜΕ ΤΕΤΡΑΓΩΝΙΔΙΑ
19 franjas horizontales	19 a strisce orizzontali	19 faixas horizontais (FH)	19 yatay çizgili	19 ΟΡΙΖΟΝΤΙΕΣ ΓΡΑΜΜΕΣ
20 franjas verticales	20 a strisce verticali	20 faixas verticais (FV)	20 dikey çizgili	20 ΚΑΘΕΤΕΣ ΓΡΑΜΜΕΣ
21 baliza eco de radar	21 radarfaro	21 Racon	21 Racon	21 ΡΑΝΤΑΡ ΜΕ ΑΠΑΝΤΩΣΑ ΣΥΣΚΕΥΗ
22 boya faro automático	22 Lanby	22 Lanby	22 büyük otomatik navigasyon şamandırası	22 ΑΥΤΟΜΑΤΗΣ ΛΕΙΤΟΥΡΓΙΑΣ ΜΕΛΑΛΙ ΤΣΑΜΑΔΟΥΡΑ

ENGLISH	FRANÇAIS	DEUTSCH	NEDERLANDS	DANSK
13 NAVIGATION	**13 NAVIGATION**	**13 NAVIGATION**	**13 NAVIGATIE**	**13 NAVIGATION**
Chartwork	**Navigation**	**Seekartenarbeit**	**Kaartpassen**	**Arbejde med søkort**
Lights	*Feux*	*Leuchtfeuer*	*Lichten*	*Fyr*
1 lighthouse (Lt Ho)	1 phare	1 Leuchtturm (Lcht-Tm)	1 vuurtoren, licht (Lt)	1 fyrtårn (Lt HO)
2 lightship	2 bateau-phare	2 Feuerschiff (F-Sch)	2 lichtschip	2 fyrskib (Lt v)
3 fixed light (F)	3 feu fixe (F f)	3 Festfeuer (F)	3 vast licht (V)	3 fast fyr (F)
4 flashing light (Fl)	4 feu à éclats (F é)	4 Blinkfeuer (Blk)	4 schitterlicht (S)	4 blinkfyr (Fl)
5 quick flashing light (Q)	5 feu scintillant (F sc)	5 Funkelfeuer (Fkl)	5 snelschitterlicht	5 hurtigblink (Q)
6 occulting light (Oc)	6 à occultations (F o)	6 unterbrochenes Feuer (Ubr)	6 onderbroken licht (O)	6 formørkelser (Oc)
7 group occulting light (Oc)	7 à occultations groupées (F 2 o)	7 unterbrochenes Gruppenfeuer (Ubr [2])	7 groep-onderbroken licht	7 gruppeformørkelser (Oc)
8 alternating light (Al)	8 à changement de coloration (F alt)	8 Wechselfeuer (Wchs)	8 kleurwisselend (Alt)	8 skiftende lys (Al)
9 intermittent	9 feu intermittent	9 periodisches Feuer	9 bij tussenpozen werkend (Int)	9 periodisk
10 interrupted quick flashing (IQ)	10 feu interrompu	10 unterbrochenes Funkelfeuer (Fkl unt)	10 onderbroken snelschitterlicht (Int Fl)	10 hurtigblink med afbrydelser (IQ)
11 fixed and flashing (F Fl)	11 fixe blanc varié par un éclat (F b e)	11 Mischfeuer: Festfeuer und Blinke (Mi)	11 vast en schitterlicht (V&S)	11 fast med blink (F Fl)
12 period	12 période	12 Wiederkehr	12 periode	12 periode
13 leading light	13 feu d'alignement	13 Richtfeuer (Rcht-F)	13 geleidelicht	13 ledefyr
14 upper light	14 supérieur (S)	14 Oberfeuer (O-F)	14 bovenste licht	14 øverste fyr
15 lower light	15 inférieur (I)	15 Unterfeuer (U-F)	15 onderste licht	15 nederste fyr
16 sector	16 secteur (Sect/S)	16 Sektor	16 sector	16 sektor
17 obscured	17 masqué	17 verdunkelt (vdklt)	17 afgeschermd	17 formørket/ikke synligt
18 visible, range	18 portée (vis)	18 Sichtweite, Tragweite	18 reikwijdte	18 synlig/synsvidde
Coastline	*Contours de la côte*	*Küstenlinien*	*Kustlijn*	*Kystlinie*
1 steep coast	1 côte escarpée	1 Steilküste	1 steile kust	1 stejl kyst
2 cliffy coastline	2 côte à falaises	2 Kliffküste	2 klipkust	2 klippekyst
3 stony or shingly	3 cailloux ou galets	3 Stein-oder Kiesküste	3 grind-of kiezelstrand	3 stenet
4 sand hills, dunes	4 dunes	4 Sandhügel, Dünen	4 duinen	4 klitter
5 foreshore	5 côte découvrant à marée basse	5 Küstenvorland	5 droogvallend strand	5 forstrand

ESPAÑOL	ITALIANO	PORTUGUÊS	TÜRKÇE	ΕΛΛΗΝΙΚΑ
13 NAVEGACION	**13 NAVIGAZIONE**	**13 NAVEGAÇÃO**	**13 NAVİGASYON**	**13 ΝΑΥΤΙΛΙΑ**
Trabajos de carta de navegación	**Carteggio**	**Cartear**	**Harita çalışması**	**ΕΡΓΑΣΙΕΣ ΕΠΙ ΧΑΡΤΟΥ**

Luces — *Luci* — *Luzes* — *Fenerler* — *ΦΑΡΟΙ*

1 faro	1 faro	1 farol	1 fener	1 ΦΑΡΟΣ
2 buque faro	2 battello faro	2 barco-farol	2 fener gemisi	2 ΠΛΟΙΟ ΦΑΡΟΣ
3 luz fija (f)	3 luce fissa (F)	3 luz fixa (F)	3 sabit fener	3 ΣΤΑΘΕΡΟΣ ΦΑΝΟΣ
4 luz de destellos (dest)	4 luce a lampi (Lam)	4 relâmpagos (Rl)	4 şimşekli fener	4 ΑΝΑΛΑΜΠΩΝ ΦΑΝΟΣ
5 luz centelleante	5 luce scintillante (Sc)	5 relâmpagos rápidos	5 seri şimşekli fener	5 ΦΑΝΟΣ ΤΑΧΕΩΣ ΑΝΑΛΑΜΠΩΝ
6 luz de ocultaciones (oc)	6 luce intermittente (Int)	6 ocultações (Oc)	6 husuflu fener	6 ΔΙΑΛΕΙΠΩΝ ΦΑΝΟΣ
7 luz de grupos de ocultaciones (grp oc)	7 intermittente a gruppi (Int)	7 grupo n ocultações (Gp n Oc)	7 grup husuflu fener	7 ΔΙΑΛΕΙΠΩΝΜΕ ΔΕΣΜΗ
8 luz alternativa (Alt va)	8 luce alternata (Alt)	8 alternada (Alt)	8 mûnetavip fener	8 ΕΝΑΛΑΣΣΟΜΕΝΟΣ
9 luz intermitente (Intr te)	9 intermittente (Int)	9 intermitente	9 kesikli/renk değiştiren fener	9 ΔΙΑΚΟΠΤΟΜΕΝΟΣ
10 luz de grupos de centelleos	10 scintillante intermittente (Sc Int)	10 interompida	10 renk değiştiren seri şimşekli fener	10 ΤΑΧΕΩΣ ΑΝΑΛΑΜΠΩΝ ΔΙΑΚΟΠΤΟΜΕΝΟΣ
11 luz fija y destellos (f dest)	11 fissa e a lampi (F Lam)	11 fixa e com relâmpagos (F Rl)	11 sabit şimşekli fener	11 ΣΤΑΘΕΡΟΣ ΚΑΙ ΑΝΑΛΑΜΠΩΝ
12 periódo	12 periodo	12 período	12 periyod	12 ΠΕΡΙΟΔΟΣ
13 luz de enfilación	13 luce d'allineamento	13 farol ou farolim de enfiamento	13 transit feneri	13 ΙΘΥΝΤΗΡΙΟΣ ΦΑΝΟΣ
14 posterior	14 luce superiore (S)	14 superior (Sup)	14 yukarıdaki fener	14 ΑΝΩ ΦΑΝΟΣ
15 anterior	15 luce inferiore (l)	15 inferior (Inf)	15 alttaki fener	15 ΚΑΤΩ ΦΑΝΟΣ
16 sector (Sect)	16 settore (set)	16 sector	16 sektör	16 ΤΟΜΕΑΣ
17 oculto	17 oscurato (Osc)	17 obscurecido	17 karanlık	17 ΣΚΟΤΕΙΝΟΣ
18 alcanca	18 visibile, portata	18 visível	18 görünür	18 ΟΡΑΤΟΣ ΑΠΟΣΤΑΣΗ

La costa — *Linea costiera* — *Linha da costa* — *Kıyı şeridi* — *ΠΕΡΙΓΡΑΜΜΑ ΑΚΤΗΣ*

1 costa escarpada 2 acantilado	1 costa scoscesa	1 costa alta	1 dik kıyı	1 ΑΠΟΤΟΜΗ ΑΚΤΗ
	2 costa a picco	2 costa escarpada	2 falezlí kıyı şeridi	2 ΓΚΡΕΜΩΔΗΣ ΑΚΤΟΓΡΑΜΜΗ
3 guijarro o grava	3 pietrosa	3 pedras ou seixos	3 taşlık veya çakıllık kıyı	3 ΠΕΤΡΩΔΗΣ Η ΜΕ ΚΡΟΚΑΛΕΣ
4 dunas	4 colline sabbiose, dune	4 dunas de areia	4 kum tepeleri kumullar	4 ΑΜΜΟΛΟΦΟΙ
5 fondos que descubren en bajamar	5 litorale	5 zona entre as linhas da bm e pm	5 cezirde suyu çekilen kıyı şeridi	5 ΑΚΤΗ

ENGLISH	FRANÇAIS	DEUTSCH	NEDERLANDS	DANSK
13 NAVIGATION	**13 NAVIGATION**	**13 NAVIGATION**	**13 NAVIGATIE**	**13 NAVIGATION**
Chartwork	**Navigation**	**Seekartenarbeit**	**Kaartpassen**	**Arbejde med søkort**

ENGLISH	FRANÇAIS	DEUTSCH	NEDERLANDS	DANSK
Quality of the bottom	*Nature des fonds*	*Grundbezeichnungen*	*Bodemgesteldheid*	*Bundarter*
1 sand (S)	1 sable (S)	1 Sand (Sd)	1 zand (Z)	1 sand (S)
2 mud (M)	2 vase (V)	2 Schlick (Sk)	2 modder (M)	2 mudder (M)
3 clay (Cy)	3 argile (Arg)	3 Ton (T)	3 klei (L)	3 ler (Cy)
4 gravel (G)	4 gravier (Gr)	4 Kies (K)	4 grind, gruis	4 grus (G)
5 shingle (Sn)	5 galets (Gal)	5 grober Kies (gb K)	5 grind, keisteen	5 rullesten (Sn)
6 pebbles (P)	6 cailloux (Caill)	6 kleine Steine (kl St)	6 kiezelsteen (Kl)	6 småsten (P)
7 stones (St)	7 pierres (Pi)	7 Steine (St)	7 stenen (St)	7 sten (St)
8 rock, rocky (R, r)	8 roches (R)	8 Felsen, felsig (Fls, fls)	8 stenen, rotsachtig (R)	8 klippe (R, r)
9 fine/coarse (f/c)	9 fin/gros (f/g)	9 fein/grob (f/gb)	9 fijn/grof (f/gr)	9 fin/grov (f/c)
10 soft/hard (so/h)	10 mou/dur (m/d)	10 weich/hart (wch/ht)	10 zacht/hard (zt/h)	10 blød/hård (so/h)
11 small (sm)	11 petit (p⁺)	11 klein (kl)	11 klein	11 lille (sm)
12 large (l)	12 grand (gᵈ)	12 groß (gß)	12 groot	12 stor (l)
13 light/dark (lt/d)	13 clair/foncé	13 hell/dunkel (h/dkl)	13 licht/donker	13 lys/mørk (lt/d)
Fog signals	*Signaux de brume*	*Nebelsignal*	*Mistsignalen*	*Tågesignaler*
1 nautophone (Nauto)	1 nautophone	1 Membransender (N-S)	1 nautofoon	1 nautofon (Nauto)
2 diaphone (Dia)	2 diaphone	2 Kolbensirene (N-S)	2 diafoon	2 diafon (Dia)
3 gun (Gun)	3 canon (Can)	3 Kanone (N-S)	3 mistkanon	3 kanon (Gun)
4 explosive (Explos)	4 par explosions	4 Knall (N-S)	4 knalmistsein	4 skud (Explos)
5 whistle (Whis)	5 sifflet (Sif)	5 Heuler (N-S)	5 misthoorn	5 fløjte (Whis)
6 bell (Bell)	6 cloche (Cl)	6 Glocke (N-S)	6 mistbel	6 klokke (Bell)
7 gong (Gong)	7 gong (Gᵍ)	7 Gong (N-S)	7 mistgong	7 gong-gong (Gong)
8 siren (Siren)	8 sirène (Sir)	8 Sirene (N-S)	8 mistsirene	8 sirene (Siren)
9 reed (Reed)	9 anche	9 Zungenhorn (N-S)	9 mistfluit	9 membran-horn (Reed)
10 submarine oscillator (SO)	10 oscillateur sous-marin	10 Unterwasser-Membransender	10 onderwateroscillator	10 undervandsmembran (SO)
11 submarine bell (Sub Bell)	11 cloche sous-marine (Cl s m)	11 Unterwasser-Glocke (U-Wss-Gl)	11 onderwaterklok, bel	11 undervandsklokke (Sub/Bell)

ESPAÑOL	ITALIANO	PORTUGUÊS	TÜRKÇE	ΕΛΛΗΝΙΚΑ
13 NAVEGACION	**13 NAVIGAZIONE**	**13 NAVEGAÇÃO**	**13 NAVİGASYON**	**13 ΝΑΥΤΙΛΙΑ**
Trabajos de carta de navegación	**Carteggio**	**Cartear**	**Harita çalışması**	**ΕΡΓΑΣΙΕΣ ΕΠΙ ΧΑΡΤΟΥ**

Naturaleza del fondo
1 arena (A)
2 fango (F)
3 arcilla (Arc)
4 cascajo (C°)
5 conchuela (Cᵃ)
6 guijarro (G°)
7 piedras (P)
8 roca, rocoso (R Rᵒ)
9 fino/grueso (f/g)
10 blando/duro (bᵒ/d)
11 pequeño
12 grande
13 claro/oscuro (cl/o)

Señales de niebla
1 nautófono (N)
2 diáfono (D)
3 cañon
4 explosiva (E)
5 pito
6 campana (C)
7 gong
8 sirena (Sir)
9 bocina (B)
10 oscilador submarino (O)
11 campana submarina

Tipo di fondo
1 sabbia (s)
2 fango (f)
3 argilla
4 ghiaia
5 ciottoli
6 sassdini
7 pietre (p)
8 roccia, roccioso (r)
9 fine/grosso
10 molle/duro
11 piccolo
12 grande
13 chiaro/scuro

Segnali da nebbia
1 nautofono (Nauto)
2 diafono (Dia)
3 cannone (Cann Neb)
4 esplosivo
5 fischio (Fi Neb)
6 campana (Cam Neb)
7 gong
8 sirena (Sir Neb)
9 corno
10 oscilatore sottomarino
11 campana sottomarina (Cam Stm)

Caracteristicas do fundo
1 areia (A)
2 lodo (L)
3 argila (Ar)
4 burgau (B)
5 calhau (C)
6 seixos (S)
7 pedras (P)
8 rocha (R)
9 fina/grossa (f/g)
10 mole/duro (ml/d)
11 miuda
12 grande
13 claro/escuro (cl/e)

Sinais de nevoeiro
1 nautofone (Nauto)
2 diafone (Dia)
3 canhão
4 explosivo
5 apito (Apt)
6 sino (Sino)
7 badalo
8 sereia (Ser)
9 limbos
10 oscilador submarino

11 sino submarino

Deniz dibinin niteliği
1 kum
2 çamur
3 balçık
4 çakıl
5 iri çakıl
6 ince çakıl
7 taş, taşlık
8 kaya, kayalık
9 ince/kalın
10 yumuşak/sert
11 küçük, dar
12 büyük, geniş
13 açık renkli/koyu renkli

Sis işaretleri
1 notofon
2 diafon
3 top
4 patlayıcı
5 düdük
6 kampana, çan
7 gonk
8 siren
9 korna
10 denizaltı osilatörü

11 sualtı kampanası

ΠΟΙΟΤΗΤΑ ΒΥΘΟΥ
1 ΑΜΜΟΣ
2 ΛΑΣΠΗ
3 ΠΗΛΟΣ
4 ΧΑΛΙΚΩΔΗΣ ΑΜΜΟΣ
5 ΚΡΟΚΑΛΕΣ
6 ΒΟΤΣΑΛΑ
7 ΠΕΤΡΕΣ
8 ΒΡΑΧΟΣ, ΒΡΑΧΩΔΗΣ
9 ΛΕΠΤΟΣ/ΧΟΝΤΡΟΣ
10 ΜΑΛΑΚΟΣ/ΣΚΛΗΡΟΣ
11 ΜΙΚΡΟΣ
12 ΜΕΓΑΛΟΣ
13 ΦΩΣ/ΣΚΟΤΑΔΙ

ΣΗΜΑΤΑ ΟΜΙΧΛΗΣ
1 ΝΑΥΤΟΦΩΝΟ
2 ΔΙΑΦΩΝΟ
3 ΟΠΛΟ
4 ΕΚΡΗΚΤΙΚΑ
5 ΣΦΥΡΙΧΤΡΑ
6 ΚΑΜΠΑΝΑ - ΚΩΔΩΝ
7 ΓΚΟΝΓΚ
8 ΣΕΙΡΗΝΑ
9 ΚΑΛΑΜΙ
10 ΥΠΟΒΡΥΧΙΟΣ ΤΑΛΑΝΤΩΤΗΣ
11 ΥΠΟΒΡΥΧΙΟΣ ΚΩΔΩΝ

ENGLISH	FRANÇAIS	DEUTSCH	NEDERLANDS	DANSK
13 NAVIGATION	**13 NAVIGATION**	**13 NAVIGATION**	**13 NAVIGATIE**	**13 NAVIGATION**
Chartwork	**Navigation**	**Seekartenarbeit**	**Kaartpassen**	**Arbejde med søkort**
Buildings etc	*Edifices etc*	*Bauten aller Art*	*Gebouwen enzovoort*	*Bygninger etc*
1 town	1 ville	1 Stadt	1 stad	1 by
2 village (Vil)	2 village (V^ge)	2 Dorf	2 dorp	2 landsby (Vil)
3 castle (Cas)	3 château (Ch^au)	3 Schloß (Schl)	3 kasteel	3 slot (Cas)
4 church (Ch)	4 église (Egl)	4 Kirche (Kr)	4 kerk	4 kirke (Ch)
5 cathedral (Cath)	5 cathédrale (Cath)	5 Kathedrale	5 kathedraal	5 domkirke
6 fort (Ft)	6 fort (F^t)	6 Fort (Ft)	6 fort (Ft)	6 fort (Ft)
7 barracks	7 caserne	7 Kaserne (Kas)	7 kazerne	7 kaserne
8 airport	8 aéroport (Aé)	8 Flughafen	8 vliegveld	8 lufthavn
9 street	9 rue	9 Straße (Str)	9 straat	9 gade
10 monument (Mont)	10 monument (Mon^t)	10 Denkmal (Dkm)	10 monument	10 monument
11 tower (Tr)	11 tour, tourelle (T^r)	11 Turm (Tm)	11 toren (Tr)	11 tårn
12 windmill	12 moulin à vent (M^in)	12 Windmühle (M)	12 windmolen	12 vindmølle
13 chimney (Chy)	13 cheminée (Ch^ee)	13 Schornstein (Schst)	13 schoorsteen (Schn)	13 skorsten
14 water tower	14 château d'eau (Ch^au)	14 Wasserturm (Wss-Tm)	14 watertoren (W Tr)	14 vandtårn
15 gasometer	15 gazomètre	15 Gasometer (Gas-T)	15 gashouder	15 gasbeholder
16 oil tank	16 réservoir à pétrole	16 Öltank (Öl-T)	16 olietank	16 olietank
17 factory	17 fabrique	17 Fabrik (Fbr)	17 fabriek	17 fabrik
18 quarry	18 carrière (Carre)	18 Steinbruch	18 steengroeve	18 stenbrud
19 railway (Ry)	19 chemin de fer (Ch de F)	19 Eisenbahn	19 spoorweg	19 jernbane
20 flagstaff (FS)	20 mât	20 Flaggenmast (Flgmst)	20 vlaggestok (Vs)	20 flagstang
21 measured mile	21 base de vitesse	21 abgesteckte Meile	21 gemeten mijl	21 målt sømil
22 conspicuous (conspic)	22 visible, en évidence (vis)	22 auffällig (auff)	22 opvallend, kenbaar	22 kendelig
23 destroyed (dest)	23 détruit (détr)	23 zerstört (zrst)	23 vernield	23 ødelagt
24 prominent	24 remarquable (rem)	24 hervorragend	24 prominent, in het oog vallend	24 fremspringende
25 approximate (approx)	25 approximatif (appr)	25 ungefähr (ungf)	25 ongeveer	25 omtrentlig
26 distant (dist)	26 éloigné (él)	26 entfernt	26 afstand	26 fjern
27 mosque	27 mosquée	27 Moschee	27 moskee	27 moské
28 ruin	28 ruine	28 Ruine	28 ruïne	28 ruin

ESPAÑOL	ITALIANO	PORTUGUÊS	TÜRKÇE	ΕΛΛΗΝΙΚΑ
13 NAVEGACION	**13 NAVIGAZIONE**	**13 NAVEGAÇÃO**	**13 NAVİGASYON**	**13 ΝΑΥΤΙΛΙΑ**
Trabajos de carta de navegación	**Carteggio**	**Cartear**	**Harita çalışması**	**ΕΡΓΑΣΙΕΣ ΕΠΙ ΧΑΡΤΟΥ**
Edificios	*Edifici, etc*	*Edifícios etc*	*Binalar*	*ΚΤΙΡΙΑ ΚΤΛ*
1 ciudad	1 città	1 cidade	1 kent	1 ΠΟΛΗ
2 pueblo, aldea	2 villaggio	2 vila, povoação	2 köy	2 ΧΩΡΙΟ
3 castillo (C^{llo})	3 castello (Cast)	3 castelo (Cast)	3 şato, kastel	3 ΚΑΣΤΡΟ
4 iglesia (Igl^a)	4 chiesa (Ch)	4 igreja	4 kilise	4 ΕΚΚΛΗΣΙΑ
5 catedral (Cat)	5 cattedrale (Catt)	5 catedral	5 katedral	5 ΜΗΤΡΟΠΟΛΗ
6 fuerte (F^{te})	6 forte (Ft)	6 forte	6 hisar	6 ΦΡΟΥΡΙΟ
7 cuartel	7 caserma	7 quartel	7 kışla	7 ΚΑΤΑΥΛΙΣΜΟΙ
8 aeropuerto	8 aeroporto	8 aeroporto	8 hava limanı	8 ΑΕΡΟΔΡΟΜΙΟ
9 calle	9 strada, via	9 estrada	9 sokak	9 ΔΡΟΜΟΣ
10 monumento (M^{to})	10 monumento (Mont)	10 monumento (Mon)	10 anıt	10 ΜΝΗΜΕΙΟ
11 torre (T^c)	11 torre (Tr)	11 moínho de vento	11 kule	11 ΠΥΡΓΟΣ
12 molino de viento	12 mulino a vento	12 tôrre	12 yeldeğirmeni	12 ΑΝΕΜΟΜΥΛΟΣ
13 chimenea (Ch^a)	13 fumaiolo	13 chaminé (Ch)	13 baca	13 ΚΑΜΙΝΑΔΑ
14 depósito de agua	14 serbatoio d'acqua	14 depósito de água (D A)	14 su kulesi	14 ΥΔΡΟΜΥΛΟΣ
15 gasómetro	15 gasometro	15 gasómetro	15 gazometre	15 ΓΚΑΖΟΜΕΤΡΟ
16 tanque de petróleo	16 serbatoio di petrolio	16 depósito de combustível (D C)	16 yağ tankı	16 ΔΕΞΑΜΕΝΗ ΠΕΤΡΕΛΑΙΟΥ
17 fábrica (F^{ca})	17 fabbrica	17 fábrica	17 fabrika	17 ΕΡΓΟΣΤΑΣΙΟ
18 cantera	18 cava	18 pedreira	18 taşocağı	18 ΝΤΑΜΑΡΙ
19 ferrocaril	19 ferrovia	19 via férrea	19 tren yolu	19 ΣΤΑΘΜΟΣ ΤΡΕΝΟΥ
20 asta de bandera	20 asta di bandiera	20 mastro para bandeira	20 bayrak direği	20 ΚΟΝΤΑΡΙ ΣΗΜΑΙΑΣ
21 milla medida	21 miglio misurato	21 a milha para experiéncia de velocidade	21 hız bazı, hız birimi	21 ΜΕΤΡΗΜΕΝΟ ΜΙΛΙ
22 notorio, conspicuo	22 cospicuo	22 conspícuo (consp)	22 görülür	22 ΠΕΡΙΒΛΕΠΤΟΣ
23 destruido (dest)	23 distrutto	23 destrúido (dest)	23 tahrip olmuş	23 ΚΑΤΕΣΤΡΑΜΕΝΟΣ
24 prominente (prom)	24 prominente	24 proeminente (proem)	24 göze çarpıcı	24 ΠΡΟΕΞΕΧΩΝ
25 aproximado (aprox)	25 approssimato	25 aproximado	25 yaklaşık	25 ΠΕΡΙΠΟΥ
26 distante	26 distante	26 distante (dist)	26 uzaklıkta	26 ΜΑΚΡΥΝΟΣ
27 mezquita	27 moschea	27 mosquetão	27 cami	27 ΤΖΑΜΙ
28 ruina	28 rovina	28 estragado	28 harabe, ören	28 ΕΡΕΙΠΙΟ

ENGLISH	FRANÇAIS	DEUTSCH	NEDERLANDS	DANSK
13 NAVIGATION	**13 NAVIGATION**	**13 NAVIGATION**	**13 NAVIGATIE**	**13 NAVIGATION**
Chartwork	**Navigation**	**Seekartenarbeit**	**Kaartpassen**	**Arbejde med søkort**
Features	*Physionomie de la côte*	*Küstenformation*	*Kenmerken*	*Kystkarakter*
1 bay (B)	1 baie (Bᵉ)	1 Buch (B)	1 baai (Bi)	1 bugt
2 fjord (Fd)	2 fjord (Fjᵈ)	2 Fjord, Förde (Fj, Fd)	2 fjord	2 fjord
3 glacier	3 glaciers	3 Gletscher (Glet)	3 gletsjer	3 gletcher
4 lake, loch (L)	4 bras de mer (L)	4 See, Binnensee	4 meer	4 indsø
5 entrance	5 entrée (Entᵉᵉ)	5 Einfahrt (Einf)	5 ingang, toegang, zeegat	5 indløb
6 passage (Pass)	6 passage, passe (Pas)	6 Durchfahrt (Drchf)	6 passage, doorvaart	6 rende
7 estuary	7 estuaire	7 Flußmündung	7 riviermond	7 flodmunding
8 mouth	8 embouchure (Embᵉᵉ)	8 Mündung (Mdg)	8 monding	8 munding
9 channel (Chan)	9 canal, chenal (Cᵃˡ)	9 Fahrwasser (Fhrwss)	9 vaarwater	9 kanal
10 anchorage (Anche)	10 mouillage (Mᵃᵍᵉ)	10 Ankerplatz (Ankpl)	10 ankerplaats	10 ankerplads
11 island,-s (I, Is)	11 ile, iles (I Is)	11 Insel (n) (I)	11 eiland, -en (E EiL)	11 ø, øer
12 cape (C)	12 cap (C)	12 Kap (K)	12 kaap (Kp)	12 forbjerg
13 mountain (Mt)	13 mont (Mᵗ)	13 Berg (Bg)	13 berg	13 bjerg
14 point (Pt)	14 pointe (pᵗᵉ)	14 Huk (Hk)	14 punt (pt)	14 pynt
15 hill	15 colline (Col)	15 Hügel (Hg)	15 heuvel	15 bakke
16 rocks (Rks)	16 rochers (Rᵉʳˢ)	16 Klippe (n) (Klp)	16 rotsen	16 klipper
Colours	*Couleurs*	*Farben*	*Kleuren*	*Farver*
1 black (B/blk)	1 noir (n)	1 schwarz (s)	1 zwart (Z)	1 sort
2 red (R)	2 rouge (r)	2 rot (r)	2 rood (R)	2 rød
3 green (G)	3 vert (v)	3 grün (gn)	3 groen (Gn)	3 grøn
4 yellow (Y)	4 jaune (j)	4 gelb (g)	4 geel (Gl)	4 gul
5 white (W)	5 blanc (b)	5 weiß (W)	5 wit (W)	5 hvid
6 orange (Or)	6 orange (org)	6 orange (or)	6 oranje (Gl)	6 orange
7 violet (Vl)	7 violet (vio)	7 violett (viol)	7 violet (Vi)	7 violet
8 brown	8 brun	8 braun (br)	8 bruin	8 brun
9 blue (Bl)	9 bleu (bl)	9 blau (bl)	9 blauw (B)	9 blå
10 grey	10 gris (gr)	10 grau (gr)	10 grijs	10 grå

ESPAÑOL	ITALIANO	PORTUGUÊS	TÜRKÇE	ΕΛΛΗΝΙΚΑ
13 NAVEGACION	**13 NAVIGAZIONE**	**13 NAVEGAÇÃO**	**13 NAVİGASYON**	**13 ΝΑΥΤΙΛΙΑ**
Trabajos de carta de navegación	**Carteggio**	**Cartear**	**Harita çalışması**	**ΕΡΓΑΣΙΕΣ ΕΠΙ ΧΑΡΤΟΥ**
Acidentes de la costa	*Fisionomia della costa*	*Fisíonomia da costa*	*Özellikler*	*ΧΑΡΑΚΤΗΡΙΣΤΙΚΑ*
1 bahia (Ba)	1 baia (B)	1 baía (B)	1 körfez	1 ΟΡΜΟΣ
2 fiord (Fd)	2 fiordo (Fd)	2 fiorde	2 fijord	2 ΦΙΟΡΝΤ
3 glaciares	3 ghiacciaio	3 campo do gêlo em movimento	3 buzul	3 ΠΑΓΕΤΩΝΑΣ
4 lago, laguna	4 lago	4 lago, lagôa (L)	4 göl, haliç	4 ΛΙΜΝΗ
5 entrada (Ent)	5 entrata	5 entrada	5 giriş	5 ΕΙΣΟΔΟΣ
6 paso (Ps)	6 passaggio (Pass)	6 passagem	6 geçit	6 ΠΕΡΑΣΜΑ
7 estuario, ría (Est)	7 estuario	7 estuário (Est)	7 nehrin girişi	7 ΕΚΒΟΛΗ
8 desembocadura (Desemb.)	8 bocca	8 foz	8 ağız, nehrin denize döküldüğü yer	8 ΣΤΟΜΙΟ
9 canal (Can)	9 canale (Can)	9 canal (Can)	9 kanal, geçit	9 ΚΑΝΑΛΙ
10 fondeadero (Fond.)	10 ancoraggio (Anc)	10 fundeadouro	10 demir yeri	10 ΑΓΚΥΡΟΒΟΛΙΟ
11 isla, islas (I, Is)	11 isola (I)	11 ilha, ilhéu (I, Il)	11 ada, adalar (Ad)	11 ΝΗΣΙ
12 cabo (C)	12 capo (C)	12 cabo (C)	12 burun (Br)	12 ΑΚΡΩΤΗΡΙ
13 monte (M.)	13 montagna (Mt)	13 monte (Mt)	13 dağ, dağı	13 ΒΟΥΝΟ
14 punta (P.)	14 punta (Pta)	14 ponta (Pta)	14 zirve, uç	14 ΑΚΡΑ
15 colina (Col)	15 collina	15 colina (Col)	15 tepe (T)	15 ΛΟΦΟΣ
16 rocas (R.)	16 Scogli (Sc)	16 rochas (R)	16 kayalar	16 ΒΡΑΧΟΙ
Colores	*Colori*	*Côres*	*Renkler*	*ΧΡΩΜΑΤΑ*
1 negro (n)	1 nero (B, blk)	1 preto (pr)	1 kara, siyah	1 ΜΑΥΡΟ
2 rojo (r)	2 rosso (R)	2 vermelho (vm)	2 kırmızı, al, kızıl	2 ΚΟΚΚΙΝΟ
3 verde (v)	3 verde (G)	3 verde (vd)	3 yeşil	3 ΠΡΑΣΙΝΟ
4 amarillo (am)	4 giallo (Y)	4 amarelo (am)	4 sarı	4 ΚΙΤΡΙΝΟ
5 blanco (b)	5 bianco (W)	5 branco (br)	5 beyaz, Ak	5 ΑΣΠΡΟ
6 naranja	6 arancione (Or)	6 côr de laranja	6 turuncu	6 ΠΟΡΤΟΚΑΛΙ
7 violeta	7 violetto (Vl)	7 violeta, lilás	7 mor	7 ΜΩΒ
8 pardo (p), marrón	8 marrone	8 castanho	8 kahverengi	8 ΚΑΦΕ
9 azul (az)	9 blu (Bl)	9 azul	9 mavi	9 ΜΠΛΕ
10 gris	10 grigio	10 cinzento	10 gri	10 ΓΚΡΙΖΟ

ENGLISH	FRANÇAIS	DEUTSCH	NEDERLANDS	DANSK
13 NAVIGATION	**13 NAVIGATION**	**13 NAVIGATION**	**13 NAVIGATIE**	**13 NAVIGATION**
Chartwork	**Navigation**	**Seekartenarbeit**	**Kaartpassen**	**Arbejde med søkort**
Ports & harbours	*Ports*	*Häfen*	*Havens*	*Havne og marinaer*
1 yacht harbour	1 bassin pour yachts	1 Yachthafen	1 jachthaven	1 lystbådehavn
2 harbourmaster's office	2 bureau du Capitaine de Port (B^cau)	2 Hafenamt (Hfn-A)	2 havenkantoor	2 havnekontor
3 custom house, custom office	3 bureau de douane (D^ne)	3 Zollamt (Zoll-A)	3 douanekantoor	3 toldkontor
4 prohibited area (Prohibd)	4 zone interdite	4 verbotenes Gebiet (Verb Gbt)	4 verboden gebied	4 forbudt område
5 dolphin (Dn)	5 duc d'Albe	5 Dalben (Dlb)	5 dukdalf, meerpaal	5 duc d'albe
6 dock	6 bassin, dock	6 Hafenbecken, Dock	6 bassin, dok	6 dok
7 careening grid	7 gril de carénage	7 Platz zum Trockenfallen	7 kielplaats, bankstelling	7 kølhalingsplads
8 slip, slipway	8 cale de halage	8 Slipp, Helling	8 helling, sleephelling	8 bedding
9 breakwater	9 brise-lames	9 Wellenbrecher	9 golfbreker	9 bølgebryder
10 mole	10 môle	10 Mole	10 havendam	10 mole
11 anchorage	11 mouillage	11 Ankerplatz	11 ankerplaats	11 ankerplads
12 anchorage prohibited	12 défense de mouiller	12 verbotener Ankerplatz	12 verboden ankerplaats	12 ankring forbudt
13 anchorage limit	13 limite de mouillage	13 Reedegrenze	13 grens ankerplaats	13 grænse for ankerplads
14 spoil ground	14 zone de déblai	14 Baggerschüttstelle	14 baggerstortplaats	14 losseplads
15 submarine cable	15 câble sous-marin	15 Unterwasserkabel	15 onderwaterkabel	15 undersøisk kabel
16 submarine pipeline	16 canalisation sous-marine	16 Rohrleitung unter Wasser	16 onderwater pijplijn	16 undersøisk rørledning
Coastguard	*Garde-côtes*	*Küstenwacht*	*Kustwacht*	*Kystvagt*
1 watch tower	1 vigie (Vig)	1 Wache (W), Wachtturm (W-Tm)	1 uitkijk, wachtpost	1 vagttårn
2 lifeboat station (LBS)	2 bateau de sauvetage (B de sauv)	2 Rettungsbootstation (R-S)	2 reddingbootstation	2 redningsbådsstation
3 pilot station	3 station de pilotage	3 Lotsenstelle (L-S)	3 loodsstation	3 lodsstation
4 storm-signal station	4 station de signaux de tempête	4 Sturmsignalstelle (Strm-S)	4 stormseinstation	4 stormvarslingsstation

ESPAÑOL	ITALIANO	PORTUGUÊS	TÜRKÇE	ΕΛΛΗΝΙΚΑ
13 NAVEGACION	**13 NAVIGAZIONE**	**13 NAVEGAÇÃO**	**13 NAVİGASYON**	**13 ΝΑΥΤΙΛΙΑ**
Trabajos de carta de navegación	**Carteggio**	**Cartear**	**Harita çalışması**	**ΕΡΓΑΣΙΕΣ ΕΠΙ ΧΑΡΤΟΥ**
Puertos y radas 1 dársena de yates 2 Comandancia de Marina 3 aduana (Ad) 4 zona prohibida (Z⁴ proh) 5 noray 6 dique 7 dique de peine, carenero 8 varadero 9 rompeolas 10 muelle 11 fondeadero 12 fondeadero prohibido (Fondᵒ/proh) 13 limite de fondeadero 14 vertedero (Vertᵒ) 15 cable submarino 16 canalización submarina, tuberia	**Porti e rade** 1 porticciolo per yacht 2 Capitaneria di porto 3 Dogana 4 area interdetta 5 briccola 6 bacino, darsena 7 scalo di carenaggio 8 scivolo d'alaggio 9 frangiflutti 10 molo 11 ancoraggio 12 divieto d'ancoraggio 13 limite d'ancoraggio 14 zona di scarico 15 cavo sottomarino 16 oleodotto sottomarino	**Portos e marinas** 1 doca de recreio 2 Capitania 3 Alfândega 4 zona proíbida 5 duque de alba 6 doca 7 grade de marés 8 plano inclinado, rampa 9 quebra-mar 10 molhe 11 fundeadouro 12 fundeadouro proíbido 13 limite de fundeadouro 14 zona para descarga de dragados ou entulhos 15 cabo submarino 16 conduta submarina	**Limanlar** 1 yat limanı 2 liman başkanlığı 3 gümrük, gümrük binası, gümrük (bürolar) 4 yasak saha 5 bağlama kazığı 6 dok, havuz 7 karina temizlik ızgarası 8 kızak ızgarası, rampa 9 dalgakıran 10 mendirek 11 demiryeri, demirleme alanı 12 demirleme yasağı 13 demirleme alanı sınırı 14 kirlenmiş deniz dibi 15 sualtı kablosu 16 sualtı boru hattı	**ΛΙΜΑΝΙΑ** 1 ΜΑΡΙΝΑ 2 ΓΡΑΦΕΙΟ ΛΙΜΕΝΑΡΧΗ 3 ΤΕΛΩΝΕΙΟ, ΤΕΛΩΝΕΙΑΚΟΣ ΣΤΑΘΜΟΣ 4 ΑΠΑΓΟΡΕΥΜΕΝΗ ΠΕΡΙΟΧΗ 5 ΔΕΛΦΙΝΙ 6 ΝΤΟΚ - ΑΠΟΒΑΘΡΑ 7 ΣΧΑΡΑ ΚΑΡΕΝΑΡΙΣΜΑΤΑΟΣ 8 ΓΛΥΣΤΡΑ 9 ΚΥΜΑΤΟΘΡΑΥΣΤΗΣ 10 ΜΩΛΟΣ 11 ΑΓΚΥΡΟΒΟΛΙΑ 12 ΑΠΑΓΟΡΕΥΕΤΑΙ Η ΑΓΚΥΡΟΒΟΛΙΑ 13 ΟΡΙΑ ΑΓΚΥΡΟΒΟΛΙΑΣ 14 ΤΟΠΟΣ ΑΠΟΡΡΙΨΗΣ ΣΚΟΥΠΙΔΙΩΝ 15 ΥΠΟΓΕΙΟ ΚΑΛΩΔΙΟ 16 ΥΠΟΓΕΙΟΣ ΣΩΛΗΝΑΣ
Guardacostas 1 vigía 2 estación de salvamento 3 caseta de prácticos 4 estación de semáforo de señales de temporal	**Guardacoste** 1 torre d'avvistamento 2 stazione battelli di salvataggio 3 stazione dei piloti 4 stazione segnali di tempesta	**Policia marítima** 1 posto de vigia 2 estação de salva-vidas 3 estação de pilôtos 4 posto de sinais de mau tempo	**Sahil güvenlik** 1 gözetleme kulesi 2 can kurtarma istasyonu 3 fırtına işaret istasyonu 4 fırtına işaret istasyonu	**ΑΚΤΟΦΥΛΑΚΗ** 1 ΠΑΡΑΤΗΡΗΤΗΡΙΟ 2 ΣΤΑΘΜΟΣ ΣΩΣΤΙΚΩΝ ΛΕΜΒΩΝ 3 ΣΤΑΘΜΟΣ ΠΙΛΟΤΟΥ 4 ΣΗΜΑΤΟΦΟΡΙΚΟΣ

ENGLISH	FRANÇAIS	DEUTSCH	NEDERLANDS	DANSK
13 NAVIGATION	**13 NAVIGATION**	**13 NAVIGATION**	**13 NAVIGATIE**	**13 NAVIGATION**
Tides	**Marées**	**Gezeiten**	**Getijden**	**Tidevand**
Tidal streams	***Courants de marée***	***Gezeitenströme***	***Getijstromen***	***Tidevandsstrøm***
1 flood stream	1 courant de flot, de flux	1 Flutstrom	1 vloedstroom	1 flodbølge
2 ebb stream	2 courant de jusant	2 Ebbstrom	2 ebstroom	2 ebbe
3 slack water	3 marée étale	3 Stauwasser	3 doodtij	3 slæk vand
4 turn of the tide	4 renverse de courant	4 Kentern des Stromes	4 kentering	4 tidevandsskifte
5 rate	5 vitesse	5 Geschwindigkeit	5 snelheid	5 fart
6 knot	6 nœud	6 Knoten	6 knoop, zeemijl per uur	6 knob
7 set	7 porter	7 setzen	7 zetten	7 sætning
8 current	8 courant	8 Strom	8 stroom	8 strøm
9 fair tide	9 courant favorable ou portant	9 mitlaufender Strom	9 stroom mee	9 med tidevandet
10 foul tide	10 courant contraire ou debout	10 Gegenstrom	10 stroom tegen, tegenstrooms	10 mod tidevandet
Tide	***Marée***	***Gezeiten***	***Getij***	***Flod og ebbe***
1 high water (HW)	1 pleine mer	1 Hochwasser (HW)	1 hoogwater (HW)	1 højvande
2 low water (LW)	2 basse mer	2 Niedrigwasser (NW)	2 laagwater (LW)	2 lavvande
3 flood (Fl)	3 marée montante	3 Flut	3 vloed	3 flod
4 ebb	4 marée descendante	4 Ebbe	4 eb	4 ebbe
5 stand	5 étale	5 Stillstand	5 stilwater, doodtij	5 slæk vande
6 range	6 amplitude	6 Tidenhub	6 verval	6 amplitude
7 spring tide (Sp)	7 eau vive, grande marée	7 Springtide	7 springtij	7 springtid
8 neap tide (Np)	8 eau morte	8 Nipptide	8 doodtij	8 niptid

ESPAÑOL	ITALIANO	PORTUGUÊS	TÜRKÇE	ΕΛΛΗΝΙΚΑ
13 NAVEGACION	**13 NAVIGAZIONE**	**13 NAVEGAÇÃO**	**13 NAVİGASYON**	**13 ΝΑΥΤΙΛΙΑ**
Mareas	**Maree**	**Marés**	**Akıntılar**	**ΠΑΛΙΡΡΟΙΕΣ**
Corrientes de marea	*Correnti di marea*	*Correntes de maré*	*Gelgit Akıntıları*	*ΠΑΛΙΡΡΟΙΚΑ ΡΕΥΜΑΤΑ*
1 corriente de creciente	1 corrente d'alta marea	1 corrente de enchente	1 gelen gelgit akıntısı med akıntısı	1 ΠΛΗΜΜΥΡΙΣ
2 corriente de vaciante	2 corrente di riflusso	2 corrente de vasante	2 çekilen gelgit akıntısı	2 ΑΜΠΩΤΙΣ
3 repunte	3 stanca	3 águas paradas	3 gelgitin durduğu an	3 ΠΑΛΙΡΡΟΙΟΣΤΑΣΙΟ
4 cambio de marea	4 cambio di marea	4 mudança de maré	4 akıntının dönmesi, yön değiştirmesi	4 ΑΝΑΣΤΡΟΦΗ ΠΑΛΙΡΡΟΙΑΣ
5 velocidad	5 velocità	5 força da corrente	5 akıntı hızı	5 ΤΑΧΥΤΗΤΑ ΠΑΛΙΡΡΟΙΑΣ
6 nudo	6 nodo	6 nó	6 deniz mili	6 ΚΟΜΒΟΣ
7 dirección	7 direzione (di corrente)	7 direcção	7 akıntı yönü	7 ΚΑΤΕΥΘΥΝΣΗ ΠΑΛΙΡΡΟΙΑΚΟΥ ΡΕΥΜΑΤΟΣ
8 corriente	8 corrente	8 corrente	8 akıntı	8 ΡΕΥΜΑ
9 corriente favorable	9 marea favorevole	9 maré favorável	9 taşıyıcı akıntı	9 ΕΥΝΟΙΚΗ ΠΑΛΙΡΡΟΙΑ
10 corriente contraria	10 marea contraria	10 maré desfavorável	10 karşıt akıntı	10 ΚΟΝΤΡΑ ΠΑΛΙΡΡΟΙΑ
Marea	*Marea*	*Maré*	*Gelgit (med-cezir)*	*ΠΑΛΙΡΡΟΙΑ*
1 pleamar	1 alta marea (A M)	1 preia-mar (PM)	1 gelgitte gel halinde denizin yükselmiş olması hali, med hali	1 ΠΛΗΜΜΗ
2 bajamar	2 bassa marea (B M)	2 baixa-mar (BM)	2 gelgitte git halinde denizin alçalmış olması hali, cezir hali	2 ΡΗΧΙΑ
3 entrante	3 flusso	3 enchente	3 denizin yükselmesi, gelen gelgit, med	3 ΠΛΗΜΜΥΡΙΣ
4 vaciante	4 riflusso	4 vasante	4 denizin alçalması, giden gelgit cezir	4 ΑΜΠΩΤΙΣ
5 margen	5 marea ferma	5 estofa da maré	5 akıntının durmuş olması	5 ΠΑΛΙΡΡΟΙΟΣΤΑΣΙΟ
6 repunte	6 ampiezza	6 amplitude de maré	6 menzil	6 ΕΥΡΟΣ ΠΑΛΙΡΡΟΙΑΣ
7 marea viva, zizigias	7 marea sigiziale	7 águas-vivas (sizígia)	7 yüksek gelgit	7 ΠΑΛΙΡΡΟΙΑ ΕΥΖΥΓΙΩΝ
8 aguas muertas	8 marea di quadratura	8 águas-mortas (quadratura)	8 alçak gelgit	8 ΠΑΛΙΡΡΟΙΑ ΤΕΤΡΑΓΩΝΙΣΜΟΥ ΚΥΚΛΟΥ

ENGLISH	FRANÇAIS	DEUTSCH	NEDERLANDS	DANSK
13 NAVIGATION	**13 NAVIGATION**	**13 NAVIGATION**	**13 NAVIGATIE**	**13 NAVIGATION**
Tides	**Marées**	**Gezeiten**	**Getijden**	**Tidevand**
Tide 9 sea level 10 mean 11 chart datum	*Marée* 9 niveau 10 moyen 11 zéro des cartes	*Gezeiten* 9 Wasserstand 10 mittlere 11 Kartennull	*Getij* 9 zeeniveau 10 gemiddeld 11 reductievlak, laag-laagwaterspring	*Flod og ebbe* 9 vandstand 10 middel 11 kortdatum
Coastal navigation	**Navigation côtière**	**Küstennavigation**	**Kustnavigatie**	**Kystnavigation**
1 North pole	1 nord	1 Nordpol	1 noordpool	1 nordpol
2 bearing	2 relèvement	2 Peilung	2 peiling	2 pejling
3 course	3 cap, route	3 Kurs	3 koers	3 kurs
4 true	4 vrai	4 rechtweisend	4 ware, rechtwijzende (koers)	4 sand
5 magnetic	5 magnétique	5 mißweisend	5 magnetisch	5 magnetisk
6 compass course	6 cap au compas	6 Kompaßkurs	6 kompaskoers	6 kompaskurs
7 variation	7 déclinaison	7 Mißweisung	7 variatie	7 misvisning
8 deviation	8 déviation	8 Deviation, Ablenkung	8 deviatie	8 deviation
9 leeway	9 dérive	9 Abdrift	9 drift	9 afdrift
10 allowance for current	10 tenir compte du courant	10 Stromvorhalt	10 stroomcorrectie	10 strømberegning
11 course through the water	11 route au compas	11 Weg durchs Wasser	11 koers door het water	11 kurs gennem vandet
12 course made good	12 route sur le fond	12 Weg über Grund	12 koers over de grond, ware koers	12 beholdne kurs
13 distance sailed	13 chemin parcouru	13 gesegelte Distanz	13 afgelegde afstand	13 udsejlet distance
14 to plot	14 tracer	14 absetzen, eintragen	14 plotten	14 at plotte
15 position	15 position	15 Schiffsort, Standort	15 positie	15 position
16 to take a bearing	16 prendre ou effectuer un relèvement	16 peilen, eine Peilung nehmen	16 een peiling nemen	16 tage en pejling
17 cross bearings	17 relèvements croisés	17 Kreuzpeilung	17 kruispeiling	17 krydspejling
18 position line	18 droite de relèvement	18 Standlinie	18 positielijn	18 stedlinie

ESPAÑOL	ITALIANO	PORTUGUÊS	TÜRKÇE	ΕΛΛΗΝΙΚΑ
13 NAVEGACION	**13 NAVIGAZIONE**	**13 NAVEGAÇÃO**	**13 NAVİGASYON**	**13 ΝΑΥΤΙΛΙΑ**
Mareas	**Maree**	**Marés**	**Akıntılar**	**ΠΑΛΙΡΡΟΙΕΣ**
Marea 9 nivel del mar 10 media 11 bajamar escorada	*Marea* 9 livello del mare 10 medio 11 livello di riferimento scandagli	*Maré* 9 nível do mar 10 média 11 zero hidrográfico	*Gelgit (med-cezir)* 9 deniz seviyesi 10 ortalama 11 harita datumu	*ΠΑΛΙΡΡΟΙΑ* 9 ΣΤΑΘΜΗ ΘΑΛΑΣΣΑΣ 10 ΜΕΣΟΣ 11 ΣΤΟΙΧΕΙΑ ΧΑΡΤΟΥ
Navegación costera	**Navigazione costiera**	**Navegação costeira**	**Kılavuz seyri**	**ΑΚΤΟΠΛΟΙΚΗ ΝΑΥΣΙΠΛΟΙΑ**
1 polo norte 2 marcación, demora 3 rumbo 4 verdadero	1 polo Nord 2 rilevamento 3 rotta 4 vero	1 polo norte 2 azimute 3 rumo 4 verdadeiro	1 Kuzey kutbu, Kuzey 2 kerteriz 3 rota 4 hakiki	1 ΒΟΡΕΙΟΣ ΠΟΛΟΣ 2 ΔΙΟΠΤΕΥΣΗ 3 ΠΟΡΕΙΑ 4 ΑΛΗΘΗΣ
5 magnético 6 rumbo de aguja 7 variación	5 magnetico 6 rotta bussola 7 variazione	5 magnético 6 rumo agulha 7 declinação	5 manyetik 6 pusla rotası 7 varyasyon, gerçek sapma	5 ΜΑΓΝΗΤΙΚΗ 6 ΠΟΡΕΙΑ ΠΥΞΙΔΑΣ 7 ΑΠΟΚΛΙΣΗ
8 desvio	8 deviazione	8 desvio	8 deviasyon, arızi sapma	8 ΠΑΡΕΚΤΡΟΠΗ
9 deriva 10 error por corriente 11 rumbo	9 scarroccio 10 compensazione per la corrente 11 rotta di superficie	9 abatimento 10 desconto para corrente 11 rumo em relação à água	9 düşme 10 akıntıya göre düzeltme 11 su içindeki rota	9 ΕΚΠΕΣΜΟΣ 10 ΔΙΟΡΘΩΣΗ ΛΟΓΩ ΡΕΥΜΑΤΟΣ 11 ΦΑΙΝΟΜΕΝΗ ΠΟΡΕΙΑ (ΣΤΟ ΝΕΡΟ)
12 rumbo verdadero	12 rotta vera	12 rumo em relação ao fundo	12 deniz dibine göre rota, gerçek rota	12 ΑΛΗΘΗΣ ΠΟΡΕΙΑ
13 distancia navegada	13 distanza percorsa	13 distância navegada	13 seyredilen mesafe	13 ΔΙΑΝΥΘΕΙΣΑ ΑΠΟΣΤΑΣΗ
14 situarse en la carta	14 tracciare	14 marcar na carta	14 plotlama, çizmek	14 ΑΠΟΤΥΠΩΝΩ ΣΤΟ ΧΑΡΤΗ
15 situación 16 tomar una marcación	15 punto 16 prendere un rilevamento	15 o ponto 16 marcar	15 konum, mevki 16 bir kerteriz almak	15 ΘΕΣΗ 16 ΠΑΙΡΝΩ ΔΙΟΠΤΕΥΣΗ
17 situación por dos marcaciones 18 línea de marcación	17 rilevamenti incrociati 18 linea di posizione	17 marcar por dois azimutes 18 linha de posição	17 çapraz kerteriz 18 mevki hattı	17 ΤΕΜΝΟΜΕΝΕΣ ΔΙΟΠΤΕΥΣΕΙΣ 18 ΕΥΘΕΙΑ ΘΕΣΕΩΣ

ENGLISH	FRANÇAIS	DEUTSCH	NEDERLANDS	DANSK
13 NAVIGATION	**13 NAVIGATION**	**13 NAVIGATION**	**13 NAVIGATIE**	**13 NAVIGATION**
Coastal navigation	**Navigation côtière**	**Küstennavigation**	**Kustnavigatie**	**Kystnavigation**
19 transferred position line	19 droite de relèvement déplacée	19 versetzte Standlinie	19 verzeilde positielijn	19 overført stedlinie
20 running fix	20 relèvements successifs d'un même amer	20 Doppelpeilung, Versegelungspeilung	20 kruispeiling met verzeiling	20 løbende stedsbestemmelse
21 four-point bearing	21 relèvement à 4 quarts	21 Vierstrichpeilung	21 vierstreekspeiling	21 fire-stregs-pejling
22 double the angle on the bow	22 doubler l'angle	22 Verdoppelung der Seitenspeilung	22 dubbelstreekspeiling	22 stedsbestemmelse ved to pejlinger
23 dead reckoning	23 navigation à l'estime	23 Koppelung, Gissung	23 gegist bestek	23 bestik
24 estimated position	24 point estimé	24 gegißtes Besteck	24 gegiste positie	24 gisset plads
25 distance off	25 distance de …	25 Abstand von …	25 afstand tot	25 afstand fra
26 seaward	26 vers le large	26 seewärts	26 naar buiten, zeewaarts	26 mod søsiden
27 waypoint	27 waypoint	27 Wegepunkt	27 waypoint	27 waypoint
28 landmark	28 point de repère	28 Landmarke	28 kenbaar punt	28 landmærke
Sailing instructions	**Instructions nautiques**	**Segelanweisungen**	**Zeilaanwijzingen**	**Farvandsoplysninger**
1 lighted channel	1 chenal éclairé	1 befeuertes Fahrwasser	1 verlicht/bevuurd vaarwater	1 farvand afmærket med fyr
2 buoyed channel	2 chenal balisé	2 ausgetonntes Fahrwasser	2 betond vaarwater	2 farvand afmærket med bøjer
3 dredged channel	3 chenal dragué	3 gebaggerte Fahrrinne	3 gebaggerd vaarwater	3 uddybet kanal

ESPAÑOL	ITALIANO	PORTUGUÊS	TÜRKÇE	ΕΛΛΗΝΙΚΑ
13 NAVEGACION	**13 NAVIGAZIONE**	**13 NAVEGAÇÃO**	**13 NAVİGASYON**	**13 ΝΑΥΤΙΛΙΑ**
Navegación costera	**Navigazione costiera**	**Navegação**	**Kılavuz Seyri**	**ΑΚΤΟΠΛΟΙΚΗ ΝΑΥΣΙΠΛΟΙΑ**
19 marcación trasladada	19 linea di posizione trasportata	19 linha de posição transportada	19 kaydırılmış konum hattı	19 ΜΕΤΑΦΕΡΘΕΙΣΑ ΕΥΘΕΙΑ ΘΕΣΕΩΣ
20 situación por dos marca ciónes a un mismo punto	20 punto nave con rilevamenti successivi	20 marcar, navegar e tornar a marcar	20 kaydırılmış kerteriz, aynı maddenin iki kez kerteriz edilmesiyle	20 ΔΥΟ ΔΙΑΔΟΧΙΚΕΣ ΔΙΟΠΤΕΥΣΕΙΣ
21 situación por marcación a 45º	21 rilevamento a 4 quarte	21 marcação as quatro quartas	21 dört kerteden mevki	21 ΔΙΟΠΤΕΥΣΗ 4 ΣΗΜΕΙΩΝ
22 distancia a la costa por angulas especiales	22 raddoppio dell'angolo da prora	22 marcação pelo ângulo duplo	22 aynı maddenin iki kez kerteriziyle. Buna 22-45"c veya 45-90"c metodları denir	22 ΠΑΡΑΛΛΑΣΣΩ - ΚΑΒΑΝΤΖΑΡΩ
23 estima	23 navigazione a punto stimato	23 navegação estimada	23 parakete konumu	23 ΣΤΙΓΜΑ ΕΞ' ΑΝΑΜΕΤΡΗΣΕΩΣ
24 situación por estima	24 punto stimato	24 posição estimada	24 yaklaşık konum	24 ΥΠΟΛΟΓΙΖΟΜΕΝΗ ΘΕΣΗ (ΣΤΙΓΜΑ)
25 distancia a …	25 distanza da …	25 distância a …	25 … den uzaklık	25 ΑΦΗΝΩ ΑΠΟΣΤΑΣΗ
26 hacia la mar, mar adentro	26 verso il largo	26 do lado do mar	26 açık denize doğru	26 ΠΡΟΣ ΤΟ ΠΕΛΑΓΟΣ
27 waypoint	27 waypoint	27 ponto de chegada/ de passagem	27 rota değişikliği noktası, menzil noktası	27 ΠΡΟΟΡΙΣΜΟΣ (ΕΝΔΙΑΜΕΣΟΣ)
28 marea fija	28 punto cospicua	28 ponto conspícuo	28 karada kerteriz noktası, alamet	28 ΧΑΡΑΧΤΗΡΙΣΤΙΚΟ ΣΗΜΕΙΟ ΣΤΕΡΙΑΣ
Derrotero	**Istruzioni di navigazione**	**Instruções para navegação**	**Seyir bilgileri, talimatı**	**ΟΔΗΓΙΕΣ ΝΑΥΣΙΠΛΟΙΑΣ**
1 canal abalizado con luces	1 canale illuminato	1 canal farolado	1 ışıklandırılmış kanal, ışıklandırılmış geçit	1 ΦΩΤΙΣΜΕΝΟΣ ΔΙΑΥΛΟΣ
2 canal balizado	2 canale segnalato con boe	2 canal balizado	2 şamandıralanmış kanal, şamandıralanmış geçit	2 ΔΙΑΥΛΟΣ ΜΕ ΣΗΜΑΝΤΗΡΕΣ
3 canal dragado	3 canale dragato	3 canal dragado	3 derinleştirilmiş kanal, derinleştrilmiş geçit	3 ΕΚΒΑΘΥΜΕΝΟΣ ΔΙΑΥΛΟΣ

ENGLISH	FRANÇAIS	DEUTSCH	NEDERLANDS	DANSK
13 NAVIGATION	**13 NAVIGATION**	**13 NAVIGATION**	**13 NAVIGATIE**	**13 NAVIGATION**
Sailing instructions	**Instructions nautiques**	**Segelanweisungen**	**Zeilaanwijzingen**	**Farvandsoplysninger**
4 navigable channel	4 chenal navigable	4 Fahrrinne	4 bevaarbaar vaarwater	4 farvandet kan besejles
5 leading line	5 alignement	5 Leitlinie	5 geleidelijn, lichtenlijn	5 ledelinie
6 in line	6 aligné	6 in Linie	6 in één lijn	6 overet
7 transit line	7 passe, alignement	7 Deckpeilung	7 peilingslijn	7 pejling
8 open two breadths	8 ouvert à deux largeurs	8 offen halten	8 twee breedten open-houden	8 at åbne to bredder
9 pass not less than one cable off …	9 passer au moins à une encâblure de …	9 mindestens eine Kabellänge Abstand halten	9 op niet meer dan een kabellengte passeren	9 passér mindst en kabellængde fra…
10 leave to port	10 laisser à bâbord	10 an Backbord halten	10 aan bakboord houden	10 holde til bagbord
11 round an object	11 contourner un amer	11 einen Gegenstand runden	11 ronden van iets	11 at runde et mærke
12 least depth	12 profondeur minimum	12 Mindestiefe, geringste Tiefe	12 minste diepte	12 mindste dybde
13 subject to change	13 irrégulier, mobile, changeant	13 Veränderungen unterworfen	13 aan verandering onderhevig	13 ændringer kan forkomme
14 offlying dangers extend 3 miles	14 dangers s'étendant sur 3 milles au large	14 Gefahren, die 3 Seemeilen vor der Küste liegen	14 voor de kust liggende gevaren tot 3 mijl	14 udeliggende fare 3 sømil fremme
15 breaking seas on bar	15 la mer déferle ou brise sur la barre	15 auf der Barre brechende Seen	15 branding op drempel	15 søen brækker på barren
16 making an offing	16 prendre le large	16 freien Seeraum gewinnen	16 vrij van de wal gaan varen	16 stå ud i frit farvand
17 lee shore	17 côte sous le vent	17 Legerwall, Leeküste	17 lage wal	17 læ kyst
18 windward shore	18 côte au vent	18 Luvküste	18 hoge wal	18 luv kyst
19 flood tide sets across entrance	19 le courant de flot porte en travers de l'entrée	19 Flutstrom setzt quer zur Hafeneinfahrt	19 vloedstroom voor ingang langs	19 flodstrømmen sætter tværs over indløbet
20 tide race during flood	20 remous violents par courant de flot	20 Stromschnellen bei Flut	20 stroomkabbeling bij vloed	20 urolig sø ved højvande
21 north-going current	21 le courant porte au nord	21 nach Nordern setzender Strom	21 noord gaande stroom	21 nordgående strøm
22 water level may be reduced	22 abaissement de niveau possible par vent de …	22 Wasserstand kann geringer sein	22 lagere waterstanden zijn mogelijk	22 vandstanden kan falde

ESPAÑOL	ITALIANO	PORTUGUÊS	TÜRKÇE	ΕΛΛΗΝΙΚΑ
13 NAVEGACION	**13 NAVIGAZIONE**	**13 NAVEGAÇÃO**	**13 NAVİGASYON**	**13 ΝΑΥΤΙΛΙΑ**
Derrotero	**Istruzioni di navigazione**	**Instruções para navegação**	**Seyir bilgileri, talimatı**	**ΟΔΗΓΙΕΣ ΝΑΥΣΙΠΛΟΙΑΣ**
4 canal navegable	4 canale navigabile	4 canal navegável	4 seyre uygun kanal/ geçit	4 ΠΛΕΥΣΙΚΟΣ ΔΙΑΥΛΟΣ
5 enfilación	5 allineamento	5 enfiamento	5 transit hattı	5 ΙΘΥΝΤΗΡΙΟΣ ΓΡΑΜΜΗ
6 en línea	6 in allineamento	6 enfiado	6 transit hattı üzerinde	6 ΣΕ ΕΥΘΕΙΑ
7 enfilación por el través	7 passaggio, transito	7 alinhado	7 transit hattı	7 ΕΥΘΕΙΑ ΔΙΕΥΛΕΥΣΗΣ
8 abierta a dos anchuras	8 aprire di due larghezze	8 aberto por duas bocaduras	8 elle kerteriz alma	8 ΑΣΕ ΧΩΡΟ ΔΥΟ ΠΛΑΤΗ ΠΛΟΙΟΥ
9 pasar a más de un cable	9 passare non meno di 1/10 di miglio da …	9 não passar a menos de 1/10 milha	9 geçit bir gominadan az uzaklıkta değil	9 ΟΧΙ ΠΙΟ ΚΟΝΤΙΝΗ ΔΙΕΥΛΕΥΣΗ ΑΠΟ…
10 dejar a babor	10 lasciare a sinistra	10 deixar a bombordo	10 iskelede bırakmak	10 ΑΣΕ ΤΟ ΑΡΙΣΤΕΡΑ
11 bojear	11 scansare un oggetto	11 rondar um obstáculo	11 bir maddeyi dönmek	11 ΠΕΡΑΣΕ ΓΥΡΩ ΑΠΟ…
12 calado minimo	12 fondale minimo	12 altura minima de água	12 en az derinlik	12 ΕΛΑΧΙΣΤΟ ΒΑΘΟΣ
13 sujete a cambiar	13 soggetto a variazioni	13 sujeito a variação	13 değişebilir, değişken	13 ΠΙΘΑΝΗ ΑΛΛΑΓΗ
14 peligro hasta 3 millas	14 pericoli al largo per 3 miglia	14 linha de resguardo de perigo a três milhas	14 kıyıdan 3 mile	14 ΟΙ ΚΙΝΔΥΝΟΙ ΕΚΤΕΙΝΟΝΤΑΙ 3 ΜΙΛΙΑ
15 rompientes en la barra	15 frangenti su barriera	15 com mar a arrebentar na barra	15 sığlıkta deniz kırılır	15 ΣΠΑΕΙ ΤΟ ΚΥΜΑ ΣΤΑ ΡΗΧΑ
16 en altamar, franquia	16 prendere il largo	16 amarar	16 denize açılmak	16 ΑΝΟΙΓΟΜΑΙ ΣΤΟ ΠΕΛΑΓΟΣ
17 costa de sotavento	17 costa sottovento	17 terra a sotavento	17 rüzgâr altındaki kıyı	17 ΠΡΟΣΗΝΕΜΟΣ ΑΚΤΗ
18 costa de barlovento	18 costa sopravvento	18 terra a barlavento	18 rüzgâr üstündeki kıyı	18 ΥΠΗΝΕΜΟΣ ΑΚΤΗ
19 la creciente tira atravesada a la entrada	19 flusso di marea di traverso all'entrata	19 corrente transversal à entrada durante a enchente	19 gelen gelgit, akıntısı girişe aykırı	19 ΠΑΛΙΡΡΟΙΑΚΑ ΡΕΥΜΑΤΑ ΣΤΗΝ ΜΠΟΥΚΑ
20 correnton durante la crecida	20 frangenti di marea durante il flusso	20 estoque de água durante a enchente	20 gelen gelgit-girişte kuvvetli anafor	20 ΧΟΝΤΡΗ ΘΑΛΑΣΣΑ ΚΑΤΑ ΤΗΝ ΠΛΗΜΜΥΡΙΔΑ
21 corriente sur	21 corrente verso nord	21 corrente em direcção ao norte	21 kuzey yönlü akıntı	21 ΡΕΥΜΑ ΜΕ ΒΟΡΕΙΑ ΚΑΤΕΥΘΥΝΣΗ
22 la sonda puede disminuir	22 possibile riduzione di livello del mare	22 nível de água pode ser reduzido	22 su seviyesi azalabilir	22 ΠΙΘΑΝΗ ΕΛΛΑΤΩΣΗ ΣΤΑΘΜΗΣ ΝΕΡΟΥ

ENGLISH	FRANÇAIS	DEUTSCH	NEDERLANDS	DANSK
13 NAVIGATION	**13 NAVIGATION**	**13 NAVIGATION**	**13 NAVIGATIE**	**13 NAVIGATION**
Inland waterways	**Eaux intérieures**	**Binnengewässer**	**Binnenwateren**	**Floder, søer og kanaler**
1 canal	1 canal	1 Kanal	1 kanaal	1 kanal
2 lock	2 écluse, sas	2 Schleuse	2 sluis	2 sluse
3 length	3 longueur, de long	3 Länge	3 lengte	3 længde
4 breadth	4 largeur, de large	4 Breite	4 breedte	4 bredde
5 depth	5 profondeur	5 Tiefe	5 diepte	5 dybde
6 to lock in	6 entrer dans le sas	6 einschleusen	6 schutten naar binnen	6 sluse ind
7 to lock out	7 sortir de l'écluse	7 ausschleusen	7 schutten naar buiten	7 sluse ud
8 lock dues	8 droits de sas	8 Schleusengebühr	8 sluisgeld	8 sluseafgift
9 opening times	9 heures d'ouverture	9 Betriebszeiten	9 openingstijden	9 åbningstider
10 bridge dues	10 droits de pont	10 Brückenzoll	10 bruggeld	10 broafgift
11 movable bridge	11 pont mobile	11 bewegliche Brücke	11 beweegbare brug	11 bro der kan åbnes
12 lifting bridge	12 pont basculant	12 Hubbrücke	12 hefbrug	12 klapbro
13 swing bridge	13 pont tournant	13 Drehbrücke	13 draaibrug	13 svingbro
14 fixed bridge	14 pont fixe	14 feste Brücke	14 vaste brug	14 fast bro
15 span	15 écartement, travée, largeur	15 Durchfahrtsweite	15 vak	15 spændvidde
16 height, headroom	16 tirant d'air	16 Durchfahrtshöhe	16 dorvaarthoogte	16 højde, fri højde
17 upstream	17 amont	17 stromauf, flußaufwärts	17 stroom opwaarts	17 ovenfor, mod strømmen
18 downstream	18 aval	18 stromab, flußabwärts	18 stroomafwaarts	18 medstrøms
19 ferry	19 bac, ferry	19 Fähre	19 pont	19 færge
20 high tension cable	20 câble à haute tension	20 Hochspannungskabel	20 hoogspanningskabel	20 højspændingsledninger
21 mooring place	21 point d'accostage	21 Festmacheplatz	21 afmeerplaats	21 fortøjningsplads
22 mooring forbidden	22 accostage interdit	22 anlegen verboten	22 afmeren verboden	22 fortøjning forbudt
23 to quant, punt	23 conduire à la gaffe, à la perche	23 staken	23 punteren	23 at stage

ESPAÑOL	ITALIANO	PORTUGUÊS	TÜRKÇE	ΕΛΛΗΝΙΚΑ
13 NAVEGACION	**13 NAVIGAZIONE**	**13 NAVEGAÇÃO**	**13 NAVİGASYON**	**13 ΝΑΥΤΙΛΙΑ**
Canales	**Acque interne**	**Cursos de água**	**İç suyolları**	**ΚΑΝΑΛΙΑ ΣΤΗΝ ΕΝΔΟΧΩΡΑ**
1 canal	1 canale	1 canal	1 kanal	1 ΚΑΝΑΛΙ
2 compuerta, esclusa	2 chiusa	2 eclusa	2 lok, geçiş havazu	2 ΑΝΥΨΩΤΙΚΗ ΔΕΞΑΜΕΝΗ
3 longitud	3 lunghezza	3 comprimento	3 uzunluk, boy	3 ΜΗΚΟΣ
4 ancho, anchura	4 larghezza	4 largura	4 genişlik, en	4 ΠΛΑΤΟΣ
5 fondo, profundidad	5 profondità	5 profundidade	5 derinlik	5 ΒΑΘΟΣ
6 entrar en la esclusa	6 entrare in chiusa	6 entrar na eclusa, docar	6 loka/kanal havuzuna girmek	6 ΑΝΕΒΑΙΝΩ ΤΗΝ ΣΤΑΘΜΗ
7 salir de la esclusa	7 uscire da chiusa	7 sair da eclusa ou doca	7 lok havuzundan çıkmak	7 ΚΑΤΕΒΑΙΝΩ ΤΗΝ ΣΤΑΘΜΗ
8 derecho de esclusa	8 diritti di chiusa	8 taxa de docagem	8 lok/havuz rüsumları	8 ΤΕΛΗ ΔΕΞΑΜΕΝΗΣ
9 tiempo de apertura	9 orario d'apertura	9 hora de abrir	9 açılış saatleri	9 ΩΡΕΣ ΑΝΟΙΓΜΑΤΟΣ
10 tarifa de puente	10 diritti di ponte	10 taxa de passagem numa ponte	10 köprü rüsumu	10 ΤΕΛΗ ΓΕΦΥΡΑΣ
11 puente móvil	11 ponte mobile	11 ponte movediça	11 mobil/açılır köprü	11 ΚΙΝΗΤΗ ΓΕΦΥΡΑ
12 puente levadizo	12 ponte levatoio	12 ponte levadiça	12 kalkar köprü	12 ΑΝΑΚΛΙΝΟΜΕΝΗ ΓΕΦΥΡΑ
13 puente giratorio	13 ponte girevole	13 ponte giratória	13 döner köprü	13 ΠΛΑΓΙΟΑΝΟΙΓΟΜΕΝΗ ΓΕΦΥΡΑ
14 puente fijo	14 ponte fisso	14 ponte fixa	14 sabit köprü	14 ΣΤΑΘΕΡΗ ΓΕΦΥΡΑ
15 anchura del puente	15 campata, luce	15 vão	15 köprü ayakları genişliği, köprü gözü genişliği	15 ΧΩΡΟΣ ΕΛΕΥΘΕΡΟΣ ΣΤΟ ΠΛΑΙ-ΑΝΟΙΓΜΑ
16 altura	16 altezza	16 altura	16 su yüzeyinden yükseklik	16 ΕΛΕΥΘΕΡΟ ΥΨΟΣ
17 aguas arriba	17 a monte	17 montante	17 akıntıya karşı	17 ΠΡΟΣ ΤΟ ΡΕΥΜΑ-ΚΟΝΤΡΑ
18 aguas abajo	18 a valle	18 jusante	18 akıntı yönünde	18 ΚΑΤΕΒΑΙΝΩ ΤΟ ΡΕΥΜΑ
19 transbordador	19 traghetto	19 ferry boat, barco da travessia	19 feribot, yolcu gemisi	19 ΦΕΡΙ
20 cable de alta tensión	20 cavo ad alta tensione	20 cabo de alta tensão	20 yüksek gerilim hattı	20 ΚΑΛΩΔΙΟ ΥΨΗΛΗΣ ΤΑΣΕΩΣ
21 amarradero	21 posto d'ormeggio	21 ponte de atracação	21 bağlama yeri, yanaşma yeri	21 ΑΓΚΥΡΟΒΟΛΙΟ
22 amarradero prohibido	22 ormeggio vietato	22 proíbido atracar	22 bağlama/yanaşma yasağı	22 ΑΓΚΥΡΟΒΟΛΙΟ ΑΠΑΓΟΡΕΥΕΤΑΙ
23 fincar	23 spingere con la pertica	23 zingar	23 botu gönderi dibine saplayarak yürütmek	23 ΠΑΚΤΩΝΑΣ

ENGLISH	FRANÇAIS	DEUTSCH	NEDERLANDS	DANSK
13 NAVIGATION	**13 NAVIGATION**	**13 NAVIGATION**	**13 NAVIGATIE**	**13 NAVIGATION**
Inland waterways	**Eaux intérieures**	**Binnengewässer**	**Binnenwateren**	**Floder, søer og kanaler**

24 sluice gate
25 lock gate
 	
26 ladder
27 bollard
28 moving bollard
	24 pertuis
	25 porte d'écluse
	
	26 échelle
	27 bollard
	28 bollard flottant
		24 Schleusentor
		25 Schleusentor
		
		26 Leiter
		27 Poller
		28 Poller auf
		    Schwimmpontons in
		    Schleusen
			24 sluisdeur
			25 sluisdeur
			
			26 ladder
			27 bolder, meerpaal
			28 bewegende bolder
				24 sluseport
				25 dokport
				
				26 stige
				27 pullert
				28 flytbar pullert

Meteorology	**Météorologie**	**Meteorologie**	**Meteorologie**	**Meteorologi**
Instruments & terms	*Instruments et termes*	*Instrumente und Ausdrücke*	*Instrumenten en uitdrukkingen*	*Instrumenter og benævnelser*

1 aneroid barometer
 	
2 barograph
3 rise/fall
4 steady
5 thermometer
6 temperature
7 rise/drop
8 anemometer
 	
9 velocity
10 pressure
11 Weatherfax
	1 baromètre anéroide
	
	2 barographe
	3 monter/baisser
	4 stable
	5 thermomètre
	6 température
	7 hausse/chute
	8 anémomètre
	
	9 vitesse
	10 pression
	11 recepteur de cartes
	    météo
		1 Aneroidbarometer
		
		2 Barograph
		3 steigen/fallen
		4 gleichbleibend
		5 Thermometer
		6 Temperatur
		7 Zunahme/Sturz
		8 Windmesser,
		    Anemometer
		9 Geschwindigkeit
		10 Druck
		11 Wetterfax
			1 aneroïde barometer
			
			2 barograaf
			3 rijzen/vallen
			4 vast
			5 thermometer
			6 temperatuur
			7 stijgen/dalen
			8 wind(snelheids)-
			    meter
			9 snelheid
			10 druk
			11 weatherfax
				1 aneroid barometer
				
				2 barograf
				3 stige/falde
				4 uforandret
				5 termometer
				6 temperatur
				7 stigende/faldende
				8 vindmåler
				
				9 hastighed
				10 tryk
				11 vejrfax

Weather forecast terms	*Termes de météo*	*Meteorologische Ausdrücke*	*Meteorologische uitdrukkingen*	*Meteorologens sprog*
1 weather forecast 2 weather report 3 area 4 low-pressure area	1 prévisions météo 2 bulletin du temps 3 région, parages 4 zone de basse pression	1 Wettervorhersage 2 Wetterbericht 3 Gebiet 4 Tiefdruckgebiet	1 weersverwachting 2 weerrapport 3 gebied 4 lagedrukgebied	1 vejrudsigt 2 vejrmelding 3 område 4 lavtryksområde

ESPAÑOL	ITALIANO	PORTUGUÊS	TÜRKÇE	ΕΛΛΗΝΙΚΑ
13 NAVEGACION	**13 NAVIGAZIONE**	**13 NAVEGAÇÃO**	**13 NAVİGASYON**	**13 ΝΑΥΤΙΛΙΑ**
Canales	**Acque interne**	**Cursos de água**	**İç suyolları**	**ΚΑΝΑΛΙΑ ΣΤΗΝ ΕΝΔΟΧΩΡΑ**
24 valvula de compuerta	24 saracinesca	24 comporta	24 lok kapısı, lok kapağı	24 ΥΔΑΤΟΦΡΑΚΤΗΣ
25 compuerta de esclusa	25 serranda di chiusa	25 grade fechada	25 lok kapısı	25 ΘΥΡΑ ΑΝΥΨΩΤΙΚΗΣ ΔΕΞΑΜΕΝΗΣ
26 escala	26 scala	26 escada	26 iskele, merdiven	26 ΣΚΑΛΑ
27 bolardo	27 bitta	27 abita	27 baba	27 ΔΕΣΤΡΑ
28 bolardo flotante	28 bitta mobile	28 abita móvel	28 hareketli baba	28 ΚΙΝΗΤΗ ΔΕΣΤΡΑ
Meteorología	**Meteorologia**	**Meteorologia**	**Meteoroloji**	**ΜΕΤΕΩΡΟΛΟΓΙΑ**
Instrumentos y terminos	*Strumenti e termini*	*Instrumentos e termos*	*Aygitlar ve terimler*	*ΟΡΟΛΟΓΙΑ ΚΑΙ ΟΡΓΑΝΑ*
1 barómetro aneroide	1 barometro aneroide	1 barómetro aneroide	1 aneroid barometre	1 ΑΝΕΡΟΕΙΔΕΣ ΒΑΡΟΜΕΤΡΟ
2 barógrafo	2 barografo	2 barógrafo	2 barograf	2 ΒΑΡΟΓΡΑΦΟΣ
3 subir/bajar	3 salire/scendere	3 subindo/descendo	3 yükseltme/alçaltma	3 ΑΝΟΔΟΣ/ΠΤΩΣΗ
4 fijo, constante	4 costante	4 constante	4 sabit	4 ΣΤΑΘΕΡΟ
5 termómetro	5 termometro	5 termómetro	5 termometre	5 ΘΕΡΜΟΜΕΤΡΟ
6 temperatura	6 temperatura	6 temperatura	6 ısı, hararet	6 ΘΕΡΜΟΚΡΑΣΙΑ
7 subida/caida	7 salire/scendere	7 subida/descida	7 gel-git	7 ΑΝΟΔΟΣ/ΠΤΩΣΗ
8 anemómetro	8 anemometro	8 anemómetro	8 anemometre	8 ΑΝΕΜΟΜΕΤΡΟ
9 velocidad	9 velocità	9 velocidade	9 hız	9 ΤΑΧΥΤΗΤΑ
10 presión	10 pressione	10 pressão	10 basınç	10 ΠΙΕΣΗ
11 Weatherfax	11 fax meteo	11 fax de meteorologia	11 hava raporu faks cihazı	11 ΟΥΕΔΕΡΦΑΞ
Previsión metereológica	*Termini meteorologici*	*Termos do boletim meteorológico*	*Hava tahmini terimleri*	*ΟΡΟΛΟΓΙΑ ΠΡΟΓΝΩΣΗΣ ΚΑΙΡΟΥ*
1 previsión metereológica	1 previsioni del tempo	1 previsão de tempo	1 hava tahmini	1 ΠΡΟΓΝΩΣΗ ΚΑΙΡΟΥ
2 boletin metereológico	2 bollettino meteo	2 boletim meteorológico	2 hava raporu	2 ΔΕΛΤΙΟ ΚΑΙΡΟΥ
3 región	3 area	3 área, zona	3 bölge	3 ΠΕΡΙΟΧΗ
4 zona de baja presión	4 area di bassa pressione	4 área de baixa pressão	4 alçak basınç alanı	4 ΠΕΡΙΟΧΗ ΧΑΜΗΛΩΝ ΠΙΕΣΕΩΝ

13 NAVIGATION | 13 NAVIGATION | 13 NAVIGATION | 13 NAVIGATIE | 13 NAVIGATION

ENGLISH	FRANÇAIS	DEUTSCH	NEDERLANDS	DANSK
13 NAVIGATION	**13 NAVIGATION**	**13 NAVIGATION**	**13 NAVIGATIE**	**13 NAVIGATION**
Meteorology	**Météorologie**	**Meteorologie**	**Meteorologie**	**Meteorologi**
Weather forecast terms	*Termes de météo*	*Meteorologische Ausdrücke*	*Meteorologische uitdrukkingen*	*Meteorologens sprog*
5 depression, low	5 dépression, bas	5 Depression, Tief	5 depressie	5 lavtryk
6 trough	6 creux	6 Trog, Ausläufer	6 dal	6 trug
7 high-pressure area	7 zone de haute pression	7 Hochdruckgebiet	7 hogedrukgebied	7 højtryksområde
8 anticyclone, high	8 anticyclone, haut	8 Hoch	8 hogedrukgebied	8 anticyklon, høj
9 ridge	9 crête	9 Rücken	9 rug	9 ryg
10 wedge	10 coin	10 Keil	10 wig	10 kile
11 front, cold, warm	11 front froid, chaud	11 Front, kalt, warm	11 front, koud/warm	11 front, kold, varm
12 occlusion	12 occlusion	12 Okklusion	12 occlusie	12 okklusion
13 fill up	13 se combler	13 auffüllen	13 opvullen	13 fyldes op
14 deepen	14 se creuser	14 sich vertiefen	14 dieper worden	14 uddybes
15 stationary	15 stationnaire	15 stationär	15 stationair	15 stationært
16 quickly	16 rapidement	16 schnell, rasch	16 snel	16 hurtigt
17 slowly	17 lentement	17 langsam	17 langzaam	17 langsomt
18 spreading	18 s'étalant, s'étendant	18 sich ausbreitend	18 uitbreidend	18 spreder sig
19 settled	19 temps établi	19 beständig	19 vast	19 stabilt
20 changeable	20 variable	20 wechselhaft	20 veranderlijk	20 omskifteligt
21 clearing up	21 éclaircies	21 aufklarend	21 opklarend	21 klarer op
22 fine	22 beau temps	22 heiter, schön	22 mooi	22 fint
23 fair	23 beau	23 klar	23 goed	23 smukt
Sky	*Ciel*	*Himmel*	*Lucht*	*Himlen*
1 clear sky	1 pur, clair, dégagé	1 wolkenlos, klarer Himmel	1 onbewokt	1 klar himmel
2 cloudy	2 nuageux	2 bewölkt, wolkig	2 bewolkt	2 skyet
3 overcast	3 couvert	3 bedeckt	3 betrokken	3 overskyet
4 high cloud	4 nuages hauts, élevés	4 hohe Wolken	4 hoge wolken	4 høje skyer
5 low cloud	5 nuages bas	5 niedrige Wolken	5 lage wolken	5 lave skyer

ESPAÑOL	ITALIANO	PORTUGUÊS	TÜRKÇE	ΕΛΛΗΝΙΚΑ
13 NAVEGACION	**13 NAVIGAZIONE**	**13 NAVEGAÇÃO**	**13 NAVİGASYON**	**13 ΝΑΥΤΙΛΙΑ**

Meteorología	**Meteorologia**	**Meteorologia**	**Meteoroloji**	**ΜΕΤΕΩΡΟΛΟΓΙΑ**
Previsión metereológica	*Termini meteorologici*	*Termos do boletim meteorológico*	*Hava tahmini terimleri*	*ΟΡΟΛΟΓΙΑΟΡΟΛΟΓΙΑ ΠΡΟΓΝΩΣΗΣ ΚΑΙΡΟΥ*
5 depresión/borrasca	5 depressione	5 depressão, baixa	5 depresyon, alçak	5 ΧΑΜΗΛΟ ΒΑΡΟΜΕΤΡΙΚΟ
6 vaguada	6 saccatura	6 linha de baixa pressão	6 alçak basınç gözü	6 ΙΣΟΒΑΡΕΙΣ ΧΑΜΗΛΟΥ
7 zona de alta presión	7 area di alta pressione	7 área de alta pressão	7 yüksek basınç alanı	7 ΠΕΡΙΟΧΗ ΥΨΗΛΩΝ ΠΙΕΣΕΩΝ
8 anticiclón, alta	8 anticiclone (o alta pressione)	8 anticiclone, alta	8 antisiklon, yüksek	8 ΑΝΤΙΚΥΚΛΩΝΑΣ – ΥΨΗΛΟ
9 dorsal, cresta	9 cresta	9 crista	9 tepe noktası	9 ΙΣΟΒΑΡΕΙΣ ΥΨΗΛΟΥ
10 cuna	10 cuneo	10 cunha	10 köşe	10 ΠΕΡΙΟΧΗ ΜΕΤΑΞΥ ΔΥΟ ΧΑΜΗΛΩΝ ΣΧΗΜΑΤΟΣ V
11 frente, frío, cálido	11 fronte, freddo, caldo	11 frente, fria, quente	11 cephe, soğuk, ılık	11 ΜΕΤΩΠΟ, ΨΥΧΡΟ, ΖΕΣΤΟ
12 oclusión	12 occlusione	12 oclusão	12 mas etme	12 ΟΡΙΟΓΡΑΜΜΗ ΜΕΤΑΞΥ ΨΥΧΡΟΥ ΚΑΙ ΖΕΡΜΟΥ ΠΕΡΙΟΧΗΣ
13 debilitamiento	13 colmarsi	13 encher	13 tamamen dolma	13 ΓΕΜΙΖΕΙ
14 intensificación	14 approfondirsi	14 agravar	14 derinleşme	14 ΒΑΘΑΙΝΕΙ
15 estacionario	15 stazionario	15 estacionária	15 sabit	15 ΣΤΑΘΕΡΟ
16 rápidamente	16 rapidamente	16 rápidamente	16 hızla	16 ΓΡΗΓΟΡΑ
17 lentamente	17 lentamente	17 lentamente	17 yavaşça	17 ΑΡΓΑ
18 extendiendo	18 che si allarga	18 alastrando	18 yayılarak	18 ΕΠΕΚΤΕΙΝΕΤΑΙ
19 sostenido, asentado	19 stabile	19 estável	19 oturmuş hava	19 ΕΓΚΑΤΕΣΤΗΜΕΝΟ
20 variable	20 variabile	20 variável, instável	20 mütehavil/değişebilir	20 ΜΕΤΑΒΛΗΤΟΣ
21 clarear, escampar	21 che si schiarisce	21 limpando	21 havanın yer yer sıyırması yer yer açması	21 ΚΑΘΑΡΙΖΕΙ
22 tranquilo, despejado	22 bello	22 bom tempo	22 güzel hava	22 ΩΡΑΙΟΣ
23 despejado	23 discreto	23 estavel	23 çok güzel hava	23 ΚΑΛΟΣ-ΔΙΑΥΓΗΣ
Cielo	*Cielo*	*Céu*	*Gök*	*ΟΥΡΑΝΟΣ*
1 claro, despejado	1 sereno	1 céu limpo	1 açık/bulutsuz gök	1 ΚΑΘΑΡΟΣ ΟΥΡΑΝΟΣ
2 nubloso	2 nuvoloso	2 nublado	2 bulutlu	2 ΣΥΝΝΕΦΙΑΣΜΕΝΟΣ
3 cubierto	3 coperto	3 coberto	3 çok bulutlu/kapalı	3 ΠΛΗΡΩΣ ΣΥΝΝΕΦΙΑΣΜΕΝΟΣ
4 nubes altas	4 nube alta	4 núvem alta	4 yüksek bulut	4 ΥΨΗΛΟ ΣΥΝΝΕΦΟ
5 nubes bajas	5 nube bassa	5 núvem baixa	5 alçak bulut	5 ΧΑΜΗΛΟ ΣΥΝΝΕΦΟ

13 NAVIGATION / 13 NAVIGATION / 13 NAVIGATION / 13 NAVIGATIE / 13 NAVIGATION

ENGLISH	FRANÇAIS	DEUTSCH	NEDERLANDS	DANSK
13 NAVIGATION	**13 NAVIGATION**	**13 NAVIGATION**	**13 NAVIGATIE**	**13 NAVIGATION**
Meteorology	**Météorologie**	**Meteorologie**	**Meteorologie**	**Meteorologi**
Visibility	*Visibilité*	*Sichtweite*	*Zicht*	*Sigtbarhed*
1 good	1 bonne	1 gut	1 goed	1 god
2 moderate	2 médiocre, réduite	2 mittel	2 matig	2 moderat
3 poor	3 mauvaise	3 schlecht	3 slecht	3 ringe
4 haze	4 brume de beau temps, ou brume sèche	4 Dunst	4 nevelig	4 dis
5 mist	5 brume légère ou mouillée	5 feuchter Dunst, diesig	5 nevel	5 let tåge
6 fog	6 brouillard	6 Nebel	6 mist	6 tåge
Wind	*Vent*	*Wind*	*Wind*	*Vind*
1 lull	1 accalmie, bonace	1 vorübergehendes Abflauen	1 luwte	1 kortvarig vindstille
2 drop, abate	2 tomber, diminuer de force	2 nachlassen	2 afnemen	2 vinden lægger sig
3 decreasing, moderating	3 décroissant	3 abnehmend	3 afnemend	3 aftagende
4 increasing, freshening	4 fraîchissant	4 zunehmend, auffrischend	4 toenemend	4 opfriskende
5 gust	5 rafale	5 Windstoß	5 windvlaag	5 vindstød
6 squall	6 grain	6 Bö	6 bui	6 byge
7 sea breeze	7 brise de mer	7 Seebrise	7 zeebries	7 søbrise
8 land breeze	8 brise de terre	8 ablandige Brise, Landbrise	8 landbries	8 landbrise
9 prevailing winds	9 vent dominant	9 vorherrschender Wind	9 heersende winden	9 fremherskende vind
10 trade winds	10 vents alizés	10 Passatwinde	10 passaatwind	10 passat
11 veer	11 virer au … (dans le sens des aiguilles d'une montre)	11 rechtdrehend, ausschießen	11 ruimen	11 højredrejende
12 back	12 adonner (dans le sens contraire aux aiguilles d'une montre)	12 zurückdrehen, krimpen	12 krimpen	12 venstredrejende

ESPAÑOL	ITALIANO	PORTUGUÊS	TÜRKÇE	ΕΛΛΗΝΙΚΑ
13 NAVEGACION	**13 NAVIGAZIONE**	**13 NAVEGAÇÃO**	**13 NAVİGASYON**	**13 ΝΑΥΤΙΛΙΑ**
Meteorología	**Meteorologia**	**Meteorologia**	**Meteoroloji**	**ΜΕΤΕΩΡΟΛΟΓΙΑ**
Visibilidad	***Visibilità***	***Visibilidade***	***Görüş***	*ΟΡΑΤΟΤΗΤΑ*
1 buena	1 buona	1 bôa	1 iyi	1 ΚΑΛΗ
2 regular	2 discreta	2 moderada	2 orta derecede, kısıtlı	2 ΜΕΤΡΙΑ
3 mala	3 scarsa	3 fraca, má	3 az, fena, çok kısıtlı	3 ΚΑΚΗ
4 calima	4 foschia	4 cerração	4 pus, iyi hava pusu	4 ΕΛΑΦΡΑ ΟΜΙΧΛΗ
5 neblina	5 caligine	5 neblina	5 hafif pus, nem taşıyan pus	5 ΨΑΘΟΥΡΑ - ΑΧΛΥΣ
6 niebla	6 nebbia	6 nevoeiro	6 sis	6 ΟΜΙΧΛΗ
Viento	***Vento***	***Vento***	***Rüzgar***	*ΑΝΕΜΟΣ*
1 encalmado	1 momento di calma	1 sota, calma temporária	1 çok sakin	1 ΚΑΛΜΑ
2 disminuir	2 attenuazione	2 acalmar	2 düşmek, kalmak	2 ΠΕΦΤΕΙ-ΚΟΠΑΖΕΙ
3 disminuyendo	3 in diminuzione	3 decrescendo de intensidade	3 azalmak	3 ΕΞΑΣΘΕΝΩΝ
4 aumentando	4 in aumento	4 aumentando	4 artmak, sertlemek	4 ΕΝΙΣΧΥΟΜΕΝΟΣ-ΦΡΕΣΚΑΡΕΙ
5 racha	5 raffica	5 rajada	5 sağnak	5 ΡΙΠΗ
6 churbasco	6 groppo	6 borrasca	6 sert sağnak	6 ΣΠΗΛΙΑΔΑ
7 brisa de mar, virazón	7 brezza di mare	7 brisa do mar	7 denizden esen rüzgar	7 ΘΑΛΑΣΣΙΑ ΑΥΡΑ, ΜΠΟΥΚΑΔΟΥΡΑ
8 terral	8 brezza di terra	8 brisa da terra	8 karadan esen rüzgar	8 ΑΠΟΓΕΙΟΣ ΖΕΦΥΡΟΣ
9 viento dominante	9 venti predominanti	9 ventos predominantes	9 hakim rüzgarlar	9 ΕΠΙΚΡΑΤΟΥΝΤΕΣ ΑΝΕΜΟΙ
10 vientos alisios	10 alisei	10 ventos alíseos	10 ticaret rüzgarları alizeler	10 ΑΛΗΓΕΙΣ ΑΝΕΜΟΙ
11 rolando en el sentido de las manillas de reloj	11 girare in senso orario	11 no sentido dos ponteiros de relógio	11 (saat ibreleri yönünde) e dönmek	11 ΓΥΡΙΖΕΙ-ΑΛΛΑΖΕΙ ΠΡΟΣ ΤΑ ΔΕΞΙΑ
12 rolando en contrario de las manillas de reloj	12 girare in senso antiorario	12 de sentido retrógrado	12 (saat ibreleri aksi yönünde) e dönmek	12 ΑΛΛΑΖΕΙ ΠΡΟΣ ΑΡΙΣΤΕΡΑ

ENGLISH	FRANÇAIS	DEUTSCH	NEDERLANDS	DANSK
13 NAVIGATION	**13 NAVIGATION**	**13 NAVIGATION**	**13 NAVIGATIE**	**13 NAVIGATION**

Meteorology	Météorologie	Meteorologie	Meteorologie	Meteorologi

Wind	*Vent*	*Wind*	*Wind*	*Vind*
13 Beaufort scale	13 Echelle de Beaufort	13 Windstärke nach Beaufort	13 windschaal van Beaufort	13 Beaufort skala
calm 0	calme 0	Windstille 0	stil 0	stille 0
light air 1	très légère brise 1	leiser Zug 1	flauw en stil 1	næsten stille 1
light breeze 2	légère brise 2	leichte Brise 2	flauwe koelte 2	svag vind 2
gentle breeze 3	petite brise 3	schwache Brise 3	lichte koelte 3	let vind 3
moderate breeze 4	jolie brise 4	mäßige Brise 4	matige koelte 4	jævn vind 4
fresh breeze 5	bonne brise 5	frische Brise 5	frisse bries 5	frisk vind 5
strong breeze 6	vent frais 6	starker Wind 6	stijve bries 6	hård vind 6
near gale 7	grand frais 7	steifer Wind 7	harde wind 7	stiv kuling 7
gale 8	coup de vent 8	stürmischer Wind 8	stormachtig 8	hård kuling 8
strong gale 9	fort coup de vent 9	Sturm 9	storm 9	stormende kuling 9
storm 10	tempête 10	schwerer Sturm 10	zware storm 10	storm 10
violent storm 11	violente tempête 11	orkanartiger Sturm 11	zeer zware storm 11	stærk storm 11
hurricane 12	ouragan 12	Orkan 12	orkaan 12	orkan 12

Sea	*Mer*	*See*	*Zee*	*Søen*
1 calm	1 plate, calme	1 glatt, ruhig	1 vlak	1 stille
2 ripples	2 vaguelettes, rides	2 gekräuselt	2 rimpels	2 krusninger
3 waves	3 vagues, ondes, lames	3 Wellen, Seen	3 golven	3 bølger
4 rough sea	4 grosse mer, mer agitée	4 große See	4 ruwe zee	4 grov sø
5 swell	5 houle	5 Dünung	5 deining	5 dønninger
6 crest	6 crête	6 Wellenkamm	6 kam, golftop	6 bølgetop
7 trough	7 creux	7 Wellental	7 trog, golfdal	7 bølgedal
8 breaking seas	8 lames déferlantes	8 brechende Seen	8 brekende zee	8 brydende sø
9 head sea	9 mer debout	9 See von vorn	9 tegenlopende zee	9 søen imod
10 following sea	10 mer arrière ou suiveuse	10 achterliche See	10 meelopende zee	10 medsø
11 choppy	11 croisée ou hachée; clapot	11 kabbelig	11 kort en steil	11 krap
12 short	12 lames courtes	12 kurz	12 kort	12 kort
13 steep	13 mer creuse	13 steif	13 steil	13 stejl
14 slight	14 mer peu agitée	14 leicht	14 lichte zeegang	14 let/ringe

ESPAÑOL	ITALIANO	PORTUGUÊS	TÜRKÇE	ΕΛΛΗΝΙΚΑ
13 NAVEGACION	**13 NAVIGAZIONE**	**13 NAVEGAÇÃO**	**13 NAVİGASYON**	**13 ΝΑΥΤΙΛΙΑ**
Meteorología	**Meteorologia**	**Meteorologia**	**Meteoroloji**	**ΜΕΤΕΩΡΟΛΟΓΙΑ**

Viento / Vento / Vento / Rüzgar / ΑΝΕΜΟΣ

ESPAÑOL	ITALIANO	PORTUGUÊS	TÜRKÇE	ΕΛΛΗΝΙΚΑ
13 escala Beaufort	13 Scala Beaufort:	13 Escala Beaufort	13 Beaufort cetveli	13 ΚΛΙΜΑΚΑ ΜΠΟΦΩΡ
calma 0	bonaccia 0	calma 0	sakin 0	ΑΠΝΟΙΑ 0
				ΕΛΑΦΡΑ ΠΝΟΗ ΑΝΕΜΟΥ 1
ventolina 1	bava di vento 1	aragem 1	hafif rüzgar 1	ΑΣΘΕΝΗΣ ΑΝΕΜΟΣ 2
flojito 2	brezza leggera 2	vento fraco 2	hafif meltem 2	ΗΠΙΟΣ ΑΝΕΜΟΣ 3
flojo 3	brezza tesa 3	vento bonançoso 3	yumuşak meltem 3	ΜΕΤΡΙΟΣ ΑΝΕΜΟΣ 4
bonancible 4	vento moderato 4	vento moderado 4	sakin meltem 4	ΦΡΕΣΚΟΣ ΑΝΕΜΟΣ 5
fresquito 5	vento teso 5	vento frêsco 5	frişka 5	ΙΣΧΥΡΟΣ ΑΝΕΜΟΣ 6
fresco 6	vento fresco 6	vento multo frêsco 6	kuvvetli rüzgar 6	ΣΧΕΔΟΝ ΘΥΕΛΛΩΔΗΣ 7
frescachón 7	vento forte 7	vento forte 7	sert rüzgar 7	ΘΥΕΛΛΩΔΗΣ 8
duro 8	burrasca 8	vento multo forte 8	çok sert rüzgar 8	ΙΣΧΥΡΗ ΘΥΕΛΛΑ 9
muy duro 9	burrasca forte 9	vento tempestnoso 9	fırtına 9	ΚΥΚΛΩΝΑΣ-
temporal 10	tempesta 10	temporal 10	kuvvetli fırtına 10	ΚΑΤΑΙΓΙΔΑ 10
borrasca 11	tempesta forte 11	temporal desfeito 11	bora 11	ΙΣΧΥΡΗ ΚΑΤΑΙΓΙΔΑ 11
huracán 12	uragano 12	furacão 12	kasırga 12	ΤΥΦΩΝΑΣ 12

Mar / Mare / Mar / Deniz / ΘΑΛΑΣΣΑ

ESPAÑOL	ITALIANO	PORTUGUÊS	TÜRKÇE	ΕΛΛΗΝΙΚΑ
1 calma	1 calmo	1 calmo, plano	1 sakin, palpa	1 ΕΠΙΠΕΔΗ
2 mar rizada	2 increspato	2 ondinhas	2 küçük dalgalı, çırpıntılı	2 ΡΕΦΛΕΣ
3 olas	3 onde	3 ondas	3 dalga	3 ΚΥΜΑΤΑ
4 mar gruesa	4 mare agitato	4 mar bravo	4 kaba deniz, kaba dalga	4 ΤΡΙΚΥΜΙΩΔΕΣ
5 mar de leva, -de fondo	5 mare lungo	5 ondulação, mar de vaga	5 ölü denizler	5 ΜΑΜΑΛΟ
6 cresta	6 cresta	6 crista da onda	6 dalga doruğu	6 ΚΟΡΥΦΗ
7 seno	7 gola	7 cava da onda	7 dalga çukuru, dalga derinliği	7 ΑΥΛΑΚΙ
8 rompientes	8 frangenti	8 arrebentação	8 kırılan dalgalar, çatlayan dalgalar	8 ΑΦΡΙΖΟΝΤΑ ΚΥΜΑΤΑ
9 mar de proa	9 mare in prora	9 mar de proa	9 baş denizleri	9 ΚΟΝΤΡΑ ΘΑΛΑΣΣΑ
10 mar de popa	10 mare in poppa	10 mar de pôpa	10 kıçtan gelen deniz	10 ΠΡΙΜΑ ΘΑΛΑΣΣΑ
11 mar picada	11 maretta	11 mareta	11 kırık dalga	11 ΠΑΦΛΑΣΜΟΣ – ΑΝΤΙΜΑΜΑΛΟ
12 mar corta	12 (mare) corto	12 mar de vaga curta	12 kısa dalga	12 ΚΟΝΤΑ
13 mar gruesa	13 (mare) burrascoso	13 mar cavado	13 derin dalgalar	13 ΑΠΟΤΟΜΑ
14 marejadilla	14 poco mosso	14 mar chão	14 hafif dalga	14 ΛΙΓΟ ΤΑΡΑΓΜΕΝΗ

ENGLISH	FRANÇAIS	DEUTSCH	NEDERLANDS	DANSK
13 NAVIGATION	**13 NAVIGATION**	**13 NAVIGATION**	**13 NAVIGATIE**	**13 NAVIGATION**
Meteorology	**Météorologie**	**Meteorologie**	**Meteorologie**	**Meteorologi**

Precipitation	*Précipitations*	*Niederschlag*	*Neerslag*	*Nedbør*
1 wet	1 humide	1 naß	1 nat	1 vådt
2 dry	2 sec	2 trocken	2 droog	2 tørt
3 rain	3 pluie	3 Regen	3 regen	3 regn
4 sleet	4 neige fondue	4 Schneeregen	4 natte sneeuw	4 slud
5 snow	5 neige	5 Schnee	5 sneeuw	5 sne
6 hail	6 grêle	6 Hagel	6 hagel	6 hagl
7 drizzle	7 bruine	7 Sprühregen	7 motregen	7 støvregn
8 shower	8 averse	8 Schauer	8 stortbui	8 byge
9 thunderstorm	9 orage	9 Gewitter	9 onweer	9 tordenvejr

ESPAÑOL	ITALIANO	PORTUGUÊS	TÜRKÇE	ΕΛΛΗΝΙΚΑ
13 NAVEGACION	**13 NAVIGAZIONE**	**13 NAVEGAÇÃO**	**13 NAVİGASYON**	**13 ΝΑΥΤΙΛΙΑ**
Meteorología	**Meteorologia**	**Meteorologia**	**Meteoroloji**	**ΜΕΤΕΩΡΟΛΟΓΙΑ**
Precipitación 1 húmedo 2 seco 3 lluvia 4 aguanieve 5 nieve 6 granizada 7 llovizna 8 aguacero 9 tempestad	*Precipitazioni* 1 umido 2 secco 3 pioggia 4 nevischio 5 neve 6 grandine 7 pioviggine 8 acquazzone 9 temporale	*Precipitação* 1 húmido 2 sêco 3 chuva 4 geáda miúda 5 neve 6 saraiva, chuva de pedra 7 chuvisco 8 aguaceiro 9 trovoada	*Yağmur/yağış* 1 nemli 2 kuru 3 yağmur 4 eriyik kar 5 kar 6 kolu 7 ince yağmur çisenti 8 sağanak yağmur 9 gök gürültüsü ile karışık fırtına	*ΒΡΟΧΕΣ —ΧΙΟΝΙΑ* 1 ΥΓΡΟΣ 2 ΣΤΕΓΝΟΣ 3 ΒΡΟΧΗ 4 ΧΙΟΝΟΕΡΟ 5 ΧΙΟΝΙ 6 ΧΑΛΑΖΙ 7 ΨΙΛΗ ΒΡΟΧΗ 8 ΒΡΟΧΗ ΜΙΚΡΗΣ ΔΙΑΡΚΕΙΑΣ 9 ΜΠΟΥΡΙΝΙ

ENGLISH	FRANÇAIS	DEUTSCH	NEDERLANDS	DANSK
14 CLASSIC BOATS	**14 BATEAUX CLASSIQUES**	**14 KLASSISCHE YACHTEN**	**14 KLASSIEKE SCHEPEN**	**14 VETERANBÅDE**
Construction	**Construction**	**Bauweise**	**Constructie**	**Konstruktion**
Hull design & construction	*Plan de coque et construction*	*Rumpfkonstruktion und Bauweise*	*Romp- ontwerp en- constructie*	*Skrogkonstruktion*
1 clinker	1 à clins	1 klinker	1 klinker, overnaadse bouw	1 klinkbygget
2 carvel	2 à franc-bord	2 karweel oder kraweel	2 karveel	2 kravelbygget
3 moulded plywood	3 contreplaqué moulé	3 formverleimtes Sperrholz	3 gevormd plakhout	3 limet finer
4 half-decked	4 semi-ponté	4 halbgedeckt	4 half open	4 halvdæk
5 overhang	5 élancement	5 Überhang	5 overhangend	5 overhang
6 canoe stern	6 arrière canoë	6 Kanuheck	6 kano-achtersteven	6 kanohæk
7 scantlings	7 échantillonnage	7 Materialstärke, Profil	7 afmeting van constructiedelen	7 scantlings
Longitudinal section	*Section longitudinale*	*Längsschnitt*	*Langsdoorsnede*	*Opstalt*
1 stem	1 étrave	1 Vorsteven	1 achtersteven	1 forstævn
2 breasthook	2 guirlande	2 Bugband	2 boegband	2 bovbånd
3 apron	3 contre-étrave	3 Binnenvorsteven	3 binnenvoorsteven	3 inderstævn
4 wood keel	4 quille de bois	4 Holzkiel	4 houten kiel	4 trækøl
5 keelson	5 carlingue	5 Kielschwein	5 kielbalk	5 kølsvin
6 ballast keel	6 lest	6 Ballastkiel	6 ballastkiel	6 ballastkøl
7 keelbolts	7 boulons de quille	7 Kielbolzen	7 kielbouten	7 kølbolte
8 sternpost	8 étambot	8 Achtersteven	8 achterstevenbalk	8 agterstævn
9 horn timber	9 allonge de voûte	9 Heckbalken	9 hekbalk	9 hækbjælke
10 stern knee	10 marsouin, courbe de poupe	10 Achterstevenknie	10 stevenknie	10 hæk-knæ

ESPAÑOL	ITALIANO	PORTUGUÊS	TÜRKÇE	ΕΛΛΗΝΙΚΑ
14 BARCOS CLÁSICOS	**14 BATTELI CLASSICI**	**14 BARCOS CLÁSSICOS**	**14 KLASIK YATLAR**	**14 ΚΛΑΣΣΙΚΑ ΙΣΤΙΟΦΟΡΑ**
Construcción	**Costruzione**	**Construção**	**İnşaat**	**ΚΑΤΑΣΚΕΥΗ**

ESPAÑOL	ITALIANO	PORTUGUÊS	TÜRKÇE	ΕΛΛΗΝΙΚΑ
Diseño y construcción del casco	***Progetto e costruzione della carena***	***Desenho e construção do casco***	***Karina dizaynı ve inşaatı***	*ΣΧΕΔΙΟ ΓΑΣΤΡΑΣ & ΚΑΤΑΣΚΕΥΗ*
1 tingladillo	1 clinker	1 tabuado trincado	1 bindirme ağaç kaplama	1 ΚΛΙΜΑΚΩΤΗ ΑΡΜΟΛΟΓΙΑ
2 unión a tope	2 a paro	2 tabuado liso	2 armuz kaplama	2 ΛΕΙΑΣ ΑΡΜΟΛΟΓΙΑΣ
3 contrachapado moldado	3 compensato marino	3 contraplacado moldado	3 kalıplanmış kontraplak	3 ΦΟΡΜΑΡΙΣΜΕΝΟ ΚΟΝΤΡΑ-ΠΛΑΚΕ
4 con media cubierta, tillado	4 semiappontato	4 meio convez	4 yarım güverteli	4 ΜΙΣΟ ΚΟΥΒΕΡΤΩΜΕΝΟ
5 sobresalir	5 slancio	5 lançamento	5 bodoslama, bodoslamanın su üzerindeki kısmının boyu	5 ΠΡΟΕΞΟΧΗ ΤΗΣ ΠΛΩΡΗΣ ΤΟΥ ΣΚΑΦΟΥΣ
6 popa de canoa	6 poppa a canoa	6 pôpa de canoa	6 kano kıç, karpuz kıç	6 ΜΥΤΕΡΗ ΠΡΥΜΝΗ
7 escantillón	7 dimensioni	7 dimensões dos materiais	7 tekne eğrilerinin çizimi	7 ΤΕΜΑΧΙΑ ΞΥΛΟΥ
Sección longitudinal	***Sezione longitudinale***	***Secção longitudinal***	***Boyuna (tülani) kesit***	*ΚΑΤΑΜΗΚΟΣ ΤΟΜΗ*
1 roda	1 dritto di prua	1 roda de proa	1 baş bodoslama	1 ΠΡΥΜΝΗ
2 buzarda	2 gola di prua	2 buçarda	2 baş güverte/ bodoslama praçolu	2 ΚΟΡΑΚΙ
3 contrarroda	3 controdritto	3 contra-roda	3 kontra bodoslama	3 ΠΟΔΙΑ
4 quilla de madera	4 chiglia di legno	4 quilha	4 ağaç omurga	4 ΞΥΛΙΝΗ ΚΑΡΙΝΑ
5 sobrequilla	5 paramezzale, controchiglia	5 sobreçame	5 kontra omurga/iç omurga	5 ΣΩΤΡΟΠΙ
6 quilla lastrada	6 chiglia zavorrata	6 patilhão	6 maden omurga	6 ΣΑΒΟΥΡΩΜΕΝΗ ΚΑΡΙΝΑ
7 pernos de quilla	7 bulloni di chiglia	7 cavilhas do patilhão	7 omurga cıvataları maden omurga cıvataları	7 ΤΣΑΒΕΤΕΣ
8 codaste	8 dritto di poppa	8 cadaste	8 kıç bodoslama	8 ΠΟΔΟΣΤΑΜΟ
9 gambota de la limera	9 volta di poppa, dragante	9 cambota	9 kepçe omurgası	9 ΞΥΛΟ (ΚΑΡΙΝΑ) ΠΟΥ ΥΠΟΣΤΗΡΙΖΕΙ ΜΕΤΑ ΤΟ ΤΙΜΟΝΙ
10 curva coral	10 bracciolo dello specchio di poppa	10 curva do painel	10 kıç ayna praçolu	10 ΓΩΝΙΑ (ΓΟΝΑΤΟ) ΠΡΥΜΝΗΣ

ENGLISH	FRANÇAIS	DEUTSCH	NEDERLANDS	DANSK
14 CLASSIC BOATS	**14 BATEAUX CLASSIQUES**	**14 KLASSISCHE YACHTEN**	**14 KLASSIEKE SCHEPEN**	**14 VETERANBÖDE**
Construction	**Construction**	**Bauweise**	**Constructie**	**Konstruktion**
Longitudinal section	*Section longitudinale*	*Längsschnitt*	*Langsdoorsnede*	*Opstalt*
11 deadwood	11 massif	11 Totholz	11 opvulhout, doodhout	11 dødtræ
12 rudder trunk	12 jaumière	12 Ruderkoker	12 hennegatskoker	12 rorbrønd
13 rudder	13 gouvernail, safran	13 Ruder	13 roer	13 ror
14 tiller	14 barre	14 Ruderpinne	14 helmstok	14 rorpind
15 deck	15 pont	15 Deck	15 dek	15 dæk
16 beam	16 barrot	16 Decksbalken	16 dekbalk	16 bjælke
17 shelf	17 bauquière	17 Balkweger	17 balkweger	17 bjælkevæger
18 rib	18 membrure, couple	18 Spant	18 spant	18 spanter
19 bilge stringer	19 serre de bouchain	19 Stringer, Kimmweger	19 kimweger	19 længskibsvæger
20 length overall/LOA	20 longueur hors-tout	20 Länge über Alles, LüA	20 lengte over alles, LOA	20 længde overalt/LOA
21 load waterline/LWL	21 ligne de flottaison	21 Konstruktionswasser-linie (KWL, CWL)	21 lengte waterlijn, LWL	21 vandlinielængde/LWL
Lateral section	*Section latérale*	*Generalplan*	*Dwarsdoorsnede*	*Halve sektioner*
1 rail	1 liston	1 Reling	1 reling	1 ræling
2 bulwark	2 pavois	2 Schanzkleid	2 verschansing	2 skanseklædning
3 scupper	3 dalot	3 Speigatt	3 spuigat	3 spygatter
4 rubbing strake	4 bourrelet, ceinture	4 Scheuerleiste	4 berghout	4 fenderliste
5 planking	5 bordage	5 Beplankung	5 huid, beplanking	5 rangene
6 skin	6 bordé	6 Außenhaut	6 huid	6 klædning
7 garboard strake	7 virure de galbord	7 Kielgang	7 zandstrook	7 kølplanke
8 king plank	8 faux-étambrai, virure d'axe	8 Fischplanke	8 vissingstuk, schaarstokplank	8 midterfisk

ESPAÑOL	ITALIANO	PORTUGUÊS	TÜRKÇE	ΕΛΛΗΝΙΚΑ
14 BARCOS CLÁSICOS	**14 BATTELI CLASSICI**	**14 BARCOS CLÁSSICOS**	**14 KLASIK YATLAR**	**14 ΚΛΑΣΣΙΚΑ ΙΣΤΙΟΦΟΡΑ**
Construcción	**Costruzione**	**Construção**	**İnşaat**	**ΚΑΤΑΣΚΕΥΗ**
Sección longitudinal	*Sezione longitudinale*	*Secção longitudinal*	*Boyuna (tülani) kesit*	*ΚΑΤΑΜΗΚΟΣ ΤΟΜΗ*
11 macizo	11 massiccio di poppa	11 coral	11 yığma, kıç yığma, praçol	11 ΠΡΟΣΤΑΤΕΥΤΙΚΗ ΚΟΝΤΡΑ ΚΑΡΙΝΑ
12 limera de timon	12 losca del timone	12 caixão do leme	12 dümen kovanı	12 ΚΟΡΜΟΣ ΤΙΜΟΝΙΟΥ
13 timón	13 timone	13 leme	13 dümen, dümen palası	13 ΠΗΔΑΛΙΟ
14 caña	14 barra (del timone)	14 cana de leme	14 dümen yekesi	14 ΛΑΓΟΥΔΕΡΑ
15 cubierta	15 ponte	15 convez	15 güverte	15 ΚΑΤΑΣΤΡΩΜΑ
16 bao	16 baglio	16 vau	16 kemere	16 ΟΛΙΚΟ ΠΛΑΤΟΣ
17 durmiente	17 dormiente	17 dormente	17 kemere/güverte ıstralyası, güverte kuşağı	17 ΓΩΝΙΑ ΓΑΣΤΡΑ/ ΚΑΤΑΣΤΡΩΜΑ
18 cuaderna	18 ordinata	18 caverna	18 triz	18 ΣΤΡΑΒΟ
19 vagra	19 corrente di sentina	19 escôa	19 alt kuşak	19 ΝΕΥΡΟ ΣΕΝΤΙΝΑΣ
20 eslora total	20 lunghezza fuori tutto (LFT)	20 comprimento fora a fora	20 tam boy, LOA	20 ΟΛΙΚΟ ΜΗΚΟΣ
21 eslora en el plano de flotación	21 linea di galleggiamento	21 comprimento na linha de água	21 dolu iken su hattı	21 ΜΗΚΟΣ ΙΣΑΛΟΥ
Sección lateral	*Sezione laterale*	*Secção lateral*	*Enine (arzani) kesit*	*ΚΑΘΕΤΟΣ ΤΟΜΗ*
1 tapa de regala	1 capodibanda	1 talabardão	1 parampet kapağı/ kupeştesi	1 ΚΟΥΠΑΣΤΗ
2 borda, regala	2 impavesata	2 borda falsa	2 parampet	2 ΥΠΕΡΥΨΩΜΑ ΓΑΣΤΡΑΣ ΠΑΝΩ ΑΠΟ ΚΑΤΑΣΤΡΩΜΑ
3 imbornal	3 ombrinale	3 embornais, portas de mar	3 frengi	3 ΜΠΟΥΝΙ
4 cintón	4 bottazzo	4 cinta, verdugo	4 yumra, borda yumrusu	4 ΠΛΑΙΝΟ ΜΡΟΣΤΑΤΕΥΤΙΚΟ
5 tablazón del casco	5 fasciame	5 tabuado	5 borda-karina kaplama tahtaları	5 ΠΕΤΣΩΜΑ ΜΕ ΣΑΝΙΔΕΣ
6 forro	6 rivestimento	6 querena	6 kaplama/borda ağacı	6 ΠΕΤΣΩΜΑ ΜΕ ΠΟΛΥΕΣΤΕΡΑ
7 aparadura	7 torello	7 tábua de resbôrdo	7 burma tahtası	7 ΔΙΑΚΟΣΜΗΤΙΚΗ ΓΡΑΜΜΗ
8 tabla de crujla	8 tavolato di coperta	8 tábua da mediania	8 güverte kaplaması	8 ΚΕΝΤΡΙΚΟ ΜΑΔΕΡΙ ΚΑΤΑΣΤΡΩΜΑΤΟΣ

217

ENGLISH

Longitudinal section

1 stem
2 breasthook
3 apron
4 wood keel
5 keelson
6 ballast keel
7 keel bolts
8 sternpost
9 horn timber
10 stern knee
11 deadwood
12 rudder trunk
13 rudder
14 tiller
15 deck
16 beam
17 shelf
18 rib
19 bilge stringer
20 length overall LOA
21 load waterline LWL

See pages 214–16

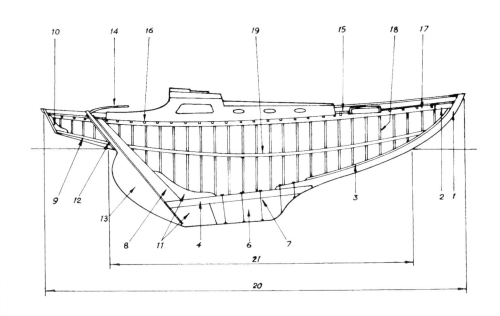

ENGLISH

Lateral section

1 rail
2 bulwark
3 scupper
4 rubbing strake
5 planking
6 skin
7 garboard strake
8 king plank
9 covering board
10 carline
11 beam
12 tie-rod
13 knee
14 timber frame
15 floor
16 cabin sole
17 limber holes
18 coaming
19 coachroof
20 depth
21 headroom
22 draught
23 waterline

See pages 216–17, 220–1

ENGLISH

9 bowsprit
10 dolphin striker
11 bobstay
12 cranze iron
13 gammon iron
14 traveller

See pages 228–9

ENGLISH	FRANÇAIS	DEUTSCH	NEDERLANDS	DANSK
14 CLASSIC BOATS	**14 BATEAUX CLASSIQUES**	**14 KLASSISCHE YACHTEN**	**14 KLASSIEKE SCHEPEN**	**14 VETERANBÅDE**
Construction	**Construction**	**Bauweise**	**Constructie**	**Konstruktion**
Lateral section	*Section latérale*	*Generalplan*	*Dwarsdoorsnede*	*Halve sektioner*
9 covering board	9 plat-bord	9 Schandeck	9 lijfhout, potdeksel	9 skandæk
10 carline	10 élongis	10 Schlinge	10 langsligger	10 kraveller
11 beam	11 barrot	11 Decksbalken	11 dekbalk	11 bjælke
12 tie-rod	12 tirant	12 Stehbolzen	12 trekstang	12 spændebånd
13 knee	13 courbe	13 Knie	13 knie	13 knæ
14 timber, frame	14 membrure	14 Spant	14 spant	14 svøb, fast spant
15 floor	15 varangue	15 Bodenwrange	15 wrang	15 bundstokke
16 cabin sole	16 plancher	16 Bodenbrett	16 vloer	16 dørk
17 limber holes	17 anguillers	17 Wasserlauflöcher	17 waterloopgaten	17 sandspor
18 coaming	18 hiloire	18 Süll	18 opstaande rand	18 lugekarm
19 coachroof	19 rouf	19 Kajütsdach	19 kajuitdek, opbouw	19 ruftag
20 depth	20 creux	20 Raumtiefe	20 holte	20 dybde indvendig
21 headroom	21 hauteur sous barrots	21 Stehhöhe	21 stahoogte	21 højde i kahytten
22 draught	22 tirant d'eau	22 Tiefgang	22 diepgang	22 dybgående
23 waterline	23 ligne de flottaison	23 Wasserlinie	23 waterlijn	23 vandlinie
Joints & fastenings	*Joints et fixations*	*Verbindungselemente*	*Verbindingen en bevestigingen*	*Samlinger og befæstigelser*
1 scarf	1 écart	1 Laschung	1 las	1 lask
2 rabbet	2 râblure	2 Sponung	2 sponning	2 spunding
3 mortise and tenon	3 mortaise et tenon	3 Nut und Zapfen	3 pen en gat	3 notgang & tap af træ, taphul & sportap
4 butted	4 bout à bout	4 Stoß	4 gestuikt	4 stød-plankeender
5 dovetail	5 en queue d'aronde	5 verzahnen, Schwalbenschwanz	5 zwaluwstaart	5 sammensænkning

ESPAÑOL	ITALIANO	PORTUGUÊS	TÜRKÇE	ΕΛΛΗΝΙΚΑ
14 BARCOS CLÁSICOS	**14 BATTELI CLASSICI**	**14 BARCOS CLÁSSICOS**	**14 KLASIK YATLAR**	**14 ΚΛΑΣΣΙΚΑ ΙΣΤΙΟΦΟΡΑ**
Construcción	**Costruzione**	**Construção**	**İnşaat**	**ΚΑΤΑΣΚΕΥΗ**
Sección lateral	*Sezione laterale*	*Secção lateral*	*Enine (arzani) kesit*	*ΚΑΘΕΤΟΣ ΤΟΜΗ*
9 trancanil	9 trincarino	9 tabica	9 küpeşte, anbar iç kapama tahtası	9 ΞΥΛΙΝΗ ΕΠΙΚΑΛΥΨΗ ΤΩΝ ΝΟΜΕΩΝ
10 gualdera	10 anguilla	10 longarina da cabine	10 kamara kovuşu	10 ΔΙΑΖΥΓΟ-ΜΠΙΜΠΕΚΙΑ
11 bao	11 baglio	11 vau	11 kemere	11 ΠΛΑΤΟΣ
12 tiranta	12 mezzobaglio	12 tirante de ligação	12 öksüz kemere takviye civatası	12 ΞΥΛΑ ΠΟΥ ΕΝΩΝΟΥΝ ΤΟ ΚΟΚΠΙΤ ΜΕ ΤΗΝ ΚΟΥΠΑΣΤΗ
13 curva, curvatón	13 bracciolo	13 curva de reforço	13 praçolu	13 ΓΟΝΑΤΟ
14 madero, pieza	14 ossatura, scheletro	14 caverna	14 triz	14 ΣΤΡΑΒΟ
15 varenga	15 madiere	15 reforços do pé caverna	15 yığma, praçol	15 ΠΑΤΩΜΑ
16 plan de la cámara	16 piano di calpestio	16 paneiros	16 kamara farşları	16 ΠΑΝΙΟΛΟ
17 imbornales de la varenga	17 ombrinali	17 boeiras	17 yığma frengi delikleri	17 ΔΙΑΚΕΝΑ ΣΤΗΝ ΚΟΥΠΑΣΤΗ ΓΙΑ ΝΑ ΦΕΥΓΟΥΝ ΤΑ ΝΕΡΑ
18 brazola	18 battente (di boccaporto)	18 braçola	18 kasara	18 ΚΑΣΑ ΚΟΥΒΟΥΣΙΟΥ - ΕΙΣΟΔΟΣ
19 tambucho	19 tetto della tuga	19 teto da cabine	19 kasara tavanı, kamara üstü	19 ΠΕΤΣΩΜΑ ΚΑΜΠΙΝΑΣ
20 puntal	20 altezza, puntale	20 pontal	20 iç derinlik (omurga üstü-kemere üstü derinliği)	20 ΒΑΘΟΣ
21 altura de techo	21 altezza in cabina	21 pé direito	21 baş yüksekliği (kamarada farş üstü-kemere altı yüksekliği)	21 ΕΣΩΤΕΡΙΚΟ ΥΨΟΣ
22 calado	22 pescaggio	22 calado	22 çektiği su	22 ΒΥΘΙΣΜΑ
23 linea de flotación	23 linea di galleggiamento	23 linha de água	23 su hattı	23 ΙΣΑΛΟΣ
Juntas y ensamblajes	*Giunti*	*Juntas e ferragem*	*Ekler ve bağlantılar*	*ΕΝΩΣΕΙΣ ΚΑΙ ΔΕΣΙΜΑΤΑ*
1 empalme	1 ammorsatura	1 escarva	1 geçme	1 ΜΑΤΙΣΜΑ (ΞΥΛΟ-ΞΥΛΟ)
2 rebajo	2 scanalatura	2 rebaixo	2 bindirme	2 ΓΚΙΝΙΣΙΑ
3 encaje y mecha	3 mortasa e tenone	3 fêmea e espiga	3 lamba ve zıvana	3 ΣΚΑΤΣΑ ΚΑΙ ΔΟΝΤΙ (ΤΟΡΜΟΣ)
4 unido a tope	4 di testa	4 topado	4 uç uca ekleme	4 ΤΕΤΡΑΓΩΝΙΣΜΕΝΟ
5 cola de milano	5 coda di rondine	5 emalhetado	5 güvercin kuyruğu geçmeli	5 ΧΕΛΙΔΟΝΙ - ΨΑΛΙΔΩΤΟΣ ΑΡΜΟΣ

221

ENGLISH	FRANÇAIS	DEUTSCH	NEDERLANDS	DANSK
14 CLASSIC BOATS	**14 BATEAUX CLASSIQUES**	**14 KLASSISCHE YACHTEN**	**14 KLASSIEKE SCHEPEN**	**14 VETERANBÅDE**
Construction	**Construction**	**Bauweise**	**Constructie**	**Konstruktion**
Joints & fastenings	*Joints et fixations*	*Verbindungselemente*	*Verbindingen en bevestigingen*	*Samlinger og befæstigelser*
6 faired	6 caréné, poncé	6 geglättet	6 gestroomlijnd	6 slette efter med skarøkse
7 wooden dowel	7 cheville	7 Holzdübel, Holzpropfen	7 houten plug	7 trædyvel
Rigging & sails	**Gréement et voiles**	**Rigg und Segel**	**Tuigage en zeilen**	**Rigning og sejl**
Yachts & rigs (see p 224–5)	*Yachts et leur gréement*	*Yachten und Takelagen*	*Jachten en tuigage*	*Fartøjer og rigning*
1 masthead cutter (*A*)	1 cotre en tête de mât	1 Kutter mit Hochtakelung	1 kotter, masttoptuig	1 mastetop-rig
2 bermudan sloop (*B*)	2 sloop bermudien	2 Slup	2 sloep, torentuig	2 bermudarig
3 gaff cutter (*C*)	3 cotre franc, aurique	3 Gaffelkutter	3 kotter, gaffeltuig	3 gaffelrigget kutter
4 bermudan yawl (*D*)	4 yawl bermudien	4 Yawl	4 yawl, torentuig	4 bermudarigget yawl
5 bermudan ketch (*E*)	5 ketch bermudien	5 Ketsch	5 kits, torentuig	5 bermuda-ketch
6 staysail schooner (*F*)	6 goélette à voile d'étai	6 Stagsegelschoner	6 stagzeilschoener	6 stagsejls skonnert
7 brig (*G*)	7 brick	7 Brigg	7 brik	7 brig
8 barque (*H*)	8 barque	8 Bark	8 bark	8 bark
Sails	*Voiles*	*Segel*	*Zeilen*	*Sejl*
1 mainsail	1 grand-voile	1 Großsegel	1 grootzeil	1 storsejl
2 topsail	2 flèche	2 Toppsegel	2 topzeil	2 topsejl
3 mizzen	3 artimon, tape-cul	3 Besan, Treiber	3 bezaan, druil	3 mesan
4 main staysail	4 grand-voile d'étai	4 Großstagsegel	4 schoenerzeil	4 store mellem stagsejl
5 fisherman staysail	5 voile d'étai de flèche	5 Fischermann-Stagsegel	5 grootstengestagzeil	5 top mellem stagsejl
6 mizzen staysail	6 foc ou voile d'étai d'artimon	6 Besanstagsegel	6 bezaansstagzeil, aap	6 mesan stagsejl
7 jib	7 foc	7 Fock	7 fok	7 fok
8 genoa	8 génois	8 Genua, Kreuzballon	8 genua	8 genua

ESPAÑOL	ITALIANO	PORTUGUÊS	TÜRKÇE	ΕΛΛΗΝΙΚΑ
14 BARCOS CLÁSICOS	**14 BATTELI CLASSICI**	**14 BARCOS CLÁSSICOS**	**14 KLASIK YATLAR**	**14 ΚΛΑΣΣΙΚΑ ΙΣΤΙΟΦΟΡΑ**
Construcción	**Costruzione**	**Construção**	**İnşaat**	**ΚΑΤΑΣΚΕΥΗ**
Juntas y ensamblajes	*Giunti*	*Juntas e ferragem*	*Ekler ve bağlantılar*	*ΕΝΩΣΕΙΣ ΚΑΙ ΔΕΣΙΜΑΤΑ*
6 encajar	6 carenato	6 desempolado	6 zımparalanmış	6 ΣΤΡΟΓΓΥΛΕΜΕΝΟ
7 espiga de madera	7 spina di legno, tassello	7 rôlha	7 ağaç düvel, ağaç takoz	7 ΞΥΛΙΝΗ ΣΦΗΝΑ
Jarcias y velas	**Attrezzatura e vele**	**Massame e velas**	**Arma ve yelkenler**	**ΑΡΜΑΤΩΣΙΑ & ΠΑΝΙΑ**
Yates y aparejos	*Yachts e attrezzature*	*Iates e armação*	*Yatlar ve armalar*	*ΤΥΠΟΙ ΙΣΤΙΟΦΟΡΩΝ*
1 balandra de mas-telero	1 cutter con fiocco in testa d'albero	1 cuter	1 markoni cutter, kotra	1 ΚΟΤΤΕΡΟ (ΔΥΟ ΠΡΟΤΟΝΟΙ)
2 balandro de Bermudas	2 sloop (Marconi)	2 sloop	2 markoni sloop	2 ΜΟΝΟΚΑΤΑΡΤΟ
3 cachemarin	3 cutter a vele auriche	3 cuter de Carangueja	3 randa armalı cutter, randa armalı kotra	3 ΚΟΤΤΕΡΟ ΜΕ ΠΙΚΙ
4 balandro de baticulo	4 yawl o iolla (Marconi)	4 yawl Marconi	4 markoni yawl	4 ΓΙΟΛΑ
5 queche bermudo	5 ketch (Marconi)	5 ketch Marconi	5 markoni ketch	5 ΚΕΤΣ
6 goleta a la americana	6 goletta a vele di taglio	6 palhabote	6 velena yelkenli uskuna	6 ΣΚΟΥΝΑ ΜΕ ΔΥΟ ΦΛΟΚΟΥΣ
7 bergantin	7 brigantino	7 brigue	7 brik	7 ΜΠΡΙΚΙ
8 barca	8 brigantino a palo	8 barca	8 barka	8 ΜΠΑΡΚΟ
Velas	*Vele*	*Velas*	*Yelkenler*	*ΠΑΝΙΑ*
1 vela mayor	1 randa	1 vela grande	1 anayelken	1 ΜΕΓΙΣΤΗ
2 escandalosa	2 freccia, controranda	2 gaff-tope	2 kontra randa	2 ΦΛΙΤΣΙ
3 mesana	3 mezzana	3 mezena	3 mizana yelkeni	3 ΜΕΤΖΑΝΑ
4 vela de estay mayor	4 fiocco	4 traquete	4 istralya anayelkeni, velenası	4 ΤΖΕΝΟΑ
5 vela alta de estay	5 fisherman	5 extênsola	5 balıkçı yelkeni	5 ΑΡΑΠΗΣ
6 entrepalos	6 carbonera	6 estai entre mastros	6 mizana velenası	6 ΣΤΡΑΛΙΕΡΑ
7 foque	7 fiocco	7 bujarrona	7 flok	7 ΦΛΟΚΟΣ
8 génova	8 genoa	8 genoa	8 genoa	8 ΤΖΕΝΟΑ

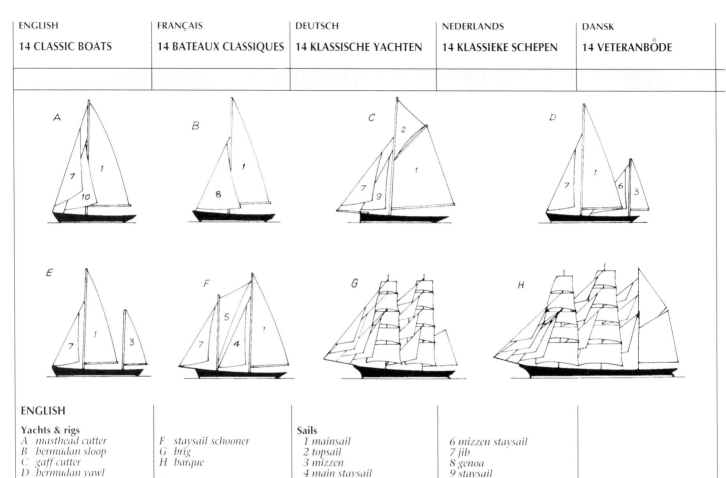

ENGLISH

Yachts & rigs
A   masthead cutter
B   bermudan sloop
C   gaff cutter
D   bermudan yawl
E   bermudan ketch

F   staysail schooner
G   brig
H   barque

See pages 222–3

Sails
1 mainsail
2 topsail
3 mizzen
4 main staysail
5 fisherman staysail

6 mizzen staysail
7 jib
8 genoa
9 staysail
10 genoa staysail

See pages 222–3, 226–7

11 yankee
12 trysail
13 spritsail
14 lugsail
15 gunter
16 square sail

See pages 226–7

ENGLISH	FRANÇAIS	DEUTSCH	NEDERLANDS	DANSK
14 CLASSIC BOATS	**14 BATEAUX CLASSIQUES**	**14 KLASSISCHE YACHTEN**	**14 KLASSIEKE SCHEPEN**	**14 VETERANBÅDE**
Rigging & sails	**Gréement et voiles**	**Rigg und Segel**	**Tuigage en zeilen**	**Rigning og sejl**
Sails	*Voiles*	*Segel*	*Zeilen*	*Sejl*
9 staysail	9 trinquette	9 Stagsegel	9 stagzeil	9 stagsejl
10 genoa staysail	10 foc ballon	10 Raumballon	10 botterfok	10 genuafok
11 yankee	11 yankee	11 grosser Klüver	11 grote kluiver	11 yankee
12 trysail	12 voile de cape	12 Trysegel	12 stormzeil, grootzeil	12 stormsejl
13 spritsail	13 livarde	13 Sprietsegel	13 sprietzeil	13 sprydsejl
14 lugsail	14 voile à bourcet, au tiers	14 Luggersegel	14 loggerzeil, emmerzeil	14 luggersejl
15 gunter	15 houari	15 Huari-, Steilgaffeltakelung	15 houari	15 gunterrig
16 square sail	16 voile carrée	16 Rahsegel	16 razeil	16 råsejl
17 peak	17 pic, empointure	17 Piek	17 piek	17 pikken (gaffelrig)
18 throat	18 gorge	18 Klau	18 klauw	18 kværken
19 mast hoop	19 cercle de mât	19 Mastring, Legel	19 hoepel	19 mastering
20 horse	20 barre d'écoute	20 Leitwagen	20 overloop	20 løjbom
21 weight of canvas	21 poids de la toile	21 Tuchstärke	21 gewicht van het doek	21 dugvægt
22 baggywrinkle	22 fourrage, gaine de hauban	22 Tausendfuß	22 lus-platting	22 skamfilings-gods
23 mildew	23 moisissure	23 Stockflecken	23 weer in het zeil	23 jordslået
Mast & boom	*Mât et bôme*	*Mast und Baum*	*Mast en giek*	*Mast og bom*
1 pinrail	1 râtelier	1 Nagelbank	1 nagelbank	1 naglebænk
2 crutch, gallows	2 support de bôme, portique	2 Baumbock, Baumstütze	2 schaar, vang	2 bomstol
3 boom claw	3 croissant	3 Baumklaue	3 schootring	3 bomklo, lyre
4 keel-stepped	4 mât posé sur la quille	4 durchgehender Mast	4 op de kiel staand (van mast)	4 står på kølen
5 mast gaiter	5 jupe de mât	5 Mastkragen	5 manchet	5 gamache

ESPAÑOL	ITALIANO	PORTUGUÊS	TÜRKÇE	ΕΛΛΗΝΙΚΑ
14 BARCOS CLÁSICOS	**14 BATTELI CLASSICI**	**14 BARCOS CLÁSSICOS**	**14 KLASIK YATLAR**	***14 ΚΛΑΣΣΙΚΑ ΙΣΤΙΟΦΟΡΑ***
Jarcias y velas	**Attrezzatura e vele**	**Massame e velas**	**Arma ve yelkenler**	**ΑΡΜΑΤΩΣΙΑ & ΠΑΝΙΑ**
Velas	*Vele*	*Velas*	*Yelkenler*	*ΠΑΝΙΑ*
9 vela de estay	9 trinchettina	9 estai	9 trinket	9 ΠΑΝΙ ΣΕ ΠΡΟΤΟΝΟ (ΑΡΑΠΗΣ)
10 foque balón	10 trinchettina genoa	10 estai de genoa	10 balon flok	10 ΣΤΕΙΣΕΙΑ - ΔΕΥΤΕΡΟΣ ΦΛΟΚΟΣ
11 trinquetilla	11 yankee	11 giba	11 yankee yelkeni	11 ΕΣΩ ΦΛΟΚΟΣ - ΓΙΑΝΚΗ
12 vela de capa	12 vela di cappa	12 cachapana	12 fırtına şeytan yelkeni	12 ΜΑΙΣΤΡΑ ΘΥΕΛΛΗΣ
13 vela tarquina, abanico	13 vela a tarchia	13 vela de espicha	13 açevela gönderli yelken	13 ΦΛΟΚΟΣ ΤΣΙΜΠΟΥΚΙΟΥ
14 vela cangreja, al tercio	14 vela al terzo	14 vela de pendão	14 çeyrek yelken	14 ΤΕΤΡΑΓΩΝΟ ΠΑΝΙ ΧΩΡΙΣ ΜΑΤΣΑ
15 vela de cortina, guaira	15 alla portoghese	15 vela de baioneta	15 sürmeli randa arma	15 ΨΗΛΟ ΠΙΚΙ
16 vela cuadra, redonda	16 vela quadra	16 pano redondo	16 kare yelken, kabasorta, arma yelkeni	16 ΤΕΤΡΑΓΩΝΟ ΠΑΝΙ
17 pico	17 angolo di penna	17 pique	17 randa yelken giz köşesi	17 ΚΟΡΥΦΗ
18 puño de driza	18 gola	18 bôca	18 randa yelken karula köşesi	18 ΛΑΙΜΟΣ
19 zuncho	19 canestrello	19 aro	19 randa yelken direk halkası	19 ΚΟΛΛΙΕΣ
20 pie de gallo	20 trasto, barra di scotta	20 varão de escota	20 anayelken ıskotası güverte rayı	20 ΜΠΟΜΠΡΕΣΟ - ΜΠΑΛΚΟΝΙ
21 peso de la lona	21 peso della tela	21 espessura da lona	21 bez ağırlığı	21 ΒΑΡΟΣ ΤΟΥ ΠΑΝΙΟΥ
22 pallete	22 filacci	22 coxim de enxárcia	22 kedi ayağı, kedí bıyığı	22 ΖΑΡΩΜΕΝΟ - ΞΕΧΥΛΩΜΕΝΟ
23 moho	23 muffa	23 garruncho	23 küf	23 ΜΟΥΦΛΑ
Palo y botavara	*Albero e boma*	*Mastro e retranca*	*Direk ve bumba*	*ΚΑΤΑΡΤΙ & ΜΑΤΣΑ*
1 cabillero	1 cavigliera	1 mesa das malagetas	1 armadora	1 ΡΑΓΑ ΤΟΥ ΤΡΑΚ
2 posa botavara	2 forchetta, capra	2 descanço da retranca	2 Bumba çatalı, çatal yastik	2 ΣΤΗΡΙΓΜΑ ΜΑΤΣΑΣ
3 media-luna	3 trozza	3 colar de fixação da escota á retranca	3 bumba boğazı	3 ΔΑΓΚΑΝΑ ΜΑΤΣΑΣ
4 mastil en quilla	4 posato in chiglia	4 mastro apoiado na quilha	4 omurgaya oturan	4 ΚΑΤΑΡΤΙ ΜΕ ΒΑΣΗ ΣΤΗΝ ΚΑΡΙΝΑ
5 funda de fogonadura	5 ghetta dell'albero	5 manga de protecção do mastro	5 direk fistanı	5 ΠΡΟΣΤΑΤΕΥΤΙΚΟ ΑΔΙΑΒΡΟΧΟ ΣΤΗ ΒΑΣΗ

14 CLASSIC BOATS / 14 BATEAUX CLASSIQUES / 14 KLASSISCHE YACHTEN / 14 KLASSIEKE SCHEPEN / 14 VETERANBÔDE

ENGLISH	FRANÇAIS	DEUTSCH	NEDERLANDS	DANSK
Rigging & sails	**Gréement et voiles**	**Rigg und Segel**	**Tuigage en zeilen**	**Rigning og sejl**
Mast & boom	*Mât et bôme*	*Mast und Baum*	*Mast en giek*	*Mast og bom*
6 ratchet and pawl	6 rochet à linguet	6 Pallkranz und Pall	6 palrad en pal	6 rebeapparat med skralle
7 worm gear	7 vis sans fin	7 Schneckenreff	7 worm en wormwiel	7 rebeapparat med snekke
Spars & bowsprit	*Espars et beaupré*	*Spieren und Bugspriet*	*Rondhouten en boegspriet*	*Rundholter og bovspryd*
1 solid	1 massif, plein	1 voll	1 massief	1 massiv
2 hollow	2 creux	2 hohl	2 hol	2 hul
3 bumpkin	3 queue-de-mallet	3 Heckausleger	3 papegaaiestok	3 buttelur, udligger
4 jib boom	4 bôme de foc ou de trinquette	4 Fock-, Klüverbaum	4 kluiverboom	4 klyverbom
5 yard	5 vergue	5 Rah	5 ra	5 rå
6 gaff and jaws	6 corne et mâchoires	6 Gaffel und Gaffelklau	6 gaffel en klem	6 gaffel & klo
7 topmast	7 mât de flèche	7 Toppstenge	7 steng, topmast	7 topmast
8 boom roller	8 enrouleur de bôme	8 Baumrollreff	8 giekrolrif	8 rullebom
9 bowsprit	9 beaupré	9 Bugspriet	9 boegspriet	9 bovspryd
10 dolphin striker	10 martingale	10 Stampfstock	10 stampstok, spaanse ruiter	10 pyntenetstok
11 bobstay	11 sous-barbe	11 Wasserstag	11 waterstag	11 vaterstag
12 cranze iron	12 collier à pitons	12 Bugsprietnockband	12 boegspriet nokring	12 sprydring med øjer
13 gammon iron	13 liure	13 Bugsprietzurring	13 boegspriet stevenring	13 sprydring
14 traveller	14 rocambeau	14 Bugsprietausholring	14 traveller	14 udhalering
Standing rigging	*Gréement dormant*	*Stehendes Gut*	*Staand want*	*Stående rig*
1 topmast, stay	1 grand étai, étai de flèche	1 Toppstag	1 topstag	1 topstag
2 preventer backstay	2 pataras, étai arrière	2 Achterstag	2 achterstag	2 fast bagstag
3 runner and lever	3 bastaque et levier	3 Backstag und Strecker	3 bakstag en hefboom	3 løst bagstag
4 jumper stay	4 étai de guignol	4 Jumpstag	4 knikstag	4 violinstag
5 ratlines	5 enflèchures	5 Webelein	5 weeflijnen	5 vævlinger

228

ESPAÑOL	ITALIANO	PORTUGUÊS	TÜRKÇE	ΕΛΛΗΝΙΚΑ
14 BARCOS CLÁSICOS	**14 BATTELI CLASSICI**	**14 BARCOS CLÁSSICOS**	**14 KLASIK YATLAR**	**14 ΚΛΑΣΣΙΚΑ ΙΣΤΙΟΦΟΡΑ**
Jarcias y velas	**Attrezzatura e vele**	**Massame e velas**	**Arma ve yelkenler**	**ΑΡΜΑΤΩΣΙΑ & ΠΑΝΙΑ**
Palo y botavara	*Albero e boma*	*Mastro e retranca*	*Direk ve bumba*	*ΚΑΤΑΡΤΙ & ΜΑΤΣΑ*
6 catalina y pal	6 cricco e nottolino	6 roquete	6 dişli ve tırnak	6 ΚΑΣΤΑΝΙΑ
7 husillo	7 ingranaggio a vite senza fine	7 sem-fim	7 sonsuz dişli	7 ΚΟΧΛΙΩΤΟ ΓΡΑΝΑΖΙ
Arboladura y botalón	*Antenne e bompresso*	*Mastreação e pau da bujarrona*	*Ahşap direkler, bumbalar ve gurcatalar & civadra*	*ΚΑΤΑΡΤΙΑ - ΜΑΤΣΑ - ΜΠΑΣΤΟΥΝΙ*
1 macizo	1 piene	1 maciço	1 içi dolu, solid	1 ΠΛΗΡΕΣ - ΜΑΣΙΦ
2 hueco	2 cave	2 ôco	2 içiboş	2 ΚΕΝΟ - ΚΟΥΦΙΟ
3 arbotante	3 buttafuori	3 pau da pôpa	3 kiç bastonu	3 ΜΟΥΡΑ ΤΟΥ ΤΡΙΓΚΟΥ
4 tangoncillo de foque	4 tangone del fiocco	4 retranca do estai	4 flok bumbası trinket bumbası	4 ΜΑΤΣΑ ΦΛΟΚΟΥ
5 verga	5 pennone	5 verga	5 çubuk	5 ΑΝΤΕΝΝΑ
6 pico y boca de cangrejo	6 picco e gola	6 carangueja e bôca	6 randa yelken piki, boğazı ve çatalı	6 ΠΙΚΙ ΚΑΙ ΔΑΓΚΑΝΑ
7 mastelero	7 alberetto	7 mastaréu	7 direk çubuğu	7 ΑΝΩ ΜΕΡΟΣ ΑΛΜΠΟΥΡΟΥ
8 enrollador de botavara	8 boma a rullino	8 enrolador na retranca	8 bumba sarma düzeneği	8 ΠΕΡΙΣΤΡΕΦΟΜΕΝΗ ΜΑΤΣΑ
9 botalón	9 bompresso	9 pau da bujarrona	9 civadra	9 ΜΠΑΣΤΟΥΝΙ
10 moco	10 pennaccino	10 pau de pica peixe	10 civadra bıyığı	10 ΔΕΛΦΙΝΙΕΡΑ
11 barbiquejo	11 briglia	11 cabresto	11 civadra kösteği	11 ΜΟΥΣΤΑΚΙ
12 raca	12 collare	12 braçadeira do pau	12 civadra cunda bileziği	12 ΣΤΕΦΑΝΙ ΣΤΕΡΕΩΣΗΣ ΜΟΥΣΤΑΚΙΟΥ
13 zuncho de botalón	13 trinca	13 braçadeira da prôa	13 civadra güverte bileziği	13 ΒΑΣΗ ΣΤΕΡΕΩΣΗΣ ΜΠΑΛΚΟΝΙΟΥ
14 racamento	14 cerchio (di mura del fiocco)	14 urraca	14 hareketli ve ayarlanabilen civadra bileziği	14 ΒΑΓΟΝΑΚΙ - ΔΙΑΔΡΟΜΕΑΣ
Maniobra	*Manovre fisse (o dormienti)*	*Aparelho fixo*	*Sabit donanım*	*ΣΤΑΘΕΡΗ ΑΡΜΑΤΩΣΙΑ*
1 estay de tope, estay de galope	1 strallo d'alberetto	1 estai do galope	1 ana ıstralya, direkbaşı ıstralyası	1 ΠΑΤΑΡΑΤΣΟ
2 poparrás	2 paterazzo	2 brandal fixo da pôpa	2 pupa ıstralyası, kıç ıstralya	2 ΕΠΙΤΟΝΟΣ - ΒΑΡΔΡΙΑ
3 burdavolante y palanca	3 sartia volante	3 brandal volante e alavanca	3 pupa çarmıhı ve levyesi	3 ΕΠΑΡΤΗΣ ΜΑΤΣΟΠΟΔΑΡΟ
4 estay de boza	4 controstrallo	4 estai de diamante	4 şeytan çarmıhı	4 ΒΟΗΘΗΤΙΚΟΣ ΠΡΟΤΟΝΟΣ - ΣΤΑΝΤΖΟΣ
5 flechadura, flechates	5 griselle	5 enfrechates	5 iskalarya	5 ΑΝΕΜΟΣΚΑΛΕΣ

ENGLISH	FRANÇAIS	DEUTSCH	NEDERLANDS	DANSK
15 GENERAL REFERENCE	**15 GENERALITES**	**15 ALLGEMEINE HINWEISE**	**15 ALGEMENE VERWIJZING**	**15 DIVERSE**
Numbers	**Nombres**	**Nummern**	**Nummers**	**Tal**
0 zero	0 zéro	0 null	0 nul	0 nul
1 one	1 un	1 eins	1 een	1 en
2 two	2 deux	2 zwei	2 twee	2 to
3 three	3 trois	3 drei	3 drie	3 tre
4 four	4 quatre	4 vier	4 vier	4 fire
5 five	5 cinq	5 fünf	5 vijf	5 fem
6 six	6 six	6 sechs	6 zes	6 seks
7 seven	7 sept	7 sieben	7 zeven	7 syv
8 eight	8 huit	8 acht	8 acht	8 otte
9 nine	9 neuf	9 neun	9 negen	9 ni
10 ten	10 dix	10 zehn	10 tien	10 ti
11 eleven	11 onze	11 elf	11 elf	11 elleve
12 twelve	12 douze	12 zwölf	12 twaalf	12 tolv
13 thirteen	13 treize	13 dreizehn	13 dertien	13 tretten
14 fourteen	14 quatorze	14 vierzehn	14 veertien	14 fjorten
15 fifteen	15 quinze	15 fünfzehn	15 vijftien	15 femten
16 sixteen	16 seize	16 sechzehn	16 zestien	16 seksten
17 seventeen	17 dix-sept	17 siebzehn	17 zeventien	17 sytten
18 eighteen	18 dix-huit	18 achtzehn	18 achttien	18 atten
19 nineteen	19 dix-neuf	19 neunzehn	19 negentien	19 nitten
20 twenty	20 vingt	20 zwanzig	20 twintig	20 tyve
30 thirty	30 trente	30 dreißig	30 dertig	30 tredive
40 forty	40 quarante	40 vierzig	40 veertig	40 fyrre
50 fifty	50 cinquante	50 fünfzig	50 vijftig	50 halvtres
60 sixty	60 soixante	60 sechzig	60 zestig	60 tres
70 seventy	70 soixante-dix	70 siebzig	70 zeventig	70 halvfjers
80 eighty	80 quatre-vingt	80 achtzig	80 tachtig	80 firs
90 ninety	90 quatre-vingt-dix	90 neunzig	90 negentig	90 halvfems
100 hundred	100 cent	100 hundert	100 honderd	100 hundrede
1000 thousand	1000 mille	1000 tausend	1000 duizend	1000 tusind
1m million	1m million	1m million	1m miljoen	1m million

ESPAÑOL	ITALIANO	PORTUGUÊS	TÜRKÇE	ΕΛΛΗΝΙΚΑ
15 REFERENCIAS GENERALES	**15 ESPRESSIONI GENERALI**	**15 REFÊRENCIAS GERAIS**	**15 GENEL REFERANS**	**15 ΓΕΝΙΚΕΣ ΑΝΑΦΟΡΕΣ**
Numeros	**Numeri**	**Números**	**Sayılar**	**ΑΡΙΘΜΟΙ**
0 cero	0 zero	0 zéro	0 sıfır	0 ΜΗΔΕΝ
1 uno	1 uno	1 um	1 bir	1 ΕΝΑ
2 dos	2 due	2 dois	2 iki	2 ΔΥΟ
3 tres	3 tre	3 três	3 üç	3 ΤΡΙΑ
4 cuatro	4 quattro	4 quatro	4 dört	4 ΤΕΣΣΕΡΑ
5 cinco	5 cinque	5 cinco	5 beş	5 ΠΕΝΤΕ
6 seis	6 sei	6 seis	6 altı	6 ΕΞΗ
7 siete	7 sette	7 sete	7 yedi	7 ΕΠΤΑ
8 ocho	8 otto	8 oito	8 sekiz	8 ΟΚΤΩ
9 nueve	9 nove	9 nove	9 dokuz	9 ΕΝΝΕΑ
10 diez	10 dieci	10 dez	10 on	10 ΔΕΚΑ
11 once	11 undici	11 onze	11 on bir	11 ΕΝΔΕΚΑ
12 doce	12 dodici	12 doze	12 on iki	12 ΔΩΔΕΚΑ
13 trece	13 tredici	13 treze	13 on üç	13 ΔΕΚΑΤΡΙΑ
14 catorce	14 quattordici	14 catorze	14 on dört	14 ΔΕΚΑΤΕΣΣΕΡΑ
15 quince	15 quindici	15 quinze	15 on beş	15 ΔΕΚΑΠΕΝΤΕ
16 dieciséis	16 sedici	16 dezaseis	16 on altı	16 ΔΕΚΑΕΞΗ
17 diecisiete	17 diciassette	17 dezasete	17 on yedi	17 ΔΕΚΑΕΠΤΑ
18 dieciocho	18 diciotto	18 dezoito	18 on sekiz	18 ΔΕΚΑΟΚΤΩ
19 diecinueve	19 diciannove	19 dezanove	19 on dokuz	19 ΔΕΚΑ ΕΝΝΕΑ
20 veinte	20 venti	20 vinte	20 yirmi	20 ΕΙΚΟΣΙ
30 treinta	30 trenta	30 trinta	30 otuz	30 ΤΡΙΑΝΤΑ
40 cuaranta	40 quaranta	40 quarenta	40 kırk	40 ΣΑΡΑΝΤΑ
50 cincuenta	50 cinquanta	50 cinquenta	50 elli	50 ΠΕΝΗΝΤΑ
60 sesenta	60 sessanta	60 sessenta	60 altmış	60 ΕΞΗΝΤΑ
70 setenta	70 settanta	70 setenta	70 yetmiş	70 ΕΒΔΟΜΗΝΤΑ
80 ochenta	80 ottanta	80 oitenta	80 seksen	80 ΟΓΔΟΝΤΑ
90 noventa	90 novanta	90 noventa	90 doksan	90 ΕΝΝΕΝΗΝΤΑ
100 ciento	100 cento	100 cem	100 yüz	100 ΕΚΑΤΟ
1000 mil	1000 mille	1000 mil	1000 bin	1000 ΧΙΛΙΑ
1m millón	1m milione	1m milhão	1m milyon	1M ΕΚΑΤΟΜΜΥΡΙΟ

ENGLISH	FRANÇAIS	DEUTSCH	NEDERLANDS	DANSK
15 GENERAL REFERENCE	**15 GENERALITES**	**15 ALLGEMEINE HINWEISE**	**15 ALGEMENE VERWIJZING**	**15 DIVERSE**

Clock times	**Heures**	**Uhrzeit**	**Kloktijden**	**Klokkeslæt**
1 o'clock, hours	1 heures	1 Uhr	1 uur	1 klokken
2 am	2 matin	2 vormittags	2 voormiddag	2 formiddag
3 pm	3 après-midi/soir	3 nachmittags	3 namiddag	3 eftermiddag
4 fifteen minutes past...	4 et quart	4 fünfzehn Minuten nach ...	4 kwart over ...	4 kvarter over
5 fifteen minutes to...	5 moins le quart	5 fünfzehn Minuten vor ...	5 kwart voor ...	5 kvarter i
6 half-past six	6 six heures et demie	6 halb sieben	6 half zeven	6 halv syv
7 noon	7 midi	7 Mittag	7 middag	7 middag
8 midnight	8 minuit	8 Mitternacht	8 middernacht	8 midnat
9 morning	9 matin	9 Morgen	9 morgen, ochtend	9 morgen
10 afternoon	10 après-midi	10 Nachmittag	10 namiddag	10 eftermiddag
11 evening	11 soirée	11 Abend	11 avond	11 aften
12 night	12 nuit	12 Nacht	12 nacht	12 nat

Colours	**Couleurs**	**Farben**	**Kleuren**	**Farver**
1 black	1 noir	1 schwarz	1 zwart	1 sort
2 red	2 rouge	2 rot	2 rood	2 rød
3 green	3 vert	3 grün	3 groen	3 grøn
4 yellow	4 jaune	4 gelb	4 geel	4 gul
5 white	5 blanc	5 weiß	5 wit	5 hvid
6 orange	6 orange	6 orange	6 oranje	6 orange
7 violet	7 violet	7 violett	7 violet	7 violet
8 brown	8 marron	8 braun	8 bruin	8 brun
9 blue	9 bleu	9 blau	9 blauw	9 blå
10 grey	10 gris	10 grau	10 grijs	10 grå

Countries	**Pays**	**Länder**	**Landen**	**Lande**
1 Britain	1 Grande-Bretagne	1 Britannien	1 Engeland	1 England
2 Denmark	2 Danemark	2 Dänemark	2 Denemarken	2 Danmark
3 France	3 France	3 Frankreich	3 Frankrijk	3 Frankrig
4 Germany	4 Allemagne	4 Deutschland	4 Duitsland	4 Tyskland
5 Greece	5 Grèce	5 Griechenland	5 Griekenland	5 Grækenland

ESPAÑOL	ITALIANO	PORTUGUÊS	TÜRKÇE	ΕΛΛΗΝΙΚΑ
15 REFERENCIAS GENERALES	**15 ESPRESSIONI GENERALI**	**15 REFERÊNCIAS GERAIS**	**15 GENEL REFERANS**	**15 ΓΕΝΙΚΕΣ ΑΝΑΦΟΡΕΣ**
La hora	**Ora**	**Horas**	**Saatler**	**ΩΡΕΣ**
1 en punto, horas	1 ore	1 horas	1 saat	1 ΩΡΑ
2 am	2 am	2 antes do meio dia	2 öğleden önce	2 Π M
3 pm	3 pm	3 depois do meio dia	3 öğleden sonra	3 M M
4 son las ... y cuarto	4 le ... e un quarto	4 quinze minutos depois	4 onbeş dakika geçe	4 ΕΝΑ ΤΕΤΑΡΤΟ ΜΕΤΑ ΑΠΟ...
5 son las ... menos cuarto	5 le ... meno un quarto	5 quinze minutos para	5 onbeş dakika kala	5 ΕΝΑ ΤΕΤΑΡΤΟ ΠΡΙΝ ΑΠΟ...
6 son las ... y media	6 le sei e mezza	6 seis e meia	6 altıbuçuk	6 ΕΞΙ ΚΑΙ ΜΙΣΗ
7 mediodía	7 mezzogiorno	7 meio dia	7 öğle vakti	7 ΜΕΣΗΜΕΡΙ
8 medianoche	8 mezzanotte	8 meia noite	8 gece yarısı	8 ΜΕΣΑΝΥΧΤΑ
9 mañana	9 mattino	9 de manhã	9 sabah	9 ΠΡΩΙ
10 tarde	10 pomeriggio	10 tarde	10 öğleden sonra	10 ΑΠΟΓΕΥΜΑ
11 tarde	11 sera	11 de tarde	11 akşam	11 ΒΡΑΔΥ
12 noche	12 notte	12 à noite	12 gece	12 ΝΥΧΤΑ
Colores	**Colori**	**Côres**	**Renkler**	**ΧΡΩΜΑΤΑ**
1 negro (n)	1 nero	1 preto	1 siyah, kara	1 ΜΑΥΡΟ
2 rojo (r)	2 rosso	2 encarnado	2 kırmızı	2 ΚΟΚΚΙΝΟ
3 verde (v)	3 verde	3 verde	3 yeşil	3 ΠΡΑΣΙΝΟ
4 amarillo (am)	4 giallo	4 amarelo	4 sarı	4 ΚΙΤΡΙΝΟ
5 blanco (b)	5 bianco	5 branco	5 beyaz	5 ΑΣΠΡΟ
6 naranja	6 arancione	6 laranja	6 turuncu	6 ΠΟΡΤΟΚΑΛΙ
7 violeta	7 violetto	7 violeta	7 mor	7 ΜΩΒ
8 marrón, pardo (p)	8 marrone	8 castanho	8 kahverengi	8 ΚΑΦΕ
9 azul (az)	9 blu, azzurro	9 azul	9 mavi	9 ΜΠΛΕ
10 gris	10 grigio	10 cinzento	10 gri	10 ΓΚΡΙΖΟ
Países	**Paesi**	**Países**	**Ülkeler**	**ΧΩΡΕΣ**
1 Gran Bretaña	1 Inghilterra	1 Inglaterra	1 Britanya	1 ΑΓΓΛΙΑ
2 Dinamarca	2 Danimarca	2 Dinamarca	2 Danimarka	2 ΔΑΝΙΑ
3 Francia	3 Francia	3 França	3 Fransa	3 ΓΑΛΛΙΑ
4 Alemania	4 Germania	4 Alemanha	4 Almanya	4 ΓΕΡΜΑΝΙΑ
5 Grecia	5 Grecia	5 Grécia	5 Yunanistan	5 ΕΛΛΑΔΑ

ENGLISH	FRANÇAIS	DEUTSCH	NEDERLANDS	DANSK
15 GENERAL REFERENCE	**15 GENERALITES**	**15 ALLGEMEINE HINWEISE**	**15 ALGEMENE VERWIJZING**	**15 DIVERSE**
Countries	**Pays**	**Länder**	**Landen**	**Lande**
6 Italy	6 Italie	6 Italien	6 Italië	6 Italien
7 Netherlands	7 Pays-Bas	7 Niederlande	7 Nederland	7 Holland
8 Portugal	8 Portugal	8 Portugal	8 Portugal	8 Portugal
9 Spain	9 Espagne	9 Spanien	9 Spanje	9 Spanien
10 Turkey	10 Turquie	10 Türkei	10 Turkije	10 Tyrkiet
Materials	**Matériaux**	**Materialien**	**Materialen**	**Materialer**
Metals	*Métaux*	*Metalle*	*Metaalsoorten*	*Metaller*
1 copper	1 cuivre	1 Kupfer	1 koper (rood)	1 kobber
2 brass	2 laiton	2 Messing	2 koper (geel)	2 messing
3 bronze	3 bronze	3 Bronze	3 brons	3 bronze
4 lead	4 plomb	4 Blei	4 lood	4 bly
5 tin	5 étain	5 Zinn	5 tin	5 tin
6 nickel	6 nickel	6 Nickel	6 nikkel	6 nikkel
7 iron	7 fer	7 Eisen	7 ijzer	7 jern
8 cast iron	8 fonte	8 Gußeisen	8 gietijzer	8 støbejern
9 mild steel	9 acier doux	9 Walzstahl	9 weekijzer	9 stål
10 stainless steel	10 acier inoxydable, inox	10 rostfreier Stahl	10 roestvrij staal	10 rustfrit stål
11 chromium	11 chrome	11 Chrom	11 chroom	11 krom
12 zinc	12 zinc	12 Zink	12 zink	12 zink
13 aluminium	13 aluminium	13 Aluminium	13 aluminium	13 aluminium
14 alloy	14 alliage	14 Legierung	14 legering	14 legering
15 gunmetal	15 bronze de canon	15 Geschützbronze	15 geschutsbrons	15 kanonmetal
16 silver	16 argent	16 Silber	16 zilver	16 sølv
17 gold	17 or	17 Gold	17 goud	17 guld
18 to galvanize	18 zinguer, chouper	18 galvanisieren, verzinken	18 galvaniseren	18 at galvanisere
19 corrosion	19 corrosion	19 Korrosion	19 corrosie, roest	19 ruste/tære
Timber	*Bois*	*Holz*	*Houtsoorten*	*Tømmer*
1 oak	1 chêne	1 Eiche	1 eikehout	1 eg
2 teak	2 teck	2 Teak	2 teakhout	2 teak
3 mahogany	3 acajou	3 Mahagoni	3 mahoniehout	3 mahogny

234

ESPAÑOL	ITALIANO	PORTUGUÊS	TÜRKÇE	ΕΛΛΗΝΙΚΑ
15 REFERENCIAS GENERALES	**15 ESPRESSIONI GENERALI**	**15 REFERÊNCIAS GERAIS**	**15 GENEL REFERANS**	**15 ΓΕΝΙΚΕΣ ΑΝΑΦΟΡΕΣ**
Países	**Paesi**	**Países**	**Ülkeler**	**ΧΩΡΕΣ**
6 Italia	6 Italia	6 Italia	6 İtalya	6 ΙΤΑΛΙΑ
7 Los Países Bajos	7 Olanda	7 Holanda	7 Hollanda	7 ΟΛΛΑΝΔΙΑ
8 Portugal	8 Portogallo	8 Portugal	8 Portekiz	8 ΠΟΡΤΟΓΑΛΙΑ
9 España	9 Spagna	9 Espanha	9 İspanya	9 ΙΣΠΑΝΙΑ
10 Turquia	10 Turchia	10 Turquia	10 Türkiye	10 ΤΟΥΡΚΙΑ
Materiales	**Materiali**	**Materiais**	**Malzemeler**	**ΥΛΙΚΑ**
Metales	*Metalli*	*Metáis*	*Metaller*	*ΜΕΤΑΛΛΑ*
1 cobre	1 rame	1 cobre	1 bakır	1 ΧΑΛΚΟΣ
2 latón	2 ottone	2 latão	2 pirinç	2 ΜΠΡΟΥΝΤΖΟΣ
3 bronce	3 bronzo	3 bronze	3 bronz	3 ΜΠΡΟΥΝΤΖΟΣ
4 plomo	4 piombo	4 chumbo	4 kurşun	4 ΜΟΛΥΒΙ
5 estaño	5 stagno	5 estanho	5 kalay	5 ΚΑΣΣΙΤΕΡΟΣ
6 níquel	6 nichel	6 níquel	6 nikel	6 ΝΙΚΕΛΙΟ
7 hierro	7 ferro	7 ferro	7 demir	7 ΣΙΔΗΡΟΣ
8 hierro calado	8 ghisa	8 ferro fundido	8 pik demir	8 ΧΥΤΟΣΙΔΗΡΟΣ
9 acero dulce	9 acciaio dolce	9 ferro temperado	9 yumuşak çelik	9 ΑΤΣΑΛΙ
10 acero inoxidable	10 acciaio inossidabile	10 aço inoxidável	10 paslanmaz çelik	10 ΑΝΟΞΕΙΔΩΤΟ ΑΤΣΑΛΙ
11 cromo	11 cromo	11 cromo	11 krom	11 ΧΡΩΜΙΟ
12 cinc	12 zinco	12 zinco	12 çinko	12 ΨΕΥΔΑΡΓΥΡΟΣ
13 aluminio	13 alluminio	13 aluminio	13 alüminyum	13 ΑΛΟΥΜΙΝΙΟ
14 aleación	14 lega	14 liga	14 alaşım	14 ΚΡΑΜΑ
15 bronce de canón	15 bronzo duro	15 liga de cobre e zinco ou estanho	15 tunç	15 ΕΡΥΘΡΟΣ ΟΡΕΙΧΑΛΚΟΣ
16 plata	16 argento	16 prata	16 gümüş	16 ΑΣΗΜΙ
17 oro	17 oro	17 ouro	17 altın	17 ΧΡΥΣΟΣ
18 galvanizar	18 zincare	18 galvanisar	18 galvaniz etmek	18 ΝΑ ΓΑΛΒΑΝΙΣΩ
19 corrosión	19 corrosivo	19 corrosão	19 çürütücü, aşındırıcı	19 ΔΙΑΒΡΩΤΙΚΟ
Maderas	*Legname*	*Madeiras*	*Ahşap/Kereste*	*ΞΥΛΕΙΑ*
1 roble	1 quercia	1 carvalho	1 meşe	1 ΔΡΥΣ
2 teca	2 tek	2 teca	2 tik	2 ΤΙΚ
3 caoba	3 mogano	3 mogno	3 maun	3 ΜΑΟΝΙ

ENGLISH	FRANÇAIS	DEUTSCH	NEDERLANDS	DANSK
15 GENERAL REFERENCE	**15 GENERALITES**	**15 ALLGEMEINE HINWEISE**	**15 ALGEMENE VERWIJZING**	**15 DIVERSE**
Materials	**Matériaux**	**Materialien**	**Materialen**	**Materialer**
Timber	*Bois*	*Holz*	*Houtsoorten*	*Tømmer*
4 iroko	4 iroko	4 Iroko	4 irokoteak	4 iroko
5 elm	5 orme	5 Ulme	5 iepehout	5 elm
6 spruce	6 spruce	6 Fichte	6 sparrehout	6 gran
7 cedar	7 cèdre	7 Zeder	7 ceder	7 ceder
8 pitch pine	8 pitchpin	8 Pitchpine, Pechkiefer	8 Amerikaans grenen	8 pitch pine
9 ash	9 frêne	9 Esche	9 essehout	9 ask
10 larch	10 mélèze	10 Lärche	10 lorkenhout, larikshout	10 lærk
11 lignum vitae	11 gaïac	11 Pockholz	11 pokhout	11 pokkenholt
12 seasoned timber	12 bois sec, bois sèché	12 abgelagertes Holz	12 uitgewerkt hout	12 lagret/tørt træ
13 rot	13 pourriture	13 Fäulnis	13 vuur, rot	13 råd
14 dry rot	14 pourriture sèche	14 Trockenfäule	14 droog vuur	14 tør råd
15 steamed	15 ployé à la vapeur	15 dampfgeformt	15 gestoomd	15 dampet/kogt
16 laminated	16 contré, laminé	16 laminiert	16 gelamineerd	16 lamineret
17 grain	17 fil ou grain du bois	17 Faser	17 draad	17 årer
Plastics	*Plastiques*	*Plastik*	*Kunststoffen*	*Plastic*
1 Cellophane™ (cellulose acetate)	1 Cellophane™ (acétate de cellulose)	1 Zellophan™ (Zelluloseazetat)	1 Cellofaan™	1 Cellofan™ (cellulose acetat)
2 nylon (polyamide)	2 nylon (polyamide)	2 Nylon	2 nylon	2 nylon (polyamid)
3 polythene (polyethylene)	3 polythène (polyethylène)	3 Polyaethylen	3 polytheen	3 polythen (polyetylen)
4 Propathene™ (polypropylene)	4 Propathène™ (polypropylène)	4 Polypropylen™	4 Propatheen™	4 polypropylen
5 PVC (polyvinyl chloride)	5 PVC	5 PVC	5 PVC	5 PVC
6 PTFE, Teflon™ (polytetrafluorethylene)	6 Téflon™	6 Teflon™	6 Teflon™	6 Teflon™
7 polyester, Terylene™ Dacron™ (polyethyl terephthallate)	7 polyester, Terylene™, Dacron™ (polyethyl terephthallate)	7 Polyester, Terylen™, Dacron™	7 polyester, Terylene™, Dacron™	7 polyester, Terylene™, Dacron™
8 Kevlar™ (polyaramid)	8 Kevlar™ (aramide)	8 Kevlar™	8 Kevlar™	8 Kevlar™
9 Neoprene™	9 Neoprène™	9 Neopren™	9 Neopreen™	9 Neopren™
10 acrylic (polyacrylonitrile)	10 acrylique (polyacrylonitrile)	10 Akryl	10 acrylic	10 akryl

ESPAÑOL	ITALIANO	PORTUGUÊS	TÜRKÇE	ΕΛΛΗΝΙΚΑ
15 REFERENCIAS GENERALES	**15 ESPRESSIONI GENERALI**	**15 REFERÊNCIAS GERAIS**	**15 GENEL REFERANS**	**15 ΓΕΝΙΚΕΣ ΑΝΑΦΟΡΕΣ**
Materiales	**Materiali**	**Materiais**	**Malzemeler**	**ΥΛΙΚΑ**

Maderas	*Legname*	*Madeiras*	*Ahşap/Kereste*	*ΞΥΛΕΙΑ*
4 iroko	4 iroko	4 iroco, madeira africana rija	4 iroko	4 ΙΡΟΚΟ
5 olmo	5 olmo	5 ulmo	5 kara ağaç	5 ΦΤΕΛΙΑ
6 abeto	6 abete (rosso)	6 spruce	6 ladin	6 ΕΛΑΤΟ
7 cedro	7 cedro del Libano	7 cedro	7 sedir	7 ΚΕΔΡΟΣ
8 pino	8 pitch pine	8 pitch pine	8 katran çamı	8 ΠΙΤΣ ΠΑΙΝ
9 fresno	9 frassino	9 freixo	9 dişbudak	9 ΜΕΛΙΚΟΥΝΙΑ
10 alerce	10 larice	10 larico	10 lariks, melez kuzey çamı	10 ΠΕΥΚΟ
11 palo santo	11 legno santo	11 lignum vitæ, gaiaco	11 peygamber ağacı	11 ΛΕΝΙΟΣΑΝΤΟ – ΑΓΙΟΞΥΛΟ
12 madera seca	12 legname stagionato	12 sêca	12 kurutulmuş/fırınlı ağaç	12 ΞΗΡΑΜΕΝΗ ΞΥΛΕΙΑ
13 putrición	13 marcio	13 garruncho	13 çürüme, çürük	13 ΣΑΠΙΟ
14 hongo de madera	14 carie secca	14 garruncho, está podre	14 küf	14 ΣΑΡΑΚΟΦΑΓΩΜΕΝΟ
15 al vapor	15 curvato a vapore	15 de estufa a vapor	15 istimlenmiş	15 ΥΓΡΑΜΜΕΝΟ ΜΕ ΑΤΜΟ
16 laminado	16 laminato	16 laminado	16 lamine	16 ΛΑΜΙΝΑΡΙΣΜΕΝΟ
17 veta	17 venatura	17 graínha	17 ağacın damarı, suyu	17 ΝΕΡΑ

Materias plásticas	*Materie plastiche*	*Plásticos*	*Plastikler*	*ΠΛΑΣΤΙΚΑ*
1 Celofán™ (celulosa acetato)	1 cellofan™ (acetato di cellulosa)	1 Celofane™ (celulose)	1 Selofan™ (selüloz asetat)	1 ΣΕΛΟΦΑΝ™
2 nilón (poliamida)	2 nylon, nailon (poliamide)	2 nilon (poliamida)	2 naylon (polyamid)	2 ΝΑΥΛΟΝ
3 politeno (poliétileno)	3 politene (polietilene)	3 politene (polietileno)	3 polietilen	3 ΠΟΛΥΑΙΘΥΛΕΝΙΟ
4 Propateno™ (polipropileno)	4 polipropilene	4 Propatene™ (polipropileno)	4 polipropilen™	4 ΠΟΛΥΠΡΟΠΥΛΕΝΙΟ™
5 PVC (cloruro de polivinilo)	5 PVC (cloruro polivinilico)	5 PVC	5 PVC (polivinil klorid)	5 ΠΙ ΒΙ ΣΙ
6 Teflon™ (politetra-fluoretileno)	6 PTFE, Teflon™ (politetrafluoroetilene)	6 Teflon™	6 PTF, Teflon™	6 ΤΕΦΛΟΝ™
7 poliester, Terylene™, Dacron™ (polietileno)	7 poliestere, Terital™, Dacron™ (tereftalato polietilico)	7 poliester, Dacron™	7 polyester, Terilen™, Dacron™	7 ΠΟΛΥΕΣΤΕΡΑΣ ΤΕΡΙΛΕΝ™-ΝΤΑΚΡΟΝ™
8 Kevlar™ (poliamida)	8 Kevlar™ (poliaramide)	8 Kevlar™	8 Kevlar™	8 ΚΕΒΛΑΡ™
9 Neopreno™	9 Neoprene™	9 Neoprene™	9 Neopren™	9 ΝΕΟΠΡΕΝΙΟ™
10 acrílico (poliacrílico)	10 resina acrilica (poliacrilonitrile)	10 acrílico	10 akrilik	10 ΑΚΡΥΛΙΚΟ

237

15 GENERAL REFERENCE

Weights & measures

METRES–FEET			CENTIMETRES–INCHES			KILOGRAMS–POUNDS		
Metres	Feet or Metres	Feet	Cm	In or Cm	In	Kg	Lb or Kg	Lb
0,31	1	3,28	2,54	1	0,39	0,45	1	2,20
0,61	2	6,56	5,08	2	0,79	0,91	2	4,41
0,91	3	9,84	7,62	3	1,18	1,36	3	6,61
1,22	4	13,12	10,16	4	1,57	1,81	4	8,82
1,52	5	16,40	12,70	5	1,97	2,27	5	11,02
1,83	6	19,69	15,24	6	2,36	2,72	6	13,23
2,13	7	22,97	17,78	7	2,76	3,18	7	15,43
2,44	8	26,25	20,32	8	3,15	3,63	8	17,64
2,74	9	29,53	22,86	9	3,54	4,08	9	19,84
3,05	10	32,81	25,40	10	3,94	4,54	10	22,05
6,10	20	65,62	50,80	20	7,87	9,07	20	44,09
9,14	30	98,42	76,20	30	11,81	13,61	30	66,14
12,19	40	131,23	101,60	40	15,75	18,14	40	88,19
15,24	50	164,04	127,00	50	19,69	22,68	50	110,23
30,48	100	328,09	254,00	100	39,37	45,36	100	220,46

1 metre = 3,280845 feet
1 foot = 0,3047995 metres

1 inch = 2,539996 centimetres
1 centimetre = 0,3937014 inches

1 kilogram = 2,20462 lb   1 lb = 0,45359 kilograms
1 ton = 1016,05 Kg   1 tonne = 2204,62 lb

BRITISH MEASURES

12	inches	=	1 foot: 3 feet = 1 yard
6	feet		1 fathom
100	fathoms		1 cable
6080	feet	=	10 cables = 1 nautical mile
1852	metres		1 nautical mile
1760	yards	=	5280 feet = 1 statute mile
16	oz (ounces)		1 lb
14	lb (pounds)		1 stone
112	lb		1 cwt
20	cwt (hundredweight)		1 ton
2	pints	=	1 quart: 4 quarts= 1 gallon

CUBIC CAPACITY

1 cu inch	16,387 c.c.
1 cu foot (1728 cu in)	0,028 c.m.
1 cu yard (27 cu ft)	0,765 c.m.
1 cu centimetre	0,061 cu in
1 cu decimetre	61,023 cu in
1 cu metre (1000 c.dm.)	35,315 cu ft
1 cu metre	1,31 cu yd

LB/IN^2–KG/CM^2

Lb/in^2	Kg/cm^2	Lb/in^2	Kg/cm^2
10	0,703	32	2,250
12	0,844	34	2,390
14	0,984	36	2,531
16	1,125	40	2,812
18	1,266	45	3,164
20	1,406	50	3,515
22	1,547	60	4,218
24	1,687	70	4,921
26	1,828	80	5,625
28	1,969	90	6,328
30	2,109	100	7,031

TEMPERATURE	
Celsius	Fahrenheit
−30	−22
−20	−4
−10	+14
−5	+23
0	+32
+5	+41
+10	+50
+20	+68
+30	+85
+36,9	+98,4
+37,2	+99
+38,8	+100
+38,3	+101
+38,9	+102
+39,4	+103
+40	+104
+41,1	+106
+50	+122
+60	+140
+70	+158
+80	+176
+90	+194
+100	+212

LITRES–IMPERIAL GALLONS		
Litres	Litres or Gals	Gals
4,55	1	0,22
9,09	2	0,44
13,64	3	0,66
18,18	4	0,88
22,73	5	1,10
27,28	6	1,32
31,82	7	1,54
36,37	8	1,76
40,91	9	1,98
45,46	10	2,20
90,92	20	4,40
136,38	30	6,60
181,84	40	8,80
227,30	50	11,10
340,95	75	16,50
454,60	100	22,00
909,18	200	44,00
2272,98	500	110,00
4545,96	1000	220,00

1,42 dcls = 1/4 pint
2,48 dcls = 1/2 pint
5,68 dcls = 1 pint
5,68 dcls = 1/8 gallon

Beaufort scale	Knots	Metres per second
0	0–1	0–0,2
1	1–3	0,3–1,5
2	4–6	1,6–3,3
3	7–10	3,4–5,4
4	11–16	5,5–7,9
5	17–21	8–10,7
6	22–27	10,8–13,8
7	28–33	13,9–17,1
8	34–40	17,2–20,7
9	41–47	20,8–24,4
10	48–55	24,5–28,4
11	56–63	28,5–32,6
12	64	32,7

METRES–FATHOMS		
Metres	Fathoms	Feet
0,91	1/2	3
1,83	1	6
3,66	2	12
5,49	3	18
7,32	4	24
9,14	5	30
18,29	10	60
36,58	20	120
54,86	30	180

METRES^2–FEET^2		
Metres^2		Feet^2
0,09	1	10,76
0,93	10	107,64
1,86	20	215,28
2,79	30	322,92
3,72	40	430,56
4,65	50	538,19
5,57	60	645,83
6,50	70	753,47
7,43	80	861,11
8,36	90	968,75
9,29	100	1076,39

ROPE

In the UK rope is measured by its circumference. On the Continent, rope is measured by its diameter. A formula to convert these dimensions is: Circumference in inches = $\dfrac{\text{Diameter in mm}}{8}$